The Social Meanings of Religion

The Social Meanings of Religion

An Integrated Anthology

William M. Newman
University of Connecticut

RAND McNALLY COLLEGE PUBLISHING COMPANY · CHICAGO

Current printing   (last digit)
15   14   13   12   11   10   9   8   7   6   5   4   3   2   1

Copyright © 1974 by Rand McNally College Publishing Company
All rights reserved
Printed in U.S.A.
Library of Congress Catalog Number 74-6560

For Sue and Vicki

Preface

This anthology brings together a diverse assortment of essays in the sociology of religion. There are undoubtedly as many opinions about what belongs in such a collection as there are people who teach about and study religion sociologically. Several explicit criteria have guided the selection of materials and editorial comments for this book. First, I have tried to provide a balanced diet of empirical studies and theoretical writing. Second, no single theoretical, analytical, or empirical approach is being "sold" here. Rather, the book is intended to counterpose different perspectives. Third, in contrast to the frequent practice of publishing short, edited excerpts from journal literature, all of the essays in this volume appear in their entire, unedited form. This decision stems from my belief that students need to know not just what our science has found, but also something about the intellectual context and craftsmanship involved in the articulation of important research findings and theoretical departures. Finally, this anthology is aimed at religion in the United States rather than comparative studies of religion.

From a broader perspective, this book attempts to bring between one set of covers some of the major issues in theory and research about religion that have occupied the efforts of sociologists over the last decade or so, and that are likely to continue to do so in the foreseeable future. The first part of the book, consisting of the editor's introduction, examines the development of the sociology of religion, with particular emphasis upon its history in the United States. Part II surveys various approaches to the problems of definition and measurement. Part III considers issues emerging from different theoretical approaches to the field. The essays in Part IV focus upon the interaction between religion and social structure, with special reference to the several major American socioreligious groups. Part V examines the forms and processes of religious organization, while the final set of essays explores the contemporary issues of secularization and religious revival.

Among those who provided suggestions during the planning for this volume, I especially wish to thank Don Ploch, Richard Fenn, and Jeff Hadden. I am also grateful to Nancy Blake, who assisted with the correspondence and manuscript typing, Larry Malley, editor-in-chief of Rand McNally College Publishing Company, and my editor, Marge Boberschmidt, for their encouragement and assistance throughout. I also wish to thank the various authors and publishers whose scholarly efforts and cooperation make this book possible. Finally, I express my deep appreciation to the two girls in my life, to whom this effort is dedicated.

William M. Newman

West Willington
March 1, 1974

Contents

Part I

Introduction

A Prologue

Perhaps the most important fact for the beginning student to grasp is that the age-old question of the truth or falsity of religious doctrines is not the subject matter of the sociology of religion. Rather, like all other branches of sociology, the sociology of religion seeks to understand the social patterns and social consequences of a particular sphere of social reality. As with all other forms of sociological inquiry, the sociology of religion assumes that, regardless of what else may be said of religion, it is also a social phenomenon—it is something that people do in groups. Accordingly, such questions as: What kinds of religious groups and doctrines are there? How are they similar or different? Who joins these groups? What are the consequences of these beliefs and practices for individuals and societies? and What are the typical processes and life histories that characterize them? are the core questions of the sociology of religion.

This is not to suggest that the sociology of religion has no implications for religion itself. As Peter Berger has suggested, all sociology has the effect of "debunking" the things it studies.[1] To study something sociologically is to view it from a new and different perspective; and once one has seen the "other side" of social reality, it becomes difficult to see it again in the accustomed way.

[1] Peter L. Berger, *Invitation to Sociology* (Garden City, N.Y.: Doubleday and Company, 1963).

3

It is indeed likely that a sociology of religion causes one to ask anew some nonsociological questions about religion. But this is far from contending that sociology is itself a sort of religion. Nor should it be assumed that a sociology of religion is inherently antireligious.

The implications of the sociology of religion for religion are at least twofold. First, sociology may provide a fuller understanding of the range and nature of religious phenomena, as well as the diverse meanings of religion for different societies, groups, and individuals. Whether this kind of knowledge about religion implies certain value judgments of religion can only be decided on an individual basis. A second possibility is that a sociological critique of religion's role in society may help us decide which theological questions are most worth asking. In this way sociology may contribute to religious dialogue. In summary, then, the student is forewarned that the sociology of religion is not likely to leave one's religious consciousness untouched. On the other hand, it is equally important to guard against the possibility of sociology assuming a priestly role.

In the fall of 1973 two academic societies involved in the study of religion, the Society for the Scientific Study of Religion and the Religious Research Association, held joint meetings under the title "Transitions to Maturity." This theme was an appropriate one for describing the present state of the sociology of religion. Even a cursory examination of the writings of sociologists of religion reveals two divergent trends. On the one hand, the field exhibits all of the characteristics of a science in its infancy. Such basic questions as: What is meant by religion? How does one measure it? What can be inferred from these measures? and Which research questions are really significant? are very much "up for grabs." At the same time there exists in the field an atmosphere charged with the excitement of new discoveries and intellectual convergence. It is indeed difficult to understand how such a situation has emerged at this point in time without considering the historical forces that have shaped the growth of the discipline.

Great Expectations

Without exception, all of the European founders of sociology believed that in order to understand modern societies, one must understand the important roles played by religion in society. In spite of the sundry differences among the writings on religion of Marx, Weber, Durkheim, Simmel, and the other classical theorists, they all shared this common theme. In this sense, the sociology of religion is as old as sociology itself. It is a major segment of social reality to which the classical period authors gave much attention. From this fact one might expect the sociology of religion to be one of the most advanced and best researched subjects in the field. Yet this is far from true. It is indeed convenient, and intellectually consoling, for the contemporary sociologist of religion to dwell upon the relationship between questions of current interest and those similar concerns of the classical "founding fathers." It is comforting to know that Weber and Durkheim were intrigued by the same things that intrigue you. But it is painfully clear that the writings of the classical theorists have had much less influence upon the development of the field than did certain trends in American sociology between the last quarter of the nineteenth century and the first quarter of the twentieth. For like most sociology, the sociology of religion has flourished most in America. Similarly, those forces that shaped the growth of sociology in America also have had a profound effect upon the unique history of the sociology of religion.

One of the major factors that propelled sociology into existence as an academic discipline in the United States was religion itself. During the last quarter of the nineteenth century much of American Protestantism was swept by a movement known as the Social Gospel. The theologians of the Social Gospel argued that the traditional faith could only have meaning for modern man if the "kingdom of God" were fulfilled here on earth through a reconstruction of the social order. A combination of religious zeal and social reformism mandated a transformation of society in Christ's name, and the new sociology was to be a pivotal technical resource in this socioreligious enterprise.[2]

It is little surprise, then, that many of the "founding fathers" of American sociology were either Protestant clergymen or sons of Protestant clergymen. Among the latter were Franklin Giddings and W. I. Thomas. Numerous others, among them William Sumner, Albion Small, George E. Vincent, Edward C. Hayes, and James P. Lichtenberger, entered sociology only after beginning their careers in the ministry.[3] The very first American textbooks on the subject did not bear the title "sociology" but "Christian sociology," and there is sufficient evidence to show that so-called

[2] See C. Howard Hopkins, *The Rise of the Social Gospel in American Protestantism 1865–1915* (New Haven: Yale University Press, 1940).

[3] See discussions in Roscoe and Gisela Hinkle, *The Development of Modern Sociology* (New York: Random House, 1954); Robert Friedrichs, *A Sociology of Sociology* (New York: Free Press, 1970); and especially Ernest Becker, *The Structure of Evil* (New York: George Braziller, 1968).

Christian sociology had gained an established place in the seminary curriculum well before sociology was being taught in the secular arts and sciences colleges.[4]

These American beginnings would appear to be no less promising for the development of a sociology of religion than were those in Europe. Yet by the early 1920s, the tenuous intermarriage between social science and religion was undergoing a divorce. In the wake of the First World War, the ethos of social optimism, and the Social Gospel with it, collapsed. Yet, perhaps the most important element in the situation was the desire of most sociologists of the day to establish the scientific status of the new discipline. In practice this meant not simply the emergence of a more quantitative orientation in social research, but a sharp demarcation between sociology and social work. Sociology had to separate itself, so they believed, from religious auspices and biases, and from entanglement in both the social and religious controversies that had surrounded the reformist doctrines of the turn of the century. Thus, as sociology set out to become "objective" and "value free" the sociology of religion, ostensibly a highly value-laden area of inquiry, became one of the first casualties. It would not be until the late 1940s that the thinking of the European classical theorists (then coming into English translation) would have a major impact upon American sociology;[5] and it was not until after the Second World War that the sociology of religion, along with a host of other special sociologies, would begin to grow and flourish as a result of the general growth in the educational establishment that characterized the postwar period.

The Douglass Tradition

This is not to suggest that no significant work in the sociology of religion was done until after the Second World War. Several im-

[4] Careful documentation of these events will be found in James Dombrowski, *The Early Days of Christian Socialism in America* (New York: Octagon Books, 1966).

[5] Aside from his essay *The Protestant Ethic and the Spirit of Capitalism*, which was in translation by 1930, the larger part of Weber's work on religion was not available in English until after the Second World War. The studies of religion in China, India, and Ancient Israel all appeared in the 1950s and his *Sociology of Religion* first appeared in 1963. While Durkheim's *Elementary Forms of the Religious Life* was in translation by 1915, the balance of his major works appeared slowly between 1933 and 1960.

portant works were written during the prewar years. But it is important to note that the authors were religious scholars, not sociologists. The two most prominent examples are H. Richard Niebuhr, a theologian at both Yale and Harvard Divinity Schools, whose classic *The Social Sources of Denominationalism* appeared in 1929, and Liston Pope, Dean of Yale Divinity School, whose *Millhands and Preachers* was published in 1942. The only significant empirical studies of religion by academic sociologists during this period were the community studies of Warner, the Lynds, and Hollingshead, all of whom encountered the salience of religious institutions in their studies of American community life.[6]

While the sociology of religion was largely ignored by academic sociologists during these years, it did not die entirely. Immediately following World War I, there were various efforts within American Protestantism to revitalize both the domestic and foreign social service efforts of the churches. Within the United States, the Interchurch World Movement, one of a host of ecumenical groups of the period, launched an ambitious program of church and community studies.[7] In many ways the emerging ecumenical groups were the remnant of the defunct Social Gospel Movement. Most importantly, these groups retained the vision of an applied sociology working in the service of both religion and society. The Interchurch World Movement quickly researched itself into financial bankruptcy and its work was continued on a less ambitious scale by the Committee for Social and Religious Surveys.

In 1921 a grant from John D. Rockefeller transformed the committee into the Institute for Social and Religious Research with the explicit goal of applying "scientific method to the study of socioreligious phenomena." The most prominent member of the institute, and for many years its director, was H. Paul Douglass. Douglass, a Baptist clergyman, was one of the most prolific and

[6] Robert and Helen Lynd, *Middletown* (1929) and *Middletown in Transition* (1937) (both volumes, New York: Harcourt-Brace); W. Lloyd Warner, *The Social Life of a Modern Community* (1941), *The Social System of American Ethnic Groups* (1945), and *The Social System of the Modern Factory* (1947) (all volumes, New Haven: Yale University Press); and A. B. Hollingshead, *Elmtown's Youth* (New York: John Wiley, 1949). Warner's most forceful statement on American religion is his later study, *American Life: Dream and Reality* (Chicago: University of Chicago Press, 1953).

[7] The definitive history of these events is yet to be written. For a concise discussion, see Yoshio Fukuyama, "The Uses of Sociology: By Religious Bodies," *Journal for the Scientific Study of Religion*, 2, no. 2 (1963): 195–203.

methodologically sophisticated sociologists of his time. The author of the first major book on American suburbs and a frequent contributor to the literature on rural sociology, Douglass guided the institute in the production of over fifty major studies and the publication of over ninety volumes between 1921 and 1934. There can be little question that Douglass' position in the institute, apart from the growing establishment of academic sociology, determined that his work would be largely overlooked by sociologists. During the very period when the sociology of religion had been abandoned by the academic sociologists, Douglass was creating a virtual library of research findings on institutional religion, ranging from studies of local churches to studies of the growing ecumenical movement both here and abroad. It was in fact through Douglass' urging that the institute provided funding for the Lynds' now famous study, *Middletown.*

Even today, many sociologists of religion disregard the work that Douglass and his associates accomplished both during the life of the institute (1921–1934) and after its demise. It is indeed fair to say that the applied nature of Douglass' work and the institutional concerns that frame it provide little guidance in social-scientific theory building. Yet on the other side, it is clear that many of the descriptive studies of mainstream religion conducted in the past two decades have not, in any significant way, gone beyond that which Douglass and his associates had already done. Nor is it clear that contemporary theorists have provided much more of an understanding of religious institutions than is provided in Douglass and Brunner's summary volume on the institute's work, *The Protestant Church as a Social Institution.*[8] Yet, as will be seen, while Douglass' sociology of religion remained marginal, apart from the academic establishment, the efforts of Douglass and his associates did have a major impact upon the organization and communication of scientific knowledge within the sociology of religion.

The Organization of Scientific Knowledge

Even before the end of the Second World War, the most prominent American social theorist of the day, Talcott Parsons, had already noted some important contributions to the sociological theory of religion on the part of European sociologists and an-

[8] H. Paul Douglass and Edmund de S. Brunner, *The Protestant Church as a Social Institution* (New York: Harper, 1935).

thropologists.[9] Just as Parsons' work served to stimulate sociological interest in religion, so an early paper by Gerhard Lenski on the social correlates of religious interest[10] marked the entrance of the sociology of religion into the era of survey research. As Hadden and Heenan have observed in their study of empirical research in the field,[11] the emergence of the alleged religious revival of the mid-1950s was accompanied by a diverse and growing assortment of sociological studies of American religion.

Nothing is more important to the growth and maturity of an academic discipline or science than the development of professional organizations within the field. For through these organizations and the journals they publish, routine channels of communication and intellectual exchange are made possible. The rapid growth of the sociology of religion in the United States in the past two decades has been greatly facilitated by the development of not one, but three such organizations, the oldest of which was a direct outgrowth of the work of H. Paul Douglass and his associates.

Following the demise of the Institute for Social and Religious Research, Douglass became the director of a technical staff of one of the divisions of the Federal Council of Churches, which became the National Council of Churches in 1950.[12] This group, consisting largely of denominationally employed researchers, created the Religious Research Fellowship in 1951. In the late 1950s this group changed its name to the Religious Research Association and began publication of its journal, *Review of Religious Research.* Even before the creation of the journal, the association had attracted to its ranks a growing number of academically based sociologists of religion. As Hadden points out, in spite of the fact that the association was created by employees of religious institutions, the new *Review* was well received and used by academic sociologists of religion.[13]

[9] Talcott Parsons, "The Theoretical Development of the Sociology of Religion," *Journal of the History of Ideas,* 5 (1944): 176–190.

[10] Gerhard Lenski, "Social Correlates of Religious Interest," *American Sociological Review,* 18 (1953): 533–543.

[11] Jeffrey Hadden and Edward Heenan, "Empirical Studies in the Sociology of Religion: An Assessment of the Past Ten Years," *Sociological Analysis,* 31, no. 3 (1970): 153–167.

[12] Jeffrey K. Hadden, "A Brief Social History of the Religious Research Association," paper presented at the joint meetings of the Religious Research Association and the Society for the Scientific Study of Religion, October 1973 and forthcoming in the *Review of Religious Research.*

[13] Ibid.

At the very same time, a parallel organization developed among academically based sociologists, psychologists, and religious scholars.[14] Founded in 1949, the Committee for the Scientific Study of Religion became the Society for the Scientific Study of Religion in 1955 and began publication of the *Journal for the Scientific Study of Religion* in 1960. The two societies have been in conversation with each other almost since their beginnings and for the past several years have held their annual meetings together. Both of the journals they publish are valuable sources of information for teachers, researchers, and students alike.

The third American scholarly organization in the area of the sociology of religion is the American Catholic Sociological Society. This group was not initially formed out of an interest in the sociology of religion, but out of the special concerns of American Catholic sociologists over the relationship between social science and religion. Paul J. Reiss describes the early period of the society's life in the following terms:

> At the time the society was founded in 1938 American sociology was not particularly congenial to those with religious commitments. Religion, even the sociology of religion, held a very low status in the eyes of American sociologists. Religion by many was seen as an outmoded hindrance to scientific study. It was to this situation that the founders of the American Catholic Sociological Society were responding.[15]

In other words, the Catholic group represented a particular response to those forces that have already been discussed here regarding the general development of sociology in America between the two world wars. It was not until 1963 that the society added the subtitle "A Journal in the Sociology of Religion" to its already established journal, *Sociological Analysis,* and changed the society's name to the Association for the Sociology of Religion. Thus the Catholic society, in the midst of examining the question of what its raison d'etre as an academic society really was, responded to the rapidly growing discipline of the sociology of religion in the early 1960s. In doing so, it created a new and meaningful role for itself as well as provided yet another publica-

[14] William M. Newman, "The Society for the Scientific Study of Religion: The Development of an Academic Society," paper presented at the joint meetings of the Religious Research Association and the Society for the Scientific Study of Religion, October 1973 and forthcoming in *Review of Religious Research.*

[15] Paul J. Reiss, "Science and Religion in the Evolution of a Sociological Association," *Sociological Analysis,* no. 3 (1970): 119–130.

tion outlet for sociological research on religion. Today these three American-based journals, along with the European-based *Archives de Sociologie des Religions, Social Compass,* and *Jewish Journal of Sociology,* provide a rich flow of scientific information about religious phenomena.

The Sociology of Religion Today

From the foregoing historical sketch it should be clear that the unique thing about the sociology of religion has been the interaction between this particular branch of sociology and the subject matter it studies. Religious doctrines played an important role in the emergence of sociology in the United States. Similarly, the confrontation between religion and science after the turn of the century relegated the sociology of religion to a marginal place in the discipline. European sociologists frequently distinguish between the *sociology of religion* and *religious sociology.* If this distinction is useful, it must be said that in America religious sociology—a sociology working in the service of religious (typically Protestant) institutions and frequently adopting the definition of research problems and value biases of those institutions—dominated until after the Second World War. It has only been in the last two decades that a sociology of religion, taking cognizance of its heritage in European classical sociology, has set out on its own as an academic discipline. There is, in fact, some evidence to suggest that this difference in orientations played an important role in keeping the Religious Research Association and the Society for the Scientific Study of Religion distinct as organizations. It is little accident that with the decline in the past decade in the number of researchers working for religious institutions, it is the former organization that has suffered a decrease in membership.[16]

The unique relationship between religion and a social science that studies religion has been a continual element in the development of the field. In this sense, the sociologist of religion occupies a unique position among sociologists. On the one hand, he has frequently been suspected by the larger discipline of letting his own religious biases influence his science. On the other hand, he has just as often been under attack by religious functionaries for being allegedly anti-religious. These problems will not soon disappear. Yet, in spite of them, immense advances in

[16] Hadden, *op. cit.*

our sociological knowledge about religion have been made in the past several decades.

Given the explosion of literature in this field in recent years, it would be impossible for any volume—short of one of encyclopedic proportions—to represent adequately all facets of the discipline. Many important areas of inquiry are not included in this collection. Yet the following essays do provide some sampling of the questions and controversies that have absorbed the energies of sociologists of religion in recent years. Similarly, they depict the diversity of the social meanings of religion in the United States.

Part II

Defining and Measuring
Religion as a Social Variable

To define "religion," to say what it *is,* is not
possible at the start of a presentation such as
this. Definition can be attempted, if at all, only
at the conclusion of this study. The essence
of religion is not even our concern, as we make
it our task to study the conditions and effects of
a particular type of social behavior.[1]
Max Weber

It is indeed ironic that the founder and perhaps most brilliant student of the sociology of religion, Max Weber, failed entirely to
define his subject matter. Today, one can at least sympathize
with the intent if not the effect of Weber's disclaimer quoted from
the opening paragraph of his monumental *Sociology of Religion*
(1922). There is little question that the basic task of the sociology
of religion is to understand not the metaphysical essence of religion, but its social aspects. As a pioneer in a new area of study,

[1] Max Weber, *The Sociology of Religion,* trans. Ephraim Fischoff (Boston:
Beacon Press, 1963), p. 1.

Weber was in effect saying that only after some period of time and only after the attainment of some cumulative knowledge on the subject would it be possible to offer a truly informed definition of religion as a social phenomenon.

Somewhat to the dismay of contemporary sociologists, Weber's assumption that the acquisition of knowledge would provide the basis for an informed definition has proved quite unfounded. Especially in the last two decades, as the quantity of research and theoretical writing about religion has increased, there has been a growing awareness among social scientists concerning the problems of operational definition and measurement. The more that is learned about religion as a social phenomenon, the more difficult it becomes to circumscribe that knowledge within the boundaries of a single definition or set of empirical measures.

The beginning student is likely to ask, Why hassle over the abstract question of definition? After all, most definitions are, in the last analysis, arbitrary. It is highly improbable that everyone will agree on any single definition. Moreover, most discussions of definitions are boring if not pedantic. Why not follow Weber's example? Shelve the question of definition and get on with the sociological study of religion.

But the matter is not quite that simple. For in both the natural and social sciences alike, to study something means to measure it, and to define a phenomenon is to prescribe the kind of yardstick by which it will be measured. It is frequently the case that different kinds of measures produce very different answers to the same question.[2] In other words, it is only through the comparison of different studies, employing fairly standardized definitions and measures, that reliable theories and generalizations may be constructed. In this context, questions of definition and measurement become problems of immense theoretical significance. As long as the field lacks some common perception of what it is one ought to measure in order to study religious phenomena, it will be exceedingly difficult to provide meaningful theories—theories that may be tested and verified by different researchers at different points in time. How then does one begin to solve such a problem?

To some extent the growing number of attempts by social scientists to define and measure religious phenomena may be viewed as signs of intellectual growth and vitality in the discipline. The

---

[2] For an excellent illustration of this point see Gibson Winter's "Methodological Reflections on the Religious Factor," *Journal for the Scientific Study of Religion,* 2, no. 1 (1962): 53–63.

past several decades of theory and research have greatly expanded our appreciation of the diversity and complexity of religious beliefs and conduct. Given the ever increasing literature on the subject, it would be impossible to include in a collection of this kind all of the various typologies, distinctions, and perspectives on the problem of defining and measuring religion as a social variable. Rather, this first set of essays provides a sampling of approaches which, taken together, illustrate the potentials and enduring problems of the sociological study of religion.

Religion, as well as attempts to define it, are probably as old as mankind. These definitions range from the simple observation of Cicero that religion is "the pious worship of God" to the more complex formulation of the eighteenth-century philosopher Friedrich Schleiermacher that religion is a "feeling of total dependence."[3] The twentieth-century theologian Paul Tillich has suggested that religion is that which involves man's "ultimate concern."[4] While these kinds of definitions may be theologically appealing, they have been extremely difficult to operationalize in empirical research.

It is important to distinguish between definition and measurement. A definition is a broad concept that provides some boundaries or limits upon what will be studied in a given field. Thus, religion may be defined as that which provides moral values in a society, or as that which involves some reference to transcendental entities, or in any other number of ways. Yet definitions of religion do not necessarily provide explicit operational or empirical measures of religion, such as frequency of church attendance, degree of belief in traditional doctrines, church membership, and the like. While there are still significant disputes among sociologists of religion over how religion should be defined, an even greater controversy has emerged since the early 1960s over how religion should be measured.

A major shift in measurement techniques has taken place in the field and most researchers are now employing multidimensional (rather than a single) measures of religion. The question at issue today is, Which specific set of measures should be employed? The first major attempt to employ multiple measures of

[3] Friedrich Schleiermacher, *On Religion: Speeches to Its Cultured Despisers,* trans. John Oman (New York: Harper & Row, Torchbooks, 1958).

[4] Paul Tillich, *Systematic Theology* (Chicago: University of Chicago Press, 1956), vol. 1.

religiosity in the same piece of research was Gerhard Lenski's now classic *The Religious Factor.*[5] Lenski makes an important distinction between religion as a form of group membership and religion as a form of belief or orientation. Within each of these two categories, he proposes two additional distinctions. Religious group membership was studied in *The Religious Factor* in terms of both *associationalism* and *communalism.* Associational religion refers to an individual's participation in an institutional setting, such as attendance at worship services. Communal religion may be measured by such things as the religion of one's spouse or of one's close friends. On the other hand, an individual's religious orientation may be measured in terms of *doctrinal orthodoxy* (the degree of belief in traditional religious doctrines) or in terms of one's communication with the infinite, prayer, and the like. Lenski calls this the individual's *pietism.*

As Lenski points out in *The Religious Factor,* the four dimensions that he operationalized produced a number of differences between religious groups. For instance, he found American Jews to be associationally weak but communally strong, as compared to both extremely high communalism and associationalism among white Catholics. On the other hand, across groups, devotionalism and orthodoxy seem to be differentially related to what he called a "unified world view."

At the very time Gerhard Lenski was collecting the data for *The Religious Factor,*[6] another group of scholars was developing yet a different set of multidimensional measures.[7] While this second approach is most frequently associated with the names of Charles Glock and Rodney Stark, it was in fact Glock's associate Yoshio Fukuyama who first used these measures in an empirical study. The differences between the Glock and Stark dimensions[8] and those used by Fukuyama, and later Fukuyama

[5] Gerhard Lenski, *The Religious Factor* (Garden City: Doubleday & Company, 1961).

[6] The data contained in *The Religious Factor* was collected during 1957 in The Detroit Area Study of the year.

[7] Charles Glock's first presentation of this typology appeared in his essay "Toward a Typology of Religious Orientation" (New York: Bureau of Applied Social Research, Columbia University, 1954), and subsequently in Glock's essay "The Religious Revival in America," in Jane C. Zahn (ed.), *Religion in the Face of America* (Berkeley: University Extension, University of California, 1959).

[8] See Charles Glock and Rodney Stark, *Religion and Society in Tension* (Chicago: Rand McNally, 1965); *Christian Beliefs and Anti-Semitism* (New York: Harper and Row, 1966); and especially Rodney Stark and Charles Glock, *American Piety: The Nature of Religious Commitment* (Berkeley: University of California Press, 1970).

and Campbell,[9] are indeed slight and it is Fukuyama's original study that is reprinted here.

As Fukuyama explains, his study was intended to address the question of the alledged "religious revival" of the 1950s. But he became increasingly aware that simply measuring church membership was an inadequate way of approaching the question. Setting out to expand upon Charles Glock's multidimension approach, Fukuyama goes on to show quite convincingly that even in the same religious denomination, different people are religious in various ways and that these differences are related to the traditional kinds of variables studied by sociologists such as age, sex, education, and social class.

[9] See Thomas Campbell and Yoshio Fukuyama, *The Fragmented Laymen* (Philadelphia: Pilgrim Press, 1970).

The Major Dimensions of Church Membership
by Yoshio Fukuyama

Sociological descriptions of the contemporary religious situation in the United States present a somewhat ambiguous picture. On the one hand are those who argue that America is experiencing a "revival" of religious interest unparalleled in its history. On the other hand, we are told that religion in America is characterized more by its decline than by its "upswing," that America is more secular and emptied of religious interest today than ever before. A third group argues that religion in our society is best described by its stability rather than by change, that the dominant themes and influences of religion are no different today than they were a century ago.

This lack of consensus among social scientists as to what is being

Yoshio Fukuyama is professor of religious studies at Pennsylvania State University. Formerly research director for the United Church of Christ, he is the author of *Ministry in Transition* (1972); and co-author of *The Fragmented Laymen* (with Thomas Campbell, 1970).

Reprinted from *Review of Religious Research*, 2, no. 4 (1961): 154–161. Used with permission of the author and publisher.

described poses the problem situation for our study. Its purpose is to define, in systematic fashion and on the basis of empirical evidence, some new and meaningful categories for the study of religion in a sociological setting. An assumption made at the outset is that the broad category of "church membership" is inadequate as a descriptive sociological category and that a fresh conceptual framework is necessary for descriptive studies of religious groups.

The primary data for this study consist of 4,095 questionnaires returned by members of twelve Congregational Christian churches located in seven cities. These churches represent the dominant varieties of city churches in the denomination and are located in the northeastern and north central regions of the nation where Congregationalists have their major strength. In addition to the questionnaires, seventy-nine interview protocols were gathered from a sample of these church members and used for illustrative purposes.

The frame of reference which we shall adopt has been informed significantly by a recent paper by Glock ("The Religious Revival in America?" in Zahn, ed., *Religion and the Face of America*). Glock suggests that "religiousness as a concept" may be thought of as one "which is divisible into four dimensions," dimensions which he calls "the experiential, the ritualistic, the ideological and the consequential." These dimensions, for Glock, have to do with religious feelings, practices, beliefs, and "works," and are comprehensive of the major ways in which church members may be said to be oriented to religion.

The present study is based on a reformulation and elaboration of Glock's proposals: *Religion is a phenomenon which can be described in terms of at least four major dimensions: the cognitive, the cultic, the creedal, and the devotional; these dimensions represent distinctive styles of religious orientation and provide meaningful categories for the sociological study of religion.*

The cognitive dimension has to do with what people *know about* religion and is manifested at one extreme by the "knowledgeable church member." He is well informed about the Bible and religious matters in general and derives great satisfaction from the intellectual stimulation received from sermons or from discussions about religion with others. This dimension is not included in Glock's categories. Presumably he intended it to be an element in his "consequential" dimension. However, it is here proposed that the cognitive element be singled out as a separate dimension.

The cultic dimension is what Glock described as the "ritualistic." It encompasses the individual's religious practices—his attendance at divine worship, his participation in church activities, and his support of church programs through voluntary service and contributions. This form of religious orientation is characterized by "the active church member."

The creedal dimension bears on what a person *believes* as distinct from what he knows about or how he practices his religion. The acceptance of traditional beliefs is central to his religious orientation. He is "the believer." The creedal dimension is equivalent to Glock's "ideological" dimension.

Finally, the devotional dimension parallels Glock's category of the "experiential" and has to do with *feelings* and *experiences* rather than with knowledge, practices, or beliefs. The Bible, for example, is appreciated more for its devotional than for its intellectual value; religious sentiment is internalized as inward feeling rather than articulated as an explicit creedal statement. "The devout" represent this style of religious orientation.

This conceptualization of the dimensions of religious orientation omits what Glock refers to as the "consequential" dimension, what people do as a result of their religious beliefs, feelings, and practices. The omission implies not that the consequences of religion are irrelevant but rather that they do not constitute a basic component of religious orientation *per se*. Our departure from Glock on this point is largely semantic; we shall later consider briefly some correlates (consequences) of differences in religious orientation as here defined.

Indexes of Religious Orientation

In order to distinguish our universe of 4,095 respondents along each of these dimensions, four indexes of religious orientation were constructed. Each index was trichotomously discrete, and each church member was classified as being "low," "moderate," or "high" on each dimension. By definition, those scoring high were classified as being oriented to that particular dimension of religion.

The index of cognitive orientation was based on the respondent's answers to three questions concerning the Bible. Cultic orientation was determined by an index based on the following indicators: frequency of church or church school attendance, regularity of financial support, participation in church organizations, and role as a leader in the church.

Belief in life after death, in Jesus Christ as Savior, and in the Bible as the revealed word of God were the criteria used to define the creedally oriented church member. Faith in the power of prayer, the practice of daily Bible or devotional reading, and belief in conversion as a necessary experience for a Christian were the indicators used for the index of devotional orientation. Table 1 summarizes the marginal distributions for the four orientation indexes.

Table 1. Marginals for Major Orientation Indexes

(4,095 = 100 percent)

Orientation index	Number			Percent		
	Low	Moderate	High	Low	Moderate	High
Cognitive	1,294	1,898	903	32	46	22
Cultic	1,124	1,183	1,788	27	29	44
Creedal	1,135	1,794	1,166	28	44	28
Devotional	1,220	1,933	942	30	47	23

Predisposing Factors

The questions we now wish to pursue, albeit briefly, are, "What factors predispose individuals to different orientations?" and "What are the consequences of different orientations for values?" Our answer to the first question will be limited to exploring the relationship of sex, age, education, and socioeconomic status to the four types of religious orientation. Our answer to the second will focus on several attitudinal correlates of religious orientation.

It is rather widely held that women are more prone to religious expression in our society than men. Our results confirm this impression but only in part. Table 2 shows separately for men and women the proportion scoring "high" on each of the four measures of orientation.

This table tells us that women are indeed more "religious" on the average than men but only on the cultic, creedal, and devotional dimensions. Men score higher than women on the cognitive dimension. Men, it would appear, are more likely than women to "know" their religion but less likely to practice, believe, and experience it. As we move across the table, the differences increase, with women differing from men most on the devotional dimension.

Like sex, age bears a different relationship to religion depending on which dimensions of orientation are used. Table 3 reports for each of seven age groups the proportion scoring high in their religious orientation.

There is little difference in cognitive orientation at different stages of the life cycle; younger people appear to be as informed religious-

Table 2. Relationship Between Sex and Four Indexes
of Religious Orientation

| Sex of respondent | Percent religiously oriented on | | | |
	Cognitive dimension	Cultic dimension	Creedal dimension	Devotional dimension
Male	25	41	23	15
Female	20	46	32	28

ly as older persons. On the cultic dimension, there is some tendency toward increased involvement up through the 50–59 age group. After this, there is a decline. This is in conformity with other studies which have examined the relationship between age and church attendance. Of more interest, however, are the figures for the creedal and devotional dimensions. Here, there is a relatively steady increase in religious orientation with increasing age.

This result may, on the one hand, be interpreted to mean that people become more religious creedally and devotionally as they move through the life cycle. On the other hand, it may also be interpreted to mean that the younger generation is simply less religious than the older generation and always will be. These data, collected as they were at only one point in time, do not permit a judgment as to which interpretation is correct. It is evident, however, that the first interpretation has very different implications for the viability of religion in our society than the second.

The next table, Table 4, reports the religious orientation of parishioners with different educational backgrounds and coming from

Table 3. Relationship of Age to Four Indexes of
Religious Orientation

| Age Group | Percent religiously oriented on | | | |
	Cognitive dimension	Cultic dimension	Creedal dimension	Devotional dimension
Under 20 years	20	35	19	12
20 to 29 years	28	29	22	12
30 to 39 years	22	46	26	19
40 to 49 years	22	49	27	19
50 to 59 years	22	51	32	27
60 to 69 years	22	45	34	31
70 years and over	19	38	32	36

different socioeconomic groups. Past studies on the relationship between socioeconomic status and religion have been peculiarly inconsistent. Table 4 provides a possible clue to the source of this inconsistency. It shows that the kind of relationship found depends very much on which index of religious orientation is used. Thus, we find that the more highly educated and the more well-to-do parishioners score higher than less educated and poorer parishioners on both the cognitive and cultic dimensions. In effect, they are more knowledgeable about their religion and they engage more frequently in ritual practice. Contrariwise, the less educated and poorer parishioners score higher on the creedal and devotional dimensions. This suggests that different social classes differ not so much in the degree to which they are religiously oriented but in the manner in which they give expression to their religious propensities.

Table 4. Relationship of Socioeconomic Indexes
to Religious Orientation

	Percent religiously oriented on			
	Cognitive dimension	Cultic dimension	Creedal dimension	Devotional dimension
Education				
Grade school or less	9	36	32	38
Some high school	12	35	30	30
Graduated high school	12	43	34	24
Some college	21	45	28	23
Graduated college	34	48	26	18
Socioeconomic status				
Low	15	35	31	32
Moderate	24	43	28	23
High	28	53	27	16
Mean distribution	22	44	28	23

Consequences in Values

These findings, then, indicate that the location of the parishioner in the general society has implications for how his religion is expressed. We were interested, therefore, to learn whether there is any relationship between an individual's religious orientation and the values he brings to bear on issues facing his denomination. In other words, do different religious orientations make for different ways of viewing the world?

For this analysis, we compared the answers of those who scored high on the four religious orientation dimensions to three questions —one having to do with the teaching of religion in public schools, a second asking parishioners whether they would grant their ministers the right to preach on controversial subjects, and a third asking parishioners whether their congregation should accept into membership persons of all races. The results are reported in Table 5.

The cognitively oriented show the greatest resistance to having religion taught in the public schools. Resistance decreases progressively across the table, with the devotionally oriented being the most supportive of having religion taught in the schools. There is a similar pattern of response to the other two questions. The cognitively oriented are most likely to grant their ministers the right to preach on controversial subjects and to favor a racially inclusive membership. There is declining support for these points of view as one moves from the cultically to the creedally, and then on to the devotionally oriented parishioners.

In part, these differences are undoubtedly a reflection of differences in the educational background of those having different religious orientations. They suggest as well, however, that traditional responses are more likely to come from those for whom the belief and devotional dimensions of their religion are important. Those

Table 5. Attitudinal Correlates of Religious Orientation*

	Percent of parishioners whose orientation is:			
	Cognitive	Cultic	Creedal	Devotional
Religion in public schools	100	100	100	100
Should be taught	32	39	41	46
Don't know	14	16	18	18
Should not be taught	54	45	41	36
Right of the minister to preach on controversial subjects	100	100	100	100
Yes	89	80	74	72
Don't know	3	10	13	14
No	8	10	13	14
Racial inclusiveness of church membership	100	100	100	100
Inclusive	87	81	80	80
Latently exclusive	7	11	10	11
Exclusive	6	8	10	8

* Table shows the distribution of responses to each question among parishioners scoring "high" on each of the indexes of religious orientation.

whose interest in religion is participation-centered or formal are more likely to adopt more liberal views of the church's responsibility.

Multidimensional Religion

In conclusion, it is to be emphasized that these findings are limited to a sample of Congregationalists from twelve urban congregations and cannot, therefore, be assumed to hold either for all Congregationalists or for members of other denominations. Their importance, we would submit, lies not so much in what they have to say descriptively about the sample as in underscoring the desirability of conceiving of religion in a multi- rather than a unidimensional way. Individuals give expression to their religion in different ways. Making the alternatives explicit is essential for gaining an understanding of the place of religion in contemporary culture.

Fukuyama presents a convincing argument for the usefulness of the four dimensions of religion that he employed. On the one hand, his approach to the cognitive aspect of religion represents an important step beyond Lenski. For while Lenski only measured the degree of an individual's doctrinal orthodoxy, Fukuyama has measured both the degree of doctrinal orthodoxy and the extent of religious knowledge. Moreover, he found that these two kinds of cognitive religious orientations are differentially related to church members' views on a number of social issues. On the other hand, by restricting his study to people who are church members, Fukuyama is unable to provide any information about the relative strength of associational religion in the general population, nor has he measured communal religion. For this reason Fukuyama's research is of little use as a retest of Lenski's claim that communalism is a central form of religious expression among American Protestants.

An intriguing aspect of Fukuyama's research is the fact that in his total sample of over 4000 church members only 28 percent scored high on his doctrinal orthodoxy index. Even when the population was viewed in terms of age, sex, class, and educational groupings, no single group scored even as high as 50 percent on this dimension. How can such an anomaly be explained?

It seems only logical that people join Christian churches because they endorse and value the basic tenets of the Christian religion. These findings cannot be understood without considering the nature of the specific religious denomination that Fukuyama studied. American Congregationalism has traditionally placed a strong emphasis upon the autonomy of the individual religious believer and the right of the individual to construct his own distinctive doctrinal outlook. The relatively low degree of doctrinal orthodoxy suggests not that this population of church members consists largely of nonbelievers, but that the diversity of religious outlooks in this population were at significant variance from the particular doctrinal questions that Fukuyama asked.

This aspect of Fukuyama's research raises an important methodological question about the use of multidimensional measures of religion. How would a population of Mormons, Episcopals, Lutherans, or Seventh Day Adventists have responded to these four dimensions of religion? It is widely recognized that different religious groups, even within the fold of American Protestantism, score differently on these kinds of multidimensional measures. Glock and Stark, for instance, have argued that in terms of theological doctrines, there are at least four distinct branches of American Protestantism. Methodists, Congregationalists, and Episcopals appear to be the most theologically liberal. The Disciples of Christ and the Presbyterians seem to exhibit a moderate doctrinal position, while American Lutherans and American Baptists are conservative. Finally, the Missouri Lutheran Synod, the Southern Baptists, and a large range of smaller so-called sectarian groups appear to be extremely conservative or fundamentalist in their doctrinal views.[10] Even Lenski found that while Jews are high on communalism and low on associationalism, Catholics appear to be high on both communalism and associationalism. In other words, even if agreement were to be reached on a given set of measures of religion, one would still have the problem of weighting these dimensions differently depending upon the specific group being studied. While it would not be surprising to encounter a group of doctrinally liberal Congregationalists, one would take great notice of a trend toward doctrinal liberalism among a group of Southern Baptists.[11] Any set of mea-

[10] Charles Glock and Rodney Stark, *Religion and Society in Tension* (Chicago: Rand McNally, 1965), p. 120.

[11] Within the past several decades organizational mergers within American Protestantism have made it even more difficult to characterize the theological and polity (church government) systems of certain denominations. For instance,

sures of religiosity must be employed with careful consideration given to the history and uniqueness of the various religious groups being studied. Rarely can a single set of measures be given equal weight and meaning across all groups.

Fukuyama, as well as most other researchers who have employed multidimensional measures of religion, has taken the individual as the basic unit of analysis. The predominant focus has been upon what individuals do and believe religiously. It is equally important to understand the religious institution as a unit of analysis. This is precisely the strategy adopted by Joseph Fichter in the following essay, "Conceptualizations of the Urban Parish." For Fichter, the Roman Catholic Church in the United States provides the best example of the many facets of religious institutions. To some extent Fichter's essay, which predates the work of Glock, Lenski, and Fukuyama by almost a decade, anticipated some of the categories that other researchers would later employ. This is especially true of his conceptualization of religious institutions as *communal groups, kinship systems,* and *institutional associations.* On the other hand, his view of the parish church as a *legal corporation,* a *superimposed association,* and a *cluster of subgroupings,* provides a perspective that is very different from that of the other researchers discussed thus far.

---

the 1957 merger that created the United Church of Christ brought together three distinct theological traditions: English Reformation (Congregationalism), Continental Lutheran (The Evangelical Church), and Continental Calvinist (The Reformed Church). See William M. Newman, "The United Church of Christ Merger: A Case Study in Organizational Structure, Policy and Ideology," in Deborah Offenbacher and Constance Poster (eds.), *Social Problems and Social Policy* (New York: Appleton-Century Crofts, 1970), pp. 137–145; and Paul M. Harrison, *Power and Authority in the Free Church Tradition* (Princeton: Princeton University Press, 1959).

Conceptualizations of the Urban Parish*

by Joseph H. Fichter, S.J.

The social structure of an urban Catholic parish is highly complex At first glance this would not seem to be true because the casual observer probably sees nothing but a large number of people who satisfy their religious needs at a particular parish Church. At closer analysis, however, it will be noted that any social unit of a few thousand persons logically structures its social relations according to multiple patterns. It seems true also that the researcher not only can but must conceptualize the parish in multiple ways in order to achieve meaningful analysis.

The normal large urban Catholic parish may be studied under the following aspects, even though each varies in importance as a conceptual frame of reference for research. The parish may be called

Joseph Fichter, S.J., is professor of sociology at Loyola University in New Orleans. His writings include: *Social Relations in the Urban Parish* (1954); *Sociology* (1957); *Priest and People* (1965); *Religion as an Occupation* (1966); *Parochial School: A Sociological Study* (1964); *Organization Man in the Church* (1973); and *One Man Research: Reminiscences of a Catholic Sociologist* (1973).

Reprinted from *Social Forces*, 31, no. 1 (1952): 43–46. Used with permission of the author and publisher.

* Read before the fifteenth annual meeting of the Southern Sociological Society, Atlanta, Georgia, March 28, 1952.

29

(a) a legal corporation, (b) a super-imposed association, (c) an institutionalized association, (d) a communal group, (e) a cluster of sub-groupings. It is also helpful for some purposes to conceive the parish as (f) a series of statistical categories and (g) a system of kinship groupings.

(a) As a *legal corporation* formed under the laws of the State, the urban Catholic parish has as its purposes and objectives: "the holding and administering of property, real, personal and mixed, so that the same may be devoted to religious services, charitable, educational and literary purposes, for the benefit of those who attend the Roman Catholic Church belonging to this corporation."

The members of this ecclesiastical corporation also constitute the Board of five Directors who manage, administer, and control it. These are the legal officers of the parish. The Bishop is *ex-officio* President, the Vicar-General of the diocese is the Vice-President; the Pastor holds the combined office of Secretary and Treasurer. The two remaining members of the Board are lay parishioners, sometimes called "trustees," who are appointed by the Bishop, usually for a term of two years. They are almost always successful professional or business men.

In practice, all legal and fiscal business of the parish is conducted by the Secretary-Treasurer, the Pastor. The corporation charter forbids him to contract any debt over two hundred dollars and stipulates that "no real estate belonging to the corporation shall be sold, mortgaged or disposed of in any way, without the vote and consent of all the five Directors."

The obvious intent of this parochial charter is that the effective legal and financial control of the parish be in the hands of the clergy. The history of lay trusteeship[1] in the United States has demonstrated the wisdom and practicality of this arrangement. The Pastor, who is himself subject to higher authority in the administration of the parish, usually recognizes that the practical advice of the lay trustees can be very valuable. At the same time he usually makes it clear that their function is consultative and not directive. The Pastor is obliged to meet with the trustees only on important financial decisions.

It is evident that the lay people in the Catholic parish are not stock-holders, or members in any way, of this corporation. They contribute the money and the properties which the corporation ad-

---

[1] For a brief and reliable discussion of trustees, see Theodore Maynard, *The Story of American Catholicism* (New York: Macmillan, 1941), pp. 187–196, 235–237.

ministers. They may be termed "beneficiaries" of the religious services, and of the charitable, educational and literary purposes for which the corporation was constituted. The two lay members of the Board are not their elected representatives. Viewed in this legal light, the American urban parish is neither a spontaneously organized social structure nor a mass-controlled organization. The lay people have no formal authority, direct or indirect, over the parochial corporation, but the corporation is an instrument of service to them.[2]

(b) The urban Catholic parish may be called a *super-imposed association* in the sense that the conditions for its existence are fixed by Rome through the local Bishop. Canon Law 216 points out that every diocese must be subdivided into definite territorial areas, each with its own permanent pastor, people and church.[3] Thus, the religious association of lay Catholics in any given parish is not a matter of choice by the people themselves as long as they reside within the designated boundaries. In practice, of course, some of the lay persons in any parish attend neighboring Catholic churches for religious services, and some participate in other parochial activities there, but a formally imposed and morally obligatory relationship still remains between them and the Pastor of their own parish.

Of more importance than the territorial assignment of people to a definite parish is the fact that the general framework of their religious functions and objectives is also prescribed by church authorities outside the parish. This means that whenever the parishioners assemble for religious activities they follow a pattern of worship and devotion which is *essentially* the same throughout the whole Catholic Church. The liturgical rituals of the Church, insofar as they are designed for public and corporate worship, can be termed ideal pat-

[2] This arrangement differs sharply from that of contemporary Canadian parishes. The "fabrique," or corporation, owns the real estate given by the parishioners for public worship; "it is the proprietor of the parish church, the rectory, and the sums of money assigned for the upkeep of those buildings and the celebration of the liturgical ceremonies." A lay warden is elected by the parishioners every year, and the three most recently elected wardens form the board of administration. They "set limits to the authority of the parish priest; they also set limits to the authority of the bishop." This is written by the Most Reverend Maurice Roy, Archbishop of Quebec, in *The Parish and Democracy in French Canada* (Toronto, Ontario: University of Toronto Press, 1950), pp. 17ff. Some American dioceses are "corporation soles" so that the parishes are merely part of the single local corporation, the diocese.

[3] See also the discussion in Joseph H. Fichter, S.J., *Dynamics of a City Church: Southern Parish*, Vol. 1 (Chicago: University of Chicago Press, 1951), chap. 2, "What is a Parish?"

terns of social relations. The moral and social behavior of parishioners, normatively posited in commandments, precepts, and rules of the Church, are also superimposed.

(c) The Catholic parish may also be conceptualized as an *institutionalized association*.[4] This is the fact which makes the parish a unique social phenomenon, different from every other parish. In other words, the patterned relationships in the urban parish have become institutionalized *locally*, by and for these particular people over a period of several generations in this designated territory of so many city blocks.

As Joachim Wach remarks, "the sociologist of religion, interested in the study of the cultic group, cannot be satisfied with reviewing its theology as the foundation of the theory and practice of fellowship among its members."[5] Even the most sympathetic observer will note that the facts of social life in the urban parish frequently fail to conform to the expectations of social thought and behavior implied in the moral and dogmatic teachings of the Catholic Church.

This is simply another way of saying that while there are many similarities among Catholic parishes all over the world there are also distinctive features in each. The associative processes and patterns are formed, maintained and transmitted by these particular parishioners. They are affected by the age and sex, and by occupational, marital, economic, and class status of the parishioners, as well as by the manner in which the parishioners perform the roles consonant with these statuses. They are affected by the various personalities which individuate each human interaction, by the goals toward which the roles *actually* function, and by the strong secular values of the American urban and industrial milieu.

(d) The fourth way in which the Catholic parish may be conceptualized is that of a *communal group*,[6] that is, of a number of

---

[4] The term "institutionalized group" used by Florian Znaniecki, seems to combine both concepts used above, "superimposed association" and "institutionalized association." His definition denotes "groups which are essentially cooperative products of their own members, but whose collective functions and statuses are partly institutionalized by other social groups." See his article, "Social Organizations and Institutions," in Gurvitch and Moore, *Twentieth Century Sociology* (New York: Philosophical Library, 1945), p. 212. Hiller's concept of the "institutional group" is partly similar to our concept of the parish as a "super-imposed association" in that the cultural system of the Church provides a common value-orientation for the members of the parish. See his article, "Institutions and Institutional Groups," *Social Forces*, 20 (March 1942), pp. 297–306.

[5] See his article, "Sociology of Religion," in Gurvitch and Moore, *Twentieth Century Sociology*, p. 428.

[6] MacIver's "communal type" of society, as distinguished from the "associational type," includes a number of factors other than "high values." See R. M. MacIver

people who are held together primarily by their high religious values. Everett Clinchy, who is a close observer of religious behavior, says that "the central element in the structure of a group's existence is religion. . . . The heart and will of every culture lie in the beliefs of the group: that is, its religion. Without convictions about what is good, and without specific beliefs about its goals and the means to attain them, the group's *espirit* will decline, and the group will perish."[7]

This concept of the parish as a communal group rests upon the negative notion that the group will perish unless it holds values of a high order. This is one of Sorokin's most emphasized sociological principles: that people are truly integrated by their "systems of meanings and values."[8] Znaniecki also uses this principle when he calls a parish "a kind of great family whose members are united by a community of moral interests."[9] Finally, Donovan remarks that "the members of the parish, both clerical and lay, share in a unity which stems from their common religious beliefs and which finds expression in their joint participation in group functions."[10]

These observations constitute the hypothesis that the *sharing of common values* is the essential sociological and psychological factor of the Catholic parish as a group. Our empirical research indicates, however, that the *sharing of functions* is a much more practical factor of unity. In simple terms, this means that when people do things together which they think are worth doing they tend to be drawn together. The interacting influence of cooperative functions seems to increase the group appreciation of values, and this again leads to progressive interaction.

It is quite possible that smaller village parishes tend toward the ideal of the communal group. In the large urban parish, however, the great majority of lay persons use the local Church as a kind of "service station" for their religious needs: a place to go to Mass and

---

and Charles H. Page, *Society: An Introductory Analysis* (New York: Rinehart, 1937), pp. 8–12, 218–229.

[7] See his article, "The Efforts of Organized Religion," *The Annals of the American Academy of Political and Social Sciences* (March 1946), p. 128.

[8] Pitirim Sorokin, *Society, Culture and Personality* (New York: Harper, 1947), p. 127.

[9] William Thomas and Florian Znaniecki, *The Polish Peasant in Europe and America* (New York: Knopf, 1927), I, p. 275.

[10] John D. Donovan, "The Sociologist Looks at the Parish," *American Catholic Sociological Review* (June 1950), p. 68. Wach similarly says that "religious communities are constituted by loyalty to an ideal or set of values which is the basis of their communion." "Sociology of Religion," *loc. cit.*, p. 428.

confession, to get married and have their children baptized, and to have their old folks buried. Their communal "social" bond with the priests and other parishioners is analogous to that which an automobile owner has with the gas station manager and with the latter's other customers. It is somewhat like the professional relationship between dentist and patients.[11]

While the concept of a genuinely integrated communal group does not apply to the whole urban parish as a social aggregate, this does not mean that there is no nuclear group which cannot be so conceived. As a matter of fact, there is at the heart of every urban parish a group of parishioners who are united primarily through their high religious values. It appears that only these can fulfill Znaniecki's definition of the parish as a "great family."

(e) The fact that various functions are performed and various objectives attained in an organized way leads to the fifth concept of the urban parish as a cluster of *sub-groupings*. Each of these has its own objectives, activities, and membership. The Pastor is theoretically and *ex-officio* the highest authority in all of them. Their ultimate objective must in some way conform to that of the parish as a whole: the sanctification and salvation of souls. But their immediate objectives help to specify the various groups.

It has been noted that the total parochial association is superimposed and maintained according to universal standards of the Catholic Church. Much more latitude is allowed in the origin and maintenance of the parochial sub-groupings. The original impetus for the formation of a group comes sometimes from the people, and sometimes from the pastor. Occasionally its formation may be requested by the Bishop.

These "parish societies" may be classified in many ways, according to age and sex composition, marital status and religious conditions of membership, although these norms are not in every instance defined. They may be placed on a continuum indicating the degree of success or failure they experienced in striving for their objectives. They may be divided as formally imposed or locally initiated, who originated them and where.

Probably the most useful sociological approach is that which considers the main functions and goals of the parish organizations. (1) The *liturgical* groups are those which assist at the religious services performed in the church itself. The Acolyte Society, the Choir

---

[11] D. W. Brogan developed a similar analogy in his article, "The Catholic Church in America," *Harper's*, 200, pp. 40—50, where he says that the Catholic Pastor is like the Postmaster who holds the local franchise for all postal transactions.

and the Ushers, take a more or less direct part in the services; the Ladies' Altar Society provides the appurtenances of the sanctuary. (2) The *socio-spiritual* groups are sufficiently distinctive in their functions and objectives that they may be considered separate from those in the above category. They are organized into social groups for the primary objective of sanctification. They are Children of Mary, Sodalities, Junior and Senior Holy Name Societies, Nocturnal Adoration Societies. (3) In the category of *educational* groupings are included the Parents' Club, the Confraternity of Christian Doctrine, and study clubs of various kinds. (4) The *ameliorative* groups do the corporal works of mercy, St. Vincent de Paul for men and the Daughters of Mercy for women. In a sense they act as the "relief agencies" of the parish for the needy families and individuals of the parish. (5) Finally, the primarily *recreational* objectives are pursued in the Boy and Girl Scouts, Brownies and Cubs, boys' and girls' sport teams, and in the adult committees which promote these groupings.

Besides the five general conceptualizations described so far it seems useful also to think of the urban parish (f) according to the statistical categories into which the membership falls and (g) as a network of kinship and family relationships.

The purpose of the classification of parishioners is the comparison of one category to another and of each to the religious ideals and practices which the parish is promoting. In the first volume of the *Southern Parish* series these categories were employed in many ways according to age, sex, marital status, socio-economic status, length of residence, amount of schooling, nationality background, and so forth.

The concept of the parish as a network of family relations is more subtle and more difficult to actualize. While it is probably false to assert as a generalization that "religion runs in families," we have found that participation in the parochial programs is frequently a "family affair." We noted this particularly in the parish organizations; the youths tend to be active in their groups when the parents are active in adult societies.

In the abstract analysis of an urban parish according to these various seven conceptual frameworks there is danger that the social roles of the persons-in-action may be neglected. For example, there can be no question that the key persons in the operation of any Catholic parish are the priests. This is true not only of the direct "care of souls" but also of the whole problem of maintaining the social structure as a going concern. Thus the pastoral roles may be separately analyzed.

At the same time, a parish is nothing without its lay membership. According to the theory of "organized Catholic Action" the lay people participate with the priests in the work of the hierarchy. The democratic ideology of the urban American culture is a social fact which cannot be neglected. In other words, the urban parish in America seems to steer a psychologically difficult course between the "congregational approach" wherein the lay people run the Church, and the "authoritarian approach" wherein the lay people are passive subjects of church administration.

There are several themes in Fichter's essay that have remained important in the subsequent development of the field. First, even though he examined institutional rather than individual aspects of religion, he clearly anticipated the contemporary interest in the multidimensionality of religious phenomena. Second, he showed that formal religious organizational membership is related to other nonorganizational expressions of religion. Lenski, for instance, later showed the importance of Fichter's concept of communal religion in his study, *The Religious Factor.* Third, Fichter's appreciation for the different internal subgroups in religious organizations would later be developed by O'Dea and others who have stressed the problems and dynamics of parish organizations.[12] In this context, while his choice of the Catholic Church as a subject for studying aspects of religious organizations seems a bit "loaded," much of what he says can be said of Protestant and Jewish congregations as well. The Catholic Church simply reveals some of the tendencies discussed in a more accentuated way.

Perhaps the most ambitious development of the multidefinitional approach to the study of religion is Morton King's 1967 essay "Measuring the Religious Variable: Nine Proposed Dimensions." King's essay is a comprehensive study of the subject, as well as a dramatic illustration of the effects of technology upon social scientific research.

A friend of this writer tells the story of having spent an entire summer during his graduate student years attempting to do a factor analysis of some data. At that point in time, some fifteen

---

[12] O'Dea's essay on this subject is reprinted on pages 271–285 of this anthology.

years ago, today's high speed computer techniques were not yet available. Working with paper, pencil, and a simple desk calculator, it took him three long months to prepare his data for a factor analysis and he never did finish the analysis! Today, factor and cluster analyses can be performed on a computer in a matter of seconds. This kind of technological advance has had a major impact upon the kinds of techniques of data analysis that social scientists employ. Some kinds of analytical techniques, that even ten years ago were infrequently done because of the time and effort required, are routinely employed today.

Before turning to King's unique study, it will be helpful to review some basic features of factor and cluster analysis. Social scientists have been using correlational statistics for many years. Suppose, for instance, in a given study we want to know the degree to which belief A is related to belief B. How great is the probability that a person who says he or she believes in God also says that he or she believes Jesus is the son of God? There are several widely employed correlational statistics that will provide an answer to this question. If, after using one of these statistical tests, we found a statistic of $+1.00$, this would mean that the relationship between belief A and belief B is both positive and high. That is, whenever belief A was present so was belief B. In another instance one might encounter a statistic of -1.00, meaning that the relationship between two beliefs was negative and high. Perhaps it was found that people who claim to be atheists never believe that Jesus is the son of God. Of course, such high correlations are rarely encountered in social scientific research. It is more frequently the case that we encounter lesser degrees of relationship between variables, that we are able to explain only part of the variation in the relationship between A and B.

Let us now examine a more complicated research situation. Suppose we are examining not just the relationship between belief A and belief B, but the relationships between belief A and beliefs B through Z. In other words, we wish to know the extent of the multiple relationships between a large number of beliefs. Moreover, we may not have yet decided upon the name of the social variable that describes this set of interrelated measures of belief. We may, for instance, find that beliefs A, C, L, M, and Z seem to "hang together" as a set. Yet none of these beliefs seem to be related to another set of interrelated items consisting of B, I, D, O, and Y. After using a factor or cluster analysis to determine these groupings of beliefs we may further inspect the substantive content of the beliefs in each group to see if they "make sense," to see if there is perhaps some unifying element or dimension that they share. In other words rather than assuming that there is a variable called "doctrinal orthodoxy" that can be measured by an index of belief statements A, B, C, and D, we are, in fact, testing the hypothesis that such a variable exists.[13] This is precisely what Morton King has done.

Morton King began by surveying the literature on multidimensional approaches to the study of religion. He then compiled a large number of statements about the cognitive and active aspects of religion. While some of these statements had been used in previous studies, including those of Lenski, Fukuyama, and Glock and Stark, other questions were entirely new. He then took the list of 121 questions and administered them to a population of nearly 600 Methodists in Dallas, Texas. He posed the question, Are there relationships between groups of these measures that reflect a number of distinct categories of religious conduct and thought? After employing three different kinds of factor and cluster techniques, he arrived at nine distinct dimensions or religious variables. In short, he asked both the inductive question, How high are the statistical relationships (factor loadings) in these groups, as well as the deductive question, Do these groups appear to make substantive sense? As a result he was able to affirm the utility of some previously employed religious categories as well as contribute several new dimensions that may be useful in future research.

[13] This is at best a figure of speech, for we are never able to directly test a hypothesis of this type. Rather, we test the null hypothesis that there are no significant relationships between variables. If we find that the relationships observed are not likely to have been produced by chance, then we discard the null hypothesis and accept the view that there are significant interrelationships at work.

Measuring the Religious Variable: Nine Proposed Dimensions[*]

by Morton King

Is the religious variable unidimensional? If not, what are its subdimensions? Glock (1954, 1959a, 1959b, 1962), Fukuyama (1960, 1961a, 1961b), Lenski (1963), Demerath (1961, 1965), and others have accepted the multidimensional theory and proposed several somewhat different dimensions. Studies of the social and psychological correlates of individual religion have produced still other dimen-

Morton B. King is professor of sociology at Southern Methodist University. He is co-author of *Measuring Religious Dimensions: Studies of Congregational Involvement* (with Richard A. Hunt, 1972).

Reprinted from *Journal for the Scientific Study of Religion*, 6, no. 2 (1967): 173–190. Used with permission of the author and publisher.

[*] Revision of a paper read at the 61st Annual Meeting of the American Sociological Association, August, 1966. Support was provided by the Graduate Council of the Humanities at Southern Methodist University and by the Division of National Missions of the Methodist Church. Useful consultations were held with research staff of the National Council of Churches, the United Presbyterian Church in the U.S.A., the United Church of Christ, the American Baptist Convention, and the Methodist Church. Special thanks are due the Dallas Area office of The Methodist Church for its cooperation and to Nurhan Findikyan, Institute of Behavioral Research, Texas Christian University, for his advice and help with programming and computer analysis.

39

sions. (See, for example: Allen and Hites, 1961; Broen, 1957; Brown, 1962; Cline and Richards, 1965; Smith, 1963). However, the uni-dimensional hypothesis has not been explicitly tested. This paper reports an exploratory attempt to do so. The main goal of the research was to test procedures which might be used in a more comprehensive survey.

Study Procedures

Selection of Items

The first problem was to construct a questionnaire containing questions about many aspects of an individual's religious beliefs, attitudes, and behaviors and of his involvement in a congregation. Hypothetical dimensions were used to guide the selection of items. Both dimensions and items were sought in three preliminary surveys and by a careful search of the relevant literature.[1] The latter was based on correspondence, "snow-balling" references cited, and use of sociological and psychological abstracts. The following eleven possible dimensions were finally chosen:

1. Assent to creedal propositions
2. Religious knowledge
3. Theological perspective (e.g., on self, society, church)
4. Dogmatism *vs* openness to growth and change
5. Extrinsic *vs* intrinsic orientation
6. Participation in and understanding of public and private worship
7. Involvement with friends in the social activities of the congregation
8. Participation in organizational activities
9. Financial support and attitudes toward the church
10. Loyalty to the institutional church
11. Attitudes toward ethical questions.

The items, 7 to 17 for each dimension, were selected or modified from questionnaires used in other studies or were constructed as possible indicators of a hypothetical dimension. The goal was items with maximum likelihood of proving useful in other localities and denominations, even non-Christian religions. Therefore, all types of

---

[1] See Bibliography. Titles followed by "**B**" provided general background for the research. Those followed by "**D**" suggested dimensions, and those by "**I**," items. A number of titles were not discovered until after fieldwork began.

parochial bias were minimized. There were 121 "religious" items in all, each with four alternatives. About 25 other questions sought data on possible correlates: (a) such socioeconomic variables as age, sex, education, and income; (b) whether the respondent had been converted to, confirmed by, or drifted into the church; and (c) a measure of ethnic tolerance.

Sample

The subjects were 575 active and inactive members of six Methodist congregations in the city of Dallas and its suburbs. The congregations, which were selected by purposive sampling methods in order to provide a wide range of subjects, differed in: size (80 to 1,000 members), socioeconomic level, age of congregation, age composition of members, location (inner-city to rural enclave), and congregational emphasis (e.g., pietistic, liturgical, "liberal"). Questionnaires were mailed to a 50 percent random sample of all resident members of each congregation over the signature of its pastor. A stamped return envelope was enclosed. Follow-up by letter and telephone over eight weeks failed to produce more than a 48 percent return. Active members are no doubt over-represented among the respondents, and illiterate and semi-literate persons excluded. Respondents, however, are heterogeneous on such relevant indices as age, self-rating of activity, education, and income. For most purposes, 500 cases are considered a satisfactory minimum for factor and cluster analyses. A representative sample is not required for the type of conclusions to be drawn.

Analysis

These 121 items, believed to be indicators of the religious variable or some dimension thereof, plus 10 items indicating ethnic tolerance, were intercorrelated using the Pearson product moment technique. A powered vector *factor analysis* was run on the resulting 131 × 131 matrix. Nineteen factors were obtained containing three or more items with a loading of .300 or above. Several bore some resemblance to the hypothetical dimensions. In order to make the desired cluster analysis, the matrix was reduced to 100 items by dropping three types of items: questions of religious knowledge which neither formed a factor nor entered importantly into others; the ethnic tolerance items which formed a cohesive factor but did not enter importantly into others; and questions which failed to appear in any factor. A new 100 × 100 matrix was computed. The same factor analysis was repeated and a hierarchal cluster analysis made. The *second factor analysis* produced seventeen factors containing three or more items with a loading of .300 or above. The *cluster analysis* produced twelve clusters of three or more items having an average intercorrelation of items of .350 or above.[2]

Findings

Factor and cluster analyses do not test hypotheses. They merely put data into a form which can be compared to a theoretical model. Since there is no accepted mathematical procedure for making such a comparison, it must be made by the researcher—using his best judgment, maximum objectivity, and familiarity with the data. Careful study of the factors and clusters in relation to the prime hypothesis and the eleven hypothetical dimensions produced the following conclusions:

1. *The hypothesis of unidimensionality must be rejected for these data,* and the multidimensional view of religious belief, commitment, and participation is given tentative support. This conclusion is based on two types of evidence.

The first type is provided by the several factors and clusters produced by the three analyses. Each such set of items was examined to see if it "made sense" as an aspect of religious belief or behavior. Some did.[3] These were given a tentative descriptive label and are presented in Appendix A in tabular form: thirteen from the first factor analysis, ten from the second, and twelve from the cluster analysis. Inspection will show that the three analyses showed agreement on the existence of several internally consistent sets of items, each of which can be interpreted as a meaningful aspect or component of religion.

Secondly, the first or "general" factor (see Appendix B) is not so general as to include items from all or most of the other factors. It controlled only a small percent of the variance. While it is true that it drew items from several of the hypothetical dimensions, the items seem to reveal only two main themes: belief and faith—assent to basic Christian doctrines and commitment to a reality which has been experienced. These 42 items would make a better measure of individual religion than most indices now in use. However, de-

---

[2] Copies of the questionnaire, factors, and clusters may be secured from the author. Space does not permit their reproduction here, but full publication is planned in a monograph.

[3] Some did not: first factor analysis, six; second factor analysis, seven. All these were sets of three or four items among which I could find no common "theme."

pendence upon such a measure would omit several important aspects of belief, attitude, and experience, as well as most aspects of congregational participation.

2. *Nine dimensions can be identified from these items and for these subjects.* They are presented in Appendix C as hypotheses for further research. The items in each dimension appear in a rough array, beginning with those believed to be of most value in measuring that dimension and ending with those probably of least value. The ordering was based on four considerations: 1. degree of agreement between the three analyses; 2. rank of items within factors and clusters; 3. size of the factor loadings and average inter-item correlations; and 4. my judgment regarding germaneness of item content. (See discussion of Dimension VI, below.)

How the nine dimensions were chosen can be seen by looking again at Appendix A. Eight derive from agreement between the cluster analysis and at least one factor analysis. Dimension V, Commitment to Intellectual Search Despite Doubt, is based on the factor analyses alone. For reasons noted in Appendix C, it is the most questionable of the nine.

The way in which the items for each dimension were selected can be illustrated by Dimension VI, Openness to Religious Growth, and its parent factors and cluster. The latter are displayed in Appendix D. The five items selected for the dimension (listed as Dimension VI in Appendix C) appear in both factors and in the cluster. The content of the fourth item *seems* inappropriate. It was used, however, because it has a high loading in all analyses. If it had been near the arbitrary cut-off points (FL, .300 or AIC, .350), it would have been dropped. Conversely, the third item, because its content is so obviously germane, would have been used even if it had been slightly below the cut-off points on all analyses (as it was on one). Two other items (the items which are fifth in the Fifth Factor and fifth in the Sixth Cluster) were not included since they appeared in only one analysis, had lower loadings, and did not seem germane. In some cases, an item from only one analysis was used, provided it seemed germane and was above the cut-off point. An intercorrelation matrix was prepared for all the prospective items in a dimension. A few items were dropped because the direction of some of their correlations contradicted the content of the dimension.

3. *Some of the nine dimensions are similar to ones proposed in the literature.*

Creedal Assent and Personal Commitment (I) seems to include what Glock calls "ideological;" Fukuyama, "creedal;" and Lenski, "doctrinal orthodoxy" items. In both the factors and the cluster, however, the creedal items never occurred alone, but were always associated with items indicating personal experience and commitment.

Participation in Congregational Activities (II) is related to or overlaps with Glock's "ritualistic," Fukuyama's "cultic," and Lenski's "associational" dimensions. Note, however, that attendance at worship services, including Communion, is included here as an "activity." No "liturgical" dimension appeared. There was no factor or cluster for worship—public, private, or a combination of the two.

Personal Religious Experience (III) seems similar to Glock's "experiential" and Lenski's "devotionalism;" less so, to Fukuyama's "devotional."

Each of these three scholars offered a different fourth dimension. What Lenski (and Demerath) have called "communal involvement" finds some support in *Personal Ties in the Congregation* (IV). Fukuyama's "cognitive" and Glock's "intellectual" dimension was tested with ten items of religious knowledge, including facts about the Bible and about church history and polity. They failed to form a usable factor or cluster. Glock's "consequential" dimension is the hardest to define operationally in questionnaire research. An attempt was made with thirteen items about attitudes on personal and social ethics, but these too failed to form a factor or cluster.

The preliminary surveys, supported by the literature, suggested a dimension between the polarities of dogmatic rigidity (liberal or orthodox) and openness to growth and change. Nine items prepared as possible indicators all appeared, but were scattered among ten factors and clusters. There, they were mixed with five of the seven "extrinsic" items (Allport, 1959, and Feagin, 1964) and ten items from still other hypothetical dimensions. From these factors and clusters, four proposed dimensions were constructed. While there is some overlap among them, there is more difference. Two were labeled: *Commitment to Intellectual Search Despite Doubt* (V) and *Openness to Religious Growth* (VI). The items for *Dogmatism* (VIIa) and *Extrinsic Orientation* (VIIb) were so associated in the parent factors and clusters that they are numbered together. Dimension VI seems closer to V than to VIIa.

The eight financial items produced two factors instead of one: five relating to *Financial Behavior* (VIIIa) and three to *Financial Attitudes* (VIIIb).

Seven items, drawn from a variety of hypothetical dimensions, formed a set dealing with *Talking and Reading about Religion* (IX).

These items may be the nucleus for an index of "salience," of how important a person's religion is to him.

Discussion

Factor and cluster analyses, with the modern computer, proved suitable and useful tools for exploring the nature of the religious variable. Certain dimensions of individual religious belief and involvement were identified for members of one denomination in one locality. The clusters and factors obtained showed some agreement with each other. Many of the factors and clusters "made sense" as different aspects of religion. Guided by rule of thumb cut-off points and common sense, it was possible to select sets of items which resemble some of the dimensions hypothesized in the literature. Nine such tentative dimensions are presented as stepping stones to further research.

Additional analysis of the same data continues. Item analyses are being made for each dimension, as well as for the parent factors and clusters. An attempt at scale construction, using alternative methods, will be made on each group of items which survives. If scales are developed, their utility will be tested by correlation with each other and with (a) a measure of racial tolerance, (b) information on how the individual first joined the Church, this denomination, and the local congregation, and (c) such personal data as age, sex, education, and income.

The exploratory work here reported was a success if it proves to be a small, preliminary step in the "slow process of beginning to build more adequate measures" of the religious variable (Glock, 1962, p. 108). The multidimensional hypothesis should be retested with greater rigor on a number of different, and larger, populations. Subjects should be drawn from a variety of religious backgrounds (Jewish as well as Christian) and from a variety of socio-cultural areas (within and outside the United States). The cooperation of several agencies, including denominations, may be required. Each replication should contain new items in addition to those found useful in this and other studies. New items should be selected both as better indicators of these nine dimensions and as indicators of other possible dimensions.

Appendix A. Comparison of Factors and Clusters[1]

First Factor Analysis	Second Factor Analysis	Cluster Analysis
1. Belief & Commitment (42)[2]	1. Belief & Commitment (42)	3. Belief & Commitment (18)
2. (Tolerance Scale (10), removed from matrix)		
3. Church activity (26)	2. Church activity (29)	4. Attendance & Activity (4)
		8. Activities (12)
4. Extrinsic/Dogmatism (15)	3. Dogmatism w/ ethics (9)	12. Dogmatism (3)
	15. Extrinsic (5)	14. Extrinsic (4)
6. Intellectual/Doubt (8)	4. Intellectual/Doubt (7)	
7. Knowledge of polity (3)		
9. Personal experience (6)	6. Personal experience (11)	2. Personal experience (10)
	21. Personal experience (5)	20. Reality of God & Sin (3)
10. Friends in congregation (3)		1. Friends and subgroups (3)
11. Knowledge of Bible (3)		
13. Open to growth (5)	5. Open to growth (7)	6. Open to growth (6)
14. "Conservative" noncontributor (4)		
21. "Liberal" non-contributor (4)		
22. Talking and Reading (4)		10. Talk about religion (7)
24. Anti-Negro/ Dogmatism (5)		
	10. Financial attitude (3)	7. Contributions (2)
	11. Contributions (4)	15. Regular contributions (2)

[1] These are factors and clusters which "made sense" enough to receive a tentative label and which contained four or more items. Sets with less than four items were included only if they were related to a hypothetical dimension.

[2] The number preceding each descriptive label gives the order in which that set of items was produced by the analysis. The number following in parentheses is the number of items in that factor or cluster.

Appendix B. The First or "General" Factor[1]

The first or "general" factor in the first factor analysis consisted of 42 items. These included the 15 items proposed as the first dimension in Appendix C and the following 27 items. Comparable factor loadings of the 15 items are given in the first column of Appendix C.

Item Loading	Content
+.600	Private prayer is one of the most important and satisfying aspects of my religious experience.[2]
+.599	I frequently feel very close to God in prayer, during public worship, or at important moments in my daily life.
+.518	How often do you ask God to forgive your sin? (Regularly-Never)
+.515	The truly religious person has the joy and peace which come from recognizing that he is a forgiven sinner.
+.509	I know what it feels like to repent and experience forgiveness of sin.
+.481	To what extent has God influenced *your* life? (Very much-Not at all)
+.477	When you have decisions to make in your everyday life, how often do you try to find out what God wants you to do? (Regularly-Never)
+.469	How often do you pray privately in places other than at church? (Regularly-Never)
+.466	I enjoy giving money to the Church.
+.450	The Church is important to me as a place where I get the understanding and courage for dealing with the trials and problems of life.
+.438	Good Christians make the best and most loyal citizens.
+.412	The truly religious person feels compelled to continue growing in understanding of his faith.
+.402	The more liberally I support the Church financially, the closer I feel to it and to God.
+.402	Life has no meaning apart from a relationship to God.
+.391	The truly religious person steadily strives to grow in knowledge and understanding of what it means to live as a child of God.
−.386	I find myself believing in God some of the time, but not at other times.
+.382	The truly religious person strives to be moral in all aspects of everyday life.
+.378	Church membership has helped me to meet the right kind of people.
+.373	People should do what is morally right regardless of the consequences.
+.361	Church is important as a place to go for comfort and refuge from the trials and problems of life.
+.359	I enjoy the intellectual stimulation of learning about the Bible and about the history and doctrines of the Church.
+.352	A Church is a group whose members know and care about what happens to each other.
+.347	How often do you read the Bible? (Regularly-Never)
+.332	The main reason I attend Church is to help me live a better life during the week.
+.328	I try to cooperate with the pastor in his program for the congregation.
+.309	If you think and live by positive religious principles, you have a better chance of being happy, healthy and prosperous.
+.305	My interest in and real commitment to religion is greater now than when I first joined the Church.

[1] The items were the same in both factor analyses. There were very minor changes in item loadings (up to .01), and hence in rank. In the first analysis, 10.6 percent of the variance was controlled; in the second, 13.3 percent.

[2] All items were followed by four response alternatives, which ranged from "very accurate" to "very inaccurate" or from "strongly agree" to "strongly disagree," unless otherwise indicated.

Appendix C. Nine Proposed Dimensions[1]

1st Factor Analysis	2nd Factor Analysis	AIC Cluster Analysis	
			Item Loadings

I. Creedal Assent and Personal Commitment

1st Factor Analysis	2nd Factor Analysis	AIC Cluster Analysis	
.831	.831	.675	I believe in God as a Heavenly Father who watches over me and to whom I am accountable. (Accurate-Inaccurate)[2]
.788	.789	.675	I know that I need God's continual love and care. (Accurate-Inaccurate)
.792	.793	.647	I believe in eternal life. (Accurate-Inaccurate)
.734	.735	.647	I believe that Christ is a living reality. (Accurate-Inaccurate)
.748	.749	.606	I believe in salvation as release from sin and freedom for new life. (Accurate-Inaccurate)
.636	.640	.561	I believe that God revealed himself to man in Jesus Christ. (Accurate-Inaccurate)
.623	.624	.536	I believe that the Word of God is revealed through the Scriptures. (Accurate-Inaccurate)
.623	.624	.510	I believe in the Church as God's agent of salvation in the world. (Accurate-Inaccurate)
.654	.655	.491	I know that God answers my prayers. (Accurate-Inaccurate)
.583	.584	.469	I believe that the Bible provides basic moral principles to guide every decision of my daily life: with family and neighbors, in business and financial transactions, and as a citizen of the nation and the world. (Accurate-Inaccurate)
.561	.561	.452	I think of the Church as a place where I can hear God's Word for me. (Accurate-Inaccurate)
.523	.523	.436	I believe that lay men and women, as well as clergy, are called by God to a ministry of witness and service in the world. (Accurate-Inaccurate)
.527	.526	.418	The purpose of worship and prayer is to find out what God wants us to do. (Agree-Disagree)
.478	.477	.403	The main purpose of the Church is to reconcile men to God and each other, thus establishing the conditions for "newness of life." (Agree-Disagree)
.467	.467	.387	Property (house, automobile, money, investments, etc.) belongs to God; we only hold it in trust for Him. (Agree-Disagree)

II. Participation in Congregational Activities

1st Factor Analysis	2nd Factor Analysis	AIC Cluster Analysis	
.739	.812	.574	How would you rate your activity in this congregation? (Very active-Inactive)
.831	.716	.667	(—) During the last year, how many Sundays per month on the average have you gone to a worship service? (None-Three or more)
.774	.673	.667	(—) How many Sundays out of the last four have you attended worship services? (None-Three or more)

[1] All items within a dimension are positively intercorrelated, except those preceded by a minus sign (—).

[2] As administered, all items were followed by four response alternatives, along the continua indicated here.

Appendix C. Nine Proposed Dimensions (continued)

1st Factor Analysis	2nd Factor Analysis	AIC Cluster Analysis	
Item Loadings			
.584	.725	.574	How often do you spend evenings at church meetings or in church work? (Regularly-Never)
.774	.666	.465	How often have you taken Communion during the past year? (Regularly-Never)
.584	.633	.542	(—) How many times during the last month have you attended Sunday School or some equivalent educational activity? (None-Three or more)
.511	.644	.520	I keep pretty well informed about my congregation and have some influence on its decisions. (Accurate-Inaccurate)
.512	.619	.447	(—) List the offices, special jobs, committees, etc., of either the congregation or denomination in which you served during the past church year. (None-Three or more)
.489	.626	.499	Church activities (meetings, committee work, etc.) are a major source of satisfaction in my life. (Accurate-Inaccurate)
.446	.604	.499	I enjoy working in the activities of the Church. (Accurate-Inaccurate)
.474	.500	.441	I try to cooperate with the pastor in his program for the congregation. (Accurate-Inaccurate)
.443	.490	.424	All in all, how well do you think you fit in with the group of people who make up your church congregation? (Very well-Rather poorly)
.456	.462	.357	When church activities conflict with your community responsibilities, how do you handle the situation? (a. I usually choose the church activities. b. I choose church activities over half the time. c. I choose church activities less than half the time. d. I am usually faithful to my civic responsibilities.)

III. Personal Religious Experience

1st Factor Analysis	2nd Factor Analysis	AIC Cluster Analysis	
.541	.497	.464	I know what it feels like to repent and experience forgiveness of sin. (Accurate-Inaccurate)
.303	.387	.688	How often do you pray privately in places other than at church? (Regularly-Never)
.266	.357	.688	How often do you ask God to forgive your sin? (Regularly-Never)
.428	.480	.304	(—) The idea of God often seems vague to me and distant from my everyday experiences. (Accurate-Inaccurate)
.396	.319	.259	(—) The idea of sin means very little to me. (Accurate-Inaccurate)
	.301	.607	When you have decisions to make in your everyday life, how often do you try to find out what God wants you to do? (Regularly-Never)
	.526	.381	Life has no meaning apart from a relationship to God. (Agree-Disagree)
	.254	.517	To what extent has God influenced *your* life? (Very much-Not at all)

Appendix C. Nine Proposed Dimensions (continued)

Item
Loadings

1st Factor Analysis	2nd Factor Analysis	AIC Cluster Analysis	
		.304[3]	(—) I find myself believing in God some of the time, but not at other times. (Accurate-Inaccurate)
		.552	Private prayer is one of the most important and satisfying aspects of my religious experience. (Accurate-Inaccurate)
		.497	I frequently feel very close to God in prayer, during public worship, or at important moments in my daily life. (Accurate-Inaccurate)
		.406	The truly religious person has the joy and peace which come from recognizing that he is a forgiven sinner. (Agree-Disagree)

IV. Personal Ties in the Congregation

1st Factor Analysis	2nd Factor Analysis	AIC Cluster Analysis	
.604		.728	Think of your five closest friends. How many of them are members of your church congregation? (None-Three or more)
.518		.728	Of all your closest friends, how many are also members of your local congregation? (None-Many)
.725			How long have you been a member of this congregation? (Under 1 year-Over 5 years)
		.414	List the church organizations to which you belong. (For example: SS Class, Women's Society, MYF, etc.) (None-Three or more)
.247			(—) Church membership has helped me to meet the right kind of people. (Accurate-Inaccurate)

V. Commitment to Intellectual Search Despite Doubt[4]

1st Factor Analysis	2nd Factor Analysis	AIC Cluster Analysis	
.605	.560		My understanding of the central doctrines of the Church has changed considerably since I first joined. (Accurate-Inaccurate)
.399	.376		How often do you read religious non-fiction books, other than the Bible? (Regularly-Never)
.336	.367		The truly religious person is likely to have sincere and searching questions about the nature of a life of faith in God. (Agree-Disagree)
.328	.313		I enjoy the intellectual stimulation of learning about the Bible and about the history and doctrines of the Church. (Accurate-Inaccurate)
.308	.305		Usually the Communion Service does not mean very much to me. (Accurate-Inaccurate)
	.341		(—) The truly religious person is sure that his beliefs are correct. (Agree-Disagree)
.300			My interest in and real commitment to religion is greater now than when I first joined the Church. (Accurate-Inaccurate)

[3] This item is intercorrelated with the 4th and 5th items in a separate sub-cluster.
[4] Four of the 21 intercorrelations do not fit the pattern. Most of the correlations are low. Therefore, this dimension should be used cautiously, while better items are sought. The last item is the least useful.

Appendix C. Nine Proposed Dimensions (continued)

Item Loadings			
1st Factor Analysis	2nd Factor Analysis	AIC Cluster Analysis	

VI. Openness to Religious Growth

.478	.415	.645	The truly religious person steadily strives to grow in knowledge and understanding of what it means to live as a child of God. (Agree-Disagree)
.518	.486	.645	The truly religious person feels compelled to continue growing in understanding of his faith. (Agree-Disagree)
.665	.694	.325	The truly religious person is so secure in his faith that his mind is always open to explore new religious ideas. (Agree-Disagree)
.624	.618	.568	The truly religious person strives to be moral in all aspects of everyday life. (Agree-Disagree)
.336	.354	.454	The truly religious person is likely to have sincere and searching questions about the nature of a life of faith in God. (Agree-Disagree)

VIIa. Dogmatism

.462		.448	The truly religious person is sure that his beliefs are correct. (Agree-Disagree)
.313		.448	The truly religious person is sure that he is living in right relationship to God and men. (Agree-Disagree)
.331		.346	The truly religious person believes honestly and wholeheartedly in the doctrines of his church. (Agree-Disagree)
.356	.540		When a congregation or its pastor are frequently criticized by respectable citizens of the community, that church is probably not preaching the true Gospel of Jesus Christ. (Agree-Disagree)
.355	.466		Being confident that I am saved, I do not need to change or increase my religious knowledge and belief. (Accurate-Inaccurate)

VIIb. Extrinsic Orientation

.640	.327		The purpose of worship and prayer is to gain personal security and happiness. (Agree-Disagree)
.473	.594		Religion helps to keep my life balanced and steady in the same way as my citizenship, friendships, and other memberships do. (Accurate-Inaccurate)
.493		.307	The Church is most important as a place to formulate good social relationships. (Agree-Disagree)
.537		.318	The purpose of worship and prayer is to ask God to help us. (Agree-Disagree)
.365	.314		The main reason I attend Church is to help me live a better life during the week. (Accurate-Inaccurate)
.304		.351	Church is important as a place to go for comfort and refuge from the trials and problems of life. (Agree-Disagree)
.357		.318	The main reason I attend Church is to learn more about religion. (Accurate-Inaccurate)

Appendix C. Nine Proposed Dimensions (continued)

Item Loadings			
1st Factor Analysis	2nd Factor Analysis	AIC Cluster Analysis	
		.436	Church membership has helped me to meet the right kind of people. (Accurate-Inaccurate)
	.305		The Church is important to me as a place where I get the understanding and courage for dealing with the trials and problems of life. (Agree-Disagree)
			VIIIa. Financial Behavior
.747		.399	(—) During the last year, what was the average monthly contribution of your family to your local congregation? (Under $5-$50 and up)
.677		.582	(—) Last year, approximately what percent of your total family income was contributed to the Church? (1 percent or less-10 percent or more)
.531		.582	In proportion to your income, do you consider that your contributions to the Church are: (Generous-Small)
.272		.399	Are your financial contributions to the Church: a) A planned amount (per week, month, etc.), b) Irregularly, but fairly often, c) Irregularly several times a year, d) Seldom or never?
		.322	During the last year, how often have you made contributions to the Church *in addition* to the general budget and Sunday School? (Regularly-Never)
			VIIIb. Financial Attitude
	.634		I enjoy giving money to the Church. (Accurate-Inaccurate)
	.512		(—) Churches talk too much about money and not enough about what it means to be a Christian. (Agree-Disagree)
	.332		The more liberally I support the Church financially, the closer I feel to it and to God. (Accurate-Inaccurate)
			IX. Talking and Reading about Religion
.510		.524	How often do you talk about religion with your friends, neighbors, or fellow workers? (Regularly-Never)
.451		.468	How often have you personally tried to convert someone to faith in God? (Regularly-Never)
.327		.420	When faced by decisions regarding social problems and issues, how often do you seek guidance from statements and publications by the Church? (Regularly-Never)
		.524	In talking with members of your family, how often do you yourself mention religion or religious activities? (Regularly-Never)
		.387	How often in the last year have you invited someone to join or visit your church? (Regularly-Never)
		.354	How often do you read religious non-fiction books, other than the Bible? (Regularly-Never)
		.354	How often do you read the Bible? (Regularly-Never)

Appendix D. Factors and Cluster Parent to Dimension VI

Thirteenth Factor: first analysis (1.6 percent of variance)

Loading

+.665   The truly religious person is so secure in his faith that his mind is always open to explore new religious ideas.

+.624   The truly religious person strives to be moral in all aspects of everyday life.

+.519   The truly religious person feels compelled to continue growing in understanding of his faith.

+.478   The truly religious person steadily strives to grow in knowledge and understanding of what it means to live as a child of God.

+.336   The truly religious person is likely to have sincere and searching questions about the nature of a life of faith in God.

Fifth Factor: second analysis (2.6 percent of variance)

Loading

+.694   The truly religious person is so secure in his faith that his mind is always open to explore new religious ideas.

+.618   The truly religious person strives to be moral in all aspects of everyday life.

+.486   The truly religious person feels compelled to continue growing in understanding of his faith.

+.415   The truly religious person steadily strives to grow in knowledge and understanding of what it means to live as a child of God.

+.392   The truly religious person believes honestly and wholeheartedly in the doctrines of his church.

+.354   The truly religious person is likely to have sincere and searching questions about the nature of a life of faith in God.

+.345   A Church is a group whose members know and care about what happens to each other.

Sixth Cluster[1]

No. AIC

     The truly religious person steadily strives to grow in knowledge and understanding of what it means to live as a child of God.

6   .645   The truly religious person feels compelled to continue growing in understanding of his faith.

12   .568   The truly religious person strives to be moral in all aspects of everyday life.

29   .454   The truly religious person is likely to have sincere and searching questions about the nature of a life of faith in God.

51   .377   The Church is important to me as a place where I get the understanding and courage for dealing with the trials and problems of life.

66   .325   The truly religious person is so secure in his faith that his mind is always open to explore new religious ideas.

90 Attached to cluster 2

---

[1] The first column is the number of the machine operation. The second column is the average intercorrelation of items after that operation. The first two items were paired on the 6th operation with an r of .645. When the third item was added on the 12th operation, the AIC of the three items was .568. And so on.

Bibliography[1]

Books, Articles, and Theses

Allen, Edmund E., and Robert W. Hites. Factors in Religious Attitudes of Older Adolescents. *J. Soc. Psychol.*, 1961, 55, 265–273.

Allport, Gordon W. *The Individual and His Religion.* N.Y.: Macmillan, 1950.

————. Religion and Prejudice. Chapter 28, 444–459 in *The Nature of Prejudice.* Cambridge: Addison-Wesley, 1954. **(B)**

————. Religion and Prejudice. *The Crane Review,* 1959, 2, 1–10. **(B, D)**

————. The Religious Context of Prejudice. *J. Scien. Study Relig.,* 1966, 5, 447–457.

————, and P. E. Vernon. *Study of Values.* N.Y.: Houghton Mifflin, 1931. **(B)**

Argyle, Michael. *Religious Behavior.* Glencoe: The Free Press, 1959.

Armatas, Philip J. A Factor Analytic Study of Patterns of Religious Belief in Relation to Prejudice. Ph.D. dissertation, University of Denver, 1962.

Armstrong, Renate G., et al. Religious Attitudes and Emotional Adjustment. *J. Psychol. Studies,* 1962, 13, 35–47.

Ashbrook, James B. The Relationship of Church Members to Church Organization. *J. Scien. Study Relig.,* 1966, 5, 396–419.

Banerjee, Debabrata. Development of Scales for Measuring Attitudes Toward Government, Morality, Religion and Society. *Indian J. Psychol.,* 1962, 37, 137–145.

Bardis, Panos D. Religiosity Among Jewish Students in a Metropolitan University. *Sociol. Soc. Res.,* 1964, 49, 90–95.

Bigman, Stanley K. Evaluating the Effectiveness of Religious Programs. *Rev. Relig. Res.,* 1961, 2, 97–121. **(D, I)**

Broen, William E., Jr. A Factor-Analytic Study of Religious Attitudes. *J. Abnorm. Soc. Psychol.,* 1957, 54, 176–179.

Brown, Gladys Guy, and Robert F. Amundsen. Research and Evaluation at Highland Park Presbyterian Church, Dallas, Texas. 63–70 in Helen F. Spaulding (ed.), *Evaluation and Christian Education.* N.Y.: National Council of Churches, 1960. **(B)**

Brown, L. B. A Study of Religious Belief. *Brit. J. Psychol.,* 1962, 53, 259–272.

---

[1] **B** indicates titles which provided general background; **D**, those which suggested dimensions; **I**, those which provided items.

_____. Classification of Religious Orientation. *J. Scien. Study Relig.*, 1964, 4, 91–99. (**B, D**)

_____. The Structure of Religious Belief. *J. Scien. Study Relig.*, 1966, 5, 259–272.

Bultena, Louis. Church Membership and Attendance in Madison, Wisconsin. *Amer. Sociol. Rev.*, 1949, 14, 384–389.

Buss, Martin J. Comment on Hadden's "An Analysis of Some Factors Associated with Religion and Political Affiliation." *J. Scien. Study Relig.*, 1964, 3, 245–246.

Chave, Ernest J. *Measure Religion: Fifty-two Experimental Forms.* Chicago: Univ. of Chicago Book Store, 1939.

_____, and L. L. Thurstone. *Scale for the Measurement of Attitude Toward God.* Chicago: Univ. of Chicago Press, 1931.

Cline, Victor B., and James M. Richards, Jr. A Factor-Analytic Study of Religious Belief and Behavior. *J. Pers. Soc. Psychol.*, 1965, 1, 569–578.

Cook, Stuart W. (ed.). *Research Plans in the Fields of Religion, Values, and Morality.* N.Y.: Religious Education Assn., 1962.

Cooke, Terence F. Interpersonal Correlates of Religious Behavior. Ph.D. dissertation, University of Florida, 1962.

Coughenour, C. M. An Application of Scale Analysis to the Study of Religious Groups. *Rural Sociol.*, 1955, 20, 197–211.

Crysdale, R. C. S. *The Changing Church in Canada: Beliefs and Social Attitudes of United Church People.* Toronto: Board of Evangelism and Social Service, United Church of Canada, 1965.

Demerath, Nicholas J., III. Social Stratification and Church Involvement: The Church-Sect Distinction Applied to Individual Participation. *Rev. Relig. Res.*, 1961, 2, 146–154. (**B, D, I**)

_____. *Social Class in American Protestantism.* Chicago: Rand McNally, 1965.

Eister, Allan W. Empirical Research on Religion and Society: A Brief Survey. *Rev. Relig. Res.*, 1965, 6, 125–130.

Fairchild, Roy W., and John C. Winn. *Families in the Church: A Protestant Survey.* N.Y.: Association Press, 1961.

Faulkner, Joseph E., and Gordon F. De Jong. Religiosity in 5-D: An Empirical Analysis. *Social Forces*, 1966, 45, 246–254.

Feagin, Joe R. Prejudice and Religious Types: A Focused Study of Southern Fundamentalists. *J. Scien. Study Relig.*, 1964, 4, 3–13. (**B, D, I**)

Fichter, Joseph. *Dynamics of a City Church* (Southern Parish, Vol. I). Chicago: Univ. of Chicago Press, 1951. (**B**)

_____. *Social Relations in the Urban Parish* (Southern Parish, Vol. II). Chicago: Univ. of Chicago Press, 1954. (**B, D, I**)

Fisher, Seymour. Acquiescence and Religiosity. *Psychol. Reports,* 1964, 15, 784–791.

Frerking, Ken. Religious Participation of Lutheran Students. *Rev. Relig. Res.,* 1965, 6, 153–162.

Fruchter, Benjamin. *Introduction to Factor Analysis.* Princeton: Van Nostrand, 1954. (**B**)

Fukuyama, Yoshio. The Major Dimensions of Church Membership. Ph.D. dissertation, Divinity School, University of Chicago, 1960. (**B, D, I**)

————. The Major Dimensions of Church Membership. *Rev. Relig. Res.,* 1961a, 2, 154–161. (**B, D, I**)

————. Functional Analysis of Religious Beliefs. *Relig. Education,* 1961b, 56, 446–451. (**B**)

Glock, Charles Y. *Toward a Typology of Religious Orientation.* N.Y.: Bureau of Applied Social Research, Columbia University, 1954. (**B, D**)

————. The Religious Revival in America? in Jane C. Zahn (ed.), *Religion and the Face of America.* Berkeley: University Extension, University of California, 1959a. (**B**)

————. The Sociology of Religion. 153–177 in Robert K. Merton et al. (eds.), *Sociology Today.* N.Y.: Basic Books, 1959b. (**B**)

————. On the Study of Religious Commitment. 98–110 in *Review of Recent Research Bearing on Religious and Character Formation.* (Research Supplement to *Religious Education,* July–August, 1962) N.Y.: Religious Research Association. Reprint A13, Survey Research Center, University of California (Berkeley). (**B, D, I**)

————, and Rodney Stark. *Religion and Society in Tension.* Chicago: Rand McNally, 1965.

————. *Christian Beliefs and Anti-Semitism.* N.Y.: Harper & Row, 1966.

Gouldner, Helen P. Dimensions of Organizational Commitment. *Adm. Science Quart.,* 1960, 4, 468–490.

Gregory, W. Edgar. Doctrine and Attitude: A Study of the Relationships between Religious Beliefs and Socio-Political-Economic Attitudes. Ph.D. dissertation, University of California (Berkeley), 1955.

Hadden, Jeffrey K. An Analysis of Some Factors Associated with Religion and Political Affiliation in a College Population. *J. Scien. Study Relig.,* 1963, 2, 209–216. (**B, I**)

————. Reply to Buss' Comment on "An Analysis of Some Factors Associated with Religion and Political Affiliation." *J. Scien. Study Relig.,* 1965, 4, 248–249.

Hagen, Elizabeth. An Overview of Evaluation. 29–38 in Helen F. Spaulding (ed.), *Evaluation and Christian Education*. N.Y.: National Council of Churches, 1960. (**B, D**)

Hammond, Phillip E. The Role of Ideology in Church Participation. Ph.D. dissertation, Columbia University, 1960. (**B, I**)

————. Contemporary Protestant Ideology: A Typology of Church Images. *Rev. Relig. Res.,* 1961, 2, 161–169. (**B**)

Hassenger, Robert. Varieties of Religious Orientation. *Sociol. Analysis,* 1964, 25, 189–199.

Havighurst, Robert J. Criteria of Christian Personality Growth. 39–43 in Helen F. Spaulding (ed.), *Evaluation and Christian Education*. N.Y.: National Council of Churches of Christ, 1960. (**B, D, I**)

Hites, Robert W. Change in Religious Attitudes during Four Years of College. *J. Soc. Psychol.,* 1965, 6, 51–63.

Jones, F. Norwell, et al. A Direct Scale of Attitude Toward the Church. *Perceptual and Motor Skills,* 1965, 20, 319–324.

Kelly, I. B. The Construction and Evaluation of a Scale to Measure Attitude toward Any Institution. *Purdue University Studies in Higher Education,* 1934, 35, 18–36. (**B**)

Kendall, M. G. *A Course in Multivariate Analysis*. N.Y.: Hafner, 1957. (**B**)

Klausner, Samuel Z. Methods of Data Collection in Studies of Religion. *J. Scien. Study Relig.,* 1964, 3, 193–203.

Kloetzli, Walter. *The City Church—Death or Renewal*. Philadelphia: Muhlenberg Press, 1961.

Kosa, John, and Clyde Z. Nunn. Race, Deprivation and Attitude Toward Communism. *Pylon,* 1964, Fourth Quarter, 337–346. (**B, I**)

Lantz, Herman. Religious Participation and Social Orientation of 1000 University Students. *Sociol. Soc. Res.,* 1949, 33, 285–290.

Lenski, Gerhard E. Social Correlates of Religious Interest. *Amer. Sociol. Rev.,* 1953, 18, 533–544. (**B**)

————. *The Religious Factor: A Sociological Study of Religion's Impact on Politics, Economics, and Family Life*. (Revised edition, Anchor Book No. A-337) Garden City: Doubleday, 1963. (**B, D, I**)

Levinson, Daniel J. The Intergroup Relations Workshop: Its Psychological Aims and Effects. *J. Psychol.,* 1954, 38, 103–126.

McDowell, M. H. *Techniques Used in Attitudinal Measurement in Religion: 1950–60*. Salt Lake City: Westminster College, 1963.

Main, Earl D. Participation and Social Characteristics of Members Attending Mid-Western Protestant Churches. M.A. thesis, Washington University, 1963a. (**B, I**)

————. *Participation in Protestant Churches.* (Research Report No. 9-1763) Chicago: Bureau of Research, Church Federation of Greater Chicago and the Illinois Council of Churches, 1963b. (**B, I**)

Maves, Paul B. Conversion: A Behavioral Category. *Rev. Relig. Res.,* 1963, 5, 41–48.

Meissner, William W. *Annotated Bibliography in Religion and Psychology.* N.Y.: Academy of Religion and Mental Health, 1961.

Nelson, Erland. Father's Vocation and Certain Student Attitudes. *J. Abnorm. Soc. Psychol.,* 1939, 34, 275–279.

Parsons, Howard L. Religious Beliefs of Student at Six Colleges and Universities. *Relig. Education,* 1963, 58, 538–544.

Pittard, Barbara B. The Meaning and Measurement of Commitment to the Church. Ph.D. dissertation, Emory University, 1963. (**B, D, I**)

————. *The Meaning and Measurement of Commitment to the Church.* (Research Paper No. 13) Atlanta: School of Arts and Sciences, Georgia State College, 1966.

Rettig, Salomon, and Benj. Pasamanick. Changes in Moral Values among College Students. *Amer. Sociol. Rev.,* 1959, 24, 856–863.

————. Differences in the Structure of Moral Values of Students and Alumni. *Amer. Sociol. Rev.,* 1960, 25, 550–555.

Ringer, Benjamin B. The Parishioner and His Church. Ph.D. dissertation, Columbia University, 1956. (**B, D**)

Ross, Murray G. *Religious Beliefs of Youth.* N.Y.: Association Press, 1950.

Salisbury, W. Seward. Religiosity, Regional Sub-Culture, and Social Behavior. *J. Scien. Study Relig.,* 1962, 11, 94–101.

Sanai, M. An Empirical Study of Political, Religious and Social Attitudes. *Brit. J. Psychol.* (Statistical Section), 1952, 5 (II), 81–92.

Satter, George A. Some Dimensions of the Religious Attitudes of Three-Hundred Engaged Couples. Ph.D. dissertation, Purdue University, 1944. (**B, I**)

Schellenberg, James, et al., Religiosity and Social Attitudes in an Urban Congregation. *Rev. Relig. Res.,* 1965, 6, 142–146.

Schroeder, W. Widick, and Victor Obenhaus. *Religion in American Culture.* N.Y.: Glencoe, 1964.

Shaw, Marvin E., and Jack M. Wright (eds.). Political and Religious Attitudes. 301–357 in *Scales for the Measurement of Attitudes.* N.Y.: McGraw-Hill Book Co., 1967.

Smith, Leona J. Religion in Living. *Character Potential,* 1963, 2, 26–39.

Spilka, Bernard, et al. The Concept of God: A Factor-Analytic Approach. *Rev. Relig. Res.,* 1964, 6, 28–36. (**B, I**)

————, and James F. Reynolds. Religion and Prejudice: A Factor-Analytic Study. *Rev. Relig. Res.*, 1965, 6, 163–168.

Stanley, Gordon. Personality and Attitude Correlates of Religious Conversion. *J. Scien. Study Relig.*, 1964, 4, 60–63.

Stark, Rodney. Social Contexts and Religious Experience. *Rev. Relig. Res.*, 1965a, 7, 17–28.

————. A Taxonomy of Religious Experience. *J. Scien. Study Relig.*, 1965b, 5, 97–116.

Steenland, Roger L. Construction and Validation of a Religious Behaviors Inventory. Ph.D. dissertation, Purdue University, 1964.

Stotts, Herbert E., and Paul Deats, Jr. *Methodism and Society: Guidelines for Strategy* (Methodism and Society, Vol. IV). N.Y.: Abingdon, 1962. (**B, I**)

Sturges, Herbert A. Methods of Comparing Orthodoxy and Piety. *Amer. Sociol. Rev.*, 1937, 2, 372–379.

Thouless, R. H. Scientific Method in the Study of the Psychology of Religion. *Character and Personality*, 1938, 7, 103–108.

Thurstone, L. L., and E. J. Chave. *The Measurement of Attitude*. Chicago: Univ. of Chicago Press, 1929.

Tisdale, John R. Selected Correlates of Extrinsic Religious Values. *Rev. Relig. Res.*, 1966, 7, 78–84.

Vernon, Glen M. An Inquiry into the Scalability of Church Orthodoxy. *Sociol. Soc. Res.*, 1955, 39, 324–327.

————. Measuring Religion: Two Methods Compared. *Rev. Relig. Res.*, 1962, 3, 159–165. (**B**)

Westie, Frank R. A Technique for the Measurement of Race Attitudes. *Amer. Sociol. Rev.*, 1953, 18, 73–78. (**B**)

Whitam, Frederick L. Subdimensions of Religiosity as Related to Race Prejudice. M.A. thesis, Indiana University, 1957. (**B, D, I**)

————. Subdimensions of Religiosity and Race Prejudice. *Rev. Relig. Res.*, 1962, 3, 166–174. (**B**)

Williams, John P. *Social Adjustment in Methodism*. N.Y.: Bureau of Publications, Teachers College, Columbia University, 1938. (**B**)

Williams, Robin M., Jr. Religion, Value-Orientations, and Inter-group Conflict. *J. Soc. Issues*, 1956, 12, 12–20.

Wilson, W. Cody. Extrinsic Religious Values and Prejudice. *J. Abnorm. Soc. Psychol.*, 1960, 60, 286–288.

Woolston, Howard. Religious Consistency. *Amer. Sociol. Rev.*, 1937, 2, 380–388.

Yinger, J. Milton. Areas for Research in the Sociology of Religion. *Sociol. Soc. Res.*, 1958, 42, 466–472. (**B**)

Questionnaires and Unpublished Material

Anders, Sarah Frances. Religious Beliefs and Family Dependence. (Mimeo.) n.d. **(B, I)**

Bardis, Panos D., Religion Scale. (Questionnaire, Mimeo.) Toledo: University of Toledo, n.d. **(I)**

Census of Church Membership. (Questionnaire) N.Y.: Division of Church Missions, American Baptist Home Mission Societies, n.d. **(I)**

Census of Church Membership. (Questionnaire) Philadelphia: Department of City Work, Division of National Missions, The Methodist Church, n.d. **(I)**

Church Participation Survey. (Questionnaire) N.Y.: Department of Research, United Church Board for Homeland Ministries, n.d. **(I)**

Crane, William E., and J. H. Coffer, Jr. Religious Attitudes Inventory. (Questionnaire) Durham, N.C.: Family Life Publications, 1964. **(I)**

Demerath, N. J., III, and Kenneth G. Lutterman. University and Society: Student Perspectives. (Questionnaire) Danforth Foundation Study of Campus Ministries, 1965. **(I)**

Detroit Area Study. A Community Survey of Greater Detroit. (Questionnaire, Project 855) Ann Arbor: Survey Research Center, University of Michigan, 1959. **(I)**

Glasner, Samuel. Self-Survey of a Congregation's Social Attitudes. (Mimeo.) N.Y.: Union of American Hebrew Congregations, 1956. **(B, I)**

Glock, Charles Y., and Rodney Stark. A Study of Religion in American Life. (Questionnaire) Berkeley: Survey Research Center, University of California, 1963. **(I)**

Hadden, Jeffrey K. Comparative Study of Campus and Parish Ministers. (Questionnaire) Danforth Foundation Study of Campus Ministries, 1965. **(I)**

Hawkins, E. M. Empirical Indication of the Effectiveness of the Church. (Questionnaire, mimeo.) n.d. **(I)**

Judy, Marvin T. Kansas Area Survey. (Questionnaire, mimeo.) Dallas: Southern Methodist University, n.d. **(I)**

Keating, Barry, and Charles Estus. I-Thou Scale: Steps and Indicators. (Mimeo.) N.Y.: Bureau of Research and Survey, National Council of Churches, n.d. **(B, I)**

Maranell, Gary M. An Instrument for the Measurement of Some Dimensions of Religiosity or Religious Attitudes. (Questionnaire, ditto) Fayetteville: University of Arkansas, n.d. **(D, I)**

Martin, James G. Religiosity Scale. (Questionnaire, ditto) n.d. **(I)**

Pringle, Bruce M. A Survey of Religious Beliefs and Practices. (Ques-

tionnaire, ditto) Dallas: Southern Methodist University, 1963.
(**B, I**)

Salisbury, W. Seward. Family-Community-Religion Experience and Value Inventory. (Questionnaire, mimeo.) n.d. (**I**)

Whitman, Lauris B. Denominational and Interdenominational Responses to the Church Membership Questionnaire: A Survey of 14,808 Responses. (Report and Tabulations, mimeo.) N.Y.: Bureau of Research and Survey, National Council of Churches, 1960. (**B, I**)

King's interesting approach to the question, How should we measure religion? raises as many problems as it solves. Yet, before considering these issues, it is first necessary to examine a brief research addendum published by King and Hunt two years after the original essay appeared. King, it will be recalled, employed factor and cluster analyses to determine the kinds of groupings of religious beliefs and practices inherent in his list of 121 questionnaire items. On the basis of this procedure, King argues that these 121 questions, when placed into groups, measure nine distinct religious categories or dimensions of religion. Said differently, each list of questions is a scale by which a particular religious variable may be measured.

An important question arises at this point. Within any given scale, how well do particular questions fit the scale? For instance, how good a measure of "Creedal Assent and Personal Commitment" (King's first religious dimension) is a person's response to the questionnaire item, "I believe in the Church as God's agent of salvation in the world"? How strongly would a person's response to that question predict his response to other questions in the Creedal Assent index? King and Hunt employed an item scale analysis to answer this question. They found that some of the measures of religion used in the original study were actually very weak measures of certain variables. Said differently, the questionnaire item, "The purpose of worship and prayer is to find out what God wants us to do," may be viewed as a measure of "Creedal Assent and Personal Commitment," but it is not a very good measure of that variable and it is not very highly intercorrelated with other items in that scale. Moreover, on the basis of this item scale analysis King and Hunt postulate the existence of two additional religious variables, making eleven rather than the original nine dimensions.

Measuring the Religious Variable: Amended Findings

by Morton B. King and Richard A. Hunt

A previous paper (King, 1967) reported an attempt to use factor and cluster analyses of questionnaire data to identify and measure dimensions of individual religious belief and practice. A unidimensional view of the religious variable was rejected, and scales were proposed for nine possible dimensions. As then noted, the items on each scale were selected by the author after a comparison of the results of two factor analyses and one hierarchical cluster analysis. No quantitative procedure was used, and no measure of scale homogeneity or reliability was developed.

Subsequently, the same data were subjected to item-scale analysis by an original computer program developed by Hunt (1969). Based on the variance-covariance matrix for all items in the domain, the program dropped and added items (according to instructions) to form successive forms of a scale. For each form, a coefficient of homogeneity was defined as the ratio of the scale covariance among items to the total scale variance. Examination of the several

Richard A. Hunt is associate professor of psychology, director of institutional research and director of psychological services at Southern Methodist University. He is co-author of Measuring Religious Dimensions: Studies of Congregational Involvement (with Morton B. King, 1972). A biographical note on Morton King appears on p. 39.

Reprinted from Journal for the Scientific Study of Religion, 8, no. 2 (1969): 321–323. Used with permission of the author and publisher.

62

forms of a scale enabled the authors to reject clusters of items whose coefficient of homogeneity was below .700 and thus too low to be useful as scales. It also made possible the selection of items for a scale which gave the highest homogeneity for the smallest number of items.

Readers of the original article are urged to consider the changes presented below in tabular form. Roman numerals indicate the titles of the nine former scales. Boldface arabic numbers and titles are used for the eleven dimensions and scales now being proposed. For each new scale, the number of items and its coefficient of homogeneity are shown.

Summary of Changes

One scale (V) was dropped altogether; and one (11), added. The number of items per scale was reduced to a maximum of seven. The items which indicate Church Attendance (2) and Organizational Activities (3), formerly combined in Scale II, are highly intercorrelated; it is possible, however, to separate them for analytical purposes. The content of several scales was considerably modified by dropping and adding items. New or modified titles (IV, 5; VI, 6; VIIa, 7; VIIIa, 9) reflect such changes.

Former Scales VI, VIIa, and VIIb are now viewed as indicating orientation toward, rather than dimensions of, religion. The homogeneity of new Scales 7, 8, and 11 is on the borderline of usefulness. Until better defined, or abandoned, those scales should be used with caution.

The authors will be glad to correspond regarding the scales and their use, based on data from a restudy now being analyzed.

References

Hunt, Richard A. A computer Procedure for Item-Scale Analysis. Educational Psychological Measurement, 1970.

King, Morton B. Measuring the Religious Variable: Nine Proposed Dimensions. *Journal for the Scientific Study of Religion*, 1967, 6, 173–190.

I. Creedal Assent and Personal Commitment (15 items)
   1. Creedal Assent (7, .906)
      a. Retain items 1–7.
      b. Drop items 8–15.

II. Participation in Congregational Activities (13 items)

    2. Church Attendance (4, .859)

        a. Composed of items 1–3, 5 from Scale II.

        b. Omit items 4, 6–13.

    3. Organizational Activities (6, .792)

        a. Composed of items 4, 6–10 from Scale II.

        b. Omit items 1–3, 5, 11–13.

III. Personal Religious Experience (12 items)

    4. Personal Religious Experience (7, .865)

        a. Retain items 2, 3, 6, 8, 10, 11.

        b. Drop items 1, 4, 5, 7, 9, 12.

        c. Add:

            "I know that God answers my prayers."

IV. Personal Ties in the Congregation (5 items)

    5. Church Work with Friends (6, .831)

        a. Retain items 1, 2.

        b. Drop items 3–5.

        c. Add four items:

            "How would you rate your activity in this congregation? (Very active—Inactive)"

            "How often do you spend evenings at church meetings or in church work? (Regularly—Seldom or never)"

            "How often do you get together with other members of your congregation other than at church or church-sponsored meetings? (Regularly—Seldom or never)"

            "How many times during the last month have you attended Sunday School or some equivalent educational activity? (None—Three or more)"

V. Commitment to Intellectual Search Despite Doubt (5 items) (These items had too little homogeneity to define a dimension or serve as a usable scale).

VI. Openness to Religious Growth (5 items)

    6. Orientation to Religious Growth and Striving (5, .763)

        a. Retain items 1, 2, 4.

        b. Drop items 3, 5.

        c. Add two items:

            "I believe that the Bible provides basic moral principles to guide every decision of my daily life."

            "The main purpose of the Church is to reconcile men to God and each other, thus establishing the conditions for 'newness of life.'"

VIIa. Dogmatism (5 items)

    7. Orientation to Religious Security or Dogmatism (3, .695)

  a. Retain items 1, 2.
  b. Drop items 3–5.
  c. Add:
  "The truly religious person has the joy and peace which comes from recognizing that he is a forgiven sinner."

VIIb. Extrinsic Orientation (9 items)
  8. Extrinsic Orientation (6, .697)
  a. Retain items 3, 6, 8, 9.
  b. Drop items 1, 2, 4, 5, 7.
  c. Add two items:
  "The more liberally I support the Church financially, the closer I feel to it and to God."
  "It is part of one's patriotic duty to worship in the church of his choice."

VIIIa. Financial Behavior (5 items)
  9. Financial Support (5, .801)
  a. Composed of same five items.
  b. Scale VIIIb, Financial Attitude, was neither homogeneous nor related to the "behavior" items in the new analysis.

  IX. Talking and Reading about Religion (7 items)
  10. Talking and Reading about Religion (6, .811)
  a. Retain items 1–4, 7.
  b. Drop items 5, 6.
  c. Add:
  "How often in the last year have you shared with another church member the problems and joys of trying to live a life of faith in God?"

No "cognitive" or "intellectual" dimension was identified by the original analysis. After recoding, however, the item-scale analysis demonstrated a homogeneous set of items.

  11. Religious Knowledge (6, .681)
  Which of the following were Old Testament prophets? (Deuteronomy; Ecclesiastes; Isaiah; Elijah; Jeremiah; Leviticus)
  Which of the following principles are supported by most Protestant denominations? (Bible as the Word of God; Separation of Church and State; Power of clergy to forgive sins; Final authority of the church; Justification by faith; Justification by good works)
  Which of the following books are in the Old Testament? (Acts; Amos; Galatians; Hebrews; Hosea; Psalms)

Which of the following denominations in the United States have bishops? (Disciples; Episcopal; Lutheran; Methodist; Presbyterian; Roman Catholic)

Which of the following books are included in the Four Gospels? (James; John; Mark; Matthew; Peter; Thomas)

And, a composite "knowledge score" constructed from the above five and four other factual items. Without this score the coefficient of homogeneity was 5, .580.

While King's study and the subsequent one by King and Hunt provide a rich array of empirical measures of religion, they also heighten some of the problems of employing such measures that were discussed earlier. The task of weighting and evaluating the relevance of these eleven variables for different kinds of religious groups would be a formidable one. Moreover, King's variables are very different in kind from one another. On the one hand, it might be argued that King's approach represents the kind of "abstracted empiricism" about which C. Wright Mills complained in his well-known book, *The Sociological Imagination.*[14] For Mills, much sociology consists of little more than the production of crude empirical measures of minutia with little concern for the larger meanings of human social action. On the other hand, it might be argued that King's work represents an important breakthrough toward sorting out the complexly interrelated aspects of religious thought and action. If nothing else King's research can be understood as a maximal extension of the kind of multidimensional analysis that has characterized the sociology of religion in the late 1960s and early 1970s.[15]

[14] C. Wright Mills, *The Sociological Imagination* (New York: Oxford University Press, 1959). See especially Chapter 3.

[15] For subsequent replication, see Morton B. King and Richard A. Hunt, "Measuring the Religious Variable: Replication," *Journal for the Scientific Study of Religion*, 11, no. 3 (1972): 240–251.

Part III

Religious Meanings
in Theoretical Perspectives

The purpose of social theory is to explain why phenomena occur, how they work or what they mean empirically, and under given conditions what is likely to happen in the future. Unfortunately, relatively few theoretical treatises in the social sciences do all these things equally well. Yet, regardless of whether a particular theorist provides precisely formulated theory propositions or broad interpretive schemas for understanding social reality, the purpose of theory remains the same—to provide generalized knowledge. Even the beginning student soon realizes that there are various alternative theoretical frameworks from which religion, or any other social phenomena, may be analyzed. From the standpoint of social science, there is no single "ultimate" meaning or significance to be assigned to a given social phenomenon. The utility of any theoretical framework, aside from its ability to predict, is largely a matter of individual choice. The following set of essays exposes some of the advantages and disadvantages that emerge as different theoretical perspectives are applied to the study of religion.

While the three classical writers, Marx, Durkheim, and Weber, all have made lasting contributions to the sociological theory of religion, there is little question that Durkheim's influence has been the most pervasive. In Durkheim's view, religion functions to provide moral order and thus both social cohesion and social control in society. Without the important ideological and ritual functions of religion, social order is all but impossible in Durkheim's theory. Most structural-functional theory in contemporary sociology stresses these very themes. While relatively few theorists today argue that society is not possible without religion (or some functional equivalent of it), there still remains an emphasis upon the ordering functions of religion for society.

As Allan Eister suggests in the following essay, there are numerous shortcomings in the structural-functional theory of religion. He begins with the observation that the functional approach ignores entirely the divisive or so-called dysfunctional consequences of religion for both personalities and society. Moreover, Eister's critique points not simply to problems that stem from the application of functional theory to religion but to some basic problems in functional theory generally.

Religious Institutions in Complex Societies: Difficulties in the Theoretic Specification of Functions[*]

by Allan W. Eister

Implicit in the methodology of structural-functional analysis, the prevailing theoretic convention among sociologists and anthropologists for describing institutions in their social context, is the demand for specification in the theory not only of the functional requisites of societies but also of functions which given parts of the whole are expected to perform in, or for, the system. The system "ends" are generally posited as (1) survival, and, as instrumental to this, if not an end in its own right, (2) the maintenance of homeostasis, or

Allan W. Eister is professor of sociology and anthropology at Wellesley College. He is the author of *Drawing Room Conversation: A Sociological Account of the Oxford Group Movement* (1950).

Reprinted from *American Sociological Review*, 22, no. 4 (1957): 387–391. Used with permission of the author and publisher, and revised by the author especially for this publication.

* Paper read at the fall meeting of the Society for the Scientific Study of Religion, Harvard University, December, 1956. An earlier version was presented at the annual meeting of the American Sociological Society, September, 1956.

of dynamic equilibrium, within the system. The theories of Malinowski, Radcliffe-Brown, Benedict, and Parsons may be regarded as examples of functionalist theories of this type. These theories usually envisage societies as social systems operating within a framework of necessity. They attempt to state explicitly what the requirements or "needs" of the social system are, usually as these are inferred from the *conditions* of human social existence, and then to trace out the implications of these and hence arrive at some idea of the functions that must (and will) be performed. Thus if religion does not perform the necessary functions, some other institution or institutions will.

In addition to theories of this type, however, there are other kinds of theoretic formulations in which the theorists have also been concerned with the functions of religion but have been content simply to enumerate various *consequences* (which may be quite random or independent of each other) that religious institutions are found, or expected, to have in various societies.[1] The latter kinds of theories have often taken the form of empirical generalizations in which a somewhat wider range of functions of religion is considered than is ordinarily done in closed system analysis.

In both cases, however, there appear to be a number of difficulties that impede the effort to designate theoretically the functions that religion, or religious institutions, perform in complex societies such as our own. This paper holds that (1) specification of expected functions of religious institutions—either on purely logical grounds or on the basis of generalization from empirical evidence—is less precise and likely to be less readily accomplished than for almost any other major area of social organization (economic, political, family, communicational, institutions), and that (2) any attempt to apply most of the available functional theories of religion to complex societies rather than to primitive ones is more likely to lead to frustration than to fruitful understanding or insight.

According to the prevailing views, the functions of religion and of religious institutions can be discussed in from two to five or six major categories, with heavy emphasis usually falling upon the integrative and supportive functions they are purported to perform. Thus religious institutions are seen, in relation to other institutions of society—and in the total system—as promoting solidarity through the provision of significant symbols, norms, supernatural sanctions,

---

[1] See, for example, J. O. Hertzler, "Religious Institutions," in R. H. Abrams (ed.), *Organized Religion in the United States, Annals of the American Academy of Political and Social Science*, 256 (March, 1948), pp. 1–13.

and so on. In relation to personalities, and hence indirectly to society, they have been seen as ego-supportive, cathartic, therapeutic, operative in the maintenance or restoration of self-confidence, in the reassertion of "life values," and in the reinforcement of collective sentiments in the face of various kinds of life crises such as famine or bereavement.[2]

Although divisive, disruptive, and ego-destructive consequences of religion or of religious institutions have been recognized—and discussed, for example, by Parsons in terms of "alienative motivation" in religious behavior[3] or by Yinger in terms of "religion in the struggle for power"[4]—it would seem to be correct to say that in the classic theories of Durkheim,[5] Malinowski,[6] Radcliffe-Brown,[7] Radin,[8] and in the more recent formulations of Nottingham,[9] Davis,[10] or Goode,[11] the emphasis tends to be on the conservative, the integrative, the supportive functions of religion rather than upon their opposites.

Much of this general pattern of interpretation rests upon the shrewd insights of Durkheim who saw in the group's *experience* of their collective power as *sacred* (and in the subsequent attempts to provide adequate symbols of this) the necessary basis for cohesion in society.

The emphasis in Malinowski's theory concerning the functions of religion, and especially of religious myths, is also upon what might be regarded as the positive contributions that these make toward maintaining the morale of the individuals and of the group and toward reaffirming and reinforcing the solidarity and the continuity of the group.

Despite the impressive array of opinion ranged on the side of the

[2] Reference in these latter instances, as social scientists will recognize, is to the work of Radin and of Malinowski.

[3] See Talcott Parsons, *Religious Perspectives of College Teaching in Sociology and Social Psychology* (New Haven: The E. W. Hazen Foundation, 1951), esp. pp. 16–21.

[4] J. M. Yinger, *Religion in the Struggle for Power* (Durham: Duke University Press, 1946).

[5] Emile Durkheim, *The Elementary Forms of the Religious Life* (London: Allen and Unwin, Ltd., 1915).

[6] B. Malinowski, *Magic, Science and Religion* (Boston: Beacon Press, 1948).

[7] A. R. Radcliffe-Brown, "Religion and Society" in *Structure and Function in Primitive Society* (Glencoe: Free Press, 1952), pp. 153–177.

[8] Paul Radin, *Primitive Religion: Its Nature and Origin* (New York: Viking, 1937).

[9] Elizabeth K. Nottingham, *Religion and Society* (Garden City: Doubleday, 1954).

[10] Kingsley Davis, "Religious Institutions," in *Human Society* (New York: Macmillan, 1949), pp. 509–545.

[11] W. J. Goode, *Religion Among the Primitives* (Glencoe: Free Press, 1951).

integrative, supportive functions of religion as its primary ones, it is difficult to accept this pattern of interpretation as valid or appropriate for the contemporary scene. Indeed the interpretation is hard to accept for any complex society where there is a high degree of specialization and functional autonomy among institutions or where religion itself is organized on a pluralistic or quasi-pluralistic pattern, as contrasted with a society in which some sort of simple monism in religious faith and practice prevails or in which, though there may be *rivals* for religious authority and for "followings," there is no rivalry among diverse or mutually contradictory *patterns of defining authority.* For each of the integrative or supportive functions of religion cited in the theories that have been so popular, it is possible—and even, as Merton[12] points out, easy—to find diametric opposites in our own society.

If religion has supplied some of the basic common value orientations of our society and buttressed these with sanctions at its disposal, it has *also* been the source of rival value orientations that have been put forward to challenge these and has also served as the excuse for rejecting or defying older prevailing norms. Religion may be said both to have sustained the *status quo,* including the underwriting of various power and prestige elites, and to have undermined it by denying sanction to such invidious distinctions or by attacking them even more directly.

On the personal level there is evidence both from clinical records and from survey research to demonstrate that feelings of unrelieved guilt, of inferiority (or of superiority), of prejudice, of hostility to critical, open-minded thought—all of which have social consequences of some sort—have been engendered, in part at least, by religion or by religious institutions.[13] One is obliged to conclude that religion lends itself (or that it can be, and has been, *used*) to foster or maintain an extraordinary variety of social interests and social processes, many of which are incongruous and many of which fail to measure up to the arbitrary standards of personal maturity, good mental health, social justice, fair play, brotherhood, intellectual honesty or even, in some cases, simple human decency. The

---

[12] R. K. Merton, *Social Theory and Social Structure* (Glencoe: Free Press, 1949), esp. pp. 30–31 ff.

[13] See, for example, B. Bettelheim and M. Janowitz, *Dynamics of Prejudice* (New York: Harper and Bros., 1950), esp. pp. 50–52, 155–156, *passim.;* L. Festinger, "Laboratory Experiments: The Role of Group Belongingness," in J. G. Miller (ed.), *Experiments in Social Process* (New York: McGraw-Hill, 1950), pp. 33–46; Ralph L. Roy, *Apostles of Discord* (Boston: Beacon Press, 1953). Not irrelevant here is William James, *The Varieties of Religious Experience* (New York: Longmans, Green, 1902).

situation is one which comes close to suggesting that the theoretically statable functions of religion are at least highly elusive if not paradoxical.

Now it is possible that the "shortcomings" in the available theoretic formulations concerning the functions of religion in society are more apparent than real, that is to say, a matter of loose usage of words, or of mistakes arising from a misreading of the theories. It does make a difference, for example, whether one is talking about the functions of *religion* or about the functions of *religious institutions,* including religious organizations. And it is at least conceivable that where *religion,* in general terms or under certain social circumstances, may be capable of providing the massive supportive or integrative "services" to the society as a whole, *specific religious organizations,* or rival religious organizations in a pluralistic society, would be quite incapable of doing so. What is possible in a relatively undifferentiated society in which a more or less homogeneous religious tradition or a single system of religious institutions and type of religious authority prevails may be entirely beyond the possibility of achievement in societies of a different order of complexity. The character of the claims each organization puts upon its members and how it trains them to look upon others (always assuming that the training "takes") are matters that are also relevant. It is perhaps the rare religious organization that does not train its members to look upon themselves as the elect of God, bearers of *the* Truth, and so on, and upon others as somehow inferior in their understanding and behavior if not in their social status or personal worth.

Another possible objection that might be raised to the assertions that have been made here concerning the inadequacies of currently available theory for use in analyzing the functions of religion in advanced societies is that we may have attempted to generalize these theories beyond the limits intended by their authors. It is true that many of the functionalist theories of religion have been erected with specific reference to primitive societies and have been so labeled explicitly. There are other theories, however, where this has not clearly been the case. Although Durkheim's major theoretic work in this area rests empirically upon data supplied by Spencer and Gillen and others on central Australian tribes, it is evident from the total context of Durkheim's work that he apparently had in mind the social functions of religion in societies generally.

Still another point in possible answer to our complaint might be that in not all functionalist theories is a specific, unequivocal, unchanging function or set of functions expected of specific institutions, religious or otherwise, or assigned theoretically to them, and that we ought not to require this of every functionalist theory. What should be posited, rather, is a situation in which given sets of conditions (which *may* vary sharply from society to society) need somehow to be met. How exactly these will be met—or by what institutions—depends upon the total range and character of all the institutions operative in the society and upon a variety of other variables present in each case. In theories of this type, it may well be, of course, that religious institutions could and would vary widely enough in their functioning so as to provide, in one context or another, or at one time or another, evidence of contradictory, diametrically opposite functions, services, consequences or effects when viewed in some total logical framework. This, however, is not quite the point against which we have been inveighing. This point is the presence of diametrically opposed functions operative at the same time in the same society.

Nothing that has been complained of so far—nor that might be said in answer to it—seems to go far enough into the matter to expose all the difficulties, or perhaps even the major difficulties, which are encountered in the attempt to specify theoretically the functions of religion—or, more precisely, of religious institutions, since religion in human society scarcely exists apart from institutional forms. The assertion here is that there are further logical difficulties that functional theorists of religion may not yet have perceived or acknowledged.

If, on the basis of what has been argued above, we may now assume that religion, operative through religious institutions, is capable of functioning in ways that are diametrically opposite, then it can be argued further that one set of functions or consequences is as legitimate or theoretically apposite as the other. It then becomes theoretically impossible to assign any fixed or necessary functions to religion or to religious institutions. Even in closed systems, where the pressure is greatest for locating all the necessary ingredients but only these, it has not been established beyond question that religion specifically is a non-replaceable or specifically necessary part of the system.[14] There is only the assertion that it *can* be useful in these

[14] In the broad sense of his being concerned with the consequences and/or the concomitants of religious beliefs and practices, Max Weber was in a sense "functionalist," but it is important to note the difference between the kind of functionalism represented in his work on one hand and that represented by "closed-system" functionalism on the other. To my knowledge Weber neither recognized nor attempted to work within a framework of the latter sort. In this sense he was not a "structural-functionalist."

respects, that it may help meet theoretically posed "system problems," and that it is not the anachronistic, functionally useless relic that the radical positivists in the Comtean tradition took it to be.

There appears to be some equivocation among functional theorists, too, as to precisely what system problem or problems religion is thought to be best qualified to serve. Is it in the area of adaptation to the environment, including an environment which may include deity, or is it in the area of internal integration within the group or social system? The specific needs that religion and religious institutions serve, whether for persons or for social systems, moreover, are apparently less a matter of common agreement (or at least of the kind of consensus that science requires) than the personal or social system needs identified and assigned to other institutions, which we conventionally label as "economic," "political," and so on.

Further evidence for the elusive character of functions that might be assigned to religion may be found in the extent to which persons and groups can avoid or evade the institutions of religion. The necessity for food-getting activities, for example, is universal and inescapable, and so, apparently, are certain of the activities identified as "political." But, except where political or economic sanc' tions are employed in the service of religious organization, religious beliefs and religious practices apparently can be ignored—and apparently without demonstrable consequences to the survival or well-being of groups or of individuals.

Another point that appears frequently to have been overlooked in theoretic formulations of the functions of religious institutions in society is that in the operating of religious institutions the beliefs and the "commitments" of individuals are relevant in a way that is unique. One of the purported functions of religious institutions is to reinforce moral norms by adding to the secular means of control sanctions of another order. Yet the efficacy of religious institutions in discharging this function rests squarely upon the acceptance by the controllee of the claims of religion. Unless he "believes" he is not controlled; threats of hell or promises of heaven are powerless in the face of disbelief. This is quite different from the way in which commitment to economic or to political ideologies works. One need not be committed to any sort of specific beliefs in nondemonstrable entities to be coerced by the operations of the physical or social environment. True, social control, whether by or for elites or by the community at large, may be facilitated by the acceptance of certain ideologies and myths with reference to the economic or the political or other institutions of the society; one need scarcely even be aware of the existence of society as an abstract phenomenon to be demonstrably controlled by it. But what is distinctive and peculiar to the situation of religious institutions is the degree of sacredness, of infallibility, of ultimate correctness which the creeds and dogmas that provide ideological support for religious institutions can command. No other institutions in society seem to enjoy either so much or such strong support (where the creeds and dogmas *are* accepted) nor to be so vulnerable (where the creeds and dogmas are rejected) as religious institutions. They appear to stand in a unique position in this respect with implications for their functioning that do not appear to have been widely recognized in the functional theories of religion.

Still another, and perhaps more vexatious, difficulty presents itself to the presumptive theorist of the functions of religion. This is posed, at least for those functional theorists who want to construct a set of *necessary conditions* that "must" be met if the society or the social system is to survive (or to remain in moving equilibrium or whatever), by the fact that one cannot erect a comprehensive or complete theoretic specification of a social system model without logically implicating in one way or another his own personal position concerning the existence of non-existence of deity *or* whatever else he takes to be the object of religious *devotion*. This shows up particularly clearly in any theoretic statement about the environment to which individuals and groups must adapt themselves or be adapted. It is not possible, I think, to speak intelligibly about this environment without revealing what it is that the theorist regards as "belonging in" or being part of that environment; and this leads one squarely to the logically necessary expression of one's own operating assumptions concerning the existence or non-existence of deity or some other supra-empirical "higher power" in the environment and the relevance or non-relevance of this to the human enterprise. In this context it does not matter what position he takes —theistic, atheistic, agnostic, or whatever—the obligation is the same if he intends to theorize responsibly within what might be called a framework of necessity, that is, if he proposes to posit social system "requirements." To leave the question of one's own personal assumptions in abeyance, as many social scientists are wont to do, does not seem to allow at least some types of functionalist theory, (including the kind that appears now [1957] to prevail), to be satisfactory.

The conclusion that seems to follow from the questions raised and from the problems posed in the foregoing pages is that the difficulties standing in the way of theoretic specification of the functions of religious institutions are very much greater than appears to have been generally recognized and that much further thinking about the logical prerequisites for theorizing in this field needs to be done.

As Eister points out, there are several different forms of functional theory. His strongest criticisms are aimed at closed systems theory, in which it is assumed that certain requisite functions must be satisfied in order for society to exist. Yet, he also warns that even the open systems theorist will stress one kind of function of religion rather than another. Traditionally this has meant an overemphasis upon the integrative functions of religion rather than the divisive consequences of religion in society. The effect of this kind of theory building is to tell but half the story.

The following essay by Elizabeth Nottingham offers an important modification of the Durkheimian approach and also avoids most of the pitfalls to which Eister points. Nottingham agrees that religion does most of the things that both Durkheim and subsequent functionalists have said that it does. Yet, she qualifies this argument by showing that how well religion does these things depends upon the kind of society being studied. The integrative functions of religion are most strongly evidenced in less socially differentiated societies. Conversely, the divisive functions of religion increase as the complexity of the social structure increases. Nottingham concludes with the idea that under conditions of extreme social differentiation, religion's integrative functions may pertain only to subgroups and not to the entire society.

Religion and Types of Society
by Elizabeth K. Nottingham

Why Use Societal Models?

Societal models* are useful because of their availability as yardsticks against which the reader may compare the concrete characteristics of the societies he encounters either at first hand or in the pages of books. It is obviously impossible to describe every society in concrete detail. Nor can we here depict the many subtle shadings of difference among the models we have chosen to present. In fact, in each case certain features are purposely exaggerated to bring out clearly the "profiles" of the model. The descriptions are of necessity oversimplified.

Model One is a type of society in which religious values predominate, Model Three a type of society in which secular values are in the ascendant, and Model Two a combination of religious and secu-

Elizabeth K. Nottingham retired in 1968 as professor of sociology at Queens College of CUNY and is presently associated with the department of sociology at the University of California at Berkeley. Her writings include *The Making of an Evangelist: A Study of John Wesley's Early Years* (1938); *Methodism and the Frontier: Indiana Proving Ground* (1941); *Religion and Society* (1954); and *Religion: A Sociological View* (1971).

Reprinted from Elizabeth K. Nottingham, *Religion: A Sociological View* (New York: Random House, 1971), pp. 32–54 and used with permission of the author and publisher. Footnotes have been renumbered.

*The term "model" is used here in a general descriptive sense and not in the precise mathematical sense in which it is sometimes used.

80

lar values.[1] These three models are not intended, however, to represent inevitable stages in historical development, although many, but by no means all, societies have passed through or are passing through these or similar stages. Yet approximations to these types of societies have existed in historical times and may also be found today—sometimes in uneasy proximity—in our rapidly shrinking world.

The reader will observe that in addition to describing the organizational features of these societal models and the structure of the religious system associated with each of them, we have given particular stress to the concomitant variations in the functions of religion.

Model One: Preliterate Societies and Religious Values

Our first model represents societies that are typically small, isolated, and preliterate.[2] They have a low level of technical development and relatively little division of labor or elaboration of social classes. The family is their most important institution, and specialization of the organization of government and economic life is rudimentary. The rate of social change is slow.

Intellectual systems of belief and myth are likely to be rather compact and undifferentiated; that is, men do not typically conceive of their objects of religious veneration as being essentially different or far removed from themselves. Their most potent religious symbols are commonly mythical figures such as tribal ancestors or culture heroes, who may be symbolized under a variety of forms.[3] The individual and his society are seen as merged in a natural-divine cosmos.

Religious action systems, therefore, are commonly directed to bringing about an *identification* between the worshiping group and that which they worship. A totem feast, in which the totem animal, in some sense symbolic of the tribe, is killed and eaten is an extreme and vivid example of the *participation mystique,* which is a common goal of religious action in such societies.

Religious organization, as such, is likely to be rudimentary or even nonexistent apart from the total organization of the society. Every member of the society, by virtue of his membership, shares in the

[1] See Logan Wilson and William L. Kolb, *Sociological Analysis* (New York: Harcourt, Brace, 1949), pp. 344–349, for a similar distinction.

[2] Compare Robert Redfield, "The Folk Society," *American Journal of Sociology,* 52 (January 1947): 293–308.

[3] See Robert Bellah, "Religious Evolution," *American Sociological Review,* 29 (June 1964): 362–363.

religion of the group. Religious organization itself constitutes not so much a separate institution as an aspect of the total activities of the group. Religion pervades other group activities, whether economic, political, familial, or recreational. For example, the Trobriand Islanders, those South Sea Islanders made known to us through the famous researches of the anthropologist Bronislaw Malinowski, build their canoes and plant their gardens (economic and technical operations) as part and parcel of their performance of the magical and religious rituals that traditionally accompany these jobs.[4]

The major functions of religion in such a society and its role in relation to the group and its members are usually readily apparent. Since this type of society is small enough for most of its customs to be known, at least by hearsay, to all its members, it follows that religion can very forcibly place its imprint on the value system of the society. Coupled with magic, it is also an important means of dealing with many situations of stress. Furthermore, in the relatively undeveloped state of the other institutions, that is, except the family, religion is likely to provide the principal focus for the integration and cohesion of the society as a whole. Religious values often, although not invariably, promote conservatism and militate against change; this is an important reason why the hand of tradition is heavy in such societies. Again, because of the absence of rival interests and the fusion of religion with almost all aspects of social life, religion exercises a dominantly cohesive, stabilizing influence. As one anthropologist has put it, "In such a society life is a one-possibility thing."[5] Consequently, life in preliterate societies affords little leverage for religion to bring about social change.

For the individual, religion puts its stamp on the entire socialization process. Socialization is marked by religious rituals at birth, puberty, marriage, and other crucial times in the life cycle.[6] Personality organization is closely related to religious values, which are handed on directly to the developing individual by family and community. In the absence of a variety of possibly competing personality models, especially secular models, religion stands unrivaled as an integrating focus for the personality patterning of individuals in societies of this type.[7]

[4] See Bronislaw Malinowski, *Magic, Science, and Religion* (Glencoe, Ill.: Free Press, 1948; reprint ed., Garden City, N.Y.: Doubleday, Anchor Book, 1954), pp. 27–28.

[5] W. E. H. Stanner, quoted in Bellah, *op. cit.*, p. 364.

[6] See Malinowski, *op. cit.*, pp. 37–41.

[7] See David Riesman et al., *The Lonely Crowd* (New Haven: Yale University Press, 1950; reprint ed., Garden City, N.Y.: Doubleday, Anchor Book, 1954),

The mode of life characteristic of our first model has been studied by anthropologists for many years. Anthropologists have enormously helped sociologists in the latter's investigation of religion in relatively simple societies where the bones, so to say, of social structure are less obscured by complex developments. Anthropologists have also drawn our attention to continuing aspects of religion's functions in more complex societies, functions that otherwise would probably have been overlooked. Nonetheless, more complex social conditions are associated with important modifications in the role played by religion. These modifications are revealed in considering societies subsumed under our Model Two.

Model Two: Changing Preindustrial Societies

Model Two societies are less isolated, change more rapidly, are larger and more expansive in both area and population, and are marked by a higher degree of technological development than are Model One societies. Considerable division of labor, distinctiveness and diversity of social classes,[8] and some degree of literacy are common features. Agriculture and hand industries are the chief means of support of a mainly village economy, with a few urban trading centers. The institutions of government and economic life are becoming specialized and distinct. Although there is more overlapping of governmental, economic, religious, familial, and recreational activities than in modern industrialized societies (Model Three), sharper lines are drawn between the occasions on which people go to work, go to play, or go to worship than, say, among the Trobrianders. This second societal model is illustrated concretely by the societies in which the great historical religions—Buddhism, prophetic Judaism, Christianity, and Islam—emerged and matured.

The intellectual and symbol systems of these historical religions differ greatly among themselves, but all share an important emphasis on *transcendentalism* that distinguishes them from the religions

---

Chapter 1. Model One societies especially, perhaps, give rise to the "tradition-directed" character type described by Riesman in his provocative sociological essay. However, modern anthropological research into so-called primitive societies has revealed a great deal of variation of which earlier writers, such as Malinowski (and Durkheim) were not aware. Thus Model One societies subsume numerous subtypes.

[8] See Bellah, *op. cit.*, pp. 367–368. Bellah sees a shift from a two-class system to a four-class system as typically accompanying the change from Model One to Model Two societies. The four classes he mentions are a political-military elite, a religious-cultural elite, a rural lower-status group (peasants), and an urban lower-status group (small merchants and artisans).

most typical of Model One societies.[9] These symbol systems portray a dualistic universe, emphasizing the contrast between life in this world and life in another specifically "religious" realm. This religious realm is viewed as man's true dwelling, and the goal of *salvation,* or entrance into this realm—whether described as heaven, enlightenment, or release—becomes the central religious quest.

The religious action system in such societies is concerned above all else with action necessary for obtaining salvation. To act religiously in a way that gains salvation becomes, in principle, the obligation of every human being. Man himself is no longer thought of mainly as a member of a particular tribe, or the devotee of a particular deity, but as an individual in a more universal sense, namely, as a human being capable of salvation. Man is also seen, however, as a being with serious flaws in his nature, and the attainment of salvation is therefore a difficult and responsible task demanding discipline and self-denial. Man is called upon to deny himself this-worldly pleasures and pursuits that might militate against his quest for an other-worldly salvation. Hence the historic religions tend to devalue the actual empirical world and to consider the most efficacious kind of religious action to be aseticism and withdrawal from worldly affairs.[10] To be sure, this denial and devaluation of the world may take a wide variety of forms, as Max Weber has pointed out.[11] Yet in one form or another Christianity, Buddhism, and Islam have each, at important periods in their history, inculcated one or more such forms of world-rejection.* World-rejection, let it be said, does not of necessity involve solitude, nor does the earnest seeker after salvation invariably abjure all contact with other humans. Hermits and other religious solitaries come close to doing this, but paradoxically (although almost inevitably) the preferred form of religious world-rejection has been carried on in like-minded groups organized under some form of monastic rule.

Religious organization is commonly of two kinds. A closely regulated quasimonastic organization of the religious elite exists side by side with a looser and more comprehensive kind of organization for

[9] *Ibid.,* p. 366.

[10] *Ibid.,* p. 367.

[11] See Max Weber, "Religious Rejections of the World and Their Directions" in *From Max Weber: Essays in Sociology,* trans. and ed. Hans H. Gerth and C. Wright Mills (New York: Oxford University Press, Galaxy Book, 1958), pp. 323–359.

* World-rejection, common at various periods in the histories of Buddhism, Christianity, and Islam, is much rarer in the history of Judaism. But even Jews had their withdrawing sects, such as the Essenes, and also some prophets who sought solitary places.

the vast majority who, from necessity or choice, remain involved in worldly affairs. Religiously, however, the latter are considered somewhat inferior to the former, who more nearly embody the religious ideal.* However, the religious organization as a whole comprises both monks (and priests) and laity, who are essential for the former's support.

In Model Two societies, then, this double-barreled organization, regarded as a whole, is a relatively separate and distinct part of the societal structure. It commonly aims at including at least as lay members all the inhabitants of a given political territory, but it usually possesses a formal, hierarchical organization of its own professional personnel.

The functions of religions in the Model Two type of society are more complex and contradictory than those in Model One societies. Religion still gives meaning and cohesion to the society's value system, but it also functions as an important stimulus to societal conflict both within societies and between them. For in these Model Two societies, the religious spheres and the secular spheres, although they continue to overlap at certain points, are becoming progressively more distinct from one another. Furthermore, the emerging institution of government is developing rapidly and consequently becoming a potential rival of the religious organization—the church—as a focus for the cohesion, integration, and stabilization of the society. Hence the possibility of internal institutional clashes is increasingly present. Of course, government in such societies is not always sufficiently secularized to be able to dispense with a religious legitimation for its authority. The Holy Roman Emperors of the medieval West, for example, tried to ensure this legitimation by being anointed by the Popes. Nevertheless, the possibility of church-state tension, and even of outright conflict, is ever present in Model Two societies. Conflicts of interest between religious and political organization are likely to be acute particularly in the later stages of their development, as each organization develops its own hierarchical structure and rationale and tends to make, each on its own level, a total claim on the loyalty of the individual members. Such conflicts of interest are complicated by the fact that although the ecclesiastical organization is typically re-

---

* This bipartite form of religious organization is very clearly seen in Buddhism, particularly in the Theravada Buddhism of Southeast Asia. The community of monks (Sangha) is clearly set off religiously from that of the laity, and monks are considered more favorably situated than are the laity for the attainment of salvation (Nirvana). The laity are thought to improve their own chances of salvation through the material support they render to the monks.

garded, at any rate officially, as "other-worldly," or even "world-denying," nevertheless religious organizations very commonly fall heir to money, lands, and buildings, and their functionaries play political roles. These worldly properties, moreover, are generally regarded by their religious owners as exempt from the payment of taxes and other "this-worldly" services to political governments. The massive church-state struggles in which medieval and early modern Christian and Islamic countries were involved are such religious-political conflicts.

The history of Model Two societies also is replete with examples of total societies locked in struggle, in large part because of religious rivalries. Model Two societies are typically expanding societies. Hence the coupling of religious organization (claiming to be the repository of a universal ethic) with the political power structure provides a setting in which attempts to spread the religion become fused with efforts to extend political domination. In medieval times, for example, the missionary drive of Islam to extend its religious beliefs westward, and of Christianity to spread its faith eastward, were also aspects of a political struggle for empire between two great rival civilizations. Such religious-political clashes may be regarded as integrative insofar as they helped to weld together the respective societies involved. From this point of view, indeed, the Crusades may be said to have helped to integrate Western Christendom.[12] But on the larger stage the bloody wars between Christianity and Islam are important examples of religion's disruptive and destructive tendencies; and even within Christendom itself it may be argued that the Crusades unleashed disintegrating forces at least as potent as those that they harnessed.

In Model Two societies, however, religion is not only a possible source of division and strife; it may also play a creative and innovating role. In contrast to the situation in Model One societies, religion is not merely an aspect and hence an implicit endorsement of custom but rather constitutes to some extent a rival system of sanctioned behavior. In these societies religion is not only of local application but is assumed to be universal; and in addition, it is thought of as representing ethical values "higher" than the everyday standards of ordinary social life. The excoriation of the prevailing customs of Israel and Judah by the Hebrew prophets Amos and Hosea because they fell short of religious standards furnishes a

---

[12] See Arnold Toynbee, *The World and the West* (New York: Oxford University Press, 1953), *passim*.

dramatic example of this disparity between religious ethic and social custom as conceived in societies of this type.

Furthermore, as such societies become increasingly complex, the dominant classes of an earlier period begin to yield before the challenge of rising classes representing a newly emergent political and economic order, while at the same time significant changes in the formulation of the religious ethic are likely to occur. These ethical innovations may themselves be important factors in helping to bring about the economic and social transformation under discussion, as Max Weber has argued in *The Protestant Ethic and the Spirit of Capitalism*.[13] Such innovations may be temporarily disintegrating, but in the long run they often contribute to the integration of a different type of society, as will be illustrated shortly.

In spite of these and other striking examples of the disruptive and innovative role played by religion in these Model Two societies (an aspect of religion's role that has sometimes been overlooked by sociologists), the important part played by religion in conserving traditional values should not be forgotten. The tendency for religion to become merged in social tradition still remains.

As far as the individual is concerned, in Model Two societies religious values continue to furnish the main focus for the integration of his behavior and the formation of his self-image. The fact that most of the members of the society are also members of a single dominant religious organization, which as a rule also controls the tools of literacy and education, lessens the likelihood of internal psychic conflicts on religious grounds. In addition, the sacred sanction given by the church to the system of statuses and vocations current in the society makes it possible for the individual to accept his social station with a minimum of internal conflict.* With the passage of time in such a society, however, both the increase of literacy and contact with other cultures may encourage religious heresy and skepticism. Societies of this type have produced a Jesus of Nazareth, a Gautama Buddha, and a Mohammed, as well as an Arius, an Averroes, and an Abelard among their dissenters.

Our description of this second model of society necessarily has

---

[13] See Max Weber, *The Protestant Ethic and the Spirit of Capitalism*, trans. Talcott Parsons (New York: Scribner, Students' Edition, 1958). This classic study should be read by all students of the sociology of religion. We are not concerned at this point to take sides in the much-debated question about the priority of economic as opposed to religious factors.

* Here, it may be surmised, is an important source of Riesman's "inner-directed" (or gyroscopically governed) character type.

been formulated in dynamic terms. The process of change that marks this type becomes increasingly apparent as such societies evolve. Not only do economic and technological developments play an indispensable part in breaking the "cake of custom," but internal developments within religion itself, in its beliefs, practices, and social organization, also contribute importantly to this end. An even greater acceleration of the tempo of change characterizes Model Three societies.

Model Three: Industrial-Secular Societies

Unlike our first two models, which were constructed from anthropological and historical materials drawn from almost every part of the world, our third model is based exclusively on the social and cultural situation in the modern West. Today the Model Three societal pattern is being rapidly diffused on a global scale (and inevitably contains a number of subtypes that our typology cannot adequately account for), but its point of origin is Western Christendom. Hence the model presented here is derived from a study of the Western world and is admittedly somewhat slanted toward urban society in the United States. The latter, however, because of its high degree of secularism, may be regarded as one of the nearest approximations to our model.

These societies are highly dynamic. Technology increasingly affects all aspects of life, having an impact most immediately on adjustments to the physical universe, but just as significantly on human relationships. The influence of science and technology has important consequences also for religion. This influence is one reason why members of these societies become more and more accustomed to applying methods of empirical common sense (and science) and efficiency to more and more human concerns. Thus the sphere of the secular is being continually enlarged, often at the expense of that of the sacred. In large part this secularizing trend accounts for the fact that religious beliefs and practices are confined to smaller and more specialized segments of the life of the society and its members.

To keep pace with this trend and in order to retain their influence, the churches themselves engage in a growing number of secular activities. In spite of the efforts of some churches to compete with secular institutions, the trend continues to relegate religion to limited times and places. In this respect the contrast with Model One societies, in which religion is an aspect of most social activity, is vivid.

The religious symbol system of Model Three societies, in part because of the secularizing tendencies just mentioned and in part because of the pluralistic nature of religious organization, is exceedingly difficult to pin down. In fact, no single universally accepted system of religious symbolism exists. Insofar as the various religious organizations are able to commend their officially sanctioned symbol systems to their membership, a plurality of symbol systems may be said to coexist simultaneously. Furthermore, many individuals, even organizational members, feel at liberty to interpret freely—or even repudiate—the traditional symbol systems handed down by hierarchical or other religious authority. Although this freedom of interpretation varies among memberships of different religious bodies, there exists a growing awareness among the religiously affiliated and nonaffiliated alike that symbols *are* symbols and that man in the last analysis is responsible for the choice of his symbolism.[14] Among the perhaps 95 percent of Americans who claim to believe in God (as reported several years ago),[15] many reinterpret religious symbols in a fashion so thorough-going that even liberal theologians and religionists are sometimes left aghast. In the world view that has emerged from the tremendous intellectual advances and upheavals of the last two centuries, there is little or no room for the "duplex" religious symbol system that characterized the historic religions of Model Two societies. Indeed, the notion of a dichotomy between a transcendent religious realm and a devalued earthly realm is increasingly repugnant to members of Model Three societies. Although conservative orthodox religionists still hold to the older "dualistic" world view, the major thrust of modern religious thought is toward the reinterpretation of religious faith and its symbolization to bring them into some kind of harmony with twentieth-century science and the economic and political conditions of the twentieth-century world.[16]

[14] Bellah, *op. cit.*, p. 373. It may be mentioned that some modern men and women are actively engaged in inventing new symbolic forms, both liturgical and creedal, which they deem more in harmony with the modern age. See, for example, C. J. McNaspy, S.J., "The Quest for Community," *America*, August 19, 1967, pp. 174–175.

[15] See Will Herberg, *Protestant, Catholic, Jew* (Garden City, N.Y.: Doubleday, Anchor Book, 1960), p. 72. Herberg quoted from the Gallup poll, *Public Opinion News Service*, December 18, 1954. Charles Y. Glock and Rodney Stark in their *Religion and Society in Tension* (Chicago: Rand McNally, 1965), p. 25, claim, on the basis of various recent polls, that between 95 and 97 percent of Americans acknowledge a belief in God. Such figures, however, as Glock and Stark point out, leave open the important question of the *saliency* of the belief for the individuals concerned.

[16] Bellah, *op. cit.*, p. 370: "How the specifically religious bodies are to adjust their time-honored practices of worship and devotion to modern conditions is of growing concern in religious circles. Such diverse movements as the liturgical

Religious action systems in the twentieth-century context increasingly emphasize action *within* the present world, action that Harvey Cox has aptly called "the sacralization of the secular."[17] Even the monastic orders, traditionally, for the most part, aloof from the world, are increasingly concerned with teaching, medicine, and other forms of social service. More and more priests and nuns, both Roman Catholic and Episcopal, are seeking professional and technical training at secular universities in order better to fulfill their religious duties in this world.[18] The Second Vatican Council has stressed the need for social relevance in respect to the Church's contemporary activities. Members of the Catholic Church in America in some areas play an active role in relation to the Negro's struggle for civil and other human rights. Nuns as well as priests have on occasion marched in civil rights demonstrations, side by side with representatives of the clergy and laity of many different faiths. Even the contemplative orders, such as the Trappists (as the writings of Thomas Merton attest) reach out, through the mass media, to help the ordinary laymen to interpret and handle their everyday "this-worldly" problems in a religious manner.

Protestants and Jews, to be sure, have been traditionally more involved with the world and have stressed more than have Catholics the *religious* significance of action within one's profession or occupation. Today Protestant, Catholic, and Jewish religious organizations are likely to have special departments for social action and social justice, as well as numerous elaborately organized philanthropic activities. Some religious bodies focus their activities on the "inner city" and maintain special services for immigrants and others who have to struggle with the extremely difficult living conditions in these areas.

Perhaps even more significantly, middle-class Americans of all faiths are becoming increasingly concerned with the ethical problems inherent in their own business, professional, political, and

---

revival, pastoral psychology, and renewed emphasis on social action are all efforts to meet the present need." The Second Vatican Council, and particularly Pope John XXIII's opening speech on "updating" (*aggiorniamento*), which has been called upon to legitimate much current liturgical and other experimentation in liberal Catholic circles, is a prominent example of the concern mentioned above.

[17] See Harvey Cox, *The Secular City* (New York: Macmillan, 1965), *passim,* for a trenchant statement of this position.

[18] See Sister M. Charles Borromeo, C.S.C. (ed.), *The New Nuns* (New York: New American Library, 1967); also, Harvey Cox, "The New Breed," *Daedalus* (Winter 1967): 135–150, in which Cox characterizes a new type of Protestant clergy.

family activities. Some churches sponsor forums, lectures, and discussions (sometimes following a sermon) in which their members may become aware of these ethical issues, express their concern, and possibly devise ways of resolving them.

The foregoing remarks should emphatically *not* be taken to imply that in existing Model Three societies "religion" has already infiltrated every area of living. Not only does religion for many individuals continue to be a "duplex" compartmentalized affair, but numerous others have abandoned the "duplex" concept only to organize their lives within an exclusively secular context. What has been said above, however, does point to a growing feeling among religiously involved individuals that if religion is to exist at all, it must prove itself in some kind of this-worldly action.

Standards for such this-worldly religious action are likely to be difficult to formulate in a complex society that changes so rapidly that the automatic application of norms handed down from former days no longer suffices. While the individual may look to religion to aid him in his search for *personal* maturity and social relevance, those responsible for the welfare of the nations of the world must seek in every available quarter for action patterns that may help to ensure world peace and human survival. In Model Three societies religious organizations and, more particularly, concerned clergy and laity within such organizations, are actively (and sometimes militantly) involved in the search for peace. But in a world society possessed of the weapons of self-destruction, religious action in general, if it is to be socially relevant in *this* world, cannot be confined to religious organizations per se, but the religiously involved must work through secular organizations to achieve their "religious" objectives.

Religious organization in industrial societies is, as noted above, both divided and pluralistic. Membership is on a voluntary basis, at least in principle. No single dominant church claims, even theoretically, the allegiance of all members of the society, as in the case of Model Two societies. With few exceptions no official tie exists between religious organizations and the secular government. In some societies of this type, such as France and the United States, such relationships are legally repudiated; and in countries like England, where there is an official state church, the latter's relation with the government has become attenuated and modified. In general there are a number of competing religious organizations, large and small, with many members of the society either nonaffiliated or what are termed "paper members" of churches. In the United States in 1964 there were some 258 religious bodies with approximately

63.4 percent of the population enrolled.[19] Hence, 36 percent of the population—a very low proportion compared to that in European countries—are nonaffiliated.[20]

Furthermore, both among those enrolled and those not enrolled in religious organizations, the "privatization" of religion appears to be becoming ever more common.[21] It has been suggested, half seriously perhaps, that one might be tempted to see in Thomas Paine's "My mind is my church" or Thomas Jefferson's "I am a sect myself" the typical expression of religious organization in the near future.[22] Nevertheless, it seems unlikely that religious organization will quickly disappear, although the function it performs may be to a decreasing extent distinctively religious.

The functions of religion in Model Three societies are profoundly affected by the changing characteristics of religion just discussed. Religious divisions combined with the growth of secularism greatly weaken religion's integrating function, and even its divisive power is somewhat blunted. Toleration of religious differences, typical of this kind of society, is partly the outcome of indifference in the face of the growing dominance of the secular value system; religious organizations themselves are not immune to this secularizing influence. Furthermore, some 36 percent of the inhabitants of the United States appear to be able to survive and maintain themselves without affiliating themselves with any kind of religious organization —a fact that raises serious questions concerning religion's function.

Religious beliefs and practices, however, may serve an integrating function within the various organizations themselves. This is particularly likely to be the case when the membership of such groups is largely drawn from class or ethnic minorities within the larger society. Here they serve a purpose as centers of "belongingness" for groups deprived or discriminated against in an increasingly depersonalized social order.

Assessing the extent of the integrative and value-forming functions of religion and striking a balance between this and its dis-

[19] See *Year Book of the American Churches* (New York: National Council of the Churches of Christ in the U.S.A., 1964), p. 252.

[20] The nonaffiliated—that is, the religious "nones"—are, as Glenn M. Vernon has aptly pointed out, an insufficiently analyzed residual category that is by no means uniform. See his unpublished paper, "The Religious 'Nones': A Neglected Category," *Journal for the Scientific Study of Religion,* 7 (Fall 1968): 219–229.

[21] See Thomas Luckman, "On Religion in Modern Society," *Journal for the Scientific Study of Religion,* 2, no. 2 (Spring 1963): 159–161, and also, *The Invisible Religion: The Problem of Religion in Modern Society* (New York: Macmillan, 1967), by the same author.

[22] Bellah, *op. cit.,* p. 373.

integrative potential is difficult. Against the weakened influence of religious organizations may be set the fact that the religious values of an earlier day persist in the society in more or less attenuated form as part of its basic tradition. In this form the values continue to contribute, to an extent extremely difficult to measure, to the cohesion of the society. Evidence of this is the frequency, especially in times of stress, of public appeals to this common heritage of religious tradition. Presidents open their inaugurals with prayer, and in times of war or national danger the help of God is solemnly and publicly invoked.

On the other hand, the state and the economic order between them have taken over important functions performed by religion in Model One and Model Two societies. For example, the secular sanctions of political law and economic supply and demand to a large extent underwrite the system of social obligations without which societies cannot persist. It is possible, moreover, that Model Three societies may be able to maintain themselves with a looser and somewhat different kind of integration than either of the previous models discussed. Hence, How secular can one get? becomes a vital question. Can the secular institutions do the minimum integrative job essential for society without borrowing back, as it were, some of the sacred values previously abandoned?

Will Herberg has supplied us with important clues that may suggest an answer to this question. He sees the "religions of America" —whether Protestant, Catholic, or Jewish—as providing the spiritual underpinnings for the "American Way of Life," a moral and democratic way of life that thus becomes invested with a sacred aura. Meanwhile, the institutionalized religions become instrumental to the preservation of national values, which are themselves increasingly regarded as ultimate.[23]

In certain other Model Three societies, to a greater extent than in the United States, governments have attempted to reinvest themselves with a sacred aura. Fascist and communist governments in particular (although not exclusively) have surrounded themselves with a panoply of quasisacred ritual and claim the total allegiance of the members of a particular society, not on the common-sense secular grounds of public services efficiently performed but rather

---

[23] Herberg, op. cit., pp. 74–90. There are, of course, great differences of opinion as to the extent to which individuals and entire religious organizations view religious faiths as instrumental to American national values. Herberg himself, it should be noted, merely describes what he takes to be the de facto situation. Personally, as a believing Jew, he deplores the conclusions that as a sociologist he draws from his observations of American society.

on some quasireligious ground.[24] Fascist governments, for example, have on occasion claimed that the state, as represented by the government in question, is a sacred end in itself. Such an example gives point to our earlier inquiry, How secular can one get? But the answer remains unclear.

The pursuit of economic power may also take on a quasisacred tinge. In many popular descriptions of the economic arrangements of modern societies, it seems at times that *monetary* values are substituted for *moral* values without either the reader or the writer being clearly aware of the difference between the two.

Religion and the Individual

The personalities of relatively few individuals in modern industrial societies are shaped solely, or even mainly, in accordance with religious values. The weakness of religious values as an integrating focus, of course, is due in part to the diversity of the value systems of various religious organizations that at times contend for the individual's loyalty. But the chief rival of all religious value systems is the increasingly dominant system of secular values. The latter are clustered around nationalism, science, economic and occupational matters, and status-striving. In view of these facts, achievement of personality integration is a more difficult and more self-conscious feat than in societies subsumed under Models One and Two.

In bringing up their children, however, perhaps the majority of American parents continue to act as if they regard traditional religious values, or a somewhat modified version of them, as a necessary background for the building of acceptable character. Parents who have themselves long ceased to attend church nevertheless often feel that their children should be taught the elements of a religious faith in Sunday or Sabbath school. A residuum of fear seems to exist among elders that unless they ensure a minimum of religious instruction for their children, the rising generation may not acquire the moral fitness to maintain, as adults, those values that the elders still feel, perhaps inarticulately, to be necessary for the welfare of society. Therefore many parents, whether they themselves are "religious" or not, persist in sending their children to parochial schools. For in the United States, where the public school not only takes over much of the socialization job once performed in the family but is also legally separated from all organized religion, a

[24] Recent reports from Russia, for example, appear to indicate that the secular religion of Communism does not suffice for a number of individuals and that there is an increase in overt and covert Jewish and Christian religious observance. See *The New York Times*, October 5, 1967, p. 1.

considerable number of people who may themselves be members of no church feel that it is neither safe nor fitting for children to be educated in an atmosphere in which the name of God is perhaps never mentioned, no prayer is uttered, and no sacred book is read. Thus the practice of many a moral maxim, which adults often disregard in their own behavior, is enjoined by the same adults on children and young people. Such practices not only widen the communication gap between the generations but also contribute to personality conflicts among members of the high school and college generation. The latter are taking the parental generation to task for failing to practice what they preach, either in person or by proxy. Today the possibilities for conflict are accentuated by the acclaim given by some members of the college generation to Oriental and American Indian religions. Although these religions are often imperfectly understood, they appeal to a certain segment of "hippie" youth precisely because, from their viewpoint, they are unconventional and espouse a philosophy that appears to be refreshingly different from the conventional and "hypocritical" religion of their parents.*

There are several prevalent types of adjustment to the problem of personality integration in modern industrial societies. First, the individual's personality may be integrated almost exclusively on the basis of the values of the particular religious organization to which he belongs. This type of integration is probably rare today. Second, the individual may frequently achieve a working personality integration by a process of compartmentalization. He may combine a more or less conventional acceptance of so-called Sabbath or Sunday religion with a workaday orientation to secular values. Thus potentially conflicting maxims, such as "Love thy neighbor as thyself" and "Business is business" or "All's fair in love and war," are not permitted to come into open conflict. Under stress, however, this compartmentalized system may break down, as the case histories of many mental patients attest. In the third type of adjustment some

---

* The above statement should *not* be taken as implying that *all* current interest in Oriental and other "foreign" religions is superficial and motivated mainly by rebelliousness against the older generation. On the contrary, there exists today much serious study of non-Christian religions by both older and younger individuals. The existence, at Harvard University, of a graduate *Center for the Study of World Religions* is evidence of this fact. Furthermore, a superficial interest in a non-Christian religion, initially triggered by rebelliousness, may well give place to a deep and genuine interest in, and possibly practice of, the religion for its own sake. Oriental religions in particular may exercise a strong appeal because they have largely retained a contemplative component that Western Christianity, especially in its Protestant branches, has almost entirely lost.

individuals may come to adopt, perhaps after a struggle or perhaps by default, an integration of their personalities in terms of secular values alone. This mode of adjustment is also rather common, but it too may break down in stress situations, such as those involved in warfare. Finally, some people, probably a minority outstanding among whom were Albert Schweitzer and Alfred North Whitehead, achieved integration in terms of ultimate religious values, which they reinterpret and reevaluate in the light of modern philosophy and science. By means of this reinterpretation they bring religious values into what for them (and for the writer) is a meaningful relationship with the secular values of modern industrialized societies.

The Intermixture of Types of Society in the Modern World

The attempt to use the three types of society as aids in understanding the functions of religion in actual societies does pose a difficulty. No one of these types exists unmixed in any of the great national societies of the modern world. For instance, Model Three societies, the most dynamic in the world today, are continually impinging their science, technology, and secular values on the more religiously oriented Model Two societies and on the few remaining representatives of Model One society. In comparison, the absence of rapid communication in medieval and early modern times meant that our own Western world experienced a period of relative isolation of several centuries during which took place the transition from a society approximating Model Two to one more nearly approaching Model Three. Even so, the accompanying changes in the role of religion in the society did not take place without prolonged and widespread social disintegration and disruption.

Today the great agricultural societies of the world, the contemporary counterparts of Model Two, are connected, whether their members desire it or not, in a worldwide network of rapid communications. Even their agricultural economics have become more and more dependent on world conditions of trade. Moreover, the kind of social life that has developed in the ports and other urban centers in direct contact with the industrialized West does not differ greatly from that of the secularized societies designated as Model Three. Hence the functions of religion in Calcutta, Bombay, Hong Kong, or Singapore are in many respects comparable to those it exercises in London, Paris, or New York. Yet in the thousands of agricultural villages that make up the greater part of such societies, the sacred values of an earlier day remain dominant. Nevertheless, the radio and movies penetrate into all but the most remote of such villages, and modern technology is being applied to ancient methods of agriculture. In Model Two societies religious observances and sacred values are intermeshed with traditional agricultural methods and are tied in with long-established patterns of social obligations and relationships. Therefore, technological innovations in agriculture, such as the introduction of "miracle rice" (a very high yield rice) in certain Asian countries recently, cannot fail ultimately to affect the sacred values themselves. When this happens, the social functions of religion in these societies will also be modified.

Even in the predominantly industrialized United States there still remain some relatively isolated rural areas, subsocieties within the larger society, where the role played by religion is often quite similar to the prevailing situation in Model Two societies. In such areas religion may still serve in part to define the position of social ranks in local communities and to preserve traditional values, as, for instance, in the Deep South, in the Kentucky Mountains, or in some of the open farm country in the West. But even in these remote and poverty-stricken areas, religious values are constantly being challenged by those of the current mass media, with its enticing commercials backed up by enterprising salesmen. The very poor may not be able to buy these tempting products, but at least they learn of their existence and to a decreasing extent are turning to religion as a substitute for material deprivation. The "Poor People's March" on Washington under religious leadership provides a striking illustration of how the dwellers in hitherto neglected and obscure rural communities are turning to political—that is, secular—action.

In spite of the changes just mentioned, religion does play a different part in remote rural areas than in metropolitan New York, Chicago, or Los Angeles. Yet even these metropolitan cities themselves, our closest approximation to Model Three societies, contain many individuals who have migrated either from rural areas in the United States or from peasant societies in southern and eastern Europe, Asia, or the Caribbean. The values of the older immigrants from such peasant societies frequently approximate those of Model Two societies. Such new immigrants to our great cities, mostly Negroes and Puerto Ricans, are often completely bewildered by the values that prevail, even among "religious" people, in American urban communities. For the expectations of such people concerning the role religion ought to play in social life are likely to be very different from those of most of their urban neighbors.

The existence of these smaller subsocieties, with their divergent conceptions of religion's role, within our larger urban societies gives rise to conflicts and discrepancies, both within the social order and within individual personalities. Some understanding of these conflicts and discrepancies, especially insofar as they result from the close and sometimes enforced contact between societies of different types, is essential for an intelligent grasp of the role of religion in the world today.

Nottingham's approach represents not a rejection of the Durkheimian tradition but a refinement of it. It is useful to remember that the particular society studied in Durkheim's most important book on religion, *Elementary Forms of the Religious Life,* was that of the Arunta, a small, undifferentiated society in Australia. Obviously it is analogous to Nottingham's Model One society. In this context, a major error of much functionalist theory about religion is its attempt to apply learnings about religion in Model One societies to religion in Model Two and especially Model Three societies.

The theoretical approach offered by Berger and Luckmann in the following essay provides some interesting contrasts to the functional approach. Both functionalism and the sociology of knowledge focus upon the problem of social order and religion's contribution to the maintenance of social order. Yet, Berger and Luckmann make no assumptions about functional requisites for the existence of societies. They do, however, assume that in some manner social order must be legitimized. In this regard they lean more heavily upon Weber's insights rather than those of Durkheim. The problem of legitimation recurs often in Weber's sociology and especially his sociology of religion.

While functional theory treats social order as a given, the sociology of knowledge, as defined by Berger and Luckmann, treats social order as a problem. If religion, broadly defined, is part of the ideological apparatus by which social legitimation is attained, then religiously pluralistic societies represent a puzzle for the social theorist. In such societies, competing religious doctrines may well hamper the attainment of legitimation (a la Weber) and value consensus (a la Durkheim). In such a framework, the sociology of religion becomes part of the broader field of the sociology of knowledge. It also becomes an important area of concern to social theorists seeking to understand the processes of order and change in modern society. Berger and Luckmann's essay is very much a manifesto for departing from the rather narrow study of the functions of religious institutions and for placing the sociology of religion in the center of the social theory-building enterprise.

Sociology of Religion and Sociology of Knowledge
by Peter L. Berger and Thomas Luckmann

Religion is both an important and an ambivalent phenomenon in contemporary western society. This is true on both sides of the Atlantic, despite significant differences between America and Europe with regard to the social situation of religion. In America, religion continues to occupy an important position in public life and, on a quite voluntary basis, continues to enlist the formal allegiance of well over *half* the population in its organized bodies. In Europe, despite the survival of various degrees of legal establishment in various countries, popular participation in organized religion lags considerably behind the conspicuous piety of the cis-Atlantic masses. This lag, however, is compensated by the political prominence of organized religion as best exemplified by the political parties identified with one or both of the two major Christian confessions. In both Europe and America religion plays an important part in the overall ideological posture *vis-à-vis* the Communist world. Moreover, again in both sectors of the emerging north-Atlantic civilization, there is widespread popular interest in religion, strongly reflected by the

Peter L. Berger is professor of sociology at Rutgers University. He is the author of *The Precarious Vision* (1961); *The Noise of Solemn Assemblies* (1961); *Invitation to Sociology* (1963); *The Sacred Canopy* (1967); and *A Rumor of Angels* (1970); and co-author of *The Social Construction of Reality* (with Thomas Luckmann, 1966); *Movement and Revolution* (with Richard Neuhaus, 1970); and *Sociology: A Biographical Approach* (with Brigitte Berger, 1972).

Thomas Luckmann has taught sociology at various colleges in both the United States and Germany and is presently affiliated with Konstanz University in Germany. He is author of *The Invisible Religion* (1967) and co-author of *The Social Construction of Reality* (with Peter L. Berger, 1966).

Reprinted from *Sociology and Social Research*, 47, no. 4 (1963): 417–427. Used with permission of the authors and publisher.

mass media but also visible on more intellectually sophisticated levels. Both Protestantism and Catholicism have given birth to intellectual movements strong enough to be called a theological revival. Interestingly enough, it is precisely among the theologians that there are to be heard severe criticisms of the sort of religion that is prominent in the society and doubts as to whether this prominence may not be profoundly deceptive. Among some theologians there has been blunt mention of a "post-Christian era" only thinly veiled by the continuing busywork of the religious organizations. The ambivalence of the religious phenomenon is thus present in the consciousness of the religious world itself, prior to any sociological imputation from without.

The ecclesiastical authorities of the two major confessions have commonly stopped short of these extreme diagnoses. Nevertheless it is a commonplace even in the inner circles of the religious bureaucracies that things are not what they ought to be and that there is something not quite real about the Christian rhetoric of public life. Minimally this ecclesiastical uneasiness can be seen in an awareness of certain obvious trouble spots on the religious scene, such as the persistent alienation of much of the working class in Europe or the problem of racial segregation within the churches of America. One of the rather surprising consequences of this uneasiness has been a turning towards sociology on the part of the churches.

In the period since World War II there has been a remarkable development of sociologically oriented research carried on under ecclesiastical auspices, to the point where today a sizable body of literature has been produced by this enterprise.[1] In this country, Protestant agencies have been engaging in this sort of research since the 1920s, largely in connection with the strategic planning of denominational and interdenominational offices, but the overall research enterprise has greatly expanded and also become more formalized in the wake of the postwar "religious revival." Catholic agencies in America have been influenced by this Protestant research-happiness as well as by the booming Catholic "religious sociology" in Europe, while Jewish organizations have been engaging in widespread research activities of their own. The most spectacular inroad of sociological techniques, however, has occurred in European Catholicism. It began in France, but today has spread to every country with a sizable Catholic population. Under various

[1] Cf. the extensive international bibliography in Dietrich Goldschmidt and Joachim Matthes, *Probleme der Religionssoziologie* (Cologne: Westdeutscher Verlag, 1962).

headings ("religious sociology," "parish sociology," "pastoral sociology," and others) a considerable number of research institutes, brought together in an international federation, are carrying on investigations under the direct sponsorship of the Catholic authorities.[2] European Protestants have not quite caught up with this development, but strenuous efforts are well under way to emulate the Catholic example.[3] This is not the place to evaluate these research enterprises, some of which have unquestionably yielded valuable data for the sociology of religion in contemporary society. However, a few comments ought to be made about the general character of this sociological activity.

This character is determined by the economic base of the enterprises in question. Generally speaking, the latter constitute a religious variety of market research. They are financed by ecclesiastical organizations facing pragmatic problems and seeking pragmatic solutions to these problems. It should not surprise anyone that this research is employer-oriented in its motivations. What is more important to see is that its conceptual framework is also determined by this employer-orientation. The focus of interest is church-affiliated religiosity, its presence or absence, constituting respectively a "good" or a "bad" situation from the management point of view. Needless to say, research carried on under ecclesiastical auspices shares this problem with the activities of sociologists employed by other types of bureaucratic management, for example in industry or government. It should also not be too surprising, consequently, that this ecclesiastically based research has borrowed its methodology from other branches of bureaucratically functional sociology. This methodology is narrowly sociographic, a fact which is both technically and ideologically functional. It avoids questions that go beyond the immediate pragmatic concerns of the employer (since such questions are not amenable to treatment by the methods utilized) and it legitimates the "scientific" respectability of the enterprise (since these methods are acceptable precisely to the most rabidly positivistic scientism outside the churches).

There is something precious in this unexpected liaison between archbishops and pollsters. What concerns us here, however, is the enormous discrepancy between this latter-day sociology of religion and the place that religion occupied in classical sociological theory.

[2] Cf. the principal international periodical published under these Catholic auspices, *Social Compass* (Brussels and The Hague).

[3] Cf. the report on the European Colloquium on the Sociology of Protestantism, held in Strasbourg in May 1959, in *Archives de sociologie des religions*, 8 (July–December 1959): 3–157.

It is hardly necessary in this context to amplify this statement in terms of the theoretical systems of Weber, Durkheim or Pareto, only to mention three crucial ones. One might recall, however, that none of the theorists just mentioned were personally "religious." They were concerned with religion for sociological reasons. Religion was perceived by them as a central phenomenon of social reality, therefore necessarily central for sociological understanding in general. Weber's recognition of religion as a prime factor in the historical process, Durkheim's insistence on the ultimately religious character of all human solidarity and Pareto's analysis of the place of religion in the perennial human pastime of self-deception—whatever one may want to do with these positions in one's own theorizing, it is clear that they are a long way, as starting points of sociological research, from the headaches of ecclesiastical bureaucrats.

This is not to say that, at any rate in American sociology, there is not some continuity with these classical sociological approaches to religion. Thus one can find strong Weberian undertones in the works on religion of Howard Becker and Gerhard Lenski, or a definite Durkheimian flavor in those of Lloyd Warner and Milton Yinger. The influence of both Weber and Durkheim on Talcott Parsons' treatment of religion is evident. It remains true that the sociology of religion is marginal in terms of the sociological enterprise proper (as distinguished from the ecclesiastical research enterprise discussed before), both in terms of its practice and in terms of its thought. Whatever may be the historical reasons for this segregation of the sociology of religion into a somewhat eccentric preserve, the implication is quite clear: —Religion is not a central concern for sociological theory or for the sociological analysis of contemporary society. Religion can, therefore, be left in the main to the social historians, to the ethnologists or to those few sociologists with an antiquarian interest in "the classics"—and, of course, to that fairly alienated group of colleagues employed by religious institutions.

Is this implication defensible? We would say that it is—but *only* if the field of the sociology of religion is defined in ecclesiastical terms, that is, if its focus is to be church-affiliated religiosity and its various degrees of presence or absence. The obvious next question is whether this definition makes sense from the standpoint of sociological theory. Our answer here is resoundingly negative. The reason for this answer is based on our understanding of the nature of the sociological enterprise.

We would say, first of all, that the sociologist who operates exclusively with an ecclesiastically oriented definition of religion has an altogether too narrow and, as it were, juridical concept of institution.[4] The latter must, of course, be taken into account by the sociologist, but it does not exhaust the pertinent social reality of this or any other phenomenon. The juridical or other "official" versions of society invariably distort sociological perspective if taken at face value. The sociologist who so takes them simply adopts the viewpoint of "management" on the matter at hand. He is well on the way from that point on towards becoming a conservative ideologist, as is best illustrated by the positivistic school of jurisprudence which became precisely that with respect to the institution of law. What happens in this case is that the "official" or "management" viewpoint comes to delimit the area of sociological relevance. Or, speaking empirically, it is not the sociologist but his employers (be they archbishops or admirals, welfare officials or business executives) who define the proper objects of his investigations. Whatever does not fall within his definition of what is relevant is either relegated to an allegedly "subjective" and "scientifically inaccessible" domain or is courteously conceded to some other academic discipline. The former solution is that of the positivists, the latter of those sociologists who are anxious not to infringe on the territory of the psychologists. A pragmatic solution somewhere between the positivistic and the psychologistic alternatives is the one that would leave these institutionally undefined phenomena to such research on "opinions" or "attitudes" as dwells in the antechambers of the temple of sociology. We would contend that none of these options is viable for a sociologist who understands and respects his own universe of discourse.

Sociology must be concerned with everything which, already on the commonsense level, is taken as social reality, even if it does not fit into the "official" definition of what the institutions of society are.[5] There is a wide range of human phenomena that are socially objectivated but not institutionalized in the narrow sense of the word. Not only is it methodologically inadmissible to exclude these phenomena from the perspective of sociology, but any concept of institution hangs theoretically in mid-air if it is not grounded in a sociological understanding of objectivation as such. The basic form of social objectivation is language. Language analyzes, recombines and "fixes" biologically based subjective consciousness and forms

[4] We would like to see a broader concept, but will not argue the point here. For a very suggestive development of the sociological concept of institution *vide* Arnold Gehlen, *Urmensch und Spaetkultur* (Bonn: Athenaeum, 1956).

[5] This understanding of the scope of sociology has been strongly influenced by the sociological theories of Alfred Schutz. Cf. Alfred Schutz, *Collected Papers, I— The Problem of Social Reality* (The Hague: Nijhoff, 1962).

it into intersubjective, typical and communicable experiences. The metaphorical and analogical potential of language facilitates the crystallization of social values and norms by which experience is interpreted. It is this edifice of semantic fields, categories and norms which structures the subjective perceptions of reality into a meaningful, cohesive and "objective" universe. This universe, "reality as seen" in a culture, is taken for granted in any particular society or collectivity. For the members of a society or collectivity it constitutes the "natural" way of interpreting, remembering, and communicating individual experience. In this sense it is internal to the individual, as his way of experiencing the world. At the same time it is external to him as that universe in which he *and* his fellow-men exist and act.[6]

Such a universe is fundamentally legitimated by the fact that it is there, confronting the individual from the beginning of his biography as the self-evident external reality which exercises unremitting constraint upon his individual experiences and actions. Nevertheless, this universe *as* a coherent configuration of meaning requires reiterated and explicitly formulated legitimation. The individual already learns in his primary socialization the fundamental formulas of this legitimation. Socialization, however, is never totally successful and never completed. The legitimating formulas must be reiterated in the ongoing life of the adult, especially in the great crises of this life (as in rites of passage). One can put this a little differently by saying that all universes, as meaning structures, are precarious. The individual's "knowledge" of the world is socially derived and must be socially sustained. Using Alfred Schutz's expression, the individual's world-taken-for-granted must be legitimated over and over again.[7] Normally this legitimation will occur in specific institutional forms. Yet one must be careful not to confound "knowledge" (i.e., the meaning configuration of the universe) with the formal institutions of learning or legitimation (i.e., the explicit —and symbolic—"explanation" of the coherence of that universe) with institutionally organized ideologies. This theoretical distinction

[6] In addition to Schutz we would point here to the classic formulations of the character of this *conscience collective* in the works of Durkheim and Maurice Halbwachs. For more recent interpretations, cf. Eric Voegelin, *The New Science of Politics* (Chicago: University of Chicago Press, 1951); Robert Redfield, *The Primitive World and Its Transformations* (Ithaca: Cornell University Press, 1953); Claude Lévi-Strauss, *La pensé sauvage* (Paris: Plon, 1962).

[7] For the phenomenological analysis of the "natural" way of looking at the world and its social relativity cf. Max Scheler, *Die Wissensformen und die Gesellschaft* (Bern: Francke, 1960).

is especially important in terms of the religious dimension of this socially constituted universe.

Throughout human history religion has played a decisive part in the construction and maintenance of universes.[8] This statement does not necessarily imply an extreme Durkheimian position that religion has done nothing else or is nothing else apart from this social function, but it does imply that this function is sociologically central. In any case, while this function of religion can be discovered cross-culturally, the institutionally specialized location of religion in churches or similar bodies is relatively rare in history. It is, of course, characteristic of the development of Christianity. But it is generally absent in ancient civilizations and is almost totally unknown in primitive societies. *Ergo,* for the purposes of a general sociology of religion, this institutional specialization cannot be used as the defining criterion of religion. The ecclesiastically oriented definition of the field of the sociology of religion betrays then, at the very least, a marked historical and cultural parochialism.

There is, indeed, a sociological problem in the relationship of institutionalized religion, where it exists, with the more general religious business of universe building. But this is not the only problem. The recent history of secularization in western and westernizing societies indicates, on the contrary, that the part of institutionally specialized religion in the fundamental processes of legitimation is on the wane. This development is of great sociological importance in itself and there already exist various theories seeking to explain it.[9] Another interesting problem lies in what has been described as the "emigration" and subsequent "privatization" of even traditionally Christian religiosity from the churches, a phenomenon especially significant in Europe.[10] Yet another sociological problem is posed by the transformation of the traditional religious meanings

---

[8] The classic sociological formulation of this is, of course, to be found in the works of Durkheim and his school. For important corroboration from the fields of the phenomenology and history of religion cf. the works of Mircea Eliade (e.g. *Cosmos and History,* New York: Harper and Brothers, 1959); and Eric Voeglin (*Order and History*) vols. I–III, Baton Rouge: Louisiana State University Press, 1956–1957). For a recent sociological interpretation cf. W. Lloyd Warner, *The Living and the Dead* (New Haven: Yale University Press, 1959).

[9] Cf. Helmut Schelsky, "Ist die Dauerreflektion institutionalisierbar?", *Zeitschrift fuer evangelische Ethik,* 4 (1957): 153–74; Talcott Parsons, *Structure and Process in Modern Societies* (New York: The Free Press of Glencoe, 1960), 295–321; Sabino Acquaviva, *L'eclissi del sacro nella civiltà industriale* (Milan: Comunità, 1961); Goldschmidt and Matthes, *op. cit.,* especially 65–77.

[10] Cf. Eberhard Stammler, *Protestanten ohne Kirche* (Stuttgart: Kreuz, 1960).

within the churches themselves, something to be observed very clearly in America but also present in varying degrees in Europe.[11] From our viewpoint, however, another problem is sociologically the crucial one: —What are the characteristics of the legitimating processes actually operative in contemporary society?

No human society can exist without legitimation in one form or another. If it is correct to speak of contemporary society as increasingly secularized (and we think that this is correct), one is thereby saying that the sociologically crucial legitimations are to be found outside the area of institutionally specialized religion. To say this, however, is only the beginning of the sociological analysis that must now take place. One must now ask what forms these legitimations take, to what extent they are institutionalized and where they are so institutionalized (since there is no longer any reason to fixate one's attention on the traditional religious institutions). At this point, needless to say, one has arrived at some of the central questions of a sociological understanding of modern society.

Before we venture on some statements concerning the implications of this for the sociology of religion in this modern society we would return for a moment to more general theoretical considerations. Legitimation cannot be discussed apart from the universe that is being legitimated. Such a universe, as we have briefly tried to indicate, is a socially constituted reality, which the individual member of society learns to take for granted as "objective" knowledge about the world. This "objectivity" (what Durkheim called the "thing-like" character of social reality) is determined by the fact that socialization is not simply individual learning of cultural items but also social constraint in the formation of the most fundamental categories of experience, memory, thinking and communication. This means that knowledge, in the broadest sense, is socially derived. The task of the sociology of knowledge is the analysis of the social forms of knowledge, of the processes by which individuals acquire this knowledge and, finally, of the institutional organization and social distribution of knowledge. It will be clear that we are here giving to the sociology of knowledge a considerably broader meaning than has hitherto been given to it. We conceive the sociology of knowledge as being properly concerned with the whole area of the re-

[11] Cf. Louis Schneider and Sanford Dornbusch, *Popular Religion* (Chicago: University of Chicago Press, 1958); Rose Goldsen e.a., *What College Students Think* (Princeton: D. Van Nostrand Company, 1960), 153–95; Peter Berger, *The Noise of Solemn Assemblies* (Garden City, N.Y.: Doubleday and Company, 1961); Hans-Otto Woelber, *Religion ohne Entscheidung* (Goettingen: Vandenhoeck & Ruprecht, 1959).

lationship of social structure and consciousness.[12] The sociology of knowledge thus understood ceases to be an idiosyncratic activity of sociologists with a penchant for the history of ideas and is placed squarely at the very center of sociological theory.[13]

The consequence for the sociology of religion as a discipline is clear: —The sociology of religion is an integral and even central part of the sociology of knowledge. —Its most important task is to analyze the cognitive and normative apparatus by which a socially constituted universe (that is, "knowledge" about it) is legitimated. Quite naturally, this task will include the analysis of both the institutionalized and the noninstitutionalized aspects of this apparatus. This will involve the sociology of religion in the study of religion in the sense in which this term is commonly understood in western civilization (that is, as a Christian or Jewish interpretation of the world and of human destiny). But the sociology of religion will also have to deal with other legitimating systems, whether one wishes to call these religious or pseudo-religious, that are increasingly important in a secularized society (such as scientism, psychologism, Communism, and so forth). Indeed, only if the latter is also done will it be possible to obtain an adequate sociological understanding of the phenomena that persist within the traditional religious systems and their institutional manifestations.

What results can be expected from this re-interpretation of the task of the sociology of religion for empirical research? First of all, such a re-interpretation leads to a detachment of the sociologist (*qua* sociologist, that is) from the ideological interests of all, not only of the traditional religious legitimating systems. This includes an emancipation from the "management" point of view within the churches, and also from any scientist ideology that may exist within the field

[12] The authors of this article, in cooperation with several colleagues in sociology and philosophy, are currently engaged in the preparation of a systematic treatise in the sociology of knowledge that will seek to integrate with what is now known as the sociology of knowledge three other streams of sociological thought hitherto largely left outside this discipline—the phenomenological analysis of the life-world (especially in the opus of Alfred Schutz), the Durkheimian approaches to the sociology of knowledge and those of American social psychology as derived from the work of G. H. Mead.

[13] The problem of ideology in its relationship to social strata and their conflicts, the original impetus and subject matter of the sociology of knowledge, remains an important area within such a broader definition of the discipline. In addition to the well-known works of Karl Mannheim cf. Robert Merton, *Social Theory and Social Structure* (New York: The Free Press of Glencoe, 1957), 439–508; Werner Stark, *The Sociology of Knowledge* (New York: The Free Press of Glencoe, 1958); Kurt Wolff (ed.), "The Sociology of Knowledge," *Transactions of the Fourth World Congress of Sociology*, IV (Louvain: International Sociological Association, 1959).

of sociology itself. In terms of research practice, there will be an obvious broadening in scope of the sociology of religion. This broader scope is especially important in a modern pluralistic society in which different legitimating systems compete for the patronage of potential consumers of *Weltanschauungen*. Indeed, we strongly believe that this market character of legitimating systems is in itself an important characteristic deserving of sociological analysis. The sociology of religion here finds itself in close proximity to the problems already investigated by the sociology of mass culture and mass communications.

This leads to further important problems. We think that the relative freedom of the consumer *vis-à-vis* the various legitimating systems influences personality structure.[14] Compared with the obligatory and unambiguous internalization of any one legitimating system in traditional societies, the consumer status of the individual *vis-à-vis* competing legitimating systems in modern society provides, if nothing else, at least the illusion of freedom. We think that the collision of this private "freedom" with the strict controls of functionally rational and bureaucratic institutions over the public conduct of the individual represents one of the central problems of the social psychology of modern society. There is a significant sociological problem involved in the loss of monopoly status incurred by the major legitimating systems of western civilization. We believe that this process is one of the social causes of the "privatization" of belief, that is, of the withdrawal of religious commitments from their traditionally designated locations in society into that curious area which German sociologists (not too happily) have called the "sphere of the intimate." The same global processes may well be related to the legitimating functions of psychoanalysis and other forms of psychologism in modern society, functions that can be said to be paradigmatic in terms of "privatization." The sociological analysis of contemporary sexuality, its myths and its rituals, would belong in the same area.

The market character of legitimation (a central aspect of what one likes to call pluralistic society) is very likely to have important consequences for the content of legitimating systems. It is one thing to preside in the role of Brahman over the metaphysical cravings

[14] *Cf.* David Riesman, *The Lonely Crowd* (New Haven: Yale University Press, 1950); Arnold Gehlen, *Die Seele im technischen Zeitalter* (Hamburg: Rowohlt, 1957); Thomas Luckmann, *Zum Problem der Religion in der modernen Gesellschaft* (Freiburg: Rombach, 1963).

of an isolated and fairly homogeneous peasant population which has no choice in the matter. It is quite another matter to try and market one legitimating system (even if it is Vedanta!) to an affluent and sophisticated clientele of suburbanites, Midwestern housewives, metropolitan secretaries, etc. A certain similarity between these social types may remain in the domains of emotion, sex, consumption, etc.—in short, in the "intimate sphere" which is relatively less dependent on class and institutional factors. The social as well as economic imperative of appealing immediately to the changeable taste of the largest possible number of "privatized" consumers may account for the importance of psychoanalysis, a legitimating system tailored to the "intimate sphere" *par excellence*. This, of course, does not preclude the success of Zen Buddhism or political chauvinism in narrower special segments of the mass market. It must not be overlooked that Presbyterianism and Reform Judaism are not exempt either from the mechanism of marginal differentiation called into play in this situation.

These considerations probably point to a comprehensive analysis of legitimation in modern society on the basis of a non-monopolistic market model. Special attention must be given here to the function of the mass media in the socialization of these consumer attitudes. The mass media are further significant in the direct, anonymous and, as it were, non-institutionalized transmission of a synthetic universe with its appropriate prefabricated legitimations. Another important area of investigation in this connection is the place of the family, the consuming entity *par excellence* with reference to all marketable commodities from television sets to "peace of mind." The ideological constellation of "familism," with its broad institutional base in contemporary society ranging from child-centered church programs to the "kiddy-korners" of the suburban shopping centers, is to be analyzed as another aspect of the overall process of "privatization."

Some of these problems have been investigated by sociologists in various sub-disciplines of the field. The re-interpretation of the sociology of religion here undertaken thus in no way pretends that the task indicated above must begin from some sort of *tabula rasa* as far as empirical data are concerned. There is already existent a wealth of data both within and without the area of research more narrowly called the sociology of religion. However, we would contend that the conception of the sociology of religion here formulated would place these data in a more comprehensive theoretical frame of reference. Beyond that it can bring into focus as yet unexplored avenues of empirical research.

Berger and Luckmann's essay is especially critical of much empirical work in the sociology of religion. It is their view that many studies of religious institutions are theoretically vacuous. It is not that such studies employ faulty theoretical frameworks, but that they have little theoretical import at all. In contrast, Berger and Luckmann argue that the sociology of religion must turn away from the study of religion in its specific institutional forms and conceptualize religion as a symbolic entity in society. The difference between their approach and that of most functionalists is partly a matter of the level of analysis. Structural-functional analysis, as its name suggests, examines religion as an aspect of social structure. In contrast, Berger and Luckmann understand religion as a cultural phenomenon. These are very different levels of the social manifestation of religion. Said differently, alternative theoretical frameworks ask different kinds of questions at different levels of analysis. It is not simply a question of which theory is best.

The final essay in this section of the book also inquires into the cultural significance of religion. Robert Bellah is concerned not simply with religion but with the cultural competition between religion and science. While he acknowledges the importance of the social scientific understandings of religion provided by Durkheim, Weber, Marx, and Freud, he also complains of the reductionism inherent in all of these approaches. He fears that by reducing religion to its objective consequences we are barred from a subjective understanding of religion in and of itself. In the final analysis, Bellah contends that the social scientific study of religion contains an anti-religious bias, regardless of which theoretical approach is employed. These concerns were, of course, a continual element in the historical development of the sociology of religion in America and were alluded to briefly in Eister's essay as well.

Christianity and Symbolic Realism [1]

by Robert N. Bellah

There is probably nothing more important than intellectual history to help us understand how our culture has become so fragmented and dissociated that we find it almost impossible to communicate the integrated meaning our young people so passionately require of us. Aware of my lack of competence in intellectual history I must nonetheless venture into it in order to deal with one central aspect of this fragmentation, namely, the split between theological and scientific (and here I mean mainly social scientific) language about Christianity or more generally the split between religious man and scientific man in the West.

Without going back before the seventeenth century one can perhaps say that from that time almost to the present the dominant theological defense of Christianity has been what may be called "historical realism." The roots of this historical realism can be traced back to biblical historicism, Greek rationalism, and the new aware-

Robert N. Bellah is professor of international studies and sociology at the University of California, Berkeley. He is the author of *Tokugawa Religion* (1957), and a collection of his essays appears under the title *Beyond Belief* (1970).

Reprinted from *Journal for the Scientific Study of Religion*, 9, no. 2 (1970): 89–96. Used with permission of the author and publisher.

ness of scientific method emerging in the seventeenth century. The figural and symbolic interpretation of scripture which was characteristic of medieval thought was almost eliminated by Reformation and counter-Reformation theology. Modern consciousness required clear and distinct ideas, definite unambiguous relationships, and a conception of the past "as it actually was." The proponents of "reasonable Christianity" worked out a theology which seemed to fit these requirements. It is true that some of the most significant theological minds—Pascal, Edwards, Schleiermacher, Kierkegaard—don't quite fit this formulation. Nevertheless for broad strata of educated laymen and above all for the secular intellectuals it was this understanding of Christianity that was decisive. Lest anyone think this kind of Christian thought is dead let him pause for a moment to consider the recent popularity of apologists who have argued that "Christ must have been who he said he was or he was the greatest fraud in history."

There have always been those willing to pick up the gauntlet with that kind of argument. Particularly in the eighteenth century many secular intellectuals argued that Christ or, if not Christ, certainly the priests were indeed frauds. Meeting Christianity on the ground of historical realism, they rejected it. When faced with the inevitable question of how something clearly fraudulent and indeed absurd could have been so powerful in human history they answered that religion was propagated for the sake of political despotism, maintained by an unholy alliance of priestcraft and political despotism. This argument was a species of "consequential reductionism," the explanation of religion in terms of its functional consequences, which in cruder or subtler form has been a standard piece of intellectual equipment in the modern secular intellectuals' understanding of religion ever since.

The nineteenth century began with a partial reaction against the abstract rationalism of the enlightenment and saw a growing awareness of the complex role of religion in the development of human consciousness. Yet at the same time the certainty grew among the secular intellectuals that Christianity, still defended largely by the old arguments and the old formulas, and with it religion generally, could not be taken seriously in its own terms. There grew up alongside of the continuing use of consequential reductionism, several varieties of what I would call "symbolic reductionism." From this point of view religion is not entirely fraudulent. It contains a certain truth. But it is necessary for the modern intellectual to discover what that truth is that is hidden in the fantastic myths and rituals of religion. Much of nineteenth-century social science developed out of the search for the kernel of truth hidden in the falsity of religion —the truth behind the symbols.

One of the great intellectual strategies of the symbolic reduction-ists was to treat religion as a phase in the history of science. Primi-tive man, unable to understand the great natural phenomena of night and day, summer and winter, storm and drought, developed the fantastic hypotheses of religion to account for them. This kind of evolutionary rationalism has been enormously pervasive and has influenced religious thought as well as secular. How convenient for the Sunday School teacher to be able to explain the strange dietary rules of the ancient Hebrews in terms of hygiene—an intuitive awareness that shellfish and pork easily spoil under the warm cli-matic conditions of the Middle East!

Another version of evolutionary rationalism which the nineteenth century developed with vast persuasiveness was the conception of religion as a stage in the development of human morality. The hid-den truth of religion was the gradually growing perception of man's ethical responsibilities. The monotheistic God of the Bible could then be considered as the expression of a high ideal of man's ethical action.

For those perplexed that religion should continue to survive even in scientifically and ethically enlightened times, more immediate, more existential forms of symbolic reductionism were developed. Following Feuerbach's treatment of religion as the projection of human nature Marx developed his famous conception of religion as the opium of the people. This is usually treated as a form of con-sequential reductionism, which it perhaps is, but if we look at the *locus classicus* we can see that it is even more an existential version of symbolic reductionism. In his Introduction to the "Critique of Hegel's Philosophy of Right" Marx wrote:

> *Religious* suffering is at the same time an *expression* of real suffering and a *protest* against real suffering. Religion is the sigh of the op-pressed creature, the heart of a heartless world, and the soul of soul-less conditions. It is the *opium* of the people.[1]

From the early decades of the twentieth-century, symbolic reduc-tionist theories of religion gained new subtlety and new complexity. Freud and Durkheim developed comprehensive formulas for the translation of religious symbols into their real meanings. Freud, first in *Totem and Taboo* and then more starkly in *The Future of an*

---

[1] Karl Marx, *Early Writings* (New York: McGraw Hill, 1964), pp. 43–44.

Illusion, disclosed that the real meaning of religion is to be found in the Oedipus complex which it symbolically expresses. The biblical God stands for the primordial father toward whom the sons feel both rebellious and guilty. Christ sums up a whole set of conflicting oedipal wishes; the wish to kill the father, the wish to be killed for one's guilty wishes, and the wish to be raised to the right hand of the father. And finally for Freud the psychologically courageous man will discard the religious symbols which cloak his neurosis and face his inner problems directly.

For Durkheim the reality behind the symbol was not the Oedipus complex but society, and the morality which expresses it. In one of his most important essays "Individualism and the Intellectuals,"[2] he attempts to describe the religion and morality appropriate to his own society. He finds this in a religion of humanity and a morality of ethical individualism. How does he treat Christianity? "It is a singular error," he says, "to present individualist morality as the antagonist of Christian morality; on the contrary it is derived from it." In contrast to the religion of the ancient city state, he says, Christianity moved the center of the moral life from outside to within the individual who becomes the sovereign judge of his conduct without having to render account to anyone but himself and God. But, he says, today this morality does not need to be disguised under symbols or dissimulated with the aid of metaphors. A developed individualism, the appropriate morality of modern society, does not need the symbolic trappings of Christianity.[3]

Unlike Marx, Freud, and Durkheim, Max Weber made no claim to have the key to the reality which lies behind the facade of religious symbolization. He treated religions as systems of meaning to be understood in their own terms, from the point of view of those who believe in them, even though in the observer they strike no personal response and in this he was at one with a whole tradition of German cultural historians and phenomenologists. For all the sensitivity with which he treats Calvinism, for example, it is the consequences for the actions of the believers which interest him, not the beliefs themselves. Without ever quite taking the position of consequential reductionism Weber still manages to convey the feeling that the scientific observer cannot finally take seriously the beliefs he is studying, even though he must take seriously the fact that beliefs have profound social consequences.

---

[2] Emile Durkheim, "L'Individualisme et les intellectuels," *Revue Bleue,* 4e serie, 10 (1898): 7–13.

[3] Ibid., 11.

For the moment I am not trying to refute any of these theories of religion. They all, I believe, have a great deal of truth in them as far as they go. But what I want to point out now is that the best minds in social science by the third decade of the twentieth century were deeply alienated from the Western religious tradition. None of them were "believers" in the ordinary sense of that word. All of them believed themselves to be in possession of a truth superior to that of religion. But since none of them, except very hesitantly and partially, wanted to fill the role that religion had previously played, they contributed to the deep split in our culture between religion and science, a break just at that highest level of meaning where integration is of the greatest importance.

Meanwhile, back at the seminary, things went on much as usual. The same old books were picked up, thumbed through, and put down again. The contemporary proponents of the historical realist position trimmed and cut what no longer seemed tenable and hoped for the best. A Karl Barth had the courage to give vivid expression to the grand themes of biblical and reformation theology as though nothing had happened intellectually in the nineteenth and twentieth centuries, at least nothing which could not be refuted with the magnificent rhetoric of divine initiative and revelation. A few (one thinks of Martin Buber and Paul Tillich) saw the problem and tried to heal the split. In their more ecstatic moments I think it is even possible to say that they did heal the split. But neither was quite able to come up with a theoretical formulation which would spell out their ecstatic insights.

It is my contention that implicit in the work of the great symbolic reductionists was another possible position with entirely different implications for the place of religion in our culture, a position I will call "symbolic realism" and will spend the rest of this paper trying to describe. Not only the great social scientists but many philosophical, literary, linguistic, and religious thinkers have contributed to this position which has been gestating for a long time and has become increasingly explicit in the last twenty years.

Both consequential reductionism and symbolic reductionism are expressions of an objective cognitive bias which has dominated Western thought ever since the discovery of scientific method in the seventeenth century. This position has held that the only valid knowledge is in the form of falsifiable scientific hypotheses. The task then with respect to religion has been to discover the falsifiable propositions hidden within it, discard the univerifiable assertions and those clearly false, and even with respect to the ones that seem valid to abandon the symbolic and metaphorical disguise in which they are cloaked. Both Durkheim and Freud, who are worth considering for a moment in this connection, ardently held to this conception of knowledge. Yet the work of both of them contains deep inner contradictions precisely with respect to this point. Durkheim came to see that the most fundamental cultural forms, the collective representations, are not the product of the isolated reflective intelligence but are born out of the intense atmosphere of collective effervescence. Collective representations are based first of all on the sentiment of respect that they exact from individuals, and it is only through their discipline that rational thought becomes possible. Rational inquiry, then, rests on a necessary substratum of sentiments and representations that has neither the form nor the function of scientific hypotheses. Nor did Durkheim believe that the element of the sacred, which is what he called the symbolic expression of the collective vitality at the basis of society and culture, could ever be outgrown. It would always be an essential feature of social life and the great terms which moved him and which he felt were so essential to modern society—individuality, reason, truth, morality, and society itself—were, as he knew, symbols, collective representations. In fact he came to see that society itself is a symbolic reality. In his own terms, finally, symbolic reductionism comes to be self-contradictory and self-destructive. It is the reality of symbols that his lifework goes to prove.

Freud's greatest discovery was the existence and nature of the unconscious. In his first and in many ways most fundamental major work, *The Interpretation of Dreams,* he showed that dreams are the royal road to the unconscious. Only through dreamlike symbolism can the primary process of the unconscious express itself. Although the rational understanding which he called secondary process can gradually increase its effective control, Freud never thought it could replace the unconscious. Indeed he emphasized the relative weakness and fragility of rational processes. And in his own work he again and again abandoned the form of scientific hypothesis for the language of myth, image, and symbol, much to the dismay of subsequent academic psychologists. He named his most important psychological complex after a Greek myth. In his late years he constructed his own myth, the myth of the struggle of Eros and the death-instinct, in order to express his deepest intuitions. The unmasker of all symbols finally if implicitly admitted the necessity and reality of symbols themselves.

In recent years the knowledge that noncognitive and nonscientific symbols are constitutive of human personality and society—are *real* in the fullest sense of the word—has deepened and consolidated. Rather than the norm of scientific objectivity invading all spheres of human experience, the role of noncognitive factors in science itself has become increasingly recognized. As the philosopher of science Michael Polanyi says, "... into every act of knowing there enters a passionate contribution of the person knowing.... This coefficient is no mere imperfection but a vital component of his knowledge."[4] What this signals is a shift away from the mechanical model of early natural science in which reality was seen as residing in the object, the function of the observer was simply to find out the laws in accordance with which the object behaves, and "subjective" was synonymous with "unreal," "untrue," "fallacious." For this mechanical model there has increasingly been substituted the interactionist model of social science, or what Talcott Parsons calls "action theory." Here reality is seen to reside not just in the object but in the subject and particularly in the relation between subject and object. The canons of empirical science apply primarily to symbols which attempt to express the nature of objects, but there are nonobjective symbols which express the feelings, values, and hopes of subjects, or which organize and regulate the flow of interaction between subjects and objects, or which attempt to sum up the whole subject-object complex, or even point to the context or ground of that whole. These symbols too express reality and are not reducible to empirical propositions. This is the position of symbolic realism.

If we define religion as that symbol system which serves to evoke what Herbert Richardson calls the "felt-whole,"[5] that is the totality which includes subject and object and provides the context in which life and action finally have meaning, then I am prepared to claim that, as Durkheim said of society, religion is a reality *sui generis*. To put it bluntly, religion is true. This is not to say that every religious symbol is equally valid any more than every scientific theory is equally valid. But it does mean that, since religious symbolization and religious experience are inherent in the structure of human existence, all reductionism must be abandoned. Symbolic realism is the only adequate basis for the social scientific study of religion.

When I say religion is a reality *sui generis* I am certainly not supporting the claims of the historical realist theologians who are still working with a cognitive conception of religious belief which makes

---

[4] Polanyi, *Personal Knowledge* (New York: Harper Torchbooks, 1964), p. xiv.

[5] Richardson, *Toward an American Theology* (New York: Harper and Row, 1967), chap. 3, esp. p. 64.

it parallel to objectivist scientific description. But if the theologian comes to his subject with the assumptions of symbolic realism as many seem to be doing, then we are in a situation where for the first time in centuries theologian and secular intellectual can speak the same language. Their tasks are different, but their conceptual framework is shared. What this can mean for the reintegration of our fragmented culture is almost beyond calculation.

But if a new integration is incipient, fragmentation still describes the present reality. Concentrating so heavily on the mastery of objects, we have too long neglected what Anais Nin calls the "Cities of the Interior,"[6] and everywhere these neglected cities are in revolt. We have concentrated too much on what Polanyi calls explicit knowledge and too little on what he calls implicit knowing. We have forgotten that the implicit knowing is the more fundamental, for all explicit knowledge depends on its unconscious assumptions.[7] As Yeats says: "Whatever flames upon the night/Man's own resinous heart has fed."[8] We see the flames, but we have forgotten the heart and its reasons that reason knows not of. The price of this neglect of the interior life (and I use interior not only to refer to the individual—there is a collective interior that contains vast forces) is the reification of the superficial, an entrapment in the world of existing objects and structures.

But the life of the interior, though blocked, is never destroyed. When thwarted and repressed the interior life takes its revenge in the form of demonic possession. Just those who feel they are most completely rational and pragmatic, most fully objective in their assessment of reality, are most in the power of deep unconscious fantasies. Whole nations in this century have blindly acted out dark myths of destruction all the while imagining their actions dictated by external necessity. In our own country both the National Security Council and the SDS claim to be acting in accordance with the iron laws of politics at the same time that they seem trapped dreamlike in their own unconscious scenarios. All of this is the price we have paid for relegating art to the periphery of life, denying the central integrating role of myth and ritual and letting our morality be dictated by our politics. For these reasons the issues of concern here are not academic, are not, to use a word that I have come to loathe

---

[6] The title of her multi-volume "continuous novel."

[7] Polanyi, p. x.

[8] William Butler Yeats, *The Variorum Edition of the Poems* (New York: Macmillan, 1968), p. 437.

in recent months, irrelevant. The future of our society, perhaps of life on this planet, depends on how we face them.

Perhaps the first fruit of symbolic realism, of taking seriously non-cognitive symbols and the realms of experience they express, is to introduce a note of skepticism about all talk of reality. "Reality is never as real as we think."[9] Since for human beings reality is never simply "out there" but always also involves an "in here" and some way in which the two are related, it is almost certain that anything "out there" will have many meanings. Even a natural scientist selects those aspects of the external world for study which have an inner meaning to him, which reflect some often hidden inner conflict. But this is true of all of us. We must develop multiple schemas of interpretation with respect not only to others but ourselves. We must learn to keep the channels of communication open between the various levels of consciousness. We must realize with Alfred Schutz that there are multiple realities[10] and that human growth requires the ability to move easily between them and will be blocked by setting up one as a despot to tyrannize over the others.

Let me conclude by applying these general remarks to the field of religion and to the problems which face those of us who think about religion today. If art and literature primarily express the realm of inner meaning and are free to explore even the most aberrant and idiosyncratic wishes, hopes, and anxieties, religion is always concerned with the link between subject and object, with the whole which contains them and forms their ground. Though religion is not primarily subjective, it is not objective either. It symbolizes unities in which we participate, which we know, in Polanyi's words, not by observing but by dwelling in them.[11] While neither the churches nor our secular culture seem to be doing a terribly good job of providing the symbols which evoke the wholeness of life and give meaning to our participation in it we must nonetheless look to whatever in our own culture or in any culture has played this role.

If we think especially of contemporary Christianity there are a number of theologians whose work seems relevant—such names as Wilfred Smith, Richard Niebuhr, Gordon Kaufmann, Herbert Richardson come to mind. But for me Paul Tillich is still the great theologian of the century, perhaps because it was through his work that

---

[9] Daniel Stern as quoted by Anais Nin in *The Novel of the Future* (New York: Macmillan, 1968), p. 200.

[10] Schutz, *Collected Papers* (The Hague: Martinus Nijhoff, 1962), vol. 1.

[11] Polanyi, p. x.

Christian symbols first began to live again for me after my adolescent loss of faith. Certainly no one had a clearer sense of the fatal consequences of objectivism in religion. When Tillich objected to such phrases as "God exists" or "God is a Being" or "the Supreme Being" it was because he felt they made God into an object, something finite, a being alongside other beings. His own conception of God was far more transcendent than the neofundamentalists ever realized. And yet even Tillich succumbed perhaps too much to the mania for interpretation, for discovering the rational core beneath the symbol, and the metaphysical structure in which he restated the fundamental Christian truths is after all not very persuasive. As one more schema of interpretation alongside others it certainly has its uses, but when he says that the statement "God is being-itself" is not symbolic[12] he seems to be engaging in a kind of metaphysical reductionism. Perhaps his greatest contribution and the line of work which is still worth pursuing today was his restless quest for the "dimension of depth" in all human social and cultural forms. This was his great contribution to breaking out of the institutional ghetto and seeing once more, as Augustine did, the figure of Christ in the whole world.

Two secular intellectuals have made major contributions in recent years to the position I am trying to set forth in this paper: Herbert Fingarette in *The Self in Transformation*[13] and Norman O. Brown in *Love's Body*.[14] Both of them oppose any kind of symbolic reductionism; both of them know that reality is inner as well as outer and that the symbol is not decoration but our only way of apprehending the real. They both have much to teach us about the multiplicity of vision—poetic, Buddhist, primitive, as well as Christian—which has become a possibility and indeed a necessity in the modern world. The work of these men is the most vivid illustration I know of the rapprochement between the language of religion and the language of the scientific analysis of religion.

As a sociologist I am by no means prepared to abandon the work of the great consequential and symbolic reductionists. They have pointed out valid implications of religious life that were not previously understood. But I am prepared to reject their assumption that they spoke from a higher level of truth than the religious systems they studied. I would point out instead their own implicit

[12] Tillich, *Systematic Theology* (Chicago: University of Chicago Press, 1951), 1:238.

[13] (New York: Basic Books, 1963); (New York: Harper Torchbooks, 1965).

[14] (New York: Random House, 1966); (New York: Vintage Books, 1968).

religious positions. Most of all I am not prepared to accept the implication that the religious issue is dead and that religious symbols have nothing directly to say to us.

Superficially the phenomenological school seems preferable on this score since it insists on describing religious symbols as closely as possible in the terms of those who hold them. But here there is the temptation to treat religious systems as embalmed specimens which could not possibly speak directly to those outside the charmed circle of believers.

I believe that those of us who study religion must have a kind of double vision—at the same time that we try to study religious systems as objects we need also to apprehend them as religious subjects ourselves. Neither evolutionist, nor historical relativist, nor theological triumphalist positions should allow us to deny that religion is one. Please don't misunderstand me when I say this. I don't mean that all religions are saying the same thing in doctrinal or ethical terms—obviously they are not. But religion is one for the same reason that science is one—though in different ways—because man is one. No expression of man's attempt to grasp the meaning and unity of his existence, not even a myth of a primitive Australian, is without meaning and value to me. Perhaps this assertion will seem less radical to many young people today (for example, to the young anthropologist Carlos Castenada who apprenticed himself to a Yaqui shaman) than it does to those trained in my generation. I am not advocating the abandonment of the canons of scientific objectivity or value neutrality, those austere disciplines which will always have their place in scientific work. But those canons were never meant to be ends in themselves, certainly not by Weber who was passionately committed to ethical and political concerns. They are methodological strictures. They do not relieve us of the obligation to study our subject as whole persons—which means in part as religious persons. Nor do they relieve us of the burden of communicating to our students the meaning and value of religion along with its analysis. If this seems to confuse the role of theologian and scientist, of teaching religion and teaching about religion,[15] then so be it. The radical split between knowledge and commitment that exists in our culture and in our universities is not ultimately tenable. Differentiation has gone about as far as it can go. It is time for a new integration.

---

[15] Randall Huntsberry has recently discussed the untenability of the distinction between teaching religion and teaching about religion in an unpublished paper, "Secular Education and its Religion."

Which theory of religion is best? Obviously the question is a loaded one. Which theoretical approach is most useful depends upon the kinds of research questions being asked and the type of information being sought. Moreover, no single theoretical understanding of religion tells us all that there is to know about religion. Bellah's plea for a "new integration" between the scientific and humanistic understanding of religion is at best utopian. While it is true that we must never remove the "whole person" from social science, we may err in the other direction by expecting social science to answer theological questions. Indeed, most sociologists of religion would be thankful for a unification of our social scientific theories of religion, not to mention a unification of scientific and religious commitment. While one may disagree with Bellah's utopian resolution of the faith-science problem, he at least reminds us to be continually aware of the limitations of our scientific knowledge of religion and the social world generally.

Part IV

Religion and Social Structure in America

Religion is intertwined in the American social structure in a host of complex ways. The relationships between religion and age, sex, social class, occupation, and geographic region are but a few of the important areas to be studied in order to understand the salience of religion in America. Unfortunately, unlike many other areas of sociological inquiry, the sociology of religion cannot turn to the United States Census for even the most basic kinds of information. In March 1957, for the first time in its history, the Census Bureau included a question on individual religiosity on a sample survey. A first report on the results of that survey was released in February 1958. This action stimulated an intense controversy. Some observers argued that the collection of information about religion by the government represented a violation of the constitutional separation of church and state. Others, particularly spokesmen for minority religious groups (especially Catholics and Jews), argued that the bureau's action was a threat to the constitutional guarantee of individual religious freedom and questioned the possible government uses of such information.[1]

In response to the controversy the Census Bureau cancelled its plans for subsequent reports on this survey. The 1957 census

[1] For a discussion, see William Petersen, "Religious Statistics in the United States," in *Journal for the Scientific Study of Religion,* 1, no. 2 (1962): 165–178.

data on religion became the only instance in which census data has been suppressed and withheld from the public. It was not until the enactment of the Freedom of Information Act (Public Law 89-489) in 1967 that the bureau was required to release the remaining information in its possession from this survey. This consisted of a small collection of tables, as the original data had already been destroyed.[2]

Prior to the 1957 survey, the bureau had collected information on religious institutions (though not on individual persons) during two different historical periods. Between 1850 and 1890, and again between 1906 and 1936, the bureau assembled membership statistics on American churches. The similar information contained in the bureau's recent census publications, like its *Pocket Data Handbook,* are actually statistics supplied to the bureau from the National Council of Churches' publication *Yearbook of the Churches.*[3] As even the past editor of the *Yearbook* readily admits, there are numerous reasons to question the accuracy of these statistics.[4] First, these figures are supplied to the council by the individual religious denominations themselves; and in most cases the denominations receive the information from individual local churches with no methodological check on the accuracy of the figures. Second, different religious groups in the United States determine membership differently. Thus, the figures in the *Yearbook* are not necessarily comparable from one group to the next.

Given the problems inherent in the information provided by religious institutions themselves and the nearly total absence of census data, sociologists must rely upon the data provided by such private polling agencies as the National Opinion Research Center at the University of Chicago, the Institute for Social Research at the University of Michigan, the Harris Poll, the Gallup Poll, and smaller studies conducted by individual researchers. The following essay by Bernard Lazerwitz examines three sample surveys conducted in 1957 at the Michigan Survey Research Center.

[2] These tables are contained in Samuel Mueller and Angela Lane, "Tabulations from the 1957 Current Population Survey on Religion," *Journal for the Scientific Study of Religion,* 11, no. 1 (1972): 76–98. The original government report released in February 1958 is "Religion Reported by the Civilian Population of the United States: March 1957," Series P-20, Number 79, Bureau of the Census, U.S. Department of Commerce, Washington, D.C.

[3] The *Yearbook* appears in annual editions.

[4] See Benson Y. Landis, "Confessions of a Church Statistician," in *National Council Outlook,* 7: (1957) p. 3.

A Comparison of Major United States Religious Groups[*]
by Bernard Lazerwitz

1. Introduction

The task of collecting information on United States religious groups now rests upon research endeavors conducted outside governmental agencies. Among recent decisions which emphasize federal reluctance to work in this field are the refusal of the United States Census Bureau to release any more information beyond a first bulletin from its March 1957, Current Population Survey [16], which included questions on religious preference, and the decision not to include questions on religious preference in the 1960 Census.

Fortunately, this information gap can be filled with data gathered on national probability sample surveys conducted by private survey research organizations. While these data are based on smaller sam-

Bernard Lazerwitz is professor of sociology at the University of Missouri at Columbia and is a member of its Research Center's Public Opinion Survey Unit. Reprinted from *Journal of the American Statistical Association*, 56 (1961): 568–579. Used with permission of the author and publisher.

  * This article was written while the author was a Research Associate of the Survey Research Center, University of Michigan. The author is indebted to the Center for use of its data and facilities and for financial support of the project. The opportunities for analysis of these religious data were pointed out by Dr. Angus Campbell, Director of the Center.

ple sizes than the rather large Census Bureau surveys and subject to sizable sampling errors for our smaller religious groups, accurate conclusions can be drawn from such findings.

Professor Donald Bogue [3] has recently published data on religious groups obtained in 1955 by the National Opinion Research Center. This present article presents religious data gathered on three national surveys conducted by the Survey Research Center of The University of Michigan.

Of the three surveys treated here, two [5, 9], conducted in the spring of 1957, asked each adult respondent[1] for his religious preference and his denominational preference if the respondent was a Protestant. The third survey [13] was conducted in November, 1958, and asked only for religious preference.[2] This latter survey is included to increase the number of Roman Catholic, Jewish, and "no religion" respondents.[3]

2. Findings

Table 1 presents the sex and marital status composition of the major United States religious groups. Note the relatively heavy female concentrations, in contrast to the national percentage, found for Negro Baptists,[4] and Episcopalians. The opposite extreme is found in the "no religion" group which is heavily male. Again, Negro Baptists and the "no religion" category rank rather low (in contrast to the national figure) on percent married. The Negro Baptists rank high on separated, divorced, and widowed; adults with no religion rank high on percents single and divorced.

[1] The three surveys accepted interviews with respondents under 21 years of age in certain cases. However, the data in this article only apply to respondents 21 years of age or older. (Very few respondents were under 21 years of age.)

[2] The lack of a question on Protestant denominational preference in the November, 1958 survey confines denominational data to the first two studies. The reader should bear this in mind when contrasting the number of interviews reported for all Protestants with that reported for specific Protestant denominations. Furthermore, only the Protestant denominations included in this article's tables were specifically coded on the two earlier surveys. Information on additional denominations can only be obtained by an expensive recoding process.

[3] Comparisons of the sets of percentages obtained on the three surveys indicate the passage of 18 months produced only random changes. With those surveys combined into one, the data may be thought of as referring to a point in time midway between the spring of 1957, and November, 1958, namely, December, 1957.

[4] The Baptists are separated by race because Negroes form 24 percent of this denomination. Negroes comprise only 10 percent of the Methodist denomination so that controlling for race did not change white or over-all Methodist percentages in any meaningful degree.

Table 1. Sex Composition and Marital Status for Adults of Major United States Religious Groups, December 1957

(in percentages)

Religious Groups	N	Men	Women	Sin-gle	Mar-ried	Wid-owed	Di-vorced	Sepa-rated	Total
Nation	5827	46	54	6	82	8	2	2	100%
Protestants	4185	45	55	5	82	8	3	2	100
Baptists	939	42	58	5	80	9	4	2	100
Whites	713	44	56	5	83	8	3	1	100
Negroes	226	34	66	5	68	12	6	9	100
Methodists	730	44	56	5	81	10	2	2	100
Lutherans	328	46	54	9	81	8	1	1	100
Presbyterians	272	42	58	8	78	9	4	1	100
Episcopalians	119	35	65	9	79	9	1	2	100
Roman Catholics	1270	46	54	8	82	7	2	1	100
Jews	188	42	58	8	85	5	1	1	100
No Religion	125	81	19	11	77	5	6	1	100

Age composition is given in Table 2. The Episcopalians are rather low in the 21 to 29 age categories and high in the 40 to 54 age categories in contrast to the national (or Protestant) figures. Similarly, the Presbyterians are high in the 55 years old and over brackets.

Number of children presently in a respondent's home and respondent's family life cycle stage are reported in Tables 3 and 4. Presbyterians, Episcopalians, and Jews have the smallest percentage of families with three or more children and relatively large percentages of their families with two children. The Methodists and the over-all Protestant percentages are between the figures reported for Presbyterians, Episcopalians, and Jews and the larger family sizes recorded for the "no religion," Lutheran, white and Negro Baptists, and Roman Catholic groups.

Note that Episcopalians, Presbyterians, and the adults with no religion groups have fairly high percentages in the "no children" category. For the "no religion" group, this concentration undoubtedly arises out of its disproportionate numbers of males and single people. For the other two religious groups a more complicated explanation seems in order which Table 4 helps provide.[5]

[5] In forming Table 4 study codes only permitted placing families into the following eight life cycle categories: (1) respondent single and under 35 years of age; (2) respondent married and under 35 years of age but with no children in the home; (3) respondent married and with at least one child under 5 years of age in the home; (4) respondent married and all children in the home 5 years of age or older; (5) respondent not now married but does have children in his home; (6), (7) and (8) are categories in which there are no children now in the respondent's home, and the respondent is of the indicated ages.

Table 2. Age Composition of Adults of Major United States Religious Groups, December 1957
(in percentages)

Religious Groups	N	21-24	25-29	30-34	35-39	40-44	45-49	50-54	55-59	60-64	65 or over	Total
Nation	5827	6	12	12	12	13	10	9	8	6	12	100%
Protestants	4185	6	12	12	11	12	11	10	8	6	12	100
Baptists	939	8	11	13	12	12	11	9	6	6	12	100
Whites	713	9	12	13	11	12	12	9	6	5	11	100
Negroes	226	7	10	15	14	10	10	11	7	7	9	100
Methodists	730	6	10	12	11	11	10	10	8	6	16	100
Lutherans	328	6	13	13	9	12	11	10	6	8	14	100
Presbyterians	272	5	10	13	9	13	8	9	11	8	14	100
Episcopalians	119	4	6	12	13	17	12	11	4	9	12	100
Roman Catholics	1270	7	13	13	12	15	9	8	7	5	11	100
Jews	188	5	9	13	16	16	8	10	9	4	10	100
No Religion	125	9	5	10	12	12	15	11	6	5	15	100

Table 3. Number of Children in the Homes of Major United States Religious Groups, December 1957

(in percentages)

Religious Groups	N	No Children	1 Child	2 Children	3 or more Children	Total
Nation	5827	44	16	18	22	100%
Protestants	4185	43	16	19	22	100
Baptists	939	42	16	17	25	100
Whites	713	41	15	19	25	100
Negroes	226	41	19	11	29	100
Methodists	730	46	14	19	21	100
Lutherans	328	43	13	20	24	100
Presbyterians	272	48	15	21	16	100
Episcopalians	119	53	13	19	15	100
Roman Catholics	1270	39	15	19	27	100
Jews	188	40	17	27	16	100
No Religion	125	48	16	13	23	100

Table 4. Family Life Cycle for Major United States Religious Groups, December 1957

(in percentages)

Religious Groups	N	R. Single and under 35 yrs.	Married, R. under 35 yrs., no children	Married, youngest child under 5 yrs.	Married, youngest child 5 yrs. or over	R. not now married, but has children	No Children in Home R. 35–44 yrs.	R. 45–64 yrs.	R. 65 yrs. and over	Total
Nation	5827	3	4	25	25	6	5	20	12	100%
Protestants	4185	3	4	25	26	5	5	21	11	100
Baptists	939	3	4	24	25	9	5	19	11	100
Whites	713	3	5	25	28	6	4	18	11	100
Negroes	226	3	3	22	17	20	7	19	9	100
Methodists	730	2	5	25	23	6	4	20	15	100
Lutherans	328	3	4	26	26	5	4	20	12	100
Presbyterians	272	3	2	23	25	4	4	23	16	100
Episcopalians	119	4	4	18	26	3	9	25	11	100
Roman Catholics	1270	5	5	27	28	5	5	16	9	100
Jews	188	6	5	25	32	2	3	19	8	100
No Religion	125	6	2	21	27	4	6	21	13	100

Episcopalians have the largest percentages with no children in the home and respondent from 35 to 64 years of age; Presbyterians have the largest percentage with no children in the home and respondent 65 years of age or older (and the second largest percentage in the previous life cycle category). These two denominations also have disproportionate concentrations in the over 45 years of age brackets as shown by Table 2.

While the data presented here cannot explain these denominational characteristics, they do suggest this possible hypothesis: that the Episcopalians and, to a lesser degree, the Presbyterians gain a fair number of new, middle-aged members from other Protestant denominations. Such recruits should have advanced their social and economic lot in life and would be seeking added status through membership in the Episcopalian or Presbyterian churches.[6] That these two churches do have large proportions of high status people is shown by the remaining tables.

Large differences appear in Table 5, which gives amount of schooling. A status array can be formed with Episcopalians on top having 53 percent with one or more years of college, followed by Presbyterians with 36 percent, and Jews with 33 percent. In the middle come people with no religion, Methodists, Lutherans, and Roman Catholics. On the bottom are the Baptists, both whites and Negroes. Finally, note the large concentration exhibited by the "no religion" group in the 0–8 grades category. Unlike the others, this group shows concentrations at both the high and low ends of the education scale.

This interesting ranking of the religious groups recurs on occupation of family head shown in Table 6. The Episcopalians have the largest professional percentage, followed by the Jews, "no religion," and then the Presbyterians. The Jews have the largest owners, managers, and officials percentage, followed by the Episcopalians and Presbyterians. The Episcopalians, Presbyterians, and Jews have very few farmers.

In the middle are found the Catholic, Methodist, and Lutheran groups. On the bottom of the occupational pile come the white and Negro Baptists.

Forty-two percent of the Catholics are found in the skilled and semi-skilled categories with the rest distributed throughout the other groupings. Catholics, too, have few farmers, and their occupational distribution resembles the white Baptists except for the latter's large farm percentage.

[6] Dr. Niles Carpenter, consultant for the General Division of Research and Field Study of the Episcopal Church, in correspondence with the author has expressed the opinion that the concentration of older adults in the Episcopal church (and, perhaps, the Presbyterian church) is a result of several factors besides status seeking. These additional factors are (1) the attraction of the Episcopalian church for dissident Roman Catholics; (2) the more liberal Episcopalian attitude toward "worldly behavior"; (3) the Episcopalian tradition of having a highly educated clergy which serves to attract and retain well educated laity.

Table 5. Amount of Education for Adults of Major United States Religious Groups, December 1957

(in percentages)

Religious Groups	N	0–8 Grades	Some High School	3 Yrs. High School	1–3 Yrs. College	4 Yrs. or More of College	Total
Nation	5827	33	20	28	10	9	100%
Protestants	4185	33	21	27	10	9	100
Baptists	939	44	24	21	7	4	100
Whites	713	39	26	24	7	4	100
Negroes	226	63	20	11	3	3	100
Methodists	730	31	20	28	10	11	100
Lutherans	328	35	22	29	9	5	100
Presbyterians	272	18	17	29	20	16	100
Episcopalians	119	8	14	25	25	28	100
Roman Catholics	1270	34	20	32	9	5	100
Jews	188	21	13	33	17	16	100
No Religion	125	40	20	18	10	12	100

Table 6. Occupation of Family Heads for Major United States Religious Groups, December 1957

(in percentages)

Religious Groups	N	Professions	Owners, Managers, and Officials	Clerical and Sales	Skilled	Semi-skilled	Unskilled	Farmers	Without an Occupation	Total
Nation	5827	9	12	10	18	15	9	9	18	100%
Protestants	4185	9	12	10	17	15	10	10	17	100
Baptists	939	5	8	7	16	20	15	11	18	100
Whites	713	6	11	9	19	19	8	12	16	100
Negroes	226	4	1	4	10	21	34	8	18	100
Methodists	730	10	11	11	16	14	8	9	21	100
Lutherans	328	7	11	13	18	14	8	15	14	100
Presbyterians	272	13	20	14	17	7	8	4	17	100
Episcopalians	119	23	23	17	12	6	4	2	13	100
Roman Catholics	1270	8	11	10	22	20	10	4	15	100
Jews	188	19	32	16	9	9	1	0	14	100
No Religion	125	15	10	5	10	20	7	11	22	100

As would be expected, the Negro Baptists have the largest unskilled percentage among all religious groups, together with the lowest percentages in the three white collar categories.

The "no religion" group continues to exhibit an atypical pattern. While outranking the Presbyterians in the professional category, it

Table 7. Total Family Income in 1956 for Major United States Religious Groups

(in percentages)

Religious Groups	N	Under $1000	$1000–$1999	$2000–$2999	$3000–$3999	$4000–$4999	$5000–$5999	$6000–$7499	$7500–$14,999	$15,000 or more	Total
Nation	5827	7	8	10	13	15	15	13	16	3	100%
Protestants	4185	8	9	11	13	14	15	12	15	3	100
Baptists	939	17	13	14	15	14	11	9	6	1	100
Whites	713	10	9	13	15	16	14	12	9	2	100
Negroes	226	27	20	17	15	9	5	5	1	1	100
Methodists	730	7	10	14	10	15	17	12	13	2	100
Lutherans	328	6	9	11	10	18	16	14	14	2	100
Presbyterians	272	5	6	9	12	14	14	14	20	6	100
Episcopalians	119	1	1	4	7	12	13	16	35	11	100
Roman Catholics	1270	4	7	8	12	17	17	17	16	2	100
Jews	188	1	2	5	9	10	15	16	31	11	100
No Religion	125	10	11	11	11	17	11	7	15	7	100

drops below the level of the white Baptists on owners, managers, and officials, clerical and sales occupations.

This hierarchical pattern is further borne out by Table 7, on total family income. On top, once more, are the Episcopalians with 46 percent of their families earning $7500 or more, followed by the Jews with 42 percent, and the Presbyterians with 26 percent of their families earning $7500 or more.

In the middle, one finds "no religion," Catholics, Lutherans, and Methodists. On the bottom, again, are white and Negro Baptists.

Once more, adults with no religion exhibit a concentration at both ends of the economic continuum. Twenty-one percent of them earn under $2000 as contrasted to the national figure of 15 percent, and 22 percent earn $7500 or more in comparison to the national figure of 19 percent.

Table 8 presents data on church attendance. The national pattern of 45 percent attending church regularly (once a week or more); 21 percent attending often (once, twice, or three times a month); 26 percent attending seldom (a few times a year or less); and 8 percent never attending is a Protestant pattern. Roman Catholics, as has been well documented, are regular attenders, and Jews seldom attend.[7]

Table 8. Church Attendance During 1957 for Adults of Major United States Religious Groups

(in percentages)

Religious Groups	N	Attends				
		Regularly	Often	Seldom	Never	Total
Nation	5827	45	21	26	8	100%
Protestants	4185	39	23	30	8	100
Baptists	939	41	31	22	6	100
Methodists	730	36	27	28	9	100
Lutherans	328	39	29	27	5	100
Presbyterians	272	41	20	29	10	100
Episcopalians	119	33	23	33	11	100
Roman Catholics	1270	72	13	11	4	100
Jews	188	13	21	51	15	100
No Religion	125	2	1	15	82[a]	100

[a] Nonresponse is classified as *never*.

In other words, four patterns of church attendance can be found in the United States:

[7] For studies of more restricted populations that have investigated the question of church attendance, see [1, 2, 4, 6, 12, 14, 15].

(1) The Catholic pattern typified by about 75 percent attending church weekly.

(2) The Protestant pattern which has one-third to 40 percent attending weekly, 20 to 30 percent attending often and seldom, and 5 to 10 percent reporting no attendance.

(3) The Jewish pattern which is predominately an annual "High Holiday" attendance.

(4) Adults with no religion who rarely (if ever) attend church services.

3. Summary

The sex, marital status, and age distribution data indicate few major differences among the religious groups. The small percentage of young Episcopalians and the large percentages of middle-aged Episcopalians and Presbyterians compared to the national percentages could be a result of sampling error. However, the repetitions of similar concentrations in the tables on number of children and family life cycle give emphasis to the hypothesis that other Protestants join the Episcopal and, to a lesser extent, the Presbyterian churches after a rise in social and economic status.

The relatively low sex ratio among Negro Baptists would well be a result of under representation of Negro males in the three surveys.[8] The pattern of more broken marriages among Negro Baptists is in accord with recent Census reports.[9]

The differences among the religious groups on numbers of children accord with the results presented in the recent Freedman, Whelpton, Campbell book [7]. Table 3 indicates that Jews have the highest percentage of two children families; the Catholics have a high percentage of their families with three or more children, and the white Baptists, Lutherans, and Methodists fall between the Catholics and Jews. Negro Baptists exceed Catholics on percentage of families with three or more children.

The high status, highly urbanized Episcopalians and Presbyterians display the small family pattern which characterizes the Jews. This, too, conforms with the conclusions reached by Goldberg [8].

---

[8] Survey Research Center national samples usually obtain slightly fewer adult males (1 or 2 percent) than would be expected on the basis of Census reports. The Census Bureau and survey organizations find that the greater mobility of Negro men produces a further reduction in sample yields for this population group.

[9] For instance, United States Bureau of the Census, "Marital Status and Family Status: March, 1958," *Current Population Reports*, Series P-20, No. 87.

The education, occupation, and income data sort the religious groups into a social hierarchy. Setting aside the "no religion" group for the moment, one can form the following ranks:

Top: Episcopalians
Jews
Presbyterians
Middle: Methodists
Lutherans
Roman Catholics
Bottom: White Baptists
Negro Baptists

The differences among the Methodists, Lutherans, and Catholics are small. The ranks in the above scale together with the data recorded in Tables 4 to 7 (except for sampling variations and some coding differences) are in substantial agreement with those reported by Bogue [3].

The bottom position of Negro and white Baptists comes as no surprise. The unfortunate position of the Negro in our society is well documented. White Baptists are a heavily Southern group—69 percent living in the South in 1957 according to Bogue's data and the South is our underprivileged region. The very high position of United States Jewry may come as a surprise to some. When one remembers that heavy Catholic and Jewish immigration began about the same time (the 1840's for Irish Catholics and German Jews; the 1880's for Eastern European Jews and other Catholic groups), the extremely rapid rise of the Jewish group becomes quite extraordinary.[10]

Finally, a word about the "no religion" group is in order. Apparently, this group is capable of being subdivided into at least two more homogeneous subgroups. The first subgroup seems to be composed of well-educated, fairly high income, professional people who account for the "top-level" concentrations previously noted.

[10] The three surveys also indicate that 31 percent of the Jews, 16 percent of the Catholics, and 3 percent of the Protestants are foreign-born. It should be borne in mind that numerical size can serve as a limiting factor on a group's social position. Relatively large religious groups, such as the Catholics or Lutherans, should have a more difficult time finding enough "better-off" social "slots" to enable as great a percentage of their groups to rank as high on education, occupation, and income as the smaller Episcopalian and Jewish groups. The numerically smaller groups, such as Episcopalians and Jews, can find a comparatively larger number of high status social "slots" relative to their numbers. On the other hand, one would expect each religious group to form as great a percentage, by chance alone, of the various social status positions as it does of the nation's population. Clearly, this is not the case.

The other subgroup seems to be composed of poorly educated, low income, blue collar workers and farmers. This latter subgroup would account for the large percentage of adults reporting no religion who belong to families having three or more children.

It is hoped that these survey data will aid in removing some of the questions presently asked about United States religious groups.

4. Appendix

A. *Sample Design:* One national sample was selected for both 1957 surveys; it was then randomly divided at the final sampling stage for the two surveys. Another sample, selected from the same primary and secondary sampling units used for the 1957 studies, was used for the November 1958 survey. The two sample designs used the 66 primary sampling units employed on standard Survey Research Center studies; the selection procedures made use of the city directory and segmentation techniques developed by the Sampling Section of the Survey Research Center. Since it is not possible to describe completely the designs of these samples in this brief paper, the interested reader is referred to [9, 10] for such a detailed presentation.

B. *Schedule Questions:* All interviewing was done by the regular field staff of the Survey Research Center. The religion question asked on the two 1957 surveys was: "What is your religious preference?" On the 1958 survey the question was: "Is your church preference Protestant, Catholic or Jewish?" Boxes were also provided for "other" or "none" responses to this question although they were not part of the question proper. In addition, interviewers for the two 1957 surveys were instructed to ask this question if a respondent stated he or she was a Protestant: "What religious denomination is that?"

The Census Bureau survey [16] used a similar question—"What is your religion?" The Census Bureau, Bogue, and the Survey Research Center all report that respondents very readily accepted the question pertaining to their religion. It is doubtful that these slight differences in question wording among the various surveys differentially affected respondents' replies in any significant degree.

C. *Sampling Errors:* Tables 9 and 10 give the sampling errors for individual percentages and for the difference between two percentages for varying numbers of interviews. The low level estimate found in the table cells gives the 95 percent confidence limits based upon the standard simple random sample formula. The high level estimate takes into consideration the additional amount of variance

Table 9. Approximate Sampling Error[a] of Percentages
(in percentages)

Reported Percentages	Number of Interviews								
	4000	2000	1500	1000	700	500	300	200	100
50	1.6–2.2	2.2–3.1	2.6–3.6	3.2–4.5	3.8–5.3	4.5–6.3	5.8–7.4	7.1–9.9	10.0–14.0
30 or 70	1.4–2.0	2.0–2.8	2.4–3.4	2.9–4.1	3.5–4.9	4.1–5.7	5.3–7.4	6.5–9.1	9.2–12.8
20 or 80	1.3–1.8	1.8–2.5	2.1–2.9	2.5–3.5	3.0–4.2	3.6–5.0	4.6–6.4	5.7–8.0	8.0–11.2
10 or 90	0.9–1.3	1.3–1.8	1.5–2.1	1.9–2.7	2.3–3.2	2.7–3.8	3.5–4.9	4.2–5.9	6.0– 8.4

[a]The figures in this table represent two standard errors. Hence, for most items the chances are 95 in 100 that the value being estimated lies within a range equal to the reported percentages, plus or minus the sampling error.
Two estimates of the sampling error are presented for each cell. The lower values are based on the standard error formula for simple random samples. The higher values are based on the computations of individual sampling errors carried out on the study data, and allow for the departure from simple random sampling in the survey design such as stratification and clustering.

Table 10. Approximate Sampling Error[a] of Differences Between Percentages

(in percentages)

Number of Interviews	Number of Interviews							
	2000	1500	1000	700	500	300	200	100
For Percentages from 35 percent to 65 percent								
4000		3.0–4.2	3.5–4.9	4.1–5.7	4.7–6.6	6.0– 8.4	7.2–10.1	10.1–14.1
2000	5.2–4.5	3.4–4.8	3.9–5.5	4.4–6.2	5.0–7.0	6.2– 8.7	7.4–10.4	10.2–14.3
1500		3.6–5.0	4.1–5.7	4.6–6.4	5.2–7.3	6.3– 8.8	7.5–10.5	10.3–14.4
1000			4.5–6.3	4.9–6.9	5.5–7.7	6.6– 9.2	7.8–10.9	10.5–14.7
700				5.4–7.6	5.9–8.3	6.9– 9.7	8.0–11.2	10.7–15.0
500					6.3–8.8	7.2–10.1	8.4–11.8	11.0–15.4
300						8.2–11.5	9.1–12.7	11.5–16.1
200							10.0–14.0	12.2–17.1
100								14.1–19.7
For Percentages around 20 percent and 80 percent								
4000		2.4–3.4	2.8–3.9	3.3–4.6	3.8–5.3	4.6– 6.4	5.8– 8.1	8.1–11.3
2000	2.5–3.5	2.7–3.8	3.1–4.3	3.5–4.9	4.0–5.6	5.0– 7.0	5.9– 8.3	8.2–11.5
1500		2.9–4.1	3.3–4.6	3.7–5.2	4.1–5.7	5.1– 7.1	6.0– 8.4	8.3–11.6
1000			3.6–5.0	3.9–5.5	4.4–6.2	5.3– 7.4	6.2– 8.7	8.4–11.8
700				4.3–6.0	4.7–6.6	5.5– 7.7	6.4– 9.0	8.6–12.0
500					5.1–7.1	5.8– 8.1	6.7– 9.4	8.8–12.3
300						6.5– 9.1	7.3–10.2	9.2–12.8
200							8.0–11.2	9.8–13.7
100								11.3–15.8
For Percentages around 10 percent and 90 percent								
4000		1.8–2.5	2.1–2.9	2.5–3.5	2.8–3.9	3.6– 5.0	4.3– 6.0	6.0– 8.4
2000	1.9–2.7	2.0–2.8	2.3–3.2	2.6–3.6	3.0–4.2	3.7– 5.2	4.5– 6.3	6.1– 8.5
1500		2.2–3.1	2.4–3.4	2.7–3.8	3.1–4.3	3.8– 5.3	4.6– 6.4	6.2– 8.7
1000			2.7–3.8	3.0–4.2	3.3–4.6	3.9– 5.5	4.7– 6.6	6.3– 8.8
700				3.2–4.5	3.5–4.9	4.1– 5.7	4.8– 6.7	6.4– 9.0
500					3.8–5.3	4.3– 6.0	5.0– 7.0	6.6– 9.2
300						4.9– 6.9	5.5– 7.7	6.9– 9.7
200							6.0– 8.4	7.3–10.2
100								8.5–11.9

[a] The values shown are the differences required for significance (two standard errors) in comparisons of percentages derived from *two different* subgroups of the study. Two values—low and high—are given for each cell. See note a to Table 9.

derived from the use of a clustered sample; it, too, gives 95 percent confidence limits. The procedures and statistical formulas used to obtain these sampling errors are presented in Kish and Hess [11].

To illustrate the use of the tables, let us find the sampling error for the 20 percent of the Methodists who have some high school training. Since the total number of Methodist interviews is 730, we enter the column of Table 9 headed 700 and the row headed 20 or

80. This tells us that chances are 95 out of 100 that the 20 percent is subject to a sampling error of plus or minus 4.2 percent (using the high level estimate). Again, to find the sampling error of the difference between the 63 percent of the Negro Baptists who have 0–8 grades of education, based on 226 interviews, and the 35 percent of the Lutherans who have 0–8 grades of education, based on 328 interviews, we enter that section of Table 10 headed "For Percentages from 35 percent to 65 percent." Finding the cell at the intersection of 300 (row) and 200 (column), we note that the chances are 95 out of 100 that the difference between 63 percent and 35 percent, namely 28 percent, is subject to a sampling error of plus or minus 12.7 percent (using the high level estimate). Since 28 percent exceeds 12.7 percent, there is a significant difference between the Negro Baptists and Lutherans on percent having 0–8 grades of education.

Frequently, the difference between two percentages of the data presented in Tables 1 to 8 exceeds the proper high level estimate of sampling error. Hence, the two percentages can be considered significantly different at a 95 percent confidence level. Occasionally,

Table 11. Comparison of Census Bureau and Survey Research Center Studies

Religious Groups	Census Bureau[a]	Survey Research Center[b]		
		March 1957	April 1957	November 1958
Protestants	66.2	70.5	71.2	72.8[d]
Baptists	19.7	21.1	21.8	
Methodists	14.0	16.3	17.0	
Lutherans	7.1	8.1	6.5	
Presbyterians	5.6	6.5	5.6	
Episcopalians	—[c]	2.9	2.6	
Other Protestants	19.8	15.6	17.7	
Roman Catholics	25.7	22.6	22.6	21.9
Jews	3.2	3.6	2.8	3.2
Other Religions	1.3	0.9	0.9	0.7
No Religion	2.7	2.2	2.3	1.3
Religion Not Reported	0.9	0.2	0.2	0.1
Nation	100.0	100.0	100.0	100.0
Sample Size	35,000	2458	1919	1450

[a] Census Bureau percentages pertain to the civilian population 14 years old or over as of March, 1957.
[b] Survey Research Center percentages pertain to the civilian population 21 years old or over as of the indicated dates.
[c] The Census Bureau has not published a separate Episcopalian percentage.
[d] Protestant denomination not asked on this survey.

some of the conclusions presented are not based upon percentages whose differences exceed their proper high level estimates. In all such cases, the percentages follow clearly discernible patterns, and it is probably correct to assert that such differences among religious groups are not functions of sampling variations.

D. *Comparison with Census Bureau Survey:* An interesting verification of the samples discussed in this article is found in Table 11 which compares the religious percentage breakdowns obtained by the Census Bureau with the three surveys treated here. The Survey Research Center surveys show a larger percentage of Protestants and a smaller percentage of Catholics than does the Census survey. These differences probably arise out of the different age groups being reported upon (the Census Bureau reports on persons 14 years old or over; the Survey Research Center reports on persons 21 years old or over), sampling errors, and from slightly different procedural definitions employed by the two organizations.

References

[1] Anonymous, "How Important Religion Is to Americans," *Catholic Digest,* 17 (February, 1953): 6–12.

[2] Argyle, Michael, *Religious Behavior.* London: Routledge and Kegan Paul, 1958. Pp. 23–38. (This book recently has been published by the Free Press.)

[3] Bogue, Donald J., "Religious Affiliation," *The Population of the United States.* Glencoe, Illinois: Free Press, 1959. Pp. 688–709.

[4] Bultena, Louis, "Church Membership and Church Attendance in Madison, Wisconsin," *American Sociological Review,* 14 (1949): 384–389.

[5] Davis, Robert, *The Public Impact of Science in the Mass Media.* Ann Arbor, Michigan: Institute For Social Research, 1958 (mimeographed).

[6] Fichter, Joseph H., *Social Relations in the Urban Parish.* Chicago: University of Chicago Press, 1954. Pp. 83–93.

[7] Freedman, Ronald, Whelpton, Pascal, and Campbell, Arthur, *Family Planning, Sterility, and Population Growth.* New York: McGraw-Hill Book Company, Inc., 1959. Chapters 4, 5, 9.

[8] Goldberg, David, "Another Look At the Indianapolis Fertility Data," *Milbank Memorial Fund Quarterly,* 38 (1960): 23–36.

[9] Gruin, Gerald, Veroff, Joseph, and Feld, Sheila, *Americans View Their Mental Health.* New York: Basic Books, 1960.

[10] Kish, Leslie and Hess, Irene, *The National Sample of Dwellings*

of the Survey Research Center. Ann Arbor, Michigan: Institute for Social Research, 1960 (mimeographed).

[11] Kish, Leslie and Hess, Irene, "On Variances of Ratios and of Their Differences in Multi-Stage Samples," *Journal of the American Statistical Association,* 54 (1959): 416–446.

[12] Landis, Benson Y., "A Guide to the Literature on Statistics of Religious Affiliation with References to Related Social Studies," *Journal of the American Statistical Association,* 54 (1959): 335–357.

[13] Miller, Warren E., *The Party and the Representative Process: A Progress Report on Research.* Ann Arbor, Michigan: Institute for Social Research, 1959 (mimeographed).

[14] Orbach, Harold L., "Aging and Religion: Church Attendance in the Detroit Metropolitan Area," *Geriatrics,* (in press, 1961).

[15] Sklare, Marshall, *Conservative Judaism.* Glencoe, Illinois: Free Press, 1955. Pp. 98–102.

[16] United States Bureau of the Census, "Religion Reported by the Civilian Population of the United States: March, 1957," *Current Population Reports,* Series P-20, No. 79.

These data show interesting variations between religious denominations in terms of age and sex characteristics, marital status, and, most importantly, social class. Both the 1957 sample census and an important study utilizing both the census and National Council of Churches' data by geographer Wilbur Zelinsky show similar patterns of variation for the different religious groups.[5] For instance, both the census and Zelinsky's analysis show dramatic patterns of religious regionalism—an aspect not considered by Lazerwitz. According to the census, most American Jews are located in the urban centers of the Northeast and North Central regions; and both Jews and Catholics are in relatively small numbers in the South and West. Zelinsky finds similar patterns within Protestantism. Thus, while it is true that there are Unitarians in almost every state of the Union, most of them are to be found in the New England states, especially Massachusetts. These

[5] Wilbur Zelinsky, "An Approach to the Religious Geography of the United States: Patterns of Church Membership in 1952," *Annals of the Association of American Geographers,* 51, no. 2 (June 1961): 139–193.

patterns of religious regionalism stem from patterns of immigration and settlement and reflect ethnic differences both within American Protestantism and among American Catholics. It can be seen, then, that in spite of the limitations of National Council of Churches' data, as well as the regrettable absence of chronological census data, these sources can be combined with information from national polling agencies to ferret out some of the basic socioreligious patterns in the United States.

An important point of convergence between the 1957 census data and the surveys upon which Lazerwitz reports is the extremely low percentage of people reporting "no religion." On the census survey, 4 percent of those responding did not report having a religion, as compared to just under 3 percent (125 of 5,827 people) of the people in the Michigan surveys. These are not necessarily valid estimates of the number of people actually joining religious organizations. Religious preference and religious organizational membership are very different measures of religion. Yet, even the National Council of Churches *Yearbook* data place church (and synagogue) membership in the United States at better than 60 percent of the population. Even this figure is higher than those for western European countries. It is frequently argued that the unusually high percentage of church membership in the United States results from the separation of church and state (as opposed to an official state church) and the resulting emphasis upon voluntary religious affiliation. By various measures, these different statistics suggest that Americans are a religious people, and that religion in America varies according to region, class, age, sex, marital status, and a host of other social variables.

While it is important to first describe the patterns of variation of religion in the social structure, it is also essential that social science consider the "hows" and "whys" of religion's impact upon society and society's impact upon religion. The most significant and still controversial attempt to answer this kind of question is Max Weber's essay, *The Protestant Ethic and the Spirit of Capitalism.* Weber attempted to show that Protestantism, especially in its Calvinist and Puritan forms, played a major role in the emergence of a rational, efficiency-oriented capitalist culture.

While some economists and historians continue to debate the adequacy of Weber's research and hypothesis, contemporary sociologists have asked whether or not the Protestant religion continues to influence the ethics and thus the economic attainment of present-day Protestants in the United States. Is the

Protestant ethic still alive? In spite of the argument that we live in a secularized society, can it be shown that religion accounts for the differential levels of social class attainment of groups in the United States? Gerhard Lenski addressed this very question in his landmark study *The Religious Factor.*[6] Based upon an analysis of data collected in the 1957 Detroit Area Study, Lenski showed that there are important patterns of difference between America's major socioreligious groups in terms of family life, political, social, and economic attitudes and conduct.

In spite of the fact that replication remains the essential means of fact-finding in science, one can point to regrettably few instances of exact replication in the social sciences. The following essay by Howard Schuman provides a valuable replication of one part of Lenski's study. Lenski argued that the Protestant ethic was "alive and well" among white Protestants and Jews as opposed to white Catholics and black Protestants in 1957. Schuman attempts to determine whether the same can be said in 1966.

[6] Gerhard Lenski, *The Religious Factor* (Garden City: Doubleday, 1961, revised 1963).

The Religious Factor in Detroit: Review, Replication, and Reanalysis[*]

by Howard Schuman

The application of Weber's Protestant Ethic thesis to the United States has two aspects that go far to explain its attractiveness to many American sociologists. On the one hand, the tracing of economic attitudes and behavior to religious values and beliefs is a nonobvious but intuitively interesting linkage. As such, it seems to provide a persuasive instance where sociology has developed insights that are not apparent to the layman. At the same time, the primary application of the hypothesis to the United States makes this more than a purely theoretical exercise. The division of the

Howard Schuman is professor of sociology at the University of Michigan, a faculty associate at the University of Michigan Survey Research Center, and was director of the Detroit Area Study from 1965 to 1971. He is co-author of *Racial Attitudes in Fifteen American Cities* (with Angus Campbell, 1970); and *The Impact of City on Racial Attitudes* (with Barry Gruenberg, 1970).

Reprinted from *American Sociological Review*, 36, no. 1 (1971): 30- 48. Used with permission of the author and publisher.

* This investigation was carried out through the University of Michigan's Detroit Area Study. I am indebted to Edward O. Laumann with whom I collaborated in designing the 1966 Detroit Area Study. Many of the specific problems involved in replication and reanalysis were solved by James House and Paula Pelletier, who worked as research assistants on this part of the project. Gerhard Lenski kindly furnished advice on use of certain codes from his 1958 study.

146

American population into one quarter Catholic and three quarters Protestant, it is argued, must be taken into account if we are to understand such nonreligious features of American life as its stratification and mobility system, economic organization, and socialization practices.

The single most influential writing on the Protestant Ethic hypothesis is probably Gerhard Lenski's *The Religious Factor* (1963).[1] As a widely available and forcefully written book, Lenski's work has been frequently cited.[2] No doubt a major reason for its impact is that it reports strikingly positive findings and concludes that the Protestant Ethic thesis *is* relevant to contemporary America, that Protestant-Catholic differences in secular attitudes are both large and manifold (more so in fact than class differences), and that these indirect effects of religion in America seem to be on the increase rather than the decrease. One other characteristic of Lenski's work that distinguishes it from most other efforts in this area is its concern to measure social psychological attitudes and values that intervene between religious identification and larger macro-social processes such as occupational mobility.[3]

Despite its intriguing nature, the Americanized version of the Protestant Ethic thesis, and more specifically Lenski's conclusions, have met with some criticism. At the theoretical level, questions have been raised as to whether Weber really intended to argue that the Protestant Ethic was an important cause of the rise of capitalism, and, even if so, whether he expected the Protestant-Catholic distinction to continue to lead to similar economic differences in the twentieth century.[4] More practical questions have focused on whether

[1] The 1963 Anchor edition is not simply a reprint of the original 1961 Doubleday edition but contains important changes in analysis and writing. All references in this paper will be to the 1963 edition.

[2] For example, the article on "The Sociology of Religion" in the new and highly regarded *International Encyclopedia of the Social Sciences* (1969, Volume 13, p. 412) describes *The Religious Factor* as "perhaps the most successful attempt to apply survey research to the sociology of religion," and briefly notes the positive findings of the book.

[3] Most other works on this topic investigate only the general connection between religious membership and socioeconomic variables such as income. See Glenn and Hyland (1967), which includes a fairly complete set of references to earlier studies. For more recent analyses emphasizing socioeconomic status, see Glockel (1969) and Warren (1970). Featherman (1969) provides one of the few analyses (other than Lenski's) which include intervening social psychological variables, though the intervention in this case is between different points in the achievement process for adults.

[4] The wide disagreements on this point indicate that *The Protestant Ethic and the Spirit of Capitalism* (Weber, 1930) can be read in different ways. I myself see Weber's citation of religious differences in education and business (pp. 38–40) as

such gross categories as "Catholic" and "Protestant" are analytically useful in the United States, since there are important ethnic lines within American Catholicism and both ethnic and denominational differences among American Protestants.[5] Finally, at the empirical level enough contradictory findings have appeared to raise some doubts about the reliability of the positive findings reported in *The Religious Factor* (see especially Greely, 1964).

The present paper will not attempt to deal with the first type of question, but will assume that whatever Weber may have intended, it is not unreasonable to determine whether there are Protestant-Catholic differences in beliefs and values relevant to economic advancement. We will deal briefly at one point with the second type of question on ethnic and denominational differences within the major religions, but that is also not our primary focus. The analysis and findings described here are mainly relevant to the third question, namely, the reliability, and therefore validity, of reported Protestant-Catholic differences, using Lenski's earlier results as the focus of investigation. More simply, we shall present results from both a replication and a reanalysis of Lenski's findings, with a review along the way of the original findings themselves.

Lenski's research was carried out in 1958 within the framework of the Detroit Area Study, a continuing survey research and training unit of the University of Michigan. It was appropriate that in 1966 the Detroit Area Study included as part of another research effort an attempt to replicate and extend certain small but important aspects of the investigation reported in *The Religious Factor*. However, the replication was by no means complete and exact, and several limitations must be stressed at the outset.

First, almost the entire focus of the 1966 replication was on the Weberian hypothesis developed and tested by Lenski in Chapter 3 ("Religion and Economics") of his book. The book deals with sev-

---

suggesting continuation into the twentieth century of Protestant-Catholic differences in secular values. That Weber, as a careful scholar, emphasized the complexity of any causal analysis of capitalism does not mean that he lacked a bold thesis himself. In any case, the impact of Weber's writing on the Protestant Ethic has certainly been largely based on this thesis, whether or not Weber himself would today subscribe to it.

[5] Glock and Stark (1965) have particularly emphasized denominational differences within Protestantism. Their dependent variables, however, are religious and moral values closely tied to the origins of American denominations, and they do not deal with values linked to the Protestant Ethic hypothesis. See Warren (1970) for a careful analysis of denominational differences in education, occupation, and income. An original review of *The Religious Factor* (Rosen, 1962) questioned the lack of attention to ethnic differences.

eral other topics, such as "Religion and Politics," which are not relevant at all here, and with still other topics such as "Religion and Family Life," that are relevant but are tested only slightly, if at all, by the present data.

Second, this replication began more as an "extension" than as a simple replication. We hoped to duplicate Lenski's results and then to carry out—more carefully than his sample and techniques allowed—several further analyses, for example, on the relevance of ethnicity to religious differences. We did not, therefore, repeat quite all the questions needed for a full replication even of the economic aspect of the 1958 DAS survey, and we did not attempt seriously to follow his exact ordering of questions.

Third, replication is not a simple concept and can obviously never be carried out perfectly.[6] Apart from sampling error, which can be estimated, and real changes over time, which often cannot, replication turns on many subtle factors in the operational definition of the population sampled and in the actual execution of the research process. The present effort is in many ways more exact than usually possible, because essentially the same organization (although not the same people) carried out much the same type of survey within almost exactly the same geographically and socially bounded population. (Indeed, successful replication in this case would still leave open the question of whether the findings could be extended beyond the Detroit Metropolitan area. Unsuccessful replication, however, does not carry this kind of ambiguity.) Despite the similar organizational and geographic frameworks, however, there are also important differences between the 1958 and 1966 sampling designs that will be discussed below.

Sample Design in 1958 and in 1966

Both the 1958 and 1966 data are based on samples from the metropolitan Detroit population—city and surrounding suburbs. The Detroit SMSA defined by the Bureau of the Census actually consists of three counties, but in both 1958 and 1966 thinly populated outlying parts of the counties (plus the city of Pontiac) were not included in

---

[6] The term "replication" is used here to refer to the deliberate repetition at a later point in time of part or all of a completed piece of research in order to determine whether the same results obtain. This usage is related to but not the same as that common to experimental designs (Fisher, 1951:58–60). A helpful discussion of the present usage appears in Lykken (1968). The type of replication used here would probably be termed "operational replication" by Lykken, as opposed to "constructive replication," which does not attempt to duplicate the research procedures of the original investigation but rather to operationalize the relevant constructs in other ways.

the survey sample boundaries, primarily to reduce time and costs.[7] The sample area was defined to be somewhat larger in 1966 than in 1958 in order to accommodate expansion of actual suburban areas, but the percentage of the total SMSA population included in the total sample area was quite similar for the two years: 87 percent in 1958 and 85 percent in 1966. Suburban towns that had experienced recent growth were all included in the 1966 boundaries, and it does not appear likely that important parts of the "1958 population" had moved beyond the 1966 boundaries. Thus, we regard the total populations available for the two studies as essentially the same, except for whatever long-distance migration may have taken place between the Detroit SMSA and the rest of the United States during the intervening eight years.

Although the geographically defined populations were essentially the same for the two studies, the 1966 survey screened out parts of the general population that were included in 1958. We need to indicate the likely effect of this differential screening on comparisons between the two sets of results.

The sample used in 1958 involved essentially a cross section selection of occupied dwelling units from the geographic area described above. Within each dwelling unit, all persons age 21 and over were listed and one was selected at random for interview. No type of household appears to have been screened out. Of the 750 households selected for interview, 656 resulted in complete interviews—a response rate of 87 percent.

The sample in 1966 drew a cross section of occupied dwelling units, but considered eligible for random selection within household, only white males, ages 21 through 64, born in the United States or Canada. A total of 1,013 cases were obtained, with a response rate of 80 percent.[8] Each of the screening factors requires brief consideration. Included in parentheses is the number of cases that were excluded from the sample as originally drawn because of the criterion discussed.

[7] Information on the 1956 sampling was obtained from Lenski (1963:16–17) and from "Sampling Design for the 1957–58 Detroit Area Study" (1959). Neither of the above sources specified the lower age limit for the 1956 sample, referring simply to "adults." The lower cut-off of 21 mentioned below is found in the "Interviewer's Instruction Booklet" for the 1957–58 study. Information on the 1966 sampling appears in Schuman (1967).

[8] The actual number of interviews obtained was 985. Twenty-eight of these interviews were weighted double for sampling reasons explained in Schuman (1967). The number involved in the weighting is assumed to be too small to require adjustments in significance tests. A design effect due to cluster sampling of about 1.1 has also been ignored here because of its trivial size.

1. Exclusion of Negroes *(N = 332):* Lenski divided the Protestant population by race in all his calculations, and his main conclusions about the effects of religion are based on differences between white Protestants and Catholics. His decision can be questioned from a theoretical standpoint, but in terms of replication it means that an all-white sample is quite adequate for retesting his findings. One simply ignores the specific results and conclusions in *The Religious Factor* that involve the Negro subsample.

2. *Exclusion of persons born outside the United States or Canada (N = 181):* The effect of this exclusion should be to *increase* Protestant-Catholic differences, according to Lenski's 1958 results. One of his most striking conclusions is that differences between "socio-religious groups" are generally heightened when third generation Americans are studied separately.

3. *Exclusion of Women (N = 268) and of Native-Born Men over 65 (N = 92):* In the chapter directly replicated by the 1966 study, certain of the tables are confined to men, and others include both sexes. There is no indication that results differ by sex where questions are relevant to both sexes. The same applies to age, except that the finding reported above on third generation effects suggests that Protestant-Catholic differences may well increase among younger people. Nonetheless, possible specification by age or sex must be allowed for and will be discussed below after presentation of major results.

4. *Differences in response rates:* The difference between the response rates for the two years is partly a function of the restriction of the 1966 sample to working age males—a particularly difficult category to reach. It may also reflect the general downward trend of response rates reported in most studies over the past two decades. Insofar as the latter is the case, the difference *may* reduce comparability between the obtained samples for the two years. While there is no particular reason to expect such an effect, especially given the relatively small percentage difference, the possibility cannot be ruled out. It provides a good example of the difficulty of achieving "literal replication" (Lykken, 1968).

Results

Lenski's major conclusion concerning Protestant-Catholic differences in economic ethic is that "as a general rule, commitment to the spirit of capitalism . . . is especially frequent among white Prot-

estants and Jews [and] is much less frequent among Catholics . . ."
(Lenski, 1963:128). We will review the evidence he offers for this
conclusion, presenting parallel results from the 1966 study where
possible. Our initial focus will be on values and attitudes, rather
than on indicators of occupational achievement or mobility, since
as noted earlier Lenski's research remains valuable mainly because
of its development of intervening social psychological variables. Our
tables will include results for Jews when these were presented by
Lenski, but our main focus will be on Protestant-Catholic comparisons. The Jewish subsample is quite small in both DAS surveys, and
it also involves other issues not directly tied to the Weberian debate.[9]

Work Values

After examining differences in upward mobility by religion, Lenski
presents the first of a series of questions on work values and work-
related attitudes. Each person in both the 1958 and the 1966 surveys
was asked to rank the following in order of their importance when
choosing a job:

1. High income
2. No danger of being fired
3. Working hours short, lots of free time
4. Chances for advancement
5. The work is important and gives a feeling of accomplishment.

The 1958 survey asked men and working women to answer for
themselves, and wives to answer in terms of what they would want
in their husbands' jobs; the 1966 survey, as mentioned earlier, did
not include women.

Lenski considers the 5th alternative the one best representing the
"Protestant Ethic" as conceived by Weber, the 4th also a partial indicator of the Ethic, and the 1st a popular but questionable approach to operationalizing the same construct. The 3rd alternative,
and to a lesser extent the 2nd, are regarded as "completely in op-

---

[9] Lenski does not always present exact N's with percentage findings. It is useful
to record here the total N's for the two studies, even though a few "don't know"
cases are usually lost for any given question.

	Protestants	Catholics	Jews	Total*
1958 Study	267	230	27	524
1966 Study	498	433	29	960

*The 1958 sample also included 100 Negro Protestants and apparently 32
"others" (Negro Catholics and white "other religion"), as calculated from figures
in Lenski (1963:16 and 370). The 1966 sample included 53 white "other religion."

position to any conception of the Protestant Ethic" (Lenski, 1963:87).

Lenski notes "how strong a hold the Protestant Ethic, in the classical sense, has on all segments of the American population": nearly half of the 1958 sample ranked the 5th alternative highest, and two-thirds selected either the 5th or the 4th alternative. Our results in 1966 are almost identical, with 47 percent of the sample making the 5th alternative first choice, and another 27 percent selecting the 4th alternative.

Turning to differences by religion, Lenski reports that the following percentages of the three religious groups rank first the "classic Protestant Ethic" alternative ("the work is important and gives a feeling of accomplishment"):[10] Protestants, 52 percent; Jews, 48 percent; Catholics, 44 percent. The difference of 8 percentage points between Protestants and Catholics is not great, but it meets the .10 level of significance (one-tailed) used in *The Religious Factor*. The small Jewish subsample does not differ significantly (p > .10, one-tailed) from either of the other categories. Lenski also notes, without presenting data, that "application of controls for class position of respondents and of their parents, and for the education of respondents . . . revealed that the differences between white Protestants on the one hand and Jews and Catholics on the other are greater among the better educated and in the middle classes than among the less well educated and the working classes." (Lenski, 1963:91).

On the other hand, Lenski finds that Jews and Catholics are high on alternatives 1 and 4 which refer to chances for advancement and high income. He reports only the percentage for the two alternatives combined and without controls:[11] Jews, 45 percent; Catholics, 40 percent; Protestants, 31 percent. This difference confirms Lenski's belief that there are two somewhat separate though related systems of work values which deserve to be distinguished. Protestants tend to be higher on the "classic" Protestant Ethic, while Jews and Catholics are higher on the more contemporary version. Finally, Lenski notes that all the reported differences are small and

[10] It is not completely clear that totals for religious groups were used, but absence of qualifications makes this likely. Here as elsewhere in this paper, Lenski's fourth "socio-religious" category of Negro Protestants is omitted; all respondents included in the three categories shown are white.

[11] This assumes that each percentage stands for first choice of one alternative or the other—an assumption implied but not explicit (Lenski 1963:91). The percentages here, it should be noted, are largely determined by the preceding set, but the determination is not complete since there were two other possible response categories to the question.

cannot account for the major part of the relative economic success of Protestants and Jews as against Catholics. Perhaps for this reason, he does not include results for this question in his summary table comparing the size of differences by religion with the size of differences by social class (Lenski, 1963:326).

Our own findings on this question are reported in Table 1. The results successfully replicate Lenski's work in part. A somewhat greater proportion of Protestants than Catholics give first rank to the sense of accomplishment and worth of work. The difference of 5

Table 1. Percent of Protestants (P), Catholics (C), and Jews (J) Giving First Rank to "Protestant Ethic Responses" (1966 Data)[*]

Religious Group	1st Choice to A[a]	1st Choice to B[b] or C[c]
P	49% (498)	40% (498)
C	44 (433)	44 (433)
J	52 (29)	38 (29)

[*] Base N's in parentheses.
[a] "The work is important and gives a feeling of accomplishment."
[b] "Chance for advancement."
[c] "High income."

percentage points between the two groups would not be significant for Lenski's sample sizes, but just makes the 10 percent level of significance (one-tailed) for our larger subsamples. There is also a trend for Catholics to be higher (by 4 percentage points) than Protestants on first choice given to income or chances for advancement. Lenski's finding that Jews were highest on first choice of advancement or income, and Protestants lowest, does not hold up well. The differences are slight and Jews are actually lowest on these combined responses (and highest on the "classical" Protestant Ethic response).

As noted above, Lenski reports, but does not present, data showing that the religious factor operates more strongly among the middle class and better educated. We have created social class (occupation and income) and educational controls as close as possible to those generally used by Lenski.[12] Comparisons between Prot-

---

[12] The social class and educational criteria used in the two surveys and the resulting distributions are shown below, with cases omitted where classificatory information is lacking:

estants and Catholics within class and educational categories for the work-values question are shown in Table 2. (There are too few Jews to allow for such controls.) Our results bear out the 1958 finding that differences between Protestants and Catholics are primarily located within the upper stratum. Among the upper-middle class and the college-educated, Protestant-Catholic differences increase slightly over that found for the total samples, while only small,

---

A. Percent in Each Social Class in 1958 and 1966

Social Class	Criteria	Lenski's Dist. (Whites only)	1966 Dist.
Upper-Middle Class	White collar occupation: Family head income $8,000 or more in 1958; $10,000 or more in 1966.	17%	29%
Lower-Middle Class	White collar occupation: Family head income less than $8,000 in 1958; less than $10,000 in 1966.	26	18
Upper-Working Class	Manual or service occupation; Family head income $5,000 or more in 1958; $7,000 or more in 1966.	32	39
Lower-Working Class	Manual or service occupation; Family head income less than $5,000 in 1958; less than $7,000 in 1966.	25	14
	Total	100	100
	N	(502)	(1004)

B. Percent in Each Category of School Years Completed in 1958 and 1966

	Lenski's Sample	1966 Sample
13 years or more	21%	35%
12 years (high school grad.)	—⎫	32⎫
9 to 11 years	—⎬ 59	21⎬ 53
0 to 8 years	20	12
	100%	100%
N=	(524)	(1008)

The 1966 study used the same occupational groupings as Lenski, but raised the cutting point for income by $2,000 to take account of changes in income level between 1958 and 1964. Partly as a result of this change, the 1966 "social class" distribution is somewhat different from Lenski's. There is also a slight difference in occupational distributions as such, since Lenski's combined middle-class categories account for 43 percent, as against 47 percent for the 1966 sample. This may represent a change in the Detroit occupational structure, but may simply be a result of sampling error plus the 1966 exclusion of older men from the sample. The greater difference between the two distributions involves income within the two occupational categories, and since this is a relative matter it should not result in marked changes in other relationships. It is also clear that the present sample is distributed somewhat differently in education than Lenski's, no doubt in part because of the 1966 age restriction. We should also note that class differences between Protestants and Catholics in the present sample are not great and educational differences are virtually nonexistent.

though consistent, differences occur among the other strata. In summary, then, our results in 1966 for this question are generally in accord with those obtained by Lenski in 1958, although all associations are small.

Attitudes Toward Work

Central to Weber's conception of the Protestant Ethic was the high valuation of work as man's vocation in this world. This contrasts with the view that work is simply a necessary evil, or indeed a consequence of Original Sin. To explore further this contrast, both the 1958 and 1966 surveys asked the following questions: "Some people tell us they couldn't really be happy unless they were working at

Table 2. Percent Protestants and Catholics Giving First Rank to "Work is important" by Social Class and Education (1966 Data)

Social Class	Protes- tants	Catholics	Education	Protes- tants	Catholics
Upper-Middle	68% (148)	58% (94)	Some College and Above	62% (165)	50% (145)
Lower-Middle	47 (86)	44 (91)	9–12 Years of School	44 (271)	42 (240)
Upper-Working	40 (181)	38 (175)	0–8 Years of School	37 (62)	35 (46)
Lower-Working	37 (78)	37 (68)		(498)	(431)
	(493)	(428)			

some job. But others say that they would be a lot happier if they didn't have to work and could take life easy. How do you feel about this? Why is that?" Respondents were then coded into one of three general categories: 1. a completely positive attitude toward work, which emphasizes its intrinsic rewards or its moral character; 2. a neutral attitude, which involves a preference for working, but one based on extrinsic factors, such as boredom with too much leisure; 3. a negative attitude, which involves a frank assertion by the respondent that he would be happier if he did not have to work.

The 1958 survey found the following percentages of males in each religious group expressing a *positive* attitude toward work: Jews, 42 percent; Protestants, 30 percent; Catholics, 23 percent. The dif-

ference between Protestants and Catholics here is significant at the
.10 level, according to the table Lenski provides (1963:372). He also
reports that controls for generation, region of birth, and class show
Protestant-Catholic differences to be on the increase rather than
on the decrease. "Catholics who were Northern-born, third-generation Americans were much more likely to have a *negative* attitude
toward work than were first- and second-generation immigrants
(36 percent vs. 14 percent)" (p. 90). The *opposite* trend occurred
among Protestants for *positive* attitudes toward work (30 percent vs.
24 percent). Moreover, positive attitudes toward work were directly
correlated with social class for Protestants, but the correlation was
inverse for Catholics (see Lenski, 1963:98, Table 10). Lenski interprets this to mean that Protestants take a more positive attitude
toward more demanding and rewarding positions, while Catholics
show a more positive attitude toward positions that are less demanding and hence less rewarding. None of the above controls are
applied to Jews because of small sample sizes, and there is no comment on the largest percentage differences in 1958 for the question,
those between Jews and *both* Protestants and Catholics.

Our own findings on this question are shown in Table 3, alongside Lenski's results where these were reported in detail. The value
of placing results from both years together is to allow direct comparisons of trends in subgroup differences. Absolute percents for
any given subgroup should not be compared, however, since as explained earlier the 1958 survey included parts of the population excluded in 1966. For the present question, the populations are somewhat closer than usual, since Lenski presents these data also only
for males, but there are still differences by age and birth place.

Our results do not replicate those of Lenski's with regard to Protestant-Catholic differences. We find only a trivial and unreliable difference on this question for the two religious groups as a whole.
When generation is introduced as a third variable, we find slight and
probably unreliable effects *opposite* to those reported by Lenski.
When social class is introduced as a third variable, there is little
variation of any kind in *negative* attitudes toward work. There is a
tendency for positive attitudes to increase with class position for
both religious groups, rather than a reversal in direction as Lenski
found. The only line of support for Lenski's original results is that
there is a greater spread between the top and bottom classes for
Protestants than for Catholics, but the figures are of uncertain reliability and meaning, and they constitute only a very partial replication of the 1958 results.

Table 3. Percent of White Males Expressing "Positive," "Neutral," and "Negative" Attitudes Toward Work*

| | Lenski's Findings | | | | 1966 Findings | | | |
Religious Group	Pos.	Neut.	Neg.	N	Pos.	Neut.	Neg.	N
Protestants	30%	(not separated)	(—)		32%	58%	11%	(481)
Catholics	23	(not separated)	(—)		33	55	12	(421)
Jews	42	(not separated)	(—)		34	55	10	(29)
By Generation:								
Protestant, 3rd Gen. or More	30%	(not separated)		(40)	33%	54%	14%	(259)
Protestant, 2nd Gen. or Less	24	(not separated)		(37)	36	56	8	(125)
Catholics 3rd Gen. or More	(not separated)		36	(22)	32	57	11	(190)
Catholic, 2nd Gen. or Less	(not separated)		14	(69)	35	52	14	(219)
By Class:								
Protestant:								
Upper-Middle	36%	52%	12%	(25)	46%	46%	9%	(145)
Lower-Middle	32	57	11	(19)	26	64	10	(84)
Upper-Working	23	56	21	(39)	28	59	12	(172)
Lower-Working	30	33	37	(27)	22	68	10	(78)
Catholic:								
Upper-Middle	19	56	25	(16)	39	53	8	(95)
Lower-Middle	18	57	25	(28)	34	57	9	(88)
Upper-Working	18	64	18	(38)	30	56	15	(171)
Lower-Working	33	48	19	(21)	30	55	15	(66)

*Where N's are not given for Lenski's groups, they were not presented in the book. The total N's in 1958 were no doubt the same or close to those reported in our ft. 9.

Class criteria here are the same as those presented in ft. 12. With regard to generational criteria, in the 1966 study 1st-generation persons were, as mentioned earlier, excluded from the target population altogether, and only Northern-born respondents are included in the generation comparison. Lenski's survey includes 1st-generation immigrants, and his tables apparently exclude Southern-born respondents from 3rd-generation or more categories, but not from 2nd-generation categories.

Spending and Saving

Shifting from attitudes toward work to values about consumption, Lenski "inquired into the manner in which families use their income." One question concerned installment buying: Changing the subject a bit, do you think it's a good idea or a bad idea to buy things on the installment plan? Lenski reports 46 percent of his total sample in favor of installment buying, 38 percent against, with the balance not decided. In 1966 we find 47 percent for, 50 percent against, and 3 percent other. The differences here are not great and could easily result from differences in sample design (e.g., Negroes included in 1958 but not in 1966), changes over time, or a combination of sampling error and format variation.[13]

Lenski reports the following percents by religious groups in terms of *dis*approval of installment buying: Jews, 56 percent; Protestants, 44 percent; Catholics, 40 percent. The Protestant-Catholic difference is not reliable even at the .10 level (one-tailed), but Lenski does find the same interaction with generation reported earlier: Catholics closer to immigrant status (1st and 2nd generation) are more disapproving of installment buying than are Catholics in or beyond the third generation; the opposite is true among Protestants. Table 4 presents the 1958 findings, along with comparable percentages from the present study.

Our overall findings by religion show even less of a Protestant-Catholic difference than the small one reported by Lenski. We also found a reversal for Jews, with the latter less rather than more disapproving of installment buying than the other two groups. This was such a puzzling finding that it led us to check our entire coding procedure for the question, but a count based on the original 29 raw questionnaires for the subsample of Jews confirmed the finding already reported.[14]

[13] This question was included at the end of a five-minute attitude form which the respondent filled out himself mid-way in the hour interview. The form was completed entirely within the larger interview and does not result in loss of respondents; such a procedure was used primarily to allow observations of the house to be made by the interviewer for purposes unconnected with the present replication. The 1958 and 1966 questions were worded identically, but the 1958 version included an interview box for "unsure" if volunteered; the 1966 item did not offer such a choice explicitly. This latter minor difference in format occurs also for the "attitude toward work" question discussed earlier.

[14] A control for occupation shows that this favorability toward installment buying is much stronger among Jewish businessmen (7 of 9 favoring) than among Jewish professionals (4 of 11). We suspect that this question may be ambiguous to some businessmen, and that they may interpret it as indicating favorability

Table 4. Percent Disapproving of Installment Buying*

Religious Group	Lenski's Findings	1966 Findings
Protestants:	44% (—)	52% (481)
Middle Class, 3rd Gen.	38 (60)	50 (159)
Middle Class, 1st & 2nd Gen.	34 (32)	49 (67)
Working Class, 3rd Gen.	51 (41)	54 (190)
Working Class, 1st & 2nd Gen.	42 (53)	52 (61)
Catholics:	40% (—)	50% (422)
Middle Class, 3rd Gen.	35 (31)	44 (94)
Middle Class, 1st & 2nd Gen.	41 (51)	49 (86)
Working Class, 3rd Gen.	35 (34)	51 (107)
Working Class, 1st & 2nd Gen.	39 (84)	53 (126)
Jews	56% (—)	59% (28)

* For the analysis by class, both studies exclude Southern-born respondents. Only Lenski's study includes 1st-generation immigrants.

Simultaneous controls for generation and class produce slight trends in the direction Lenski noted: third-generation Protestants are more disapproving of installment buying than second-generation Protestants, while the reverse effect is found among Catholics. However, the percentage differences are very tiny and could easily result from chance or from other differences correlated with religion, e.g., socioeconomic differences not controlled by the crude categorization into "middle class" and "working class." Certainly the net "interaction effect" found in the present study is much less than that reported in *The Religious Factor*.

---

toward allowing installment buying by customers, rather than in terms of personal preference.

Other Attitudes and Values Regarding Work and Consumption

The Religious Factor presents the results for several relevant attitude questions which we did not attempt to replicate exactly in the 1966 study. Lenski's findings on these questions will be briefly reviewed, with our reason for omitting the question or the results of modifying it also noted.

(a) *Belief in the Possibility of Success:* Lenski asked two questions designed to determine whether a respondent believed it is possible to rise from the working class to the middle class and whether he believed that ability rather than family connections makes for success. He reports that with class held constant (dichotomized into Middle class vs. Working class), over 10 percent more Protestants than Catholics hold such beliefs. We did not attempt to replicate these questions because we could not see a clear connection between them and Weber's central focus on the Protestant Ethic. As Lenski himself had earlier stressed, the concern with work that supposedly developed out of early Protestant views had to do not with the striving after extrinsic success, but with positive satisfaction in pursuing one's vocation in this world.

(b) *Divine Concern with Economic Striving:* A somewhat more relevant question seemed to be one that asked whether "God is more pleased when people try to get ahead, or when people are satisfied with what they have and don't try to push ahead." But Lenski found only a five percentage points difference between Protestants and Catholics on this question, though in the "right direction." He also reports that the question was difficult for respondents to answer and that many tried to avoid the forced choice. For these reasons, the question was not included in the 1966 study.

(c) *Use of Leisure Time:* In another chapter of *The Religious Factor,* Lenski reports data from an earlier (1953) Detroit Area Study, which shows a trend for Protestants to say they would use extra leisure time productively (e.g., social service work, reading, gardening) rather than indulgently (e.g., loafing, going to movies, shopping). This seems to be directly relevant to Weber's conception of a puritan work ethic, and we included the following similar (although not identical) question in our study immediately after the question on whether the respondent would be happier working or not working: "Suppose you *did* have a lot of free time. What would you most like to do with it?" Responses were coded into two basic categories of "Productive" (mainly self-improvement in content) and "Indulgent" (mainly casual social contacts, sports, and recreation). Differences by religion in 1966 were as follows:

	Productive	Indulgent	Total	N
Protestant	22	78	100%	(476)
Catholic	26	74	100%	(424)
Jewish	21	79	100%	(28)

Differences are slight, and if anything the trend is for Catholics to be less "indulgent" than Protestants.

(d) *Concern with Thrift:* Respondents in 1958 were asked how important it is to save regularly, and why? This "ant-and-grasshopper" inquiry was used to determine whether respondents emphasized ascetic self-discipline in the early Calvinist tradition or indulged themselves in more consummatory directions. Results are not reported in detail, but apparently Protestants and Catholics did *not* differ in belief in the desirability of saving. The only difference found between the two groups was that a greater proportion of Protestants (28 percent) than Catholics (19 percent) gave more than one reason for saving. We did not find this numerical result as pertinent to the thrift argument as other questions, and therefore did not attempt to repeat the long series of inquiries used to obtain it.

(e) *Follow-up to Installment Buying:* After the question on installment buying reported earlier, the 1958 study asked: "Why do you feel this way?" Lenski reports that in explaining their disapproval, Protestants more often cited moral reasons than Catholics: 30 percent of the working-class Protestants, as against 18 percent of the working-class Catholics. Figures for middle-class respondents are not given, but by implication are less clear. Of the additional attitude questions treated in this section, this is the only one which seems both directly relevant to the main argument and somewhat promising in terms of reported results. It is unfortunate that we were not able to include it in the 1966 study.

Positional and Performance Measures

Although Lenski does not explicitly distinguish between attitudes and values on the one hand and performance indicators on the other hand, such a distinction appears essential. Weber's emphasis, although historical in its source of data, was basically social-psychological in nature. Individual Protestants were seen as developing beliefs and values which in turn led to distinctive performance in the world. Such performance finally led to changes in social position, for example, to a rise in one's occupation, income, and general status. If only one of these links can be focused upon, the psychological dimension seems most proximate for investigating the construct "Protestant Ethic." Differences in social position or even in performance cannot by themselves tell us very much about their origins. With this qualification in mind, we will examine the remaining evidence that Lenski offers for differences in Work Ethic between the two religious groups.

(a) *Labor Union Activity:* As suggested above, Lenski believed that "in many respects the values for which the unions stand are in opposition to the values embodied in the 'Protestant Ethic' and the 'spirit of capitalism.' " This is because unions view work as a necessary evil and emphasize security rather than achievement. The Benjamin Franklins of today should presumably be men who wish to escape from the union rank and file, not contribute to its solidarity.

Lenski focuses on the lower middle class (clerks and salesmen) as the place in the social structure where union membership is possible but not taken for granted. He finds that 38 percent of the Catholics in the middle class (N = 27) belong to unions, while only 15 percent of the middle class Protestants (N = 33) have such membership. (No difference appears among working class men.) Our results do not replicate the white collar difference: among clerical and sales workers we find that 23 percent of the Protestants (N = 66) and 23 percent of the Catholics (N = 49) belong to unions.

The 1958 study did not include other questions on union involvement. But Lenski refers to other surveys done through the Detroit Area Study and elsewhere which show Protestant-Catholic differences. He cites the 1952 Detroit Area Study data showing that Protestant union members attend union meetings less often than Catholics and also say they are less "interested" in their union than Catholics. We did not repeat either of these questions exactly, but we did ask union members whether they felt "very involved" or "not very involved" in their union. Exactly 28 percent of the union members (177 Protestant union members, 166 Catholics) of each religious group claimed to be "very involved." A control for occupational level did not change this indication of no difference.

(b) *Self-Employment:* Just as unions are seen by Lenski as the locus of collectivistic and security-minded sentiments, so the self-employed are viewed as representatives of individualism. He finds little difference between Protestant and Catholic males in overall rates of self-employment (8 percent and 10 percent, respectively). Controls for immigrant generation and region of birth alter the picture, with Protestants showing a greater representation among the self-employed (see Table 5). Lenski concludes from these trends (and similar trends for past self-employment) that "even in the bureaucratized modern metropolis there are real and significant differences among the major socio-religious groups in the degree to which they value occupational independence and autonomy, with Jews ranking first, white Protestants second, and Catholics third" (1963:104). The findings of the present study, however, confirm these earlier results only with regard to Jews. As Table 5 shows, we find no difference at all between Protestants and Catholics on this measure.

(c) *Budgeting:* Lenski was interested in discovering whether Protestants were more likely than Catholics to budget family expenditures. He found, however, no difference between the two religious groups on this question, and we therefore did not attempt to replicate the question.

(d) *Vertical Mobility:* We have saved until last the question of "vertical mobility," which Lenski treats first. Although it is obviously important to discover such differences if they exist, their origin is bound to be ambiguous. Even given the same attitudes and values, groups starting from different points will end at different points.

Lenski reports on the conflicting evidence in this area, and then presents data (p. 85) from the 1958 study showing greater Protestant than Catholic intergenerational mobility among white males. His data are not unambiguous, and this is an area where there is a fair amount of replication, often with larger national samples and using more recent analytic techniques.[15] Nevertheless, we have closely

Table 5. Percent of Each Religious Group Self-Employed*

Religious Group	Lenski's Findings		1966 Findings	
1st & 2nd Generation				
Protestants	15%	(39)	11%	(266)
Catholics	8	(71)	11	(193)
3rd Generation Northern-born				
Protestants	12	(42)	14	(118)
Catholics	4	(24)	13	(211)
Total				
Protestants	10	(—)	12	(384)
Catholics	8	(—)	12	(404)
Jews	">50%"	(27)	36	(25)

* 1st-generation men were not included in the 1966 sample. Both samples used only males. Lenski does not report the N's for the two missing entries.

[15] See Glockel, *op. cit.,* and Featherman, *op. cit.*

Table 6. Occupational Level of White Male Respondents by Father's Occupation and Religion (1966 Data)*

Respondent's Occupational Level	Middle		Father's Occupation Upper Working		Lower Working		Farmer	
	Prot.	Cath.	Prot.	Cath.	Prot.	Cath.	Prot.	Cath.
Upper Middle	54%	47%	32%	28%	22%	27%	18%	21%
Lower Middle	18	17	12	10	12	10	10	0
Upper Working	10	17	23	34	27	35	26	53
Lower Working	17	19	33	28	39	28	46	26
Total	100	100	100	100	100	100	100	100
N	153	95	112	144	147	162	77	20

* Occupational levels here and in Lenski (1963, Table 8, p. 85) are not the class levels described in ft. 12, but instead involve distinctions between: (1) professional and managerial, (2) clerical and sales, (3) craftsmen and foremen, and (4) operatives, service workers, and laborers. (Based on communication from Gerhard Lenski.) Note also that males over 64 and foreign-born are excluded from the 1966 sample and the above table, but not from Table 8 in *The Religious Factor*.

comparable data on this subject for the Detroit metropolitan area for 1966, presented in Table 6. Following the same mode of analysis that Lenski uses, we do not find much consistent support for his conclusion concerning greater Protestant mobility. Evidence in one part of the table is contradicted by evidence in another part, and the N's are too small to allow diverse conclusions based on specific pairs of cells.

Religious Involvement and the Protestant Ethic

A problem with comparisons of "Protestants" and "Catholics" is the vague and omnibus nature of such labels. For one thing, "Protestant" covers many different denominations and sects in America, and Weber was at pains to detail differences as well as similarities among these. In addition, within religious groups, individuals differ widely in the depth of their involvement, and if indeed it is religion that is a source of attitudes and values, we might expect these variations in involvement to lead to variations in adherence to the "Protestant Ethic."

Lenski handles the first problem by arguing that "denominational groupings within Detroit Protestantism no longer constitute self-contained socio-religious groups" (1863:21). He notes that his 1958 data show large "amounts" of marriage and friendship across denomination lines, and that half the Protestant respondents were in favor of denominational mergers. Most significantly, he reports that dependent variables in his data show few differences by denomination that are not simply accounted for by class position or regional background (1963:396–398).

Our own larger sample allows a somewhat more adequate analysis of denominational effects, and shows them to be about as impressive as simple Protestant-Catholic differences. Using only the four denominations on which we have at least 75 respondents, and employing the "work values" question discussed earlier, we obtain the results shown in Table 7. Even with controls for three indicators of socioeconomic status, five of the six between-denomination comparisons are as large as the original Protestant-Catholic difference we reported in Table 1, and four of the six are as large as the Protestant-Catholic difference reported for this question in *The Religious Factor*. It is not clear that the ordering of denominations is what a careful reader of Weber would anticipate, since the more "Calvinistic" Presbyterians score closest to the Catholics, while the Lutherans are unexpectedly high in giving the classic Protestant Ethic response. However, it does appear that "Protestants" constitute a rather heterogeneous category, and that at the very least we must expect responses for that category to vary depending on the varying proportions of these denominations in different parts of the United States.[16]

Table 7. Percent Choosing "The Work Is Important and Gives a Feeling of Achievement"[a], by Denomination (1966 Data)

Religious Group	Without Controls		Controlled for Socioeconomic Status[b]	
Baptists	35%	(103)	39%	(103)
(Catholics)[c]	44	(433)	—	(433)
(All Protestants)[c]	49	(498)	—	(498)
Presbyterians	52	(75)	47	(75)
Lutherans	53	(110)	53	(110)
Methodists	59	(87)	57	(87)

[a] The "work values" question was dichotomized into the fifth alternative quoted here vs. the other four combined.

[b] The four denominations shown here were included as one set of predictors in a multiple classification analysis. The other predictors used as controls were education, occupation, and income. Results are not changed appreciably if only education is included as a control.

[c] Protestant and Catholic figures from Table 1 are also shown here for comparison purposes. Note that "all Protestants" include respondents from other denominations in addition to the four separated out here.

[16] We also attempted to learn to what extent a control for ethnicity affected the Protestant-Catholic difference reported in Table 1. We included our three religious groups (Protestants, Catholics, Jews) and also eight nationality groupings

Let us turn now to individual differences in personal involvement in religion. Lenski deals with the important issue of depth of commitment by constructing one index of "associational involvement" in the church as a formal organization, and another index of "communal involvement" in the informal but encompassing subcommunity of co-religionists. The former is operationalized by frequency of attendance at church services, the latter by the degree to which primary relationships are limited to members of the same religion. (See Lenski, 1963:23, for details of index construction.) He shows that the two indices are only slightly related to each other, hence can usefully be treated as separate measures.

Although Lenski makes a convincing case for the general importance of "communal involvement" as a vehicle for religious influence, it turns out that the index does *not* distinguish within religious groups in terms of economic attitudes and behaviors. He concludes that "the churches, rather than the sub-communities, are the primary source of the differences in economic behavior" between Protestants and Catholics (pp. 124–125).

As the above quotations suggest, associational involvement does appear to be an important specifying variable for the 1958 data. In most of the questions where comparisons were possible, frequency of church attendance among Protestants was positively associated with the Weberian "spirit of capitalism." There was no, or even a slight negative, relationship for the same variables among Catholics. The quantitative results for each question are not presented by Lenski in tabular form, but most of the questions which are reported to show the relationship involve social positions (e.g., self-employment) rather than values or attitudes. In particular, neither the question on what is valued about work nor positive attitudes toward work as against leisure showed any relation in 1958 to degree of associational involvement. This lack of a relationship is not treated by Lenski as a negative finding concerning the influence of the religious factor on economic behavior, but rather as a sign that "the Protestant churches have allowed the doctrine of the calling to be neglected."

(based on the question "What nationality background do you think of yourself as having—that is, besides being an American?") as predictors in a single multiple classification analysis. With nationality controlled, the original five point percentage difference between Protestants and Catholics on the "work values" question is halved. Thus ethnicity does seem to be a relevant variable, as Rosen (1962) and others have argued. Both ethnic and denominational effects are much slighter when the dependent variable shifts to the "attitudes toward work" question. Apparently the latter variable is simply not a useful one in this study, for as we saw earlier it fails to show any significant relation to religion.

Our own findings, reported in Table 8, differ considerably from Lenski's, insofar as comparisons can be made.

1. Lenski reports that the "work values" question showed little relation to associational involvement; we find a consistent trend for the more actively involved among both Protestants and Catholics to say that the significance of the work is their main concern in choosing a job. This may simply reflect uncontrolled variations within crude class categories that are related to associational involvement.

2. For attitudes toward work, we find a relation that Lenski apparently expected: positive attitudes going with frequent church attendance among Protestants but not among Catholics. However, Lenski's own *findings* appear to have been in the opposite direction.

3. Lenski finds both occupational self-employment and disapproval of installment buying greater among more actively involved Protestants. We find weak trends in the opposite direction for both religious groups.

4. Lenski reports that both membership and interest in unions are least among active Protestant church-goers. We find opposite trends.

Table 8. Percent of "Protestant Ethic" Responses for High and Low Associational Categories within Religious and Social Class Categories (1966 Data)*

"Protestant Ethic" Response	Protestants				Catholics			
	Middle Class		Working Class		Middle Class		Working Class	
	Active	Marg.	Active	Marg.	Active	Marg.	Active	Marg.
	(79)	(154)	(58)	(201)	(144)	(37)	(155)	(85)
Intrinsic work valuation in job choice	67%	56%	43%	38%	54%	43%	42%	29%
Positive attitude toward work	43	36	32	25	37	38	31	29
Disapproves of installment buying	43	53	47	55	46	46	48	60
Presently self-employed	16	18	2	4	22	27	4	6
Member of union**	31	21	57	64	19	36	61	67
Very involved in union**	23	4	19	16	5	9	17	20

* The measure of associational involvement here is slightly different from Lenski's. Lenski classifies as Active "those who attend worship services every week, plus those who attend services two or three times a month and also some church-related group at least once a month," with all others classified as Marginal. The 1966 questionnaire included only a question on frequency of attendance at religious services, and we have distinguished only between those who attend at least once a week (Active) and those who attend less often (Marginal).

** For these two questions, Middle Class refers only to clerical and sales workers, and the relevant N's are reduced to 13 (Protestant-Active), 53 (Protestant-Marginal), 37 (Catholic-Active), and 11 (Catholic-Marginal).

More generally we find little systematic or meaningful difference in the effect of associational involvement on Protestants and Catholics. We have not been able to attempt replication of certain questions used by Lenski in this analysis because they were not included in the 1966 survey, but the results we can check are not encouraging.

Lenski reports several other ways in which some of the dependent variables under discussion seem to be influenced by type of religious commitment. For example, he finds that a "devotional" orientation, as indicated by personal prayer and concern to determine God's will when making decisions, is positively associated with a commitment to work. But in this instance, as elsewhere in these supplementary findings, the relation of religious variables to other variables is not associated with Protestant-Catholic differences, but holds equally for both religious groups. Therefore, we do not attempt here to replicate such results.

Reanalysis of Lenski's 1958 Data

We have reviewed Lenski's 1958 findings bearing directly on the application of the Protestant Ethic hypothesis to Protestant-Catholic differences in the United States, and have presented evidence from a 1966 replication of most of the more promising 1958 results. The 1966 survey provides a single important confirming replication regarding work values, and we will explore it further below. Against this lone successful replication, a variety of failures to replicate have been presented.

As indicated earlier, our 1966 sample omitted women, the foreign-born, and men over 65, and it also had a somewhat lower response rate than did the 1958 study. It is conceivable that these differences in target populations account for some of the differences in results. Although we have not attempted a complete reanalysis of Lenski's 1958 data, we have done so using age, sex, and nativity controls on the initial Protestant-Catholic differences for three main items: "work values," "attitudes toward work," and "installment buying." It is worth noting that the reanalysis proved a great deal more difficult than anticipated, because of the problems encountered first of all merely in reproducing the original results reported in *The Religious Factor,* before proceeding to introduce sample controls. In only one of the attitudes reviewed here were we able to obtain Lenski's published results perfectly, although in the other two cases the discrepancies were minor and very likely due to differences in placement of one or two cases. The possible explanations for such minor discrepancies are manifold: errors in our, or Lenski's, use of computing equipment; errors by Lenski in preparation of tables or at later stages in writing; errors by us in interpretation of Lenski's codes and recodes; actual damage to the data over the intervening decade. The whole effort left us with a healthy respect for the variability of percentages for reasons other than either sampling or measurement error, and with a sense of how easily borderline significance levels can be altered in this size sample by minor changes in coding conventions (for example, inclusion or not of missing data when calculating percents). We suspect that these problems in reanalysis are not unique to Lenski's data, and that only with the greatest care is it possible to transmit data and codes in reliable form from one investigator to another.

When controls for age, sex, and nativity were applied to bring Lenski's sample to essentially the same composition as the 1966 replication, the results did in fact tend to converge. For the "work values" item this means that in the 1958 tables rerun using only 21- to 64-year-old, native-born males, Protestant-Catholic differences were reduced to almost the exact sizes of the 1966 results given in Table 1. For example, "the work is important..." shows a 6 percent Protestant-Catholic difference in Table 9, as compared with our 5 percent difference in 1966. Thus our earlier report of a successful replication for this item holds and is even improved when the 1958 and 1966 samples are brought more closely into line.

The two other items in Table 9 show a similar movement toward the 1966 results when similar age, sex, and nativity controls are

Table 9. Percent of 21–64 Year Old Native-Born Men in Each Religious Group Giving "Protestant Ethic" Responses (Reanalysis of 1958 Data)

Religious Group	% Saying "The work is important . . ."			N
Protestants	50%			(93)
Catholics	44			(88)
	Attitude toward work			
	Positive	Neutral	Negative	
Protestants	26%	52%	22%	(89)
Catholics	26	57	17	(86)
	Disapprove Installment Buying			
Protestants	29%			(91)
Catholics	27			(88)

applied. This means, however, that Protestant-Catholic differences for these items tend to disappear among 1958 native-born men under 65. For the "attitude toward work" item, the original difference reported by Lenski appears to come entirely from men over 64 and men born outside the United States—relegating the result either to the record of a disappearing generation or an indicator of the religious correlates of old age. Because of the difficulties noted above in this reanalysis, along with the small N's within subsample categories and the generally small percentage differences by religion found for all these items, we are reluctant to place great emphasis on such specific findings.

Further Pursuit of Our One Positive Finding

Most of our conclusions about an intrinsically religious factor must, therefore, be negative. But not quite all, for a single question on work values repeated in 1966 did, as already reported, replicate Lenski's results; moreover, stronger findings were produced in favor of his hypothesis than were apparent in his own 1958 data. Also, the question seems theoretically closer to the conceptual meaning of the "Protestant Ethic" than most of the other variables introduced by Lenski. It is possible, of course, that the finding is due to chance, given the large number of results that have been reviewed here. But it is important to avoid Type II as well as Type I errors, and for that reason the "work values" result bears closer examination.

The 1966 difference between Protestants and Catholics in their basis for evaluating jobs has proven surprisingly tenacious. In particular, under a variety of controls Protestants, significantly more often than Catholics, rank as most important their attitude that "the work is important and gives a feeling of accomplishment." Examination of this response using combinations of socioeconomic background factors has specified the religious difference, but in the process generally sharpens rather than eliminates it. Several such controls are shown in Table 10.

The difference on this question is rather clearly located in upper middle-class and, to a lesser extent, upper blue-collar occupations. These occupational differences in turn are not much changed when either respondent's education or father's education is held constant. An interesting interpretation of the results might note that the three occupational areas in question—professional, managerial, and craftsmen—are probably the most nonroutinized parts of the occupational structure. They are types of occupations that can be en-

Table 10. Percent Emphasizing Importance of Work (5th Alternative) in Choosing a Job, by Religion, Occupation, and Education (1966 Data)*

Respondent's Occupation

Religion	Profes-sional	Managerial	Clerical	Sales	Craftsman	Operative & Laborer
Prot.	69 (99)	59 (68)	53 (36)	40 (30)	48 (103)	33 (157)
Cath.	58 (67)	49 (71)	52 (25)	38 (24)	41 (134)	34 (109)
Dif.	+11	+10	+ 1	+ 2	+ 7	− 1

Respondent's Occupation (Selected) and Education

Religion	Professional			Managerial			Craftsman		
	0–8	9–12	13+	0–8	9–12	13+	0–8	9–12	13+
Prot.	(0)	54(22)	72(77)	(4)	58(31)	64(33)	60(20)	46(76)	(7)
Cath.	(2)	54(11)	57(54)	(1)	51(35)	46(35)	29(24)	37(84)	42(26)
Dif.		0	+15		+ 7	+18	+31	+ 9	

Respondent's Occupation (Selected) and Father's Education

Religion	Professional			Managerial			Craftsman		
	0–8	9–12	13+	0–8	9–12	13+	0–8	9–12	13+
Prot.	68(41)	66(32)	80(20)	57(30)	79(19)	44(16)	44(70)	59(17)	(9)
Cath.	53(17)	55(33)	69(16)	49(47)	42(19)	(5)	40(77)	42(36)	47(15)
Dif.	+15	+11	+11	+ 8	+37		+ 4	+17	

* Each percent is shown with its base N in parentheses. Percents are not calculated for N < 15.

tered *both* for intrinsic reasons relating to the content of the work and for extrinsic reasons having to do with advancement in income and status. Religious sources of values could thus operate to fill these positions not with differential frequency, but rather for different reasons and perhaps with different consequences in terms of actual role performance.

In the light of previous sections of this report, we will wish to regard this line of thought as merely an intriguing hypothesis for further investigation, certainly not as a conclusion based on broad empirical evidence. The findings first of all require urgent replication, since they have been selected as the only "reliable differences" from among a large number of comparisons.[17] If replicable, they

[17] The application of significance tests to complex survey analysis has been attacked and defended regularly at least since Hanon Selvin's (1957) "A Critique of Tests of Significance in Survey Research." However, none of the more controversial issues are involved in the present point, which concerns only the loss of clear meaning to conventional significance levels as an analyst scans many tables and selects for interpretation the few that are "significant."

then suggest the value of concentrating the search for a current equivalent of the Protestant Ethic in particular directions. This means not only locating it more specifically in the social structure, but also both clarifying and, if possible, validating the secular value dimension involved. Rather than expanding the Protestant Ethic thesis in many and diverse ways, construct specification seems very much in order.

Discussion

The 1966 Detroit Area Study replication of parts of the 1958 Detroit Area Study has called into question conclusions derived from the earlier survey that bear on "religion and economics." Four explanations are available.

(1) There may have been a genuine change in Protestant or Catholic attitudes and values during the intervening eight years. This explanation seems the least plausible one to me, because the variables involved do not appear subject to rapid change on the basis of transient events. Lenski's own conclusions point toward gradual widening of Protestant-Catholic differences.

(2) Variations between the two surveys may result from the more limited population defined by the 1966 study. Women, men over 64, and the foreign-born were deliberately excluded, and the response rate was also somewhat lower in 1966. There is little in Lenski's analysis to suggest that these factors *should* affect major conclusions, but our reanalysis of Lenski's 1958 data does seem to point to such special but not especially meaningful subpopulations as the source of some of his findings.

(3) Lenski's results may point toward religious differences of a much more specific and limited character than he expected and concluded. This is the import of the one successful replication in 1966, which concerns a single but strategic question on work values and locates the religious difference mainly among men in professional and managerial occupations. Those interested in the Protestant Ethic hypothesis would seem well advised to follow up this result, staying close to whatever the item represents. It must also be kept in mind that the difference discovered here is by no means a large one.

(4) There is the real possibility that all the differences reported by Lenski, as well as the one most successfully pursued in the 1966 data, are due to "chance." The reader who has followed the detailed comparison of the 1958 and 1966 results may have noted by now that the original findings presented by Lenski were by no means

uniform and large in their implications for a "religious factor" in the economic realm. For a number of variables introduced by Lenski, there were no reliable differences even in 1958, and in other cases the differences barely met the rather lenient demand of a one-tailed significance level of .10. In still other cases, there were no 1958 differences between Protestants and Catholics as a whole, but differences appeared in certain subgroups when controls were applied. Such subgroups were often quite small, and selective attention to them capitalized on sampling error. A more general problem that runs through *The Religious Factor* is a tendency to assume a basic Protestant-Catholic difference as fact, and therefore to interpret negative findings as adding specific nuances in meaning to the nature of this fact, rather than as calling it into general question. For example, when "communal involvement" turns out to be unrelated to economic values, Lenski's conclusion is that "the churches, rather than the subcommunities, are the primary source of the [religious] differences in economic behavior" (1963:124–125). But another, and at least equally reasonable conclusion, would have been that an important linking hypothesis had been tested and disconfirmed, raising the problem of whether the earlier findings meant what they seemed to mean about religious differences.

While the specific implications of this paper have to do with the Protestant Ethic thesis as developed by Lenski, there is surely a larger implication concerning the place of replication in empirical sociology. *The Religious Factor* was an original and stimulating work, and while the analysis carried out within it seems somewhat problematic in 1969, the primary issue lies not with the book but with the need to strengthen traditions that make replication an assumed part of sociological research. This is particularly true when the original finding is a nonobvious but intuitively interesting one. As with all science, the development of sociology can be greatly stimulated by unexpected results, but the more remarkable an empirical finding, the more it requires careful scrutiny and systematic replication.

References

Bellah, Robert N.
  1968   "The sociology of religion." In International Encyclopedia of the Social Sciences. Volume 13, pp. 406–414. New York: The Macmillan Co. and The Free Press.
Detroit Area Study.
  1959   "Sampling design for the 1957–58 Detroit area study." Mimeograph. Ann Arbor: Detroit Area Study.

Featherman, David.
  1969 The Socioeconomic Achievement of White Married Males in the United States: 1957–67. Ph.D. Dissertation, University of Michigan.
Fisher, Ronald A.
  1951 The Design of Experiments. New York: Hafner.
Glenn, Norval and Ruth Hyland.
  1967 "Religious preference and worldly success: Some evidence from national surveys." American Sociological Review 32 (February):73–85.
Glock, Charles Y. and Rodney Stark.
  1965 Religion and Society in Tension. Chicago: Rand McNally.
Glockel, Glen L.
  1969 "Income and religious affiliation." American Journal of Sociology 74 (May):632–649.
Greely, Andrew M.
  1964 "The Protestant ethic: Time for a moratorium." Sociological Analysis 24 (Spring): 20–33.
Lenski, Gerhard.
  1963 The Religious Factor. Garden City, N.Y.: Anchor Books.
Lykken, David T.
  1968 "Statistical significance in psychological research." Psychological Bulletin 70 (September):151–159.
Rosen, Bernard C.
  1962 "Review of The Religious Factor" American Sociological Review 27 (February):111–113.
Schuman, Howard.
  1967 "Sampling memorandum on the 1965–66 Detroit area study." Multilith. Ann Arbor: Detroit Area Study.
Selvin, Hanan.
  1957 "A critique of tests of significance in survey research." American Sociological Review 22 (October):1957.
Warren, Bruce.
  1970 The Relationship Between Religious Preference and Socioeconomic Achievement of American Men. Ph.D. dissertation, University of Michigan.
Weber, Max.
  1930 The Protestant Ethic and the Spirit of Capitalism. New York: Charles Scribner's Sons.

Does religion affect peoples' economic attitudes and conduct? It is painfully clear that how one answers this question depends upon how one measures both religious and economic phenomena. For instance, while both Lenski and Schuman's data show important differences between Protestants' and Catholics' attitudes toward work and achievement (see Table 7, p. 166), the introduction of specific denominational categories by Schuman reveals some previously undiscovered differences between the various Protestant groups. Baptists differ more greatly in terms of economic attitudes from Presbyterians than do Catholics. Schuman has not simply validated the hypothesis that religion influences economic attitudes and conduct. Rather, he has shown that these patterns of influence are much more varied and subtle than was suggested by Lenski's research.

The fact that Schuman was unable to replicate some of Lenski's findings should not be taken to mean that Lenski's research (or Schuman's) is somehow in error. As Lenski himself observes, there is no reason to believe that the relationships described in *The Religious Factor* will not change over time.[7] Replication must be understood not simply as a means for testing the validity of previous studies but also as an essential technique for documenting changing trends in society.

An important theme in Schuman's essay is that while religion does appear to affect economic attitudes and conduct, religion is far from an independent variable in the social order. At numerous junctures in his discussion Schuman demonstrates that religion is interrelated with age, generational, occupational, and social class differences. An important variable that he discusses, but for which he provides no data, is ethnicity. It is this variable and its impact upon religion that takes center stage in the following essay by Harold Abramson.

As was seen in Schuman's essay, the general categories of Protestant, Catholic, and Jew are often too broad for meaningful sociological analysis. They mask important differences. In this context, Andrew Greeley has argued that denominationalism among Protestants is an ethnic phenomenon.[8] Said differently, denominational difference is an expression not just of theological diversity but of ethnic diversity as well. But what may be said of

[7] Gerhard Lenski, "The Religious Factor in Detroit: Revisited," *American Sociological Review,* 36, no. 1 (1971): 48–50.

[8] Andrew Greeley, *The Denominational Society* (Glencoe, Ill.: Scott, Foresman and Co., 1972), especially chapter 5.

American Catholics in this regard? There are, of course, several non-Roman Catholic churches in the United States that reflect distinct ethnic communities. Among these are the Greek Orthodox Catholic Church, the Polish National Catholic Church, and the Russian Orthodox Catholic Church. While it is widely recognized that Roman Catholic parishes are sharply distinguished at the local level in terms of ethnic differences, there have been relatively few studies of the meaning and consequences of the ethnic factor within the Roman church. Harold Abramson's essay examines the impact of ethnicity upon Roman Catholicism.

Inter-Ethnic Marriage Among Catholic Americans and Changes in Religious Behavior[1]

by Harold J. Abramson

A question for the sociology of religion is the extent of contemporary heterogeneity in religious behavior in the light of social assimilation and the forces of society which propel different social and cultural groups toward unity and conformity. In this context, focus may be placed on the Catholic population of the United States, with its considerable tradition of ethnic diversity. The historical facts of different immigration periods and waves, the distinct nationality churches and parish communities, and the various

Harold J. Abramson is associate professor of sociology at the University of Connecticut and is the author of *Ethnic Diversity in Catholic America* (1973).

Reprinted from *Sociological Analysis*, 32, no. 1 (1971): 31–44. Used with permission of the author and publisher.

[1] This is a revised version of a paper delivered at the meetings of the Society for the Scientific Study of Religion, Chicago, October 1966. For their assistance at various stages of data preparation, and for their helpful comments, I wish to thank Andrew M. Greeley, Jerold S. Heiss, Dennison Nash, and C. Edward Noll. The study from which these data were obtained was financed by a grant from the Carnegie Corporation and by supplementary funds from the Office of Education of the U.S. Department of Health, Education, and Welfare.

cultural orientations which the Catholic immigrants brought with them, point up the importance of studying this group in the face of socio-religious change.

The relationship of ethnicity and religion is an area which has received little attention in the recent past. To be sure, American social history has amply documented the variety of ethnic and religious institutions which European immigrant groups have developed in the United States (Park and Miller, 1921; Niebuhr, 1929; Handlin, 1951; Cross, 1958). But while past sociological investigation has drawn attention to the relevance and distinctiveness of the immigrant church, there is relatively little comparative research in the association between religious and ethnic behavior (cf. scattered portions in Anderson, 1938; Warner and Srole, 1945; Glazer and Moynihan, 1963).

More recent studies in the sociology of religion, such as those by Herberg (1960) and Lenski (1961), do not account for persisting ethnic distinctions within the contemporary Catholic Church. The Herberg thesis rests on the Kennedy (1944; 1952) findings of a "triple melting pot," according to which Americans intermarry and assimilate across ethnic lines but within each of the three major religious faiths. One of the problems with this notion is its assumption that ethnicity has ceased to be important for social and cultural behavior. The idea that the ethnic factor is no longer salient for religious behavior remains to be solidly demonstrated.

A second and related question is the nature of socio-religious change for Catholic Americans. Inter-ethnic or exogamous marriage within the Church may be viewed as an indicator of change in social structure, and presumably, a measure of the loss of ethnic association and identity. In anthropological terms, endogamous marriage, as a prescribed rule in traditional societies or as a preferential normative practice in modern communities, may be expected to contribute to the maintenance of the group's culture, while exogamy may contribute to the change of such culture (White, 1959: 101–116). Given the diversity of religious behavior of ethnic groups, what changes emerge when ethnic mixing takes place within the Church? How influential is the ethnic factor in Catholic religious behavior?

Data and Method of Analysis

The data to be used come from a national sample of 2,071 white Catholic Americans, interviewed by the National Opinion Research Center, as a part of a larger study investigating the effects of parochial school education (Greeley and Rossi, 1966).[2] All of the respondents were Catholic at the time of the interview, and the subsequent analysis is limited to Catholics born of Catholic parents.

Ethnicity is determined by the respondent's report of the main nationality background of his parents and that of his spouse's parents. The six largest ethnic groups among Catholic Americans are selected for analysis: the Italians, the Irish, the Germans, the Poles, the French-Canadians, and the combined Spanish-speaking Mexicans and Puerto Ricans.

For the parental generation, an endogamous marriage is one in which both parents share the same ethnic or nationality background, and an exogamous marriage is one where both parents are reported as having different ethnic backgrounds. For the respondent's generation, an endogamous marriage is defined by the ethnicity of the respondent's father and that of the spouse's father reported as the same; an exogamous marriage is defined by different nationality backgrounds reported for both fathers.[3] The father is chosen in preference to the mother for reasons of the family name and the ethnic identity which is presumed to adhere to the surname. It is not meant to deny the relevance of the mother's role in ethnic behavior.[4]

Ethnic Heterogeneity Among Catholic Americans

When compared as a single religious category with other American religious groups, Catholics show relatively greater involvement in formal religious association. Distinguishing between communal and associational measures, Lenski (1961:18–24, 35–42) points to the strong bonds among Catholics on the obligation of frequent church attendance.

Viewed as a heterogeneous religion, however, we may expect to

[2] The national sample is representative of the universe of the total, non-institutionalized, white Catholic population in the United States, inclusive of ages twenty-three to fifty-seven. See Greeley and Rossi (1966) for details of the survey and the sampling procedure.

[3] For the parental generation, there are 1,194 endogamous marriages and 298 exogamous ones. Among the respondents themselves, the figures are 600 and 497, respectively. See the footnoted distribution of data in Tables 1 and 3, below.

[4] Obvious questions in this connection are the numbers and kinds of other combinations which might define conditions of ethnic endogamy and exogamy. A related problem refers to specific exogamous combinations, e.g., Irish-German, or Polish-Italian, marriages, and to sex differentials. The numbers of cases for any specific combinations are too few to permit any analysis in this study; thus, all exogamous combinations are included in a single category. For a detailed discussion of these questions, along with descriptions of the extent and antecedents of inter-ethnic marriage among Catholic Americans, see Abramson (1969).

find signs of diversity. The cultural traditions historically associated with different ethnic groups within Catholicism serve as a reminder that ethnicity may persist as a distinguishing factor within the same religious affiliation. The six ethnic groups, selected for this study by virtue of their size and roles within American Catholicism, illustrate this diversity.[5]

For the parental generation, Table 1 shows the levels of involvement for six endogamous ethnic groups. As measured by father's and mother's attendance at Mass and reception of Communion, the

Table 1. Religious Behavior of Endogamous Ethnic Groups: Parental Generation

Ethnic Groups	Mass Attendance (percent weekly or more)		Communion (percent monthly or more)	
	Mother	Father	Mother	Father
Irish	91	81	79	62
	(163)	(160)	(150)	(142)
French-Canadian	89	80	80	61
	(115)	(115)	(103)	(99)
German	89	82	74	60
	(170)	(169)	(163)	(159)
Polish	81	76	62	40
	(147)	(148)	(133)	(127)
Italian	71	39	61	23
	(300)	(294)	(266)	(249)
Spanish-speaking	58	36	55	24
	(108)	(107)	(78)	(74)
Total[a]	79	63	66	42
	(1,162)	(1,148)	(1,033)	(980)

[a] Total refers to all ethnically endogamous parents of respondents, and is not the sum of the six selected ethnic groups shown in the table.

N =	1,162	1,148	1,033	980
Exogamous parents =	298	298	298	298
NAP ethnicity =	83	83	83	83
NAP (DK, NA) =	32	46	161	214
Total working N =	1,575	1,575	1,575	1,575
Converted respondents =	252	252	252	252
Non-Catholic fathers =	186	186	186	186
Non-Catholic mothers =	58	58	58	58
Total N =	2,071	2,071	2,071	2,071

[5] For the Irish and the French-Canadians, the historical fusion of religion and nationality in Ireland and Quebec, when confronted with a Protestant England and Canada, may help explain their more consistent association with formal Catholicism. Religion and nationality may be said to have become closely integrated in Irish and French-Canadian culture. At the other extreme, the Italians,

Irish, the French-Canadians, and the Germans are the more involved in the formal religion. The Polish Catholics tend to level at the national total figures, and the Italians and Spanish-speaking Mexicans and Puerto Ricans show a pattern of limited involvement in the Church.

A further point might be made of the differences between mothers and fathers in church attendance and Communion reception. For every instance, as expected from numerous studies, women are more likely to be involved than men. However, the differences

Table 2. Parochial School Support by Endogamous Ethnic Groups: Parental Generation

Ethnic Groups	Parents Sent Respondents to Available Parochial Schools (percent Yes)	
	Catholic Elementary	Catholic High School
Irish	87	62
	(135)	(122)
French-Canadian	88	67
	(100)	(55)
German	81	54
	(106)	(59)
Polish	87	31
	(120)	(81)
Italian	35	14
	(215)	(149)
Spanish-speaking	35	9
	(65)	(32)
Total[a]	67	39
	(850)	(573)

[a] Total refers to all ethnically endogamous parents of respondents, and is not the sum of the six selected ethnic groups shown in the table.

N =	850	573
Exogamous parents =	298	298
NAP ethnicity =	83	83
No schooling =	3	315
No school available =	338	303
NAP (DK, NA) =	3	3
Total working N =	1,575	1,575

Puerto Ricans, and Mexicans are among the least involved in formal requirements. In these cases, some explanation may be found in the histories of the relationships between the Catholic Church and the political movements of nationalism in the respective countries of emigration, as well as the mission status of much of Latin America. Societal conflict within each of these countries between religious and populistic or nationalistic movements helped to create strains of indifference to the formal religious institutions. For a more extensive comparative discussion of ethnic diversity within Catholicism, and a cross-cultural analysis of the relationship between religion and ethnicity, see Abramson (1971).

between the sexes are considerably greater for the less involved ethnic groups. It would seem that the more highly involved groups absorb some of the sex differential in religious practice. This underlines the role of the spouse in influencing religious practice, and this idea will be examined directly later in this study.

Another measure of religious behavior is involvement in the Catholic parochial school system. Table 2 offers the percentages of different ethnic group parents who sent their children (the respondents of the survey) to locally available Catholic elementary and Catholic high schools. The findings are the same as for the measures of Mass attendance and Communion reception. The Irish and the French-Canadians are the most consistently involved, while the Italians and the Spanish-speaking are the most indifferent. The

Table 3. Religious Behavior of Endogamous Ethnic Groups: Respondent's Generation

Ethnic Groups	Mass Attendance (percent weekly or more) Respondent	Communion (percent monthly or more) Respondent	Respondent Sends Children to Available Parochial Schools (percent Yes)
Irish	94	66	86
	(78)	(78)	(56)
French-Canadian	84	42	91
	(76)	(75)	(56)
German	92	72	78
	(72)	(72)	(41)
Polish	82	42	86
	(67)	(67)	(57)
Italian	68	40	64
	(170)	(169)	(135)
Spanish-speaking	44	24	43
	(77)	(78)	(60)
Total[a]	76	45	72
	(599)	(597)	(452)

[a] Total refers to all ethnically endogamous respondents, and is not the sum of the six selected ethnic groups shown in the table. This footnote also pertains to subsequent tables 4 through 9.

N =	599	597	452
Exogamous marriages =	497	497	497
NA =	1	3	3
No school available =	—	—	99
No children =	—	—	46
Total working N =	1,097	1,097	1,097
Not married =	190	190	190
Non-Catholic spouses =	175	175	175
NAP ethnicity =	113	113	113
N =	1,575	1,575	1,575

German and Polish Catholics are high in support of parochial elementary schools, but they fall somewhat at the high school level.

Table 3 refers to the respondent's own generation, and the religious behavior of the contemporary ethnic groups show a pattern similar to that of their parents. Seventy-six percent of the total attends Mass as often as once a week or more, and this figure corresponds to the proportion cited by Lenski (1961: 37) as the measure of associational involvement among Detroit Catholics. But the important fact of the table is the range of diversity persisting for the six endogamous ethnic groups. This range may be qualified or explained by structural factors, such as social class or generation in the United States, and these will be examined as endogamy is compared with exogamy.

Ethnic Marriage and Religious Behavior

Under the assumption that religious and cultural behavior is maintained by the practice of group endogamy, what kind of change in religious practice is associated with ethnic exogamy? The proportions of the total, in Table 4, show no difference in Mass attendance or parochial school support for respondents of either type of marriage, but the findings are variable for specific ethnic groups.

The Irish and the French-Canadians show consistently less involvement with both church-going and religious school involvement when they marry out of their respective ethnic backgrounds. The German and Polish Catholics do not display any patterned change for both measures of religious association. The Italians and the Spanish-speaking Mexicans and Puerto Ricans, as well, reveal no consistent behavioral change with inter-ethnic marriage. The increase from 43 percent of the endogamous Spanish-speaking to 71 percent of the exogamous, in parochial school association, must be tentative because of the very small case base of exogamous Mexicans and Puerto Ricans.

Since women are more likely than men to be church-goers, as noted above, it would be of some value to see if exogamy has any influence on their religious involvement. The data of Table 5, which controls for the sex of the respondent, suggests that this is the case. The Irish of both sexes show the same pattern: decline in church attendance. The French-Canadian females show no difference, but the males of this ethnic group display considerable loss of involvement once they choose wives from some other ethnic background.

In Table 5, the German and Polish Catholics of both sexes reveal

Table 4. Mass Attendance and Parochial School Support, by Type of Marriage and Ethnicity

Ethnic Groups	Respondent's Mass Attendance (percent weekly or more)		Respondent Sends Children to Available Parochial Schools (percent Yes)	
	Endogamous	Exogamous	Endogamous	Exogamous
Irish	94	76	86	75
	(78)	(101)	(56)	(64)
French-Canadian	84	73	91	77
	(76)	(36)	(56)	(22)
German	92	90	78	88
	(72)	(93)	(41)	(60)
Polish	82	80	86	80
	(67)	(68)	(57)	(45)
Italian	68	72	64	60
	(170)	(86)	(135)	(55)
Spanish-speaking	44	50	43	71
	(77)	(10)	(60)	(7)[a]
Total	76	76	72	76
	(599)	(497)	(452)	(322)

[a] Too few cases for adequate percentaging.

N =	1,096	774
NA =	1	3
No children =	—	161
No school available =	—	159
Total N =	1,097	1,097

Table 5. Mass Attendance, by Type of Marriage, Ethnicity, and Sex of Respondent

Ethnic Groups	Respondent's Mass Attendance (percent weekly or more)			
	Female		Male	
	Endogamous	Exogamous	Endogamous	Exogamous
Irish	96	85	90	72
	(47)	(48)	(31)	(53)
French-Canadian	85	86	83	57
	(41)	(22)	(35)	(14)
German	95	90	87	89
	(41)	(48)	(31)	(45)
Polish	81	82	83	79
	(37)	(39)	(30)	(29)
Italian	69	80	67	64
	(94)	(41)	(76)	(45)
Spanish-speaking	56	67	33	25
	(41)	(6)[a]	(36)	(4)[a]
Total	79	80	72	72
	(334)	(254)	(265)	(243)

[a] Too few cases for adequate percentaging.

N =	1,096
NA =	1
Total N =	1,097

no difference by type of marriage. As for the Italians, the women are more likely to attend weekly Mass if they have married outside of their group, but there is no comparable difference for the men. The fact of ethnic exogamy apparently is influential enough to affect the traditional behavior of Irish and Italian women (in their different ways) as well as have a bearing on Irish and French-Canadian men.

Since ethnic groups tend to predominate in either the newer or older waves of immigration, the association between ethnicity and generation in the United States is an obviously important one. The decline of religious involvement for the exogamous Irish and French-Canadians may be a function of generational residence in the United States, rather than a weakening of the ethnic factor through exogamy. In other words, the decline may be due to the fact that exogamy is limited to those generations further removed from the immigration experience (Abramson, 1969: 89–97), and the fact that Irish and French-Canadian levels of religious involvement diminish somewhat among these third and later generations (despite the contrary statements and findings of the "third generation hypothesis" in Herberg, 1960, and in Lenski, 1961: 43–48).

What happens to the frequency of Mass attendance among the first and second generation Irish and French-Canadians when they become exogamous? If the force of ethnicity is relevant among the immigrants and their children, it would be reasonable to expect signs of such relevance with ethnic exogamy. Table 6 examines this question by pointing out the persistence of decline for the exogamous Irish and French-Canadians.

Indeed, it is among the more recent immigrants that the change is greater. Among the first- and second-generation Catholics, those Irish and French-Canadians who have left their respective nationality groups and have chosen spouses from other Catholic ethnic backgrounds are now among the *least* likely to fulfill the requirement of weekly Mass attendance. For Irish and French-Canadian Catholics, ethnicity is bound up with religion, and the act of ethnic marriage appears to be as important, if not more so, for religious behavior, as the fact of generation.

For German Catholics, there is no difference at all between types of marriages, for either generation. But it is clear that for the Germans, generation in the United States itself is an important factor. Among Polish Catholics, there is a mixed phenomenon; the newer generations become less church-going when they become exogamous, and the older generations become more so.

The Spanish-speaking are overwhelmingly endogamous, and of recent immigration to the United States; the cases in other categories

Table 6. Mass Attendance, by Type of Marriage, Ethnicity, and Generation in the United States

	Respondent's Mass Attendance (percent weekly or more)			
Ethnic Groups	First or Second Generation		Third or Later Generation	
	Endogamous	Exogamous	Endogamous	Exogamous
Irish	96	53	92	79
	(26)	(17)	(48)	(82)
French-Canadian	90	64	86	81
	(41)	(11)	(21)	(21)
German	80	80	94	96
	(15)	(35)	(47)	(51)
Polish	84	76	73	86
	(44)	(41)	(15)	(22)
Italian	69	71	61	73
	(149)	(59)	(16)	(22)
Spanish-speaking	41	56	67	0
	(70)	(9)[a]	(9)[a]	(1)[a]
Total	71	69	86	83
	(389)	(235)	(162)	(220)

[a] Too few cases for adequate percentaging.

$$N = 1,006$$
$$\text{NAP generation (DK, NA)} = 90$$
$$NA = 1$$
$$\text{Total } N = 1,097$$

are too few for any adequate comparison. For Italian Catholics, however, it is clear that there is no change in religious behavior among the newer generations; the pattern of relative indifference persists, regardless of the spouse's background. Among the older generation Italians, there is increased Mass attendance with inter-ethnic marriage. Perhaps the alleged acculturation of Italian Catholics to the "Irish norm" of religious behavior in the United States depends not so much on generational background alone, but rather on the combined influence of generation and ethnic exogamy.[6]

If one considers the total percentages of church attendance in Table 6, alone, there is evidence of more involvement among the

[6] The Irish-Italian comparison has recently been raised by Russo (1969), who presents data on the religious behavior of three generations of Italians in New York City, and argues the case for increased involvement of Italian Catholics within the Church. This is consistent with Lenski's (1961) findings, and his data dispute Herberg's thesis (1960) of some rejection of tradition by the second generation. Closer examination of Russo's data suggests, however, that the Italians of New York are becoming more similar to the Irish in terms of *informal* religious practice, but they are not becoming more involved in attendance at Mass or reception of Communion.

third and later generations, regardless of type of marriage. This confirms the general findings reported by Lenski (1961: 43–48), and as suggested by Herberg (1960). The ethnic factor, however, is an important qualification. The German Catholics are the only group within the Church to display this expected behavior. The other ethnic groups are variably influenced by generation of residence and by the fact of ethnic attachments through marriage.

The general association of church-going and generation in the United States is, as Lenski has noted, connected with the Americanization of the immigrants and the degree of socio-economic status. As one measure of social class, Table 7 examines the influence of educational attainment. The total percentages clearly show the influence of class position on church-going, even though they again mask the ethnic factor within Catholicism.

Among the better-educated, type of marriage makes little difference for frequencies of church attendance, except for the Irish; there is some loss in this religious practice for the exogamous Irish. It is among those who never completed high school that the ethnic attachments of marriage have more influence. The effect is most sharply seen among the Irish and the French-Canadians, as before. In this connection, Greeley and Rossi (1966: 53–76, 138–157) offer a number of relevant data. In their study it was pointed out that Catholics with higher levels of formal education tended to receive this schooling in the parochial school system, and both of these factors contribute to increased religious observance. Since the Irish and the French-Canadians are among the most active supporters of the Catholic schools, those among them who received limited education in the public schools are for purposes of this analysis deviant, and probably less likely to be frequent church-goers. In this case, it is apparently ethnic marriage which is responsible for their maintaining the ethnic culture; choosing spouses from other nationality backgrounds, as the fourth column of Table 7 shows, makes them the *least* likely of all ethnic groups to continue tradition.

In addition to the factors of the social structure, some clarification of these findings of the Irish and the French-Canadians may be introduced by looking into the relevance of specific religious influences. It is reasonable to expect that the Irish and the French-Canadians who do leave their ethnic backgrounds for marriage purposes do so because they are disposed to for reasons of an atypical background. In other words, the exogamous Irish and French-Canadians may be those whose parental homes had less religious influence to begin with, or those whose exogamous spouses were and are not as inclined to attend weekly church services. The data of

Table 7. Mass Attendance, by Type of Marriage, Ethnicity, and Educational Attainment

| Ethnic Groups | Respondent's Mass Attendance (percent weekly or more) | | | |
| | High School Graduate or More | | Some High School or Less | |
	Endogamous	Exogamous	Endogamous	Exogamous
Irish	94	83	93	61
	(64)	(78)	(14)	(23)
French-Canadian	92	95	80	43
	(26)	(22)	(50)	(14)
German	92	95	91	76
	(39)	(64)	(33)	(29)
Polish	81	86	82	74
	(27)	(36)	(40)	(31)
Italian	73	73	65	70
	(67)	(59)	(103)	(27)
Spanish-speaking	40	33	47	57
	(15)	(3)[a]	(62)	(7)[a]
Total	83	82	70	65
	(268)	(320)	(331)	(176)

[a] Too few cases for adequate percentaging.

$$N = 1,095$$
$$NA = 2$$
$$Total\ N = 1,097$$

the survey do not allow for an examination of the respondent's own disposition toward religion during the years before his marriage, but the influence of parents and spouse can be ascertained. These factors can further specify the strength of the ethnic factor itself.

Table 8 controls for the degree of parental religious involvement, based on an index of parental religious practice; high involvement indicates that both parents attended Mass as frequently as once a week, and one or both were weekly communicants, while low involvement measures any less frequent religious expression (Greeley and Rossi, 1966: 44).

The total figures suggest quite clearly the influence of parental practice, but they obscure the ethnic effect for Catholics raised in less devout households. Among the Irish from homes with less religious influence, the fact of ethnic exogamy reduces Mass attendance by thirty percentage points. For the French-Canadians, as for the other groups, exogamy does not make as much difference as does the extent of parental influence. With Irish Catholics, however, the importance of ethnicity persists.

Table 8. Mass Attendance, by Type of Marriage, Ethnicity, and Parental Religious Involvement

| Ethnic Groups | Respondent's Mass Attendance (percent weekly or more) | | | |
| | High Parental Involvement | | Low Parental Involvement | |
	Endogamous	Exogamous	Endogamous	Exogamous
Irish	97	90	80	50
	(63)	(70)	(15)	(30)
French-Canadian	88	80	69	64
	(60)	(25)	(16)	(11)
German	95	96	75	73
	(60)	(67)	(12)	(26)
Polish	90	89	61	65
	(49)	(45)	(18)	(23)
Italian	90	88	56	62
	(62)	(33)	(108)	(53)
Spanish-speaking	61	0	37	62
	(23)	(2)[a]	(52)	(8)[a]
Total	90	87	54	60
	(357)	(298)	(239)	(197)

[a] Too few cases for adequate percentaging.

$$N = 1{,}091$$
$$NA = 6$$
$$\text{Total } N = 1{,}097$$

The influence of the spouse, as suggested above in the discussion of Table 1, would seem considerable and a direct examination of this factor in Table 9 confirms the expectation. While individuals with church-going spouses attend Mass themselves in high proportions, be they of endogamous or exogamous marriages, there is notable change for both the Irish and the French-Canadians who have married out of their respective backgrounds and whose spouses are less devout.

The endogamous Irish with less involved spouses tend to remain high on church attendance; 83 percent go to Mass weekly or more. When their spouses are not Irish, the proportion drops to 23 percent. Similarly, if less spectacularly, 33 percent of the endogamous French-Canadians with less devout spouses attend weekly services, but only 18 percent go this often when their spouses are not French-Canadian. Thus, the previous findings are not solely due to the idea that Irish and French-Canadian Catholics who marry into other backgrounds are more likely to be marrying Catholics less involved in the Church. The fact of ethnic marriage itself is clearly important.

Table 9. Mass Attendance, by Type of Marriage, Ethnicity, and Mass Attendance of Spouse

Ethnic Groups	Respondent's Mass Attendance (percent weekly or more)			
	Spouse's Mass Attendance (Weekly or More)		Spouse's Mass Attendance (Less than Weekly)	
	Endogamous	Exogamous	Endogamous	Exogamous
Irish	95	94	83	23
	(65)	(79)	(12)	(22)
French-Canadian	95	96	33	18
	(65)	(24)	(12)	(11)
German	97	95	60	40
	(62)	(83)	(10)	(10)
Polish	92	89	50	50
	(51)	(54)	(16)	(14)
Italian	87	93	36	35
	(107)	(55)	(63)	(31)
Spanish-speaking	67	67	26	25
	(36)	(6)[a]	(38)	(4)[a]
Total	91	92	38	33
	(433)	(368)	(162)	(126)

[a] Too few cases for adequate percentaging.

N = 1,089
NA =   8
Total N = 1,097

Conclusions

On the basis of the data and secondary analysis presented in this study, it is clear that conclusions need to be stated carefully. The small case bases in some instances, the lack of supporting data on ethnic identification, and the wider meaning of ethnic group membership, do pose problems to the analysis.

It seems reasonable, however, to suggest that the Irish and French-Canadian Catholics do tend to fall away from the high level of association with the Church which has long been traditional for these two groups. The falling away, of course, is not at all a sign of apostasy, but merely a modification of the Irish and French-Canadian religio-ethnic systems taking place through the marital assimilation of Catholic Americans.

The role of ethnicity within religion and the Catholic Church is all the more striking for the traditions of the Irish and French-Canadians because of the absence of any patterned change when other ethnic groups intermarry. Those groups—the Germans, the Poles, the Italians, and the Spanish-speaking Mexican and Puerto Ricans—for whom involvement in religious practice has been characteristically less of a function of nationality, or even one of traditional indifference to the meaning of nationality, show no consistent changes with ethnic exogamy.[7] Furthermore, one could argue that if any groups would show tendencies of patterned change, one would expect it from those precise groups for whom the meanings of ethnicity and religion are so historically integrated.

It would appear at this point in the research that the fact of ethnicity itself has implications for the area of religious behavior. The fusion of religion and nationality in the histories of Ireland and Quebec was such that changes in ethnic attachments, as examined here through marriage choice, have relevance for changes in religious attachments. Where historical developments did not foster the interpenetration of religion with a sense of peoplehood, the specific relevance probed here did not emerge.

Finally, it is not merely a question of ethnic persistence that needs to be raised for future research, but also the idea that ethnicity—the underlying traditional and distinctive culture—is a source of heterogeneity. As such, it seems reasonable to expect ethnic variation in change itself, as subcultural forms interact with the wider structural currents of religion and society.

References

Abramson, Harold J.
  1969   "The Ethnic Factor in American Catholicism." Unpublished Ph.D. dissertation, University of Chicago.
  1971   "Ethnic diversity within Catholicism: a comparative analysis of contemporary and historical religion." Journal of Social History 4: 359–388.
Anderson, Elin L.
  1938   We Americans. Cambridge: Harvard University Press.
Cross, Robert D.
  1958   The Emergence of Liberal Catholicism in America. Cambridge: Harvard University Press.
Glazer, Nathan, and Daniel Patrick Moynihan.
  1963   Beyond the Melting Pot. Cambridge: M.I.T. Press.

---

[7] A summary of the percentage changes in the comparisons of religious behavior between endogamous and exogamous conditions in the tables above reflects the findings. The size of the Spanish-speaking group, under the various controls, is inadequate for comparison, but the Italians, Germans, and Poles all display no pattern; most of the percentage changes are negligible, and in the few instances where the differences are considerable they run in inconsistent directions. Patterns are evident only for the Irish, and to a lesser extent, for the French-Canadians.

Greeley, Andrew M., and Peter H. Rossi.
   1966   The Education of Catholic Americans. Chicago: Aldine.
Handlin, Oscar.
   1951   The Uprooted. New York: Grosset and Dunlap.
Herberg, Will.
   1960   Protestant-Catholic-Jew. New York: Doubleday.
Kennedy, Ruby Jo Reeves.
   1944   "Single or triple melting-pot? Intermarriage trends in New
           Haven, 1870–1940." American Journal of Sociology 49:
           331–339.
   1952   "Single or triple melting-pot? Intermarriage in New Haven,
           1870–1950." American Journal of Sociology 58: 56–59.
Lenski, Gerhard.
   1961   The Religious Factor. New York: Doubleday.
Niebuhr, H. Richard.
   1929   The Social Sources of Denominationalism. New York:
           Henry Holt.
Park, Robert E., and Herbert A. Miller.
   1921   Old World Traits Transplanted. New York: Harper.
Russo, Nicholas John.
   1969   "Three generations of Italians in New York City: their re-
           ligious acculturation." International Migration Review 3:
           3–17.
Warner, W. Lloyd, and Leo Srole.
   1945   The Social Systems of American Ethnic Groups. New
           Haven: Yale University Press.
White, Leslie A.
   1959   The Evolution of Culture. New York: McGraw-Hill.

Abramson's study, like Schuman's, points to the complexity of the relationships between religion and other social variables. In one sense the two studies are very different. While Schuman has illuminated the effect of religion upon other aspects of social thought and conduct, Abramson has demonstrated the effect of at least one important social variable (ethnicity) upon religion. Both studies point to the hazards of broad generalizations and to the need for detailed research on socioreligious relationships as they are manifest from one group situation to the next. From the very outset of his study Abramson demonstrates that it is even misleading to view Roman Catholicism as a single religious category, for different ethnic Catholics appear to exhibit very different norms of religious practice. Predictably, since these different patterns of religiosity involve ethnic traditions, ethnic inter-marriage affects each of these different religioethnic subcultures in different ways.

An important characteristic of both Catholicism and Judaism in the United States is that both religious groups are ascribed minority social status. They have traditionally been accorded lower social prestige than the dominant Protestant religious groups. Understandably, much of the literature about American Jews focuses upon the problems of prejudice and discrimination, specifically anti-Semitism. While the social relevance of this kind of research is hardly to be denied, there are, of course, other important questions about the way in which minority communities, religious or otherwise, cope with their unique position in the social structure. As Abramson points out, the assimilation and/or survival of religioethnic communities in the United States is the broader context in which his study must be understood. In the following essay, S. J. Gould provides an excellent overview of the diverse studies of both the religious and social characteristics of American Jews, viewed as a distinctive community making its way in a society that evidences pressures toward both accom-modation and pluralism.

American Jewry—
Some Social Trends
by S. J. Gould

I

The sociology of the Jews can, and should, take a variety of forms. Some of these forms are conventionally "minority" studies—naturally so. For everywhere outside Israel the Jews form "minority" groups embedded in the social systems of the "majority" and acculturated within those systems. The "minority" questions which thus arise are important and familiar. How coherent and self-conscious is the minority? How marginal is it to the majority culture? Does the "minority" member feel overwhelmed by it or does the minority tradition, in part or in whole, appear to him significant or superior? What impact does the minority have on the surrounding society? How does the status accorded to the "minority" member (by law or convention)—and the "minority's" self-image—reflect leading features of the wider social system? Are there different kinds of answers to these questions if we classify "minority" members by

S. J. Gould is reader in social institutions at the London School of Economics, England. He has taught at both the University of California, Berkeley, and Cornell University, and is author of *The Rational Society* (1971).
Reprinted from *Jewish Journal of Sociology*, 3, no. 1 (1961): 55-75. Used with permission of the author and publisher.

age, sex, or length of settlement among (or contact with) the majority? These are the kinds of questions which are bound to arise from any serious minority study. And if Jewish life in the diaspora is scrutinized in this way, it soon becomes clear that, to large measure, each diaspora community can only with caution be compared to other such communities. For to scrutinize Jewish life in this way makes us focus our attention on the wider social system—its structure, history, and prevailing ideologies. In this way specialized "minority" studies can be, in practice and in theory, integrated into general sociology.

Ancillary to such essays in sociology are a variety of problems which are, broadly speaking, statistical. They are concerned with demographic and, more widely, with occupational data. In the case of some minorities such work may be facilitated by the available census data. Such data on the Jews are not generally available;[1] and, in the absence of national census data available on a cumulative basis, demographic data are fugitive and the inferences drawn from them highly speculative. Criteria of Jewishness are neither so clear nor uniform as to make for ease in counting and assessment. Yet, for methodological and substantive reasons, demographic insights, and evidence on occupational distribution and status, are basic raw material for social analysts. In addition there is a practical demand, articulated keenly by Jewish institutions, for such demographic data as will help them to plan ahead. The supply of adequate data seldom satisfies this requirement, not to speak of wider appetites for insight into the "survival chances" of Jewry. Yet the efforts to fulfill the demand partially answer some questions and help to raise others. There is a third form of inquiry of great and obvious importance. These inquiries attempt to survey the structure of Jewish life and institutions among the population described by itself and others as Jewish. What forms of voluntary associations survive, arise, and maintain themselves? And, since the Jews are not simply a social group but inherit a religious tradition, what do they make of this tradition? What elements are adapted to the pressures of the wider social system? Is the traditional always the dependent variable acted upon by "social" factors? Or do some elements within the tradition have a dynamic of their own as autonomous, independent factors? What, in short, happens to the religious tradition in new institutional settings? If acculturation means disintegration of an

---

[1] An important exception may be found in studies of the census data on religious preference available in Canada. See L. Rosenberg, "The Demography of the Jewish Community in Canada," *Jewish Journal of Sociology*, I, no. 2, 1959.

earlier structure of ideas and practice, what factors, internal and external to that structure, limit the break-down?

There is a fourth area of study which is equally important and about which there is a remarkable lack of hard data or verified knowledge. It might be called the social psychology of the Jew—but the borderlines between sociology and social psychology are hard to draw and need not be too closely demarcated for our present purposes. Here we inquire about the character and personality of the Jew—and more particularly about his motivations. What prompts him, often surprisingly, to say that he is Jewish? What religious significance does this have for him in a modern, predominantly secular, culture? How does he act out this religious significance—and what does it mean to him in other sociocultural contexts, i.e. how does being, or feeling, Jewish (at various "strengths" of commitment) affect or determine his standards in public or private life?

II

These problem areas, difficult to survey and to integrate, arise with regard to all Jewish "minorities," large or small. They arise with especial vigour and interest in the study of contemporary Jewish life in the United States. Here an estimated Jewish population of over five million persons constitutes the largest single Jewish settlement in the world. The very size of the field is intimidating—even though the vast majority of these five million Jews live in a relatively small number of urban metropolitan regions. To set American Jewish life in an ordered pattern in the light of the questions we have raised would be a lifetime work for an interdisciplinary team. Naturally, and unfortunately, no such team exists. In recent years, however, there has been an accumulation of serious studies of Jewish life in America—much of it sociological in intention and execution—from which some important trends of development clearly emerge. While it is true that no full-dress history of Jewish life in America is yet available, for many purposes Mr. Nathan Glazer's short, compact book *American Judaism*[2] admirably fills the gap. Mr. Glazer records the development of American Jewry from its seventeenth-century beginnings—patterning it to the story of successive immigrations, the German immigration of the early and mid-nineteenth century and the East European immigration which gathered force from the eighteen-eighties. Central to his narrative is the social mobility of

[2] N. Glazer, *American Judaism* (University of Chicago Press, 1957).

the East European Jews and their descendants, their "internal migration" from generation to generation. If Mr. Glazer is, for the most part, concerned to trace the movement *into* suburbia, Dr. Gordon in *The Jews in Suburbia*[3] paints a picture of present-day Jewish life which, for all its discursiveness, yields useful information and insights. Two books for which Dr. Marshall Sklare is responsible are equally informative and, in a more stringent way, sociological. In his study of *Conservative Judaism*[4] Sklare has produced an admirable account of the growth and evolution of a peculiarly American pattern of Jewish life, the social sources of its strength, and some of its inner tensions and weaknesses. It provides a remarkable case study of the adaptation of a religious tradition to wider social developments—and if, at times, he appears to overstress the degree of adaptation which has taken place, his approach has the merit (among many others) that it is both cogent and revealing. In the volume *The Jews—Social Patterns of An American Group*[5] Dr. Sklare has assembled a rich, and only occasionally indigestible, bill of fare. Historical analyses are combined with essays on demographic and occupational data available for Jewish research. There is an especially useful study of suburban life, a pioneer of its genre, provided by Mr. Herbert Gans. There is some attempt to delineate features of Jewish attitudes and personality as well as some further data on the changing significance of the concept of the "Rabbi." There is included a shortened version of a well-known study by Mr. Glazer on the sources and direction of the middle-class orientation of American Jews. Throughout the volume, concern with detail is blended with a careful attention to the wider American social scene.

We have discussed these works in rather summary terms. In what follows an attempt is made to present some of the leading features which emerge from these, and other, contemporary analyses.

III

It will be convenient to set out first of all some of the demographic evidence to be found in Dr. Sklare's volume *The Jews* and to relate it to collateral evidence that has subsequently appeared. No attempt will be made here to summarize in full the two demographic studies contained in *The Jews*—the essay "Some Aspects of Jewish Demog-

---

[3] Albert I. Gordon, *Jews in Suburbia* (Beacon Press, 1959).

[4] M. Sklare, *Conservative Judaism* (Free Press, 1955).

[5] M. Sklare (ed.), *The Jews—Social Pattern of an American Group* (Free Press, 1958).

raphy" by Ben B. Seligman and A. Antonovsky and the companion piece by Seligman on *The Jewish Population of New York City: 1952.* We shall for the most part examine the evidence on age structure and fertility—two areas in which some new and later data are available. Seligman is quite frank in declaring that "little is really known of the dynamic changes in Jewish population growth. For this information on birth rates and death rates is essential."[6] Only tentative conclusions may therefore be derived from the analysis he offers of the attempts made by a variety of U.S. Jewish communities to arrive at population estimates and the techniques and methods (the Yom Kippur method, the death records method, community sample surveys, etc.) employed in these calculations. Special attention is given to the data available for 13 communities which were studied between 1947 and 1950. A marked feature visible in these studies is the well-known feature of "hollow classes" in the age structure. The Census data for the total population reveal this phenomenon among the young and teen-age groups. But the evidence assembled by Seligman shows that for the Jewish communities it "seems more marked and appears to extend beyond the 20-year group . . . often . . . to the 35-year group."[7] This was noted also in Seligman's separate study of the 1952 Health Insurance Plan study for New York City.[8] Here the 20–24 year age-group for males and the 15–19 year age-group for females were "hollow" in this way, especially when contrasted with the relatively large age-groups born from 1943 onwards. The dynamics of this are of course obscure—but the "hollow class" phenomenon is evidently related to the unfavourable economic conditions of the 1930's and the impact of these conditions on the white population as a whole. There seems ground for the view that the Jewish middle class reacted somewhat more strongly to these conditions than the general white population. Another way of looking at the age structure is to look at the differential pattern of "aging." Despite the wartime and post-war boom in births this phenomenon is visible in the overall national statistics: but the Seligman study shows that this feature is accentuated among the Jews.[9] This is even more marked in the New York City study where Seligman draws attention to the fact that the Jews of New York are "structurally" older than they appear to be elsewhere. It is not clear how much of this difference is the result of migration from New

[6] See *The Jews,* p. 99.
[7] Ibid., p. 53.
[8] Ibid., p. 95 et seq.
[9] Ibid., p. 97.

York to the suburbs—but this factor is clearly substantial. The main trend in these analyses has since been confirmed by data of an unusually reliable and comprehensive nature. In March 1957, as a supplement to its monthly employment survey, the U.S. Bureau of the Census included a question on religious preference in interviews with its national sample. Some of the results were published in February of the following year[10] and some further results were made available in a later volume, Statistical Abstract of the United States 1958.[11] From this material it is clear that the age-groups between 45 and 64 were, in 1957, significantly (7 percent) larger in the Jewish population than in the country's white population taken as a whole.[12]

The topics of fertility and of family or household size are especially difficult in Jewish demography—given the general absence of reliable cumulative data. Seligman clearly recognizes the limitations of the material which he analyses on these fields. No conclusive evidence can be provided on the much discussed possibility of a declining Jewish rate of reproduction. In all but two of the 13 studies he discusses, the average Jewish household size appears lower than in the general white population: the 1952 data for New York City are not dissimilar to those found in these eleven communities. Fertility ratios (the number of children under 5 per 1,000 women of childbearing years) also show, in Seligman's account, lower indices for Jewish females as contrasted with the general white female population. The Census Bureau data for 1957 to which we have referred show that in the age-groups from 15 to 44 (and in the older age-groups as well) the number of children born per 1,000 Jewish women is markedly lower than for Protestant and Catholic women and that these differences are, as expected, associated with the general Jewish propensity for urban residence. Some additional material is now available on this topic. This may be found in the report of the "Growth of American Families" study, based on a sample drawn

[10] U.S. Bureau of the Census. Current Population Reports: Population Characteristics. Series P-20, No. 79, 2 February 1958. This study confirms the overall estimates of the total Jewish population as of the order of five and one quarter millions strong. There is a useful discussion of the material in American Jewish Yearbook, Vol. 60, 1959.

[11] See Table 40 in that volume.

[12] If the data are adjusted to increase their comprehensiveness, it appears that 27.8 percent of the Jews were in this age-group as compared with 20.8 percent in the total white population. For the older group (those over 65) the Jewish proportion was 10.1 percent as contrasted with the white population's proportion of 9 percent. It may be noted that all the more general indices confirm Seligman's view on the relatively greater "aging" of the Jewish population of New York City.

from 17 million white couples with wives between the ages of 18 and 39. This study was conducted in 1955: it examined by interview a sample of 2,713 women, 74 of whom were Jewesses. It is reported in *Family Planning, Sterility and Population Growth* by R. Freedman, P. K. Whelpton and A. A. Campbell (McGraw-Hill, 1959). The subsample of Jewish women is too small for many of the more refined analyses, but some of the material is highly relevant. The most striking new evidence relates to the family-planning habits of Jewish couples: "Jews are much more likely to have completely planned fertility."[13] The proportion of those couples using some method of avoiding conception is highest among the Jews.[14] More than eight out of ten Jewish wives started birth control measures before the first pregnancy—for Protestant wives the comparable figure is 57 percent and for Catholic wives only 32 percent.[15] The authors comment

> the proportion of Jews with completely planned fertility is so large that it will not be surprising to find that the average family size is considerably smaller for them than it is for Protestants and Catholics[16] [and] the Jewish couples covered expect significantly fewer children (2.4) than either Catholics (3.4) or Protestants (2.9). Unfortunately the small size of the Jewish sample . . . makes detailed comparisons impossible. The low fertility of the Jews in the United States as a whole is apparently attributable in large measure to their concentration in large cities where the fertility of all groups is low. In the 12 largest cities included in the sample the Jews and the Protestants expect the same average number of births (2.3) while the Catholics expect 3.1. In the large cities the Jews and the Protestants are alike in wanting fewer children than do the Catholics and in using more effective methods of preventing conception.[17]

IV

From this demographic material we will now turn to some historical and sociological issues. Three propositions about the Jews of America will surely go unchallenged. Firstly, they have survived as a distinctive social group. Secondly, they have "acculturated"—they are, as is rightly made explicit in the very title of Dr. Sklare's collection of studies, "an American group." And, thirdly, the America into which

[13] Freedman and others, op. cit., p. 112.
[14] Op. cit., p. 104.
[15] Op. cit., p. 110.
[16] Op. cit., p. 115.
[17] Op. cit., pp. 287–288.

they have acculturated has been, and remains, a unique and complex setting for diaspora life—a kind of civilization which, in all its changes, is unique in world history, let alone in the experience of the Jews. About the acculturation there can be no question—the only questions that arise are questions about its processes and its limits. The whole history of Jewish life in the United States, especially since the beginning of the present century, turns upon the spread of acculturation among successive generations. Today even the spokesmen for Orthodoxy at times speak the language of advanced acculturation and examine their problems from its perspective. Rabbi Rackman, for example, urges that in order to present its case to American Jews "Orthodoxy must have leaders who are not only articulate in English but also masters of Western thought and its temper." That is why Yeshiva University and the Hebrew Teachers' College advocate the mastery of all Western thought in order to create an ultimate synthesis with Jewish learning. Dr. Rackman is convinced that this goal will be attained "as more of the graduates of these schools and other Yeshivoth become expert in the natural and social sciences."[18] With the practicability of this ambitious programme we need not here be concerned. It may well be that Dr. Rackman, for all his distinction, is not a "typical" Orthodox Rabbi. Nevertheless the spokesmen for moderate Orthodoxy in England, for example, would feel neither able nor obliged to couch their programme in such "modern" terms—terms which have about them so authentic an American ring.

Well before the formative years of mass immigration the Jews of the United States were being moulded by a unique environment. Mr. Halpern in his essay in *The Jews* pinpoints this uniqueness and scrutinizes its sources. In the first place, "emancipation was never an issue"[19] among American Jews. There has never, in the short history of the United States, been a "Jewish Question" on traditional European lines nor the occasion for familiar Jewish reactions to the "problem." Secondly, from the "openness" of American society, from the fact that America at the time of the heaviest Jewish immigration was a nation of immigrants, it followed that America enjoyed no fixed corporate framework into whose subtle modes of exclusiveness the Jews had to be accommodated. From the perspective of the closing decades of the nineteenth century it was unclear whether the Jews would be assimilated or acculturated. But there was a still more

[18] See Dr. Rackman's contribution to *Jewish Life in America*, ed. by T. Friedman and R. Gordis (Horizon Press, 1955).
[19] Ben Halpern, "America Is Different" in *The Jews*, ed. M. Sklare, p. 24.

open question to be asked at that time: "Into what kind of society will such acculturation or assimilation take place?" Jews, like so many other immigrants, were moving into a future which had no definable shape. On the one hand the norms of white Anglo-Saxon Protestant America were to retain their vitality and, very largely, their primacy. On the other hand these norms were to be blended with those of the European immigrants, Catholic as well as Jewish. They were to be modified by new and unprecedented developments of industry and urbanism. They were to be affected in a myriad of ways by cultural novelties and fashions not yet dreamed of; and they were to be modified by the social mobility, for groups and for individuals, which decades of economic growth were to bring in their train. The tensions between freedom, privilege, and equality have never been unknown in America[20]—the status preservers are as old as, if not older than, the status seekers. Yet, as Mr. Halpern's essay reminds us, "the initial status is that of freedom"—and, we might add, this is so in a variety of spheres and senses. So far as the Jews were concerned, they were to be freely acculturated—once they became willing to abandon the more obvious signs of foreignness. Multiple social and economic pressures were working in that direction—even if countervailing pressures were to make for social segregation and to discourage any tendencies towards social assimilation.

A second sense in which America was to be different was in the extent and speed with which one generation's proletariat became the next generation's middle class. The white population was to enjoy a high measure of social mobility—not, perhaps, as high or as uniform as has often been supposed, but none the less substantial. This mobility was the consequence of unprecedented economic growth, modernity, and differentiation—and enjoyed the support of powerful normative traditions. Of these opportunities the Jews were to take full advantage. Mr. Glazer cautions us against reading too much into comparisons of Jewish with non-Jewish social mobility. He points out[21] that if compared with high status groups of long standing such as Presbyterians and Episcopalians, the Jewish headway over the last fifty years may seem less conspicuous. Yet the evidence from

[20] Mr. Vance Packard in *The Status Seekers* often appears to suggest that the existence of class and status barriers was first revealed in recent sociological research and argues that there has been a hardening of status lines in recent decades. He is wrong on both counts. His book does, however, provide a popular account of the social restrictions under which American middle-class Jews, despite acculturation, still labour.

[21] N. Glazer in *The Jews*, p. 146.

communities of all sizes shows,[22] as he himself demonstrates, a remarkable concentration of the Jews in self-employment and in the "open" professions. There are important differences reported from New York by Seligman—here skilled and unskilled workers were up to 28 percent of the Jewish labour force—and here too there was a higher proportion than elsewhere of Jews who were in private employment rather than self-employed.[23]

Glazer, like many other commentators, stresses the rapidity of this Jewish advance to middle-class status and incomes—and observes that in this context, as in so many others, the Jewish minority followed general American patterns, only faster and more energetically. He interprets this aptitude in terms of the traditional Jewish concern for learning and education and the urban trading background which the East European Jewish proletariat, uniquely among the immigrants, brought with them to America. Dr. Sklare adds the significant point that, since this mobility was group-mobility and so rapid in its tendencies, the traditional religious framework had no possible chance to modify itself through the niceties of gradualism. The challenge to traditional Judaism, already latent in the change of scene and in the early tensions between the generations, was thus reinforced by the spatial, as well as the social, mobility of the Jews and by the growth of new aspirations to status. Dr. Sklare sees in this process of movement the major sources of Conservative Jewish institutions—and to this point we will later return.

There are special features of the modern American middle-class style of life by which Jewish life is constantly moulded. To these features a good deal of sociological attention has, of recent years, been directed. High standards of living, suburban life in a mobile society, the values of achievement and success, child-centredness in family patterns, "democratic" permissive family relations, new op-

[22] This evidence is familiar and need not be laboured. See the table of data from thirteen communities in Seligman's article, "Some Aspects of Jewish Demography," in Sklare (ed.), *The Jews*, pp. 76–77.

See also the article by D. Goldberg and H. Sharp in the same collection, p. 107 et seq., on "Some characteristics of Detroit Area Jewish and non-Jewish Adults." They report that in 1955 Jewish family heads were very largely (75 percent) in white collar jobs "... particularly clustered in the 'proprietor, manager and official' classification. The proportion of Jews in these 'tradesman' jobs (42 percent) is between three and four times greater than that for Catholics or white Protestants. ... an intermediate position between the relatively proletarian Jews of New York City and the virtually complete white collar concentration of Jews in some of the smaller communities of this country," op. cit., p. 113.

[23] B. Seligman, "The Jewish Population of New York City" in *The Jews*, ed. Sklare, p. 102.

portunities, sanctions, and tensions—all these have come under the sociological microscope and macroscope. These values are in part deeply rooted in American culture and their novelty should not be exaggerated. But in recent decades they have become more articulate and, probably, more dominant than hitherto—and, as we shall see, they present especial problems and conflicts for the Jewish middle class.

A third important sense in which America was to be "different"— and quite uniquely so—remains to be cited. Nowhere but in America is there a semi-formal acceptance of three great religious communities—Protestant, Catholic, and Jewish—as providing a socially recognized pattern of group difference and group distinctiveness. This phenomenon has been much debated in recent years—much of the debate being inspired by Mr. Herberg's important book, *Protestant, Catholic, Jew*. Mr. Herberg, like other religious commentators, was concerned to trace the origins of this phenomenon in American history and to explore it in the light of the religious "revival" of America in the nineteen-fifties.[24] He also relates the phenomenon to the growing tendencies within the three major faiths towards convergence—in a watered-down, packaged allegiance to a common creed of Americanism. All the practicality and moralism long noted in American religion was to be reinforced in the mid-nineteen-fifties —moulding all religious institutions to a new and disturbing norm. Another writer has complained that

> For the American citizen, the Protestant, Catholic and Jewish faiths tend to furnish a psychological resting place. This is in contrast to the sort of faith which allegedly enshrines the final truth of God, a being to whom men ought to commit themselves quite independently of specific "good" consequences that may follow. Protestantism, Catholicism, and Judaism combine with less institutional aspects of American folk piety to form a body of religion distinguished and limited by elements of utilitarianism, this worldly activism . . . surrounded by an atmosphere of religious pluralism, tolerance and optimism.[25]

And the editor of the *Christian Century* has inveighed against "the wearing waters of generalized religion," a sanctioned "national religion-in-general," lacking any sense of inner tension or struggle.

[24] W. Herberg, *Protestant, Catholic, Jew* (first edition, 1955: second and revised edition, Doubleday, 1960).

[25] A. Roy Eckardt, *The Surge of Piety in America* (Association Press, 1958), p. 57.

This national mood often leads Americans to assume that God is a good fellow with whom they may "collaborate" in a gently permissive manner. Its hallmark is externality and mediocrity—and it has come in for consistent attack by thoughtful critics, anxious to examine what has often looked like a major religious boom.[26] Jewish life has been clearly influenced by this trend. The suburban Jew is, as some may argue, often consciously Jewish or actively Jewish because religious affiliation is generally "acceptable" in middle-class circles and one is expected to "belong." But the significant point is not the accusation of "conformity"—nor, indeed, the reality. The prevailing national ethos has given Jewish community and institutional life an added source of vitality. Contrary to the patterns of earlier decades this life now clusters around the synagogue and the Rabbi. As Sklare and Glazer both point out, in the prewar period a sense of Jewishness with no trace of attachment to formally religious bodies was not only possible but, in the circumstances, natural. This is no longer the norm—and the retreat from this norm is in part the result of the general American expectation that cultural or ethnic differences may be socially approved and encouraged within a *religious* community. It may well be that, for all its shallowness and bias towards mediocrity, this ethos will continue to act as one barrier against Jewish assimilation and to reinforce the others.

V

The special forms which have developed in American Jewish life all involve departures from the standards of East European orthodox practice which, ideally, demanded the most exact adherence to the provisions of the Shulchan Aruch and prescribed a body of ritual to be observed rather than a set of mandatory, theologically formulated beliefs. There are, of course, important creedal items within orthodox Judaism—but it has been ritual which has predominated. In traditional Judaism of the East European mode, the religious leader, the Rabbi, has been a student and expositor of the Talmud rather than a synagogue functionary, preacher or cleric. He has enjoyed the status of a legal expert—pronouncing, within the closed circle of Jewish settlement, upon ritual questions and upon disputes over family status, property rights, and kindred topics. Rabbis of this kind had never flourished in America before the East European immigra-

---

[26] See Martin E. Marty, *The New Shape of American Religion* (Harper, 1959), *passim*—particularly pp. 26–27 and 73.

tions—nor were they to do so subsequently. Neither the social nor the legal status of the Jew were favourable to this role.[27] Over time the American term "rabbi" has come to cover a vast range of functions which are quite new and exacting. He has become a synagogue official rather than an independent scholar or a community expert on Jewish law. This change mirrors the prevailing congregationalism of American Jewry. The European Kehila was never transplanted to the United States. Congregationalism was the American norm—one which America's Jewish immigrants found congenial.[28] A national framework for Jewish life has been equally repugnant—and all attempts to build one have been foiled by the congregationalism, by the consequences of new immigrations, as well as by personal/factional or ideological blocks. A third distinctive retreat from the orthodox pattern has been in the growing role of the women within the congregation—the disruption of the Eastern element in Jewish practice which, for example, prescribed segregation of the sexes at places of worship and assigned to women relatively few, though important, ritual duties. We shall subsequently discuss the evidence which recent studies have provided upon the impact of these changes—especially within the suburban setting that has added an impact of its own. But these structural changes—all part of a sustained departure from the orthodox pattern—have long been functionally connected.

The background to this structure is amply illuminated by Dr. Sklare's *Conservative Judaism*—for, despite the earlier shifts promoted by Reform Judaism, it was the Conservative movement that came to focus, in a special set of ways, the adaptation of Judaism, and Jewish practices, to the American scene. It is not necessary here to trace in detail the development of American Jewish religious institutions. Mr. Glazer's[29] account rehearses, with great succinctness, the familiar story. He tells of the first American attempt, from the mid-ninteenth century on, to modernize Judaism—of the advance of, and resistances to, Reform Judaism, from the eighteen-forties a developing movement among the German Jews. Reform has not been halted—but its pace and character was to be affected, like everything in American Jewry, by the arrivals from Eastern Europe.

[27] For a fuller discussion of this, see J. E. Carlin and S. H. Mendlovitz, "The American Rabbi: A Religious Specialist Responds To Loss of Authority," in M. Sklare (ed.), *The Jews*, pp. 377–382.

[28] For a useful discussion on "congregationalism" the reader is referred to the study by Joseph I. Blau, "The Spiritual Life of American Jewry, 1654–1954" in the *American Jewish Yearbook*, Vol. 56, 1955, p. 112 et seq.

[29] N. Glazer, *American Judaism*, chapters III–V.

The social distance between the Germans and the East Europeans was great. Even so, economic, professional, and philanthropic relationships brought the older settlement into contact with the new. And, as Mr. Glazer acutely observes, the effect of this contact upon the Reform-oriented German Jews was to stem the movement towards naturalism and extreme Protestantization.[30] The Reform position, and its status barriers, made no serious impact upon the newcomers. They were otherwise preoccupied—and where they were not religiously indifferent, agnostic, or atheist, they clung to a kind of Orthodoxy which reminded them of their East European past. To their needs and, ultimately, to the needs of their children, another approach, the Conservative approach, had greater affinity. As Dr. Sklare records, the Conservative movement antedated the arrival of the East Europeans. It was a reaction against the sweeping alterations of mood and ritual inherent in the Reform position—but it had made little headway. The students graduating from the Conservative "Jewish Theological Seminary" were graduates into an uncertain future—and "at the turn of the century the school was in virtual bankruptcy."[31] It revived because its leaders sensed the new opportunities—an uncovenanted consequence of Russian pogroms. The processes of acculturation and mobility were to create a demand for the kind of "middle way" for which Conservatism stood. From this time on Conservatism was to have an East European slant. Unlike old-line Reform it never stood aloof from such concerns as Zionism. In matters of religious observance Conservative leaders were to advocate such non-orthodox arrangements as mixed seating in the synagogues and to stress the need for greater "decorum" at times of worship. They were to recognize that the daily cycle of ritual and prayer had broken down. Yet they were careful to stress that the changes were changes of form rather than content—a distinction that is always difficult to establish—and to claim that "the traditional ritual has been retained in all its essentials."[32] Modified traditionalism of this kind did not make easy a coherent advance in matters of ideology or religious policy. Many observers have noted, not always with approval, the reluctance of the Jewish Theological Seminary to make rapid modifications of Jewish Law.[33] Indeed, as Sklare shows, this middle-road position makes for some inner con-

[30] N. Glazer, op. cit., p. 99 et seq.

[31] M. Sklare, *Conservative Judaism*, p. 161.

[32] *United Synagogue Recorder*, VIII, 1 February 1928, 25, quoted in M. Sklare, op. cit., p. 113.

[33] See the recent paper by M. J. Rottenberg in *The Reconstructionist*, Vol. XXVI, No. 11, p. 19 et seq., and No. 12, p. 14 et seq.

flict within the rabbi's mind as well as interesting debates when the rabbis meet. They occupy a middle position themselves—between the laity who are not too preoccupied with the sanctity of tradition and the professors of the seminary who are aloof from the mundane concerns of the typical congregation. For all its dilemmas the movement has been able to reap the fruits of eclecticism. Rejecting in large measure the full force of the innovations proposed by Mordecai Kaplan, it has followed him so far as was necessary to bridge the gap between the community centre and the synagogue—a gap which, as we shall see, yawned in the areas of second settlement but which has been largely closed in the suburbs. It has long concerned itself with the changing character of Jewish educational needs—both for the direct purposes of raising existing low levels of "Jewish knowledge" and for more long-range ends of institutional self-maintenance and perpetuation. And as Jews moved into the suburbs, with the old controversies between Germans and East Europeans irrelevant and dead, Conservatism has set benchmarks for all Jewish activity—including that of the Reform groups. The ideological and institutional vested interests remain very powerful—but at a period of rapid overall advance, peaceful coexistence is the order of the day. Such coexistence is, also, to some measure a reflection of the general American pattern of religious life which de-emphasizes the kind of theological exclusiveness and rancour so prevalent, historically, in many other societies.

VI

We turn now to the place where these trends have met and, by meeting, been intensified—the suburbia whose Jews form the subject of Dr. Gordon's book and whose life-style is dominant among American Jews. We have already noted the spatial mobility of the East European Jews and their descendants—concomitant with their rise to middle-class status and their prosperity. This mobility has been a two-stage affair. Firstly the ghettoes were deserted for better areas—which were to be second-settlement zones of a transitional kind. Then, in the interwar years and more rapidly since 1945, there has been a further movement to the fringes of the great cities and beyond their formal limits. Thus in New York City "in 1940 only one Jew in every eight in the region was living in the suburbs: in 1955 over one in five was living in the suburbs: and in 1965 one in every three Jews in the region will be living in the suburbs."[34] There is no

---

[34] *Jewish Population Trends in New York* (Federation of Jewish Philanthropists Report, January 1956).

question but that this migration has altered the entire perspective of Jewish life. The second-settlement areas were heavily populated by Jews: there was little need to be over-conscious of one's Jewish-ness—it was in the air. The religious bodies in such areas were mainly orthodox in character—but with declining religious ob-servance they had no wide significance either for most of the Jews or for the predominantly low-status non-Jews who lived in such neighbourhoods. The Jews were able to live a life which had many powerful Jewish overtones: they did not mix socially with non-Jews; they could belong to Jewish social or cultural or political or-ganizations without any synagogal bias or connexion whatsoever. Very often there was a Jewish community centre in the district which was quite distinct from the synagogue and sometimes in conflict with religious leaders. Jewish education was not typically a syna-gogal responsibility—being conducted by a number of distinct bod-ies, on a community basis or following one or another of the non-religious movements which at that phase flourished among the Jews. When the children of the original immigrants moved on into third-settlement areas, they found that the whole context had changed. They had little or no synagogal attachments: those who did could not always even attempt to reproduce the limited orthodox patterns to which they were accustomed. Orthodoxy had about it an aura of foreignness and of the low-status past. Middle-class acculturation re-quired them to turn their backs upon the past—even where they had some nostalgia for the good old days. It was in these areas that the Conservative synagogues were to be liberally established—here the middle road was the only viable one.

There is no typical suburb. Even a cursory glance at the variety of areas surveyed by Dr. Gordon would suffice to show this. They differ in the manner of their settlement, in their inner structure, and the accidents of their local history. But Dr. Gordon's evidence and much other material is of a kind which enables something of a suburban profile to emerge. The first element is the return to the synagogue—not by every Jew but by at least five out of ten American Jews. Sec-ondly, this return to the synagogue does not involve any widespread revival of religious observance or, indeed, vastly increased attend-ances at worship. Thirdly, the impulse to return to the synagogue is associated with the coalescence around the synagogue of a variety of social and educational activities to which a great deal of time and attention is devoted—and the synagogue's function as a place of prayer is largely subordinated to these other functions. The separate community centre gives place to the synagogue centre. Fourthly, the return to the synagogue is child-centred to an extent which is not uniform but is generally apparent. The child's needs for Jewish indoctrination is a matter for anxious, explicit concern in such sub-urban settings. The religious import of this indoctrination is sec-ondary—despite recent and fairly general efforts to upgrade this aspect of Jewish education. Much evidence supports the view that it is the children whose future as Jews bring their parents, often ig-norant of Judaism or reluctant to become too "involved," into a min-imal relationship with the synagogue. There is evidence that this child-centredness in the American setting is bound to make a return to old-time religious forms more than implausible but that, inter-estingly, it is linked with parental fears about intermarriage as a risk to be contained. Fifthly, there is no doubt that at present social in-timacy and mixing between Jews and non-Jews is still remarkably rare. There is a good deal of social self-segregation—even in those suburbs whose Jewish population is a relatively small proportion of the total. Sixthly, the suburbs are places where Jewish women spend their days while their husbands work elsewhere. The Jewish father has less and less direct responsibility for bringing up his children on Jewish lines. The perspectives of the next generation of Jewish adults are thus dominated by the roles at present played by their mothers. These mothers now have the leisure, opportunity, and money with which to engage actively in the life of the synagogue centre. And finally the role of the Rabbi, as has been indicated above, has been drastically altered. He is now less and less free to pursue scholarly avocations. He is expected not only to preach and teach but also to be a pastoral counsellor, to have skills as an educational adminis-trator and general bureaucrat, to be a promoter of an expanding enterprise, in harness with well-intentioned but often narrow and ignorant laymen, and to act as a representative of the Jews at those interfaith occasions so dear to the American heart.

There is an illuminating study by Mr. Herbert Gans, included in the volume on *The Jews,* in which some, but not all, of these devel-opments are mirrored.[35] Mr. Gans studied the "village" of Park For-est near Chicago shortly after its foundation in 1948 and again, more briefly, in 1955.[36] At both times the Jewish families numbered about 10 percent of the total number of families in the suburb. The first stirrings of community life came with the early foundation of social clubs for men and women. The first great controversies arose over the need felt by the parents of young children that, in the new en-

[35] H. Gans, "The Origins and Growth of a Jewish Community in the Suburbs" in M. Sklare (ed.), *The Jews,* p. 205 et seq.

[36] Park Forest gained a wider celebrity as it was featured as a suitable example of modern suburbia by William H. Whyte, Jr., in his study of *The Organization Man* (1956).

vironment, the youngsters should receive a "Jewish education." The mothers were at once playing a dominant role—and were adamant in promoting a child-centred Jewish institution. "They wanted," said one of the embattled men, "a non-sectarian Sunday school." And they got what they wanted. They were anxious to ensure that, as far as possible, the adults would be free to "abstain from religious-cultural activity and involvement in the community."[37] The result may be illustrated by the undertaking given by the community school to the parents:

> The children will not be taught that parents have to light candles: the children will be informed of the background of candles. . . . We're teaching the child not that he must do these things: we just teach him the customs.[38]

There was no majority support at that time for a synagogue but what support there was also stemmed from a feeling that it would be good for the children but either not necessary or unimportant for the adults. The adults felt the need to give their children a sense of Jewish identity and being unable to do it themselves wanted simply, in the American way, to hire an expert in these affairs and then to be left alone. Eventually, after several years, those actively desirous of a synagogue succeeded in establishing one, with aid from the developer of the suburb, a prominent national Jewish figure. Typically this synagogue, following "warm Reform" patterns of worship, embarked upon providing a school of its own, to bring education into closer relation to Jewish *practices*. This too aroused a complex controversy of a subtle kind—but when Gans paid his second visit to Park Forest the congregational school was well established. The Rabbi was facing the task of reaching a balance between his own view that children should be educated as potential adult congregants and the prevailing sentiment in favour of child-centred procedures and activities.

This child-centredness has several results. One of them, of course, is the high level of American Jewish concern with Chanukah. This has become a child-oriented festival *par excellence* and it is celebrated variously as a kind of articulate counter to Christmas or as an uneasy ancillary to it or through the invention of symbols which possess some of the flavour of both holidays. A more important structural consideration is, of course, that many parents are in fact

[37] See Gans, op. cit., p. 215.
[38] See Gans, op. cit., p. 217.

drawn into synagogal life through their children. For one reason—
Park Forest is an example—the system of fees for education makes
it an economy for parents to join the temple themselves and get
free or reduced-cost education for their children. Temple officials
have been quick to utilize this pressure. Secondly, the child-centred
family offers many opportunities for the children to influence their
parents—such influence is more likely to confine itself to externals
and the introduction of *some* minimal Jewish customs into the home
rather than in any deep spiritual unease or renewal.[39]

Despite the fact that the study relates to a Canadian suburb (near
Toronto) and not to an American one, the study *Crestwood Heights*
by J. R. Seeley and others is very relevant here.[40] This study was not
in its main emphasis a *Jewish* community study. It had wider theoretical and practical concerns than has been the case with the bulk
of Jewish community portraits. But as Crestwood Heights has a
large and growing Jewish population the book's insights are relevant
to our present theme. Its authors present what is at once the most
acute and most dispiriting of all the analyses of religion in suburbia.
They stress the dominance of the values of "maturity" and "democracy" within the family—and the values of success, health, happiness, peace of mind which are general to the suburban middle class.
They make the interesting point about the middle-class outlook in
North America. ". . . to many of its members [it is] a mere stepping
stone . . . a precarious resting point, in a vertical movement in which
upward hopes and downward fears have, or are felt to have, a very
high probability of realization."[41] One wonders whether the urban
and other traditions of the Jewish new middle class insulate them
from these tensions to any extent: and one is reminded that since
Jewish mobility in America has been an *upward* movement of a
group we hear nothing of the causes or amount of *downward* movement.

In this middle-class environment at Crestwood Heights, religion,
like the school which is in the foreground of the study, aims "to gird
the child with the minimum of spiritual armour which can be shed

---

[39] It is of interest that the study of *The Jewish Population of Greater Washington*
(by S. K. Bigman, 1957) inquired into the reasons for *non-membership* of congregations: over 53 percent of the families studied were non-affiliated. No tabula-
tion of the answers was apparently made but the most frequent answers made
reference to the age of the family's children, e.g., "We won't join until our
children are old enough for Sunday school" or "Our children are grown up now,
so we no longer need to belong," p. 93.

[40] J. R. Seeley, R. A. Sim, and E. W. Looseley, *Crestwood Heights* (Basic Books,
1958).

[41] Ibid., p. 356.

easily in favour of other defences, should it be experienced as obsolete or cumbersome."[42] It is "rather a guide to a style of behaviour than to any particular line of conduct."[43] "Parents asked again and again whether a given theological teaching was 'bad for the child,' that is, damaging to his personality or the likelihood of his success in any one of its innumerable meanings—*excluding* salvation."[44] With this instrumental view of religion it is hardly likely that even when parents are obliged to become themselves "involved" they will bring to the home any practices which might unsettle the child or conflict with the permissive directives so important for success in the wider world. The evidence from *Crestwood Heights* does not point to a pattern of *deep-seated* religious conviction and revival.

Commenting on the role of the women in American Jewry, Dr. Gordon suggests that "no synagogue in America could function well these days if it were not for the women . . . who support it with their devoted efforts."[45] "The wife has become the modern matriarch of Jewish suburbia. Her ideas, opinions and values clearly dominate."[46] He praises their devotion and loyalty—but is evidently uneasy about their dominance. He expresses two main sources of unease. Firstly he is anxious about the consequences for Jewish family life of the present day dominance of the suburban mother. On the one hand there is the risk of maternal over-protection: on the other there is a decline of the father's authority and his physical absence from the suburbs for long periods of each day. In the absence of reliable evidence based upon systematic study of Jewish families of varied types, it is difficult to assess the results of this changing pattern of parental roles or to compare the consequences of this pattern with those of earlier patterns. The Jewish mother has always been a powerful force in the lives of her children and it is hard to measure whether we are witnessing a change for the "worse." The second source of Dr. Gordon's unease is the fact that the level of her education in Jewish matters is low and she is not, in his view, really prepared for the kind of leadership roles she is assuming. We would add a third reason for unease. Surely the women are bound to mould yet further the role and personality of the Rabbi—and perhaps add to the problems which beset him. The kind of Rabbi who is appointed and becomes successful must now be the kind of man

[42] Ibid., p. 215.
[43] Ibid., p. 239.
[44] Ibid., p. 240.
[45] A. I. Gordon, *Jews in Suburbia,* p. 65.
[46] Ibid., p. 59.

who is acceptable to the ladies. After all he will see more of his female congregants in many cases than he will of his male. A reform Rabbi recently said aloud what many other Rabbis must long have felt. "There is a great personal anxiety arising out of this suburban constellation. Have we in suburbia been spending too much time with the women of our temple? How will Judaism be affected if we continue to tailor it to fit the needs of our female congregants?"[47]

We have mentioned earlier the new and exacting tasks which the American Rabbi performs. In their essay "The American Rabbi"[48] Carlin and Mendlovitz distinguish seven rabbinic roles as found in the U.S.A.—the traditional rabbi, the free-lancer, the modern orthodox rabbi, the intellectual reform rabbi, the social reform rabbi, the traditionalistic reform rabbi, and the conservative rabbi. Within this typology the roles of the modern orthodox, traditionalistic reform, and conservative rabbis converge at salient points. They all aspire to the scholar-saint role of traditional rabbi but they are pre-eminently organizers, performers of priestly functions, teachers, pastoral counsellors and spokesmen for the Jews in the wider community. This, say the writers, is the core of an emerging common rabbinic role. Within this role there is no place for the skills in talmudic disputation once characteristic of the Rabbi—nor is the Rabbi needed as a legal expert. The Rabbi's position, so far as he works within the limits tacitly or explicitly imposed by his flock, carries considerable status—this is drawn in part from his prestige within the Jewish community as *the* expert, a kind of surrogate through whom the bulk of the Jews maintain an often vicarious contact with a centuries-old tradition, and in part from the Rabbi's standing in the non-Jewish community. As Herberg pointed out in his *Protestant, Catholic, Jew*, the Jewish zeal for "corporate self-validation" is reflected in "the extraordinary high salaries Jewish rabbis receive in comparison with those received by Protestant ministers of equal status and service."[49] These rewards may be some compensation for the tensions which, according to Sklare, are built into the Conservative rabbi's role—they are certainly not rewards for sinecures. Allow-

---

[47] Rabbi Alvan D. Rubin of Long Island, Central Conference of American Rabbis, 69th Annual Convention, *Yearbook*, Vol. LXVIII, 1958, p. 177.

[48] *The Jews*, ed. M. Sklare, pp. 377–414.

[49] W. Herberg, op. cit., p. 240. Mr. Herberg later (p. 250) notes that in 1958 Protestant clergymen's salaries averaged $4,432. According to Carlin and Mendlovitz (in *The Jews*, p. 411), "If we include perquisites, the average Conservative Rabbi earns between $10,000 and $12,000." They add that there are insufficient Conservative rabbis to fill all the openings available.

ing for a certain measure of exaggeration, there can be no doubt that in the "revived" synagogues of the suburbs the Rabbi is a very busy man, with little time to read or think.[50] He is incessantly involved with *human relations* and in the suburbs this can be very time-consuming. He must, as many Rabbis increasingly argue, fight for the time needed for reflection and scholarship. Much evidence supports the view that modern rabbis value, often guiltily, the older scholarly norm and its intellectual rewards.[51] But human relations, especially counselling work, are more central to the role. One Rabbi prides himself: "I am now one of the best known lay practitioners in the field of personal problems. . . . I've reconciled more couples who were going into divorce and sent more people to psychiatrists than any other minister in town."[52] There are all sorts of suburban tensions which the Rabbi may help to resolve.[53] To do so he may himself turn to psychiatry and psychotherapy—primarily to become better equipped to handle counselling work. One is sometimes tempted to suggest that this concern with psychotherapy is an index of rabbinical uncertainties, an expression of his feeling that his seminary training and/or his religious beliefs require supplementation. It would be interesting to survey those Rabbis who have themselves been psycho-analysed and to assess whether they have emerged as more committed, less problem-haunted occupants of religious roles or whether they are now practising a kind of applied psychiatry from a synagogue office.

VII

Is all this *really* Judaism? We can make no attempt here even to summarize the widespread debate there has been on this question—or on the related question—"Have American Jews a Jewish Future?"[54] Only the briefest conclusions are possible here.

---

[50] Even so a number do find time to write papers and books.

[51] Of course the failure to study may often be the result of the Rabbi's activist preferences. Certainly the recent expansionist phase has made activism indispensable. One can, however, see a defensive undertone in the recent hope of a distinguished Reform Rabbi that "when our Rabbis are less preoccupied with the construction of buildings and the organization of new groups, they will surely give more time to study" (Dr. B. J. Bamberger, at Central Conference of American Rabbis, 69th Annual Convention. 1958, *Yearbook,* Vol. LXVIII, p. 268).

[52] See Carlin and Mendlovitz, op. cit., p. 396; also Gordon, op. cit., p. 89 et seq.

[53] See R. E. Gordon and others, *The Split-Level Trap,* Geis, 1961, for a useful account of these problems.

[54] This is the title of a perceptive recent article by Dr. Marie Syrkin in *Jewish Frontier,* January 1961, pp. 7–12.

(a) There has not been a *religious awakening*—if by that term one means a return to traditional practices or the penetration of daily life by a religious ethic. All the data suggests that, in matters of formal observance and worship, Jews are secularized even more than most other Americans.

(b) The return to the synagogue has been the result of the sub-urban migration as well as the other features of middle-class American life to which we have referred. In the suburbs, as Mr. Glazer puts it, Jews are a captive audience for the synagogue centre and for professional religious experts. But one feels that Mr. Gans, for example,[55] may be wrong to suggest that the revival is largely "a transfer to traditionally intense ingroup sociability patterns from the informal groups in which they were practised in the cities to a set of formal organizations in the suburbs." This is to underrate the importance of formal organizations—and the loyalties and vested interests which they build up over the years. Nor do we yet know what will be the result of the increased emphasis in recent years upon Jewish education. Amid all the externality of Jewish life in the suburbs there is a small thin voice of commitment— an anxiety, even among adults, to "know more" about Judaism. It may well be that the answer to this demand is supplied in a conventionally packaged American form, and that the pervasive smoothness of popular culture—including religious culture—seldom rises above mediocrity. But there is, as yet, no way of assessing the long-run effects.

(c) Mr. Glazer is right to see in the return to the synagogue something more than conformity or the need to belong. Belongingness is an empty category: while men are not entirely free to choose *how* to belong and *to what* they will belong, there is *some* range of freedom. Some 40 percent of America's Jews exercise this freedom by joining no synagogue—even if they occasionally enter one. The greater numbers who do belong are often "joiners" for a variety of superficial reasons—as Dr. Gordon's survey records—but they may not always be aware of their deeper motivations. The result is—and here Mr. Glazer is surely correct—that they are choosing to relate themselves to a particular set of values and to co-operative activity with Jewish people. They have not become so acculturated as to relax the traditional Jewish barriers against exogamy. (The data on intermarriage are, like all the demographic material, inadequate—but the rates of intermarriage reported in various surveys do not spell Jewish extinction.)[56] Nor for the most part do they spend their

---

[55] See Gans in *The Jews*, p. 247.

[56] There may be, as Dr. Syrkin suggests (*Jewish Frontier*, January 1961), a differential rate of intermarriage. Jewish intellectuals may have a greater tendency to

leisure time with non-Jews.[57] The zeal for identification as Jews has, as we have seen, many apparent causes. Social self-segregation, endogamy, Jewish education for the children, the growth (and acceptance by non-Jews) of a "Jewish" popular culture[58] are all likely to strengthen this identification in the decades ahead. This pattern of Jewish life does not lack its critics. Not only the habitual cynic will question some of the co-operative activity in which Jews indulge. There is, for example, no special merit in playing bingo with Jews rather than with non-Jews. Indeed there may be greater merit in not playing it at all. Nor is there any obvious virtue in Jewish theatre parties to Broadway productions—even when, as often, such productions have a mediocre, shallow or perverse Jewish content. Yet this triviality need not be mistaken for the total picture. Further trivialities will, no doubt, emerge. Much that is basic to American life seems to exclude significance from the cultural sphere. Yet none can say that a new thoughtfulness or awareness cannot arise. This may happen in many spheres of American life—and only a dogmatic cultural determinism can deny the possibility.[59] So far at least, there are millions of American Jews who, though not profoundly religious, are maintaining contact with some significant Jewish traditions. Can we exclude the possibility that, at some levels of consciousness, they feel that Judaism is not only "different" but also "better?" Perhaps for many this *is* excluded by ignorance and by its frequent corollary

---

marry out; and this may impair the quality—let alone the quantity—of the Jewish population. But there is no means of knowing whether this will be so.

[57] The survey evidence on this is quite impressive. See, for example, H. Gans, loc. cit., p. 226, for the Park Forest data: elsewhere in *The Jews* (p. 311 et seq.) for data on Elmira reported by J. P. Dean. For evidence on commensalism in the Greater Washington area see S. K. Bigman, *The Jewish Population of Greater Washington,* pp. 80–81.

[58] The success which greets the efforts of Mr. Harry Golden is only one of innumerable instances. Equally significant are such plays as *A Majority of One* in which Jewish and Japanese practices are compared with a view to showing how "alike" they are. Plays like *The Tenth Man* are more subtle in their presentation and, some might add, misrepresentation of Jewish themes. Films like *Exodus* combine the mood of the conventional Western with a Zionist flavour—a sure recipe for box office success.

[59] Some conflicting evidence on this possibility may be found in the symposium "Jewishness and the Younger Intellectuals" in *Commentary*, April 1961, p. 306 et seq. Many of the contributors sound complacent and superior persons—with an inclination at times to boast their ignorance of Judaism and their distance from it. Remarkable too is their overall failure to recognize the positive contribution (especially cultural and philanthropic) which Jews now make to American life. But interestingly one of the writers in the symposium, Miss Sonya Rudikoff, in a perceptive glance at the future, leaves open the possibility that ". . . the Jews, whose very existence speaks of history, are necessary to American life not in the old way but in some relation that is still to be revealed. Religion may bcome more significant than culture" (*Commentary,* April 1961, p. 353).

of cultural relativism. But they may not constitute a permanent majority. There are even some who, as Mr. Glazer observes in his concluding paragraph, have shown "a readiness to listen," however indirectly, to "the voice of God."[60]

[60] N. Glazer, *American Judaism*, p. 149.

The final question raised by Gould, "Is this *really* Judaism?," is perhaps better answered by theologians and philosophers than by sociologists. Yet the question is not without its sociological dimension. It can at least be said that some of the changes that have occurred in the American Jewish community in the last several decades can be characterized sociologically as instances of religious change. Moreover, much of what has been said about the Jewish life-style and religiosity in the suburbs has also been said about Catholicism[9] and the major branches of Protestantism.[10] The child-oriented family, greater emphasis upon the educational rather than the ritualistic functions of religious institutions, and the alleged privatization of religious belief are characteristic of much American religion, not just Judaism. This is not to deny the distinctiveness of American Jews as a social and religious group. Just as Abramson has shown the importance of ethnicity for different American Catholics, so it can be argued that American Jews exhibit both religious and communal distinctiveness. Said differently, Judaism functions both in religious and social-communal ways for its adherents in the United States. Gould and others examine both aspects of being Jewish without explicitly stressing such a distinction. One must ask which of the trends described by Gould derive from the explicitly religious aspect of the Jewish community and which derive from the designation of Jews as a distinctive social group?

The preceding several essays have depicted the intricate relationships between religion and other social variables in three major religious collectivities: Protestants, Catholics, and Jews. The concluding essay in this set turns to the fourth major socio-

[9] Andrew Greeley, *The Church and the Suburbs* (New York: Sheed and Ward, 1959).

[10] Gibson Winter, *The Suburban Captivity of the Churches* (Garden City, N.Y.: Doubleday and Company, 1961).

religious group examined in Lenski's *The Religious Factor,* black Christians.[11]

It has frequently been observed that one of the most interesting elements in the transition from Civil Rights to Black Power in the late 1960s was the emergence of both a secular rationale and secular leadership in the struggle for racial justice in the United States. Even prior to the shocking murder of the Reverend Martin Luther King Jr., his role in the movement had been abruptly over-shadowed by secular leaders such as Stokely Carmichael. Similarly, the appeal for equal justice was made increasingly upon secular, not religious, grounds. Black leaders stressed not the nature of God's will but the hypocrisy of the established social system.

In the following essay, Gary Marx examines the role of religion in the emergence of black militancy in the United States. He is concerned not with the degree of religiosity of leaders in the black community, but with the relationship between social militancy and religion for the rank-and-file members of that community.

[11] Lenski actually studied only black Protestants, while Marx's study contains data on both Protestants and Catholics in the black community.

Religion: Opiate or Inspiration of Civil Rights Militancy Among Negroes?*

by Gary T. Marx

The relationship between religion and political radicalism is a confusing one. On the one hand, established religious institutions have generally had a stake in the status quo and hence have supported conservatism. Furthermore, with the masses having an otherworldly orientation, religious zeal, particularly as expressed in the more fundamentalist branches of Christianity, has been seen as an alternative to the development of political radicalism. On the other hand, as the source of universal humanistic values and the strength that can come from believing one is carrying out God's will in political

Gary T. Marx is lecturer in sociology at Harvard University and faculty associate at the Joint Center for Urban Studies. He is the author of *Protest and Prejudice* (1967).

Reprinted from *American Sociological Review*, 32, no. 1 (1967): 64–72. Used with permission of the author and publisher.

* Revision of paper read at the annual meeting of the American Sociological Association, August, 1966. This paper may be identified as publication A-72 of the Survey Research Center, University of California, Berkeley. I am grateful to Gertrude J. Selznick and Stephen Steinberg for their work in the early phase of this project, and to the Anti-Defamation League for support.

matters, religion has occasionally played a strong positive role in movements for radical social change.

This dual role of religion is clearly indicated in the case of the American Negro and race protest. Slaves are said to have been first brought to this country on the "good ship Jesus Christ."[1] While there was occasional controversy over the effect that religion had on them it appears that most slave-owners eventually came to view supervised religion as an effective means of social control. Stampp, in commenting on the effect of religion notes:

> . . . through religious instruction the bondsmen learned that slavery had divine sanction, that insolence was as much an offense against God as against the temporal master. They received the Biblical command that servants should obey their masters, and they heard of the punishments awaiting the disobedient slave in the hereafter. They heard, too, that eternal salvation would be their reward for faithful service . . .[2]

In discussing the period after the Civil War, Myrdal states that ". . . under the pressure of political reaction, the Negro church in the South came to have much the same role as it did before the Civil War. Negro frustration was sublimated into emotionalism, and Negro hopes were fixed on the afterworld."[3] Many other analysts, in considering the consequences of Negro religion from the end of slavery until the early 1950's reached similar conclusions about the conservatizing effect of religion on race protest.[4]

---

[1] Louis Lomax, When the Word Is Given (New York: New American Library, 1964), p. 34.

[2] Kenneth Stampp, The Peculiar Institution (New York: Alfred A. Knopf, 1956), p. 158.

[3] Gunnar Myrdal et al., An American Dilemma (New York: Harper, 1944), pp. 851–853. About the North he notes that the church remained far more independent "but on the whole even the Northern Negro church has remained a conservative institution with its interests directly upon otherworldly matters and has largely ignored the practical problems of the Negro's fate in this world."

[4] For example Dollard reports that "religion can be seen as a mechanism for the social control of Negroes" and that planters have always welcomed the building of a Negro church on the plantation but looked with less favor upon the building of a school. John Dollard, Caste and Class in a Southern Town (Garden City: Doubleday Anchor, 1957), p. 248. A few of the many others reaching similar conclusions are, Benjamin E. Mays and J. W. Nicholson, The Negro's Church (New York: Institute of Social and Religious Research, 1933); Hortense Powdermaker, After Freedom (New York: Viking Press, 1939), p. 285; Charles Johnson, Growing Up in the Black Belt (Washington, D.C.: American Council of Education, 1941), pp. 135–136; St. Clair Drake and Horace Cayton, Black Metropolis (New York: Harper and Row, 1962), pp. 424–429; George Simpson and Milton Yinger, Racial and Cultural Minorities (New York: Harper, rev. ed., 1958), pp. 582–587. In a more

However, the effect of religion on race protest throughout American history has by no means been exclusively in one direction. While many Negroes were no doubt seriously singing about chariots in the sky, Negro preachers such as Denmark Vesey and Nat Turner and the religiously inspired abolitionists were actively fighting slavery in their own way. All Negro churches first came into being as protest organizations and later some served as meeting places where protest strategy was planned, or as stations on the underground railroad. The richness of protest symbolism in Negro spirituals and sermons has often been noted. Beyond this symbolic role, as a totally Negro institution, the church brought together in privacy people with a shared problem. It was from the church experience that many leaders were exposed to a broad range of ideas legitimizing protest and obtained the savoir faire, self-confidence, and organizational experience needed to challenge an oppressive system. A recent commentator states that the slave churches were "the nucleus of the Negro protest" and another that "in religion Negro leaders had begun to find sanction and support for their movements of protest more than 150 years ago."[5]

Differing perceptions of the varied consequences religion may have on protest have continued to the present time. While there has been very little in the way of empirical research on the effect of the Negro church on protest,[6] the literature of race relations is rich with impressionistic statements which generally contradict each other about how the church either encourages and is the source of race protest or inhibits and retards its development. For example, two observers note, "as primitive evangelism gave way to a more sophisticated social consciousness, the church became the spearhead of

---

general context this social control consequence of religion has of course been noted throughout history from Plato to Montesquieu to Marx to Nietzsche to Freud to contemporary social theorists.

[5] Daniel Thompson, "The Rise of Negro Protest," *Annals of the American Academy of Political and Social Science,* 357 (January, 1965).

[6] The empirical evidence is quite limited. The few studies that have been done have focused on the Negro minister. Thompson notes that in New Orleans Negro ministers constitute the largest segment of the Negro leadership class (a grouping which is not necessarily the same as "protest leaders") but that "the vast majority of ministers are primarily interested in their pastoral role . . . their sermons are essentially biblical, dealing only tangentially with social issues." Daniel Thompson, *The Negro Leadership Class* (Englewood Cliffs, New Jersey: Prentice-Hall, 1963), pp. 34–35. Studies of the Negro ministry in Detroit and Richmond, California also stress that only a small fraction of Negro clergymen show any active concern with the civil rights struggle. R. L. Johnstone, *Militant and Conservative Community Leadership Among Negro Clergymen,* Ph.D. dissertation, University of Michigan, Ann Arbor, 1963, and J. Bloom, *The Negro Church and the Movement for Equality,* M.A. thesis, University of California, Berkeley, Department of Sociology, 1966.

Negro protest in the deep South,"[7] while another indicates "the Negro church is a sleeping giant. In civil rights participation its feet are hardly wet."[8] A civil rights activist, himself a clergyman, states: ". . . the church today is central to the movement . . . if there had been no Negro church, there would have been no civil rights movement today."[9] On the other hand, a sociologist, commenting on the more involved higher status ministers, notes: ". . . middle class Negro clergymen in the cities of the South generally advocated cautious gradualism in race activities until the mid-1950s when there was an upsurge of protest sentiment among urban Negroes . . . but most of them [ministers] did not embrace the more vigorous techniques of protest until other leaders took the initiative and gained widespread support."[10] Another sociologist states, "Whatever their previous conservative stance has been, the churches have now become 'spearheads of reform.' "[11] Still another indicates: ". . . the Negro church is particularly culpable for its general lack of concern for the moral and social problems of the community . . . it has been accommodating. Fostering indulgence in religious sentimentality, and riveting the attention of the masses on the bounties of a hereafter, the Negro church remains a refuge, and escape from the cruel realities of the here and now."[12]

Thus one faces opposing views, or at best ambiguity, in contemplating the current effect of religion. The opiating consequences of religion are all too well known as is the fact that the segregated church is durable and offers some advantages to clergy and members that might be denied them in a more integrated society. On the other hand, the prominent role of the Negro church in supplying

[7] Jane Record and Wilson Record, "Ideological Forces and the Negro Protest," *Annals, op. cit.,* p. 92.

[8] G. Booker, *Black Man's America* (Englewood Cliffs, N.J.: Prentice-Hall, 1964), p. 111.

[9] Rev. W. T. Walker, as quoted in William Brink and Louis Harris, *The Negro Revolution in America* (New York: Simon and Schuster, 1964), p. 103.

[10] N. Glenn, "Negro Religion in the U.S." in L. Schneider, *Religion, Culture and Society* (New York: John Wiley, 1964).

[11] Joseph Fichter, "American Religion and the Negro," *Daedalus* (Fall, 1965), p. 1087.

[12] E. U. Essien-Udom, *Black Nationalism* (New York: Dell Publishing Co., 1962), p. 358.

Many other examples of contradictory statements could be offered, sometimes even in the same volume. For example, Carleton Lee stresses the importance of religion for protest while Rayford Logan sees the Negro pastor as an instrument of the white power structure (in a book published to commemorate 100 years of emancipation). Carleton Lee, "Religious Roots of Negro Protest," and Rayford Logan, "Educational Changes Affecting American Negroes," both in Arnold Rose, *Assuring Freedom to the Free* (Detroit: Wayne University Press, 1964).

much of the ideology of the movement, many of its foremost leaders, and an institution around which struggle might be organized—particularly in the South—can hardly be denied. It would appear from the bombings of churches and the writings of Martin Luther King and other religiously inspired activists that for many, religion and protest are closely linked.

Part of this dilemma may lie in the distinction between the church as an institution in its totality and particular individual churches within it, and the further distinctions among different types of individual religious concern. This paper is concerned with the latter subject; it is an inquiry into the relationship between religiosity and response to the civil rights struggle. It first considers how religious denomination affects militancy, and then how various measures of religiosity, taken separately and together, are related to civil rights concern. The question is then asked of those classified as "very religious" and "quite religious," how an "otherworldly orientation"— as opposed to a "temporal" one—affects militancy.

In a nationwide study of Negroes living in metropolitan areas of the United States, a number of questions were asked about religious behavior and beliefs as well as about the civil rights struggle.[13] Seven of the questions dealing with civil rights protest have been combined into an index of conventional militancy.[14] Built into this index are a number of dimensions of racial protest such as impatience over the speed of integration, opposition to discrimination in public facilities and the sale of property, perception of barriers to Negro advancement, support of civil rights demonstrations, and expressed willingness to take part in a demonstration. Those giving the militant response to five or more of the questions are considered militant, those giving such a response to three or four of the questions, moderate, and fewer than three, conservative.[15]

[13] This survey was carried out in 1964 by the Survey Research Center, University of California, Berkeley. A non-Southern metropolitan area probability sample was drawn as well as special area samples of Negroes living in New York City, Chicago, Atlanta, and Birmingham. Since the results reported here are essentially the same for each of these areas, they are treated together. More than 90 percent of the interviews were done with Negro interviewers. Additional methodological details may be found in Gary Marx, *Protest and Prejudice: A Study of Belief in the Black Community* (New York: Harper & Row, 1969).

[14] Attention is directed to conventional militancy rather than to that of the Black Nationalist variety because a very small percentage of the sample offered strong and consistent support for Black Nationalism. As in studying support for the KKK, the Birch Society or the Communist Party, a representative sample of normal size is inadequate.

[15] Each of the items in the index was positively related to every other and the index showed a high degree of internal validity. The index also received external

Denomination

It has long been known that the more fundamentalist sects such as the Holiness groups and the Jehovah's Witnesses are relatively uninterested in movements for secular political change.[16] Such transvaluational movements with their otherworldly orientation and their promise that the last shall be first in the great beyond, are said to solace the individual for his lowly status in this world and to divert concern away from efforts at collective social change which might be brought about by man. While only a minority of Negroes actually belong to such groups, the proportion is higher than among whites. Negro literature is rich in descriptions of these churches and their position on race protest.

In Table 1 it can be seen that those belonging to sects are the least likely to be militant; they are followed by those in predominantly Negro denominations. Ironically those individuals in largely white denominations (Episcopalian, Presbyterian, United Church of Christ, and Roman Catholic) are those most likely to be militant, in spite of the perhaps greater civil rights activism of the Negro denominations. This pattern emerged even when social class was held constant.

In their comments members of the less conventional religious groups clearly expressed the classical attitude of their sects toward

Table 1. Proportion Militant (%) by Denomination*

Denomination	% Militant
Episcopalian	46 (24)
United Church of Christ	42 (12)
Presbyterian	40 (25)
Catholic	40 (109)
Methodist	34 (142)
Baptist	32 (658)
Sects and Cults	20 (106)

* 25 respondents are not shown in this table because they did not specify a denomination, or belonged to a non-Christian religious group or other small Christian group.

validation from a number of additional questions. For example, the percentage belonging to a civil rights organization went from zero among those lowest in militancy to 38 percent for those who were highest, and the percentage thinking that civil rights demonstrations had helped a great deal increased from 23 percent to 58 percent. Those thinking that the police treated Negroes very well deceased from 35 percent to only 2 percent among those highest in militancy.

[16] Liston Pope, *Millhands and Preachers* (New Haven: Yale University Press, 1942), p. 137; J. Milton Yinger, *Religion, Society, and the Individual* (New York: The Macmillan Company, 1957), pp. 170–173.

participation in the politics of the secular world. For example, an Evangelist in the Midwest said, "I don't believe in participating in politics. My church don't vote—they just depends on the plans of God." And an automobile serviceman in Philadelphia stated, "I, as a Jehovah's Witness, cannot express things involving the race issue." A housewife in the Far West ventured, "In my religion we do not approve of anything except living like it says in the Bible; demonstrations mean calling attention to you and it's sinful."

The finding that persons who belong to sects are less likely to be militant than the non-sect members is to be expected; clearly this type of religious involvement seems an alternative for most people to the development of radicalism. But what of the religious style of those in the more conventional churches which may put relatively less stress on the after-life and encourage various forms of secular participation? Are the more religiously inclined within these groups also less likely to be militant?

Religiosity

The present study measured several dimensions of religious involvement. Those interviewed were asked how important religion was to them, several questions about orthodoxy of belief, and how frequently they attended worship service.[17] Even with the sects excluded, irrespective of the dimension of religiosity considered, the greater the religiosity the lower the percentage militant. (See Tables 2, 3, and 4.) For example, militancy increases consistently from a low of only 29 percent among those who said religion was "extremely

Table 2. Militancy by Subjective Importance Assigned to Religion*

Importance	% Militant
Extremely important	29 (668)
Somewhat important	39 (195)
Fairly important	48 (96)
Not too important	56 (18)
Not at all important	62 (13)

* Sects are excluded here and in all subsequent tables.

[17] These dimensions and several others are suggested by Charles Y. Glock in "On the Study of Religious Commitment," *Religious Education Research Supplement,* 57 (July–August, 1962), pp. 98–100. For another measure of religious involvement, the number of church organizations belonged to, the same inverse relationship was noted.

Table 3. Militancy by Orthodoxy

Orthodoxy	% Militant
Very high	27 (414)
High	34 (333)
Medium	39 (144)
Low	47 (68)
Very low	54 (35)

important" to a high of 62 percent for those who indicated that religion was "not at all important" to them. For those very high in orthodoxy (having no doubt about the existence of God or the devil) 27 percent were militant while for those totally rejecting these ideas 54 percent indicated great concern over civil rights. Militancy also varies inversely with frequency of attendance at worship service.[18]

Each of these items was strongly related to every other; when taken together they help us to better characterize religiosity. Accordingly they have been combined into an overall measure of religiosity. Those scored as "very religious" in terms of this index attended

Table 4. Militancy by Frequency of Attendance at Worship Services

Frequency	% Militant
More than once a week	27 (81)
Once a week	32 (311)
Once a month or more but less than once a week	34 (354)
Less than once a month	38 (240)

[18] There is a popular stereotype that Negroes are a "religious people." Social science research has shown that they are "over-churched" relative to whites, i.e., the ratio of Negro churches to the size of the Negro population is greater than the same ratio for whites. Using data from a nationwide survey of whites, by Gertrude Selznick and Stephen Steinberg, some comparison of the religiosity of Negroes and whites was possible. When these various dimensions of religiosity were examined, with the effect of education and region held constant, Negroes appeared as significantly more religious *only* with respect to the subjective importance assigned to religion. In the North, whites were more likely to attend church at least once a week than were Negroes; while in the South rates of attendance were the same. About the same percentage of both groups had no doubts about the existence of God. While Negroes were more likely to be sure about the existence of a devil, whites, surprisingly, were more likely to be sure about a life beyond death. Clearly, then, any assertions about the greater religiosity of Negroes relative to whites are unwarranted unless one specifies the dimension of religiosity.

church at least once a week, felt that religion was extremely important to them, and had no doubts about the existence of God and
the devil. For progressively lower values of the index, frequency of
church attendance, the importance of religion, and acceptance of
the belief items decline consistently until, for those scored "not at
all religious," church is rarely if ever attended, religion is not considered personally important and the belief items are rejected.

Using this measure for non-sect members, civil rights militancy
increases from a low of 26 percent for those labeled "very religious"
to 30 percent for the "somewhat religious" to 45 percent for those
"not very religious" and up to a high of 70 percent for those "not at
all religious"[19] (Table 5).

Table 5. Militancy by Religiosity

Religiosity	Very Religious	Somewhat Religious	Not Very Religious	Not at All Religious
% Militant	26	30	45	70
N	(230)	(523)	(195)	(36)

Religiosity and militancy are also related to age, sex, education,
religious denomination, and region of the country. The older, the
less educated, women, Southerners, and those in Negro denominations are more likely to be religious and to have lower percentages
scoring as militant. Thus it is possible that the relationship observed
is simply a consequence of the fact that both religiosity and militancy are related to some third factor. In Table 6 it can be seen,
however, that even when these variables are controlled the relationship is maintained. That is, even among those in the North, the
younger, male, more educated, and those affiliated with predominantly white denominations, the greater the religiosity, the less
the militancy.

[19] When the sects are included in these tables the results are the same. The
sects have been excluded because they offer almost no variation to be analyzed
with respect to the independent variable. Since virtually all of the sect members
scored as either "very religious" or "somewhat religious," it is hardly possible to
measure the effect of their religious involvement on protest attitudes. In addition
the import of the relationships shown in these tables is considerably strengthened
when it is demonstrated that religious involvement inhibits militancy even when
the most religious and least militant group, the sects, are excluded.

Table 6. Proportion Militant (%) by Religiosity, for Education, Age, Region, Sex, and Denomination

	Very Religious	Somewhat Religious	Not Very Religious	Not at All Religious
Education				
Grammar school	17 (108)	22 (201)	31 (42)	50 (2)
High school	34 (96)	32 (270)	45 (119)	58 (19)
College	38 (26)	48 (61)	59 (34)	87 (15)
Age				
18–29	33 (30)	37 (126)	44 (62)	62 (13)
30–44	30 (53)	34 (180)	48 (83)	74 (19)
45–59	25 (71)	27 (131)	45 (33)	50 (2)
60+	22 (76)	18 (95)	33 (15)	100 (2)
Region				
Non-South	30 (123)	34 (331)	47 (159)	70 (33)
South	22 (107)	23 (202)	33 (36)	66 (3)
Sex				
Men	28 (83)	33 (220)	44 (123)	72 (29)
Women	26 (147)	28 (313)	46 (72)	57 (7)
Denomination				
Episcopalian, Presbyterian, United Church of Christ	20 (15)	27 (26)	33 (15)	60 (5)
Catholic	13 (15)	39 (56)	36 (25)	77 (13)
Methodist	46 (24)	22 (83)	50 (32)	100 (2)
Baptist	25 (172)	29 (354)	45 (117)	53 (15)

The incompatibility between piety and protest shown in these data becomes even more evident when considered in light of comments offered by the respondents. Many religious people hold beliefs which clearly inhibit race protest. For a few there was the notion that segregation and a lowly status for Negroes was somehow God's will and not for man to question. Thus a housewife in South Bend, Indiana, in saying that civil rights demonstrations had hurt Negroes, added: "God is the Creator of everything. We don't know why we are dark-skinned. We should try to put forth the effort to do what God wants and not question."[20]

[20] Albert Cardinal Meyer notes that the Catholic Bishops of the U.S. said in their statement of 1958: "The heart of the race question is moral and religious." "Interracial Justice and Love," in M. Ahmann, ed., Race Challenge to Religion (Chicago: H. Regnery, 1963), p. 126. These data, viewed from the perspective of the activist seeking to motivate Negroes on behalf of the civil rights struggle, suggest that this statement has a meaning which Their Excellencies no doubt did not intend.

A Negro spiritual contains the lines "I'm gonna wait upon the Lord till my change comes." For our respondents a more frequently stated belief stressed that God as the absolute controller of the universe would bring about change in his own way and at his own time, rather than expressing segregation as God's will. In indicating her unwillingness to take part in a civil rights demonstration, a Detroit housewife said, "I don't go for demonstrations. I believe that God created all men equal and at His appointed time He will give every man his portion, no one can hinder it." And in response to a question about whether or not the government in Washington was pushing integration too slowly, a retired clerk in Atlanta said: "You can't hurry God. He has a certain time for this to take place. I don't know about Washington."

Others who desired integration more strongly and wanted immediate social change felt that (as Bob Dylan sings) God was on their side. Hence man need do nothing to help bring about change. Thus a worker in Cleveland, who was against having more civil rights demonstrations, said: "With God helping to fight our battle, I believe we can do with fewer demonstrations." And in response to a question about whether Negroes should spend more time praying and less time demonstrating, an Atlanta clergyman, who said "more time praying," added "praying is demonstrating."[21]

Religion Among the Militants

Although the net effect of religion is clearly to inhibit attitudes of protest it is interesting to consider this relationship in the opposite direction, i.e., observe religiosity among those characterized as militant, moderate, and conservative with respect to the civil rights struggle. As civil rights concern increases, religiosity decreases (Table 7). Militants were twice as likely to be scored "not very religious" or "not at all religious" as were conservatives. This table is also of interest because it shows that, even for the militants, a majority were scored either "very religious" or "somewhat religious." Clearly, for many, a religious orientation and a concern with racial protest are not mutually exclusive.

[21] A study of ministers in Richmond, California, notes that, although almost all questioned were opposed to discrimination, very few had taken concrete action, in part because of their belief that God would take care of them. One minister noted, "I believe that if we all was as pure . . . as we ought to be, there would be no struggle. God will answer my prayer. If we just stay with God and have faith. *When Peter was up, did the people march to free him? No. He prayed, and God did something about it.*" (Bloom, *op. cit.,* italics added.)

Table 7. Religiosity by Civil Rights Militancy

	Militants	Moderates	Conservatives
Very religious	18%	24%	28%
Somewhat religious	48	57	55
Not very religious	26	17	16
Not at all religious	8	2	1
Total	100	100	100
N	332	419	242

Given the active involvement of some churches, the singing of protest spirituals, and the ideology of the movement as it relates to Christian principles of love, equality, passive suffering,[22] and the appeal to a higher moral law, it would be surprising if there were only a few religious people among the militants.

A relevant question accordingly is: Among the religious, what are the intervening links which determine whether religion is related to an active concern with racial matters or has an opiating effect?[23] From the comments reported above it seemed that, for some, belief in a highly deterministic God inhibited race protest. Unfortunately the study did not measure beliefs about the role of God as against the role of men in the structuring of human affairs. However, a related variable was measured which would seem to have much relevance—the extent to which these religious people were concerned with the here and now as opposed to the after-life.

The classical indictment of religion from the Marxist perspective is that by focusing concern on a glorious after-life the evils of this life are ignored. Of course there are important differences among religious institutions and among individuals with respect to the importance given to other worldly concerns. Christianity, as with most ideologies, contains within it, if not out-and-out contradictory themes, then certainly themes which are likely to be in tension with one another. In this fact, no doubt, lies part of the explanation of religion's varied consequences for protest. One important strand of Christianity stresses acceptance of one's lot and glorifies the after-

[22] Nonviolent resistance as it relates to Christianity's emphasis on suffering, sacrifice, and privation, is discussed by James W. Vander Zanden, "The Non-Violent Resistance Movement Against Segregation," *American Journal of Sociology*, 68 (March, 1963), pp. 544–550.

[23] Of course, a most relevant factor here is the position of the particular church that an individual is involved in. Unfortunately, it was difficult to obtain such information in a nationwide survey.

life;[24] another is more concerned with the realization of Judeo-Christian values in the current life. King and his followers clearly represent this latter "social gospel" tradition.[25] Those with the type of temporal concern that King represents would be expected to be higher in militancy. A measure of temporal vs. otherworldly concern has been constructed. On the basis of two questions, those interviewed have been classified as having either an otherworldly or a temporal orientation.[26] The evidence is that religiosity and otherworldly concern increase together. For example, almost 100 percent of the "not at all religious" group were considered to have a temporal orientation, but only 42 percent of the "very religious" (Table 8). Those in predominantly white denominations were more likely to have a temporal orientation than those in all-black denominations.

Among the religious groups, if concern with the here and now is a relevant factor in overcoming the opiating effect of religion then it is to be anticipated that those considered to have a temporal reli-

---

[24] The Muslims have also made much of this theme within Christianity, and their militancy is certainly tied to a rejection of otherworldly religiosity. The Bible is referred to as a "poison book" and the leader of the Muslims states, "No one after death has ever gone any place but where they were carried. There is no heaven or hell other than on earth for you and me, and Jesus was no exception. His body is still ... in Palestine and will remain there." (As quoted in C. Eric Lincoln, *The Black Muslims in America* (Boston: Beacon Press, 1961), p. 123.

However, while they reject the otherworldly theme, they nevertheless rely heavily on a deterministic Allah; according to E. U. Essien-Udom, this fact leads to political inactivity. He notes, "The attainment of black power is relegated to the intervention of "Almighty Allah" sometime in the future ... Not unlike other religionists, the Muslims too may wait for all eternity for the coming of the Messiah, the predicted apocalypse in 1970 notwithstanding." E. U. Essien-Udom, *Black Nationalism, op. cit.,* pp. 313–314.

[25] He states: "Any religion that professes to be concerned with the souls of men and is not concerned with the slums that damn them, the economic conditions that strangle them, and the social conditions that cripple them is a dry-as-dust religion." He further adds, perhaps in a concession, that "such a religion is the kind the Marxists like to see—an opiate of the people." Martin Luther King, *Stride Toward Freedom* (New York: Ballantine Books, 1958), pp. 28–29.

John Lewis, a former SNCC leader and once a Baptist Divinity student, is said to have peered through the bars of a Southern jail and said, "Think not that I am come to send peace on earth. I came not to send peace, but a sword." (Matthew 10:34.)

[26] The two items used in this index were: "How sure are you that there is a life beyond death?"; and "Negroes should spend more time praying and less time demonstrating." The latter item may seem somewhat circular when observed in relation to civil rights concern. However, this is precisely what militancy is all about. Still it would have been better to measure otherworldly vs. temporal concern in a less direct fashion; unfortunately, no other items were available. Because of this the data shown here must be interpreted with caution. However it does seem almost self-evident that civil rights protest which is religiously inspired is related to a temporal religious outlook.

Table 8. Proportion (%) with Temporal (as Against Otherworldly) Concern, by Religiosity

Religiosity	% with Temporal Concern
Very religious	42 (225)
Somewhat religious	61 (531)
Not very religious	82 (193)
Not at all religious	98 (34)

gious orientation would be much higher in militancy than those scored as otherworldly. This is in fact the case. Among the otherworldly religious, only 16 percent were militant; this proportion increases to almost 40 percent among those considered "very religious" and "somewhat religious" who have a temporal religious outlook (Table 9). Thus it would seem that an important factor in determin-

Table 9. Proportion Militant (%) by Religiosity and Temporal or Otherworldly Concern

Concern	Very Religious	Somewhat Religious
Temporal	39 (95)	38 (325)
Otherworldly	15 (130)	17 (206)

ing the effect of religion on protest attitudes is the nature of an individual's religious commitment. It is quite possible, for those with a temporal religious orientation, that—rather than the effect of religion being somehow neutralized (as in the case of militancy among the "not religious" groups)—their religious concern serves to inspire and sustain race protest. This religious inspiration can, of course, be clearly noted among some active civil rights participants.

Conclusion

The effect of religiosity on race protest depends on the type of religiosity involved. Past literature is rich in suggestions that the religiosity of the fundamentalist sects is an alternative to the development of political radicalism. This seems true in the case of race protest as well. However, in an overall sense even for those who belong to the more conventional churches, the greater the religious involvement, whether measured in terms of ritual activity, orthodoxy of religious belief, subjective importance of religion, or the three taken together, the lower the degree of militancy.

Among sect members and religious people with an otherworldly orientation, religion and race protest appear to be, if not mutually exclusive, then certainly what one observer has referred to as "mutually corrosive kinds of commitments."[27] Until such time as religion loosens its hold over these people or comes to embody to a greater extent the belief that man as well as God can bring about secular change, and focuses more on the here and now, religious involvement may be seen as an important factor working against the widespread radicalization of the Negro public.

However, it has also been noted that many militant people are nevertheless religious. When a distinction is made among the religious between the "otherworldly" and the "temporal," for many of the latter group, religion seems to facilitate or at least not to inhibit protest. For these people religion and race protest may be mutually supportive.

Thirty years ago Donald Young wrote: "One function which a minority religion may serve is that of reconciliation with inferior status and its discriminatory consequences ... on the other hand, religious institutions may also develop in such a way as to be an incitement and support of revolt against inferior status."[28] The current civil rights struggle and the data observed here certainly suggest that this is the case. These contradictory consequences of religion are somewhat reconciled when one distinguishes among different segments of the Negro church and types of religious concern among individuals.

[27] Rodney Stark, "Class, Radicalism, and Religious Involvement," *American Sociological Review,* 29 (October, 1964), p. 703.

[28] Donald Young, *American Minority Peoples* (New York: Harper, 1937), p. 204. These data are also consistent with Merton's statement that it is premature to conclude that "all religion everywhere has only the one consequence of making for mass apathy" and his insistence on recognizing the "multiple consequences" and "net balance of aggregate consequences" of a given institution such as religion. Robert Merton, *Social Theory and Social Structure* (Glencoe: Free Press, 1957, revised edition), p. 44.

Marx's study, like the others presented here, conveys the message that religion has a powerful effect upon the social structure and upon the lives of people with strong religious beliefs. Yet, a corollary of this theme is that religion's meaning in social life and its consequences for the social order vary from one religious group to the next and from one *type* of religious group to the next.

One is compelled to ask whether the forceful theoretical statements about religion offered by the classical theorists, Marx, Weber, Durkheim, and others, are still relevant today? Clearly they are. In large part, contemporary research has not allowed us to discard our classical heritage, but has helped us to refine and specify some of the social meanings of religion about which the classical founders of the discipline wrote. Weber was perhaps correct about the unique effects of the Protestant social ethic in the United States. But over time, we have learned that the Protestant ethic has become reshaped and diffused in various ways by the different forms of latter-day Protestantism. Marx was indeed correct in seeing religion as an opiate that retarded social change. Yet both Marx's and Durkheim's observations about the role of religion in maintaining social order can be refined by what contemporary research tells us concerning the variety of religions in the modern world. The several preceding essays are of value not just because they enhance our empirical knowledge about religion in society and hence our ability to theorize about it, but also because they are valuable exemplars in showing how the process of scientific knowledge about religion advances.

Part V

Organizational Forms and Processes of Religion

The categorization of different types of phenomena is a basic task in any branch of science. It is no less so for the sociology of religion. The differences and similarities between religious groups, the processes by which they wither and grow, and the typical social correlates and consequences of different forms of religion are all essential areas of inquiry within the field. While there have been significant advances in our knowledge in the past several decades, this does not mean that these questions are easily answered. Both the number and diversity of religious groups in the United States are immense. There are well over 300 different Protestant groups alone, and even those scholars that have attempted a simple description and listing of them admit that their efforts are far from complete.[1] The following four essays provide a sampling of ways of conceptualizing this diversity. Each of them offers a somewhat different strategy of analysis and, as might be expected, each paints a different picture of the organizational expressions of religion in the United States.

[1] See Elmer T. Clark, *The Small Sects in America* (Nashville: Abingdon Press, rev. ed., 1965); Frank S. Mead, *Handbook of Denominations in the United States* (Nashville: Abingdon Press, rev. ed., 1965); and *Yearbook of American Churches* (New York: National Council of Churches of Christ, annual editions).

The most persistent and most controversial avenue of analysis of types of religious groups stems from the Troelstch-Weber church-sect dychotomy. Just as it is likely that these two concepts will continue to be used by sociologists of religion, so it is likely that there will continue to be periodic revisions of how they should be defined and employed.[2] Even Benton Johnson, the author of the following essay, has expressed views on the subject that are different from those he provides here. This essay, which was the first of several he has written on church and sect,[3] traces the history of these concepts and offers at least one important set of criteria for defining and utilizing these two terms.

[2] A symposium on the church-sect distinction appears in *Journal for the Scientific Study of Religion*, 6, no. 1 (1967): 64–90. Much of the literature in the controversy is discussed in J. Milton Yinger, *The Scientific Study of Religion* (New York: Macmillan, 1970), pp. 256, 280–281.

[3] His other writings on the subject include the following: "Do Holiness Sects Socialize to Dominant Values?," *Social Forces*, 39 (1961): 309–316; "On Church and Sect," *American Sociological Review*, 28 (1963): 539–549; and "Church and Sect Revisited," *Journal for the Scientific Study of Religion*, 10, no. 2 (1971): 124–137.

A Critical Appraisal of the Church-Sect Typology[*]
by Benton Johnson

Church and Sect are two much-used concepts in the sociology of religion. They have been applied to many manifestations of the Christian faith and today seem to be in as good favor as ever as basic tools in the analysis of the structure of groups in the Christian tradition. Though sociologists are only partly agreed on the defini-

Benton Johnson is professor of sociology at the University of Oregon. He is a past editor of the *Journal for the Scientific Study of Religion* and is co-editor (with Phillip Hammond) of the book *American Mosaic: Social Patterns of Religion in the United States* (1970).

Reprinted from *American Sociological Review*, 22, no. 1 (1957): 88–92. Used with permission of the author and publisher.

[*] Revised version of paper read at the annual meeting of the American Sociological Society, September 1955.

tions of Church and Sect, the concepts have been applied frequently, especially to the complex and interesting field of American Protestantism.

The way that sociologists have construed these concepts seems to have narrowed their range of applicability and limited their usefulness in new fields of research. This paper has two aims: (1) to examine the accepted definitions of Church and Sect with an eye to sharpening them and attempting to delineate the path by which they may be integrated into a general sociology of religion, and (2) to develop some immediate implications of the reformulated typology in the area of American Protestantism.

The classical statement of the Church-Sect typology was made by Ernst Troeltsch. Max Weber also made substantial contributions. Although the typology was posed as an ideal type, thereby consisting in a set of general structural features all of which need not be manifested in every case, the low state of development of ideal-type methodology has meant that for practical purposes each of the two concepts refers to a loosely integrated listing of empirical characteristics.[1]

The main attention of this paper is given to those sociologists who have endeavored to bring conceptual order out of an array of characteristics. It is they who have used the typology most profitably from a research standpoint, but even so it appears that in reducing it to manageable proportions they have discarded precisely those aspects that may be most promising both in new research areas and in conceptual growth. The reformulation proposed below will modify the significance of the research undertaken under the previous definition but it will not jeopardize established insights. Perhaps it will clarify the place of Church and Sect in the sociology of religion and lay down an important methodological principle in this field.

Troeltsch conceived of Church and Sect as separate and distinct, representing two radically different structural and value orientational tendencies in Christianity. He defined the Church as an institution that is sole keeper of the means of grace[2] and that dispenses this to its communicants through rites which may be performed only by ordained functionaries. Connection with the Church is a recognized obligation of maturing children of affiliated families. In social ethic

---

[1] This type of approach is exemplified by the following works: Elmer T. Clark, *The Small Sects in America* (Nashville: Abingdon-Cokesbury Press, rev. ed., 1949), pp. 6, 9–24; Charles S. Braden, "The Sects," *The Annals of the American Academy of Political and Social Science*, 56 (March 1948): 53–54.

[2] Ernst Troeltsch, *The Social Teaching of the Christian Churches*, trans. by Olive Wyon (New York: The Macmillan Company, 1932), v. 1, p. 331 ff.

the Church is conservative, accepting as much of the secular social order as it can. The Sect is a voluntary association of persons committed to an ethico-religious ideal, which its members attempt to manifest in their own behavior.[3] There is no priestly mediation of grace nor is grace conceived to be the property of the Sect. In social ethic the Sect is either revolutionary, seeking radically to reform the existing social order, or passively critical, ultimately withdrawing into small communities where the pure religious ideal can be practiced.

Since Troeltsch was primarily interested in the social ethic of Christian groups, their attitudes toward the secular culture assumed a definitive position in his typology. He assumed that Sects were essentially at sharp variance with secular values and that in order to survive they had to come to some *modus vivendi* with the "world." This usually involved their extinction or their settling down into socially isolated, ingrown communities.[4]

Guided by this formulation one may readily classify as Churches the Roman Catholic, Anglican, Lutheran, and Orthodox communions. When it comes to classifying Sects there is not much trouble with most of the pre-Reformation groups, with the Quakers and the Anabaptists, or even with the modern Holiness movement. Calvinism, on the other hand, presents some difficulties with which Troeltsch himself grappled but which he did not resolve. He perceived that its religious ideal did not reject society and its functional requirements. For this reason alone he regarded Calvinism as basically Churchly. In addition it aimed at an orderly incorporation of all persons within its fold. But there were also Sectarian aspects of Calvinism,[5] which as it was planted in new environments loomed large. There was a clear distinction between the "worldly" and the righteous, there was not priesthood, and morality was rigidly enforced.

Troeltsch's "Free Church" concept was intended to point the way out of the mixture of types that Calvinism seemed to represent. This concept, however, was not well spelled out and at best is simply a recognition of an empirical type manifesting mixed features.[6] The

---

[3] *Ibid.*

[4] *Ibid.,* pp. 344–346.

[5] *Ibid.,* v. 2, p. 593 ff., p. 656 ff.

[6] *Ibid.,* v. 2, pp. 707–708. Von Wiese and Becker have recommended that the term "denomination" be used for essentially the same phenomenon. For our purposes the term has descriptive merit since it refers to a Sect that has grown tame after becoming large. (Leopold von Wiese and Howard Becker, *Systematic Sociology* [New York: J. Wiley and Sons, Inc., 1932], pp. 621–628.)

basic difficulties remained. Research that made use of the typology in studying American Protestantism should have been immediately on guard, for it is generally agreed that Calvinism has exerted an exceedingly powerful influence on the religion of this country.

Richard Niebuhr deserves the credit for adapting the typology to research in American Protestantism.[7] Recognizing it as unwieldy and perceiving its "static" nature, he attempted a reformulation based upon what he considered the essential differentiating criteria between Church and Sect. Assuming the definitiveness of attitude toward the secular culture, Niebuhr simplified the original statement of the typology and developed certain implications he saw as logically following from a clear statement of the underlying features of the two types. Troeltsch had observed that Sects must make some reconciliation with the "world" or suffer extinction. Niebuhr proposed that the typology be used to study the processes by which Sects effect this reconciliation. This is the origin of the well-known hypothesis that Sects develop ultimately into Churches—that is, that the attitude toward the secular culture in time undergoes a change from harsh rejection to a degree of toleration or even acceptance.

The findings of Niebuhr, Liston Pope[8] and others seem to point to important changes in the development of newly formed Protestant Sects in America. These changes involve a lessening of the original rigidly drawn line between the "saved" and the "worldly." Mention is made of accommodation to standards of the larger society, relaxing a strict moral code, letting down rigorous membership requirements as the second generation is maturing, etc.

Since this statement of the typology is based squarely and unambiguously on attitude toward the secular culture, it is concluded that once Sects have relaxed their opposition to worldly ways, they are Churches. Other aspects of Troeltsch's formulation are ignored or treated as empirical adjuncts. The conceptual difficulty with Calvinism drops out of view and the large, established Protestant denominations plus many of the newer or smaller ones are classified as Churches together with the Lutheran, Anglican, Orthodox and Roman Catholic.

While there can be no doubt that the Niebuhr formulation has been instrumental in producing some significant findings, it is ap-

[7] H. Richard Niebuhr, *The Social Sources of Denominationalism* (New York: Henry Holt and Company, 1929), pp. 17–21.

[8] Liston Pope, *Millhands and Preachers* (New Haven: Yale University Press, 1942), pp. 117–124.

parent that its usefulness is now more or less limited to the conceptualizing of a developmental sequence that seems to take place in some areas of American Protestantism. New theoretical explorations are needed.

In aiming at developing the typology for the broadest possible use it will be necessary to examine once more the underlying criteria used to distinguish the two types. In attempting the structural analysis of a social system it is necessary to focus internally in the first instance, that is upon the nature of its various roles. The Niebuhr formulation has not done this. Attitude toward the secular culture is at best a derivative of other beliefs that provide the actual rallying point for adherents and furnish the basis for the precipitation of a social system. Attitude toward the world refers to outer things not immediately connected with the sacred itself, which is the heart and soul of religion.

To focus on the nature of roles within the system one should state clearly what aspects of this rather complex field are being selected for study. It is fairly well agreed that religious behavior involves the attainment by committed individuals of a favorable relationship to sacred objects and ideals. This behavior is not instrumental or utilitarian but symbolic and ritualistic. The individual who is committed to a set of beliefs about the ultimate nature of things attempts to "uphold" them by certain regularly prescribed acts. In this way he not only secures a more thorough identity with the ideals from a psychological standpoint, he also reaffirms his status in the religious system. Our interest, then, will not be in the totality of accepted behavior associated with religions, nor even in the wide assortment of acts of "piety." It will be specifically in that regularly undertaken set of behaviors which out of all other permissible behaviors enjoys a primacy in the affirming of religious status. This central aspect of the ritual system may be called the *process of justification*. The question that next arises is, "What *kind* of justification do given religions have?"

This approach is judged to be a necessary and logical one if we are to construct systematic theory in the field of the sociology of religion. A sound comprehension of paramount aspects of the ritual system of a religion would seem to be essential to assessing the significance of the great mass of usage that makes up the other structural features found with it. The lack of sharp methods of analysis has made the comparative study of religion a rather confusing, descriptive business.

The Church-Sect typology may now be built according to the above criteria. Both Troeltsch and Weber mentioned elements in their formulation of the typology that bear directly upon the process of justification, or "salvation" in the Christian sense. The sacramental system of the Church, with its conception of the transmission of grace through ceremonies performed by qualified priests, is such an element. Troeltsch clearly regarded this to be the crucial means of securing "grace" or religious assurance in a Church situation.[9] This basic institutional pattern, as well as the orientation to securing religious status through participation in sacred ceremony performed by functionaries, may be called the *liturgical* means of justification.

The attainment of justification in the Sect does not take place within a liturgical framework despite the presence of some ritual or sacramental usage. Both Troeltsch and Weber have noted that the Sect is characterized by a strict ethical code that its adherents are expected to live up to.[10] The Sect is an association of ethical virtuosos who attempt to realize in their own conduct the principles in terms of which they are united. This primacy, then, of an *ethical* orientation to justification (whatever the actual content of the ethic) distinguishes the Sect from the Church from the point of view of behavior crucial to religious status.[11]

The liturgical-ethical orientation to justification is not an exhaustive account of the possible kinds of ritual systems in religion. It is simply a way of noting what the two most important structural types in Christianity seem to incorporate. What is now needed is a search for such an exhaustive list of kinds of ritual systems and their implications for the larger structure of religions. Church and Sect would then be only two types in a field of several. Although this abstract pursuit cannot be undertaken now, we will turn to some preliminary implications of the new formulation in the immediate, empirically relevant field of American Protestanism.

Troeltsch's difficulty with Calvinism may be completely resolved if one accepts the primacy of the process of justification in defining the type. The large American Protestant denominations are without doubt structurally Sectarian. The reasons for so typing them may be briefly reviewed. First, it is hard to find a genuinely sacramental tendency in American Protestantism. Except within the Episcopal

---

[9] Troeltsch, *op. cit.*, v. 1, p. 338.

[10] *Ibid.*, v. 1, p. 348 ff.

[11] The objection may be raised that this formulation neglects the factor of "faith through grace" in Protestant justification and places undue emphasis upon "works." The preferred state of motivational commitment to the religious ideal (a principal referent of "faith" for the sociologist) must of course be taken into consideration in any full and extended analysis, but our present focus is upon systems of behavior manifesting commitment.

church, which is ambivalently Protestant and has never been without a formal liturgical framework, there is no movement self-consciously aimed at channeling grace to communicants through sacred ceremonies. This can be affirmed despite the long-term tendency to greater formalism or "dignity" in worship. Though this trend should be watched by sociologists, the new forms are anything but "means of grace" in the sacramental sense. Throughout most of American Protestantism the Sectarian sentiment persists that the sincerity of a person's spiritual exercises, professions, even church attendance, is measurable by the quality of his daily life. Such a full-blown ethical position is impossible in Catholicism. Second, there is no indication of a change in the ministerial role in the direction of converting it into one endowed with a monopoly on the distribution of grace to the laity. The traditional Calvinist ministerial function of instructing and setting an example among a group of religious peers is changing, but it seems bound in the direction of an executive, secular-bureaucratic definition.

If the bulk of non-Lutheran, non-Anglican Protestantism in America is to be called Sectarian, what is the fate of the Niebuhr hypothesis that Sects must develop into Churches? Certainly the proposition cannot continue to be entertained in its present form because most of Protestantism can not be placed in the Church category.

There is very good reason to suspect that the Sect-to-Church hypothesis was a generalization of rather limited application anyway. Most research within this framework has been done on Calvinist-type denominations, indeed denominations of a revivalistic, moralistic sort. Their development toward a more sedate middle-class norm has been noted. In other words a particular kind of ethico-ritual system has been focused on. Paradoxically those radically "anti-worldly" groups, which Troeltsch would unhesitatingly have called Sects, cannot be understood so clearly in terms of the Sect-to-Church hypothesis. The major historical trend of the Amish, the Shakers, or to a lesser extent the Quakers can scarcely be understood as a simple process of "accommodation" to the values of the outer society. It seems safe to say that despite some astute and valid observations that Niebuhr makes in presenting his Sect-to-Church hypothesis,[12] the actual developmental sequence he poses is pretty much confined to voluntarist Calvinist Sects in a mobile society.

[12] Niebuhr (op. cit.) makes the point that family solidarity of necessity impairs the fervor of a religion. While this is true we do not believe that factors such as this make Sectarianism impossible on a long-term basis unless one uses the term in some pure, utopian form.

What is needed now in this field is an understanding of how particular kinds of ethical belief systems affect the overall structure and developmental potential of Sects. One of the reasons why most expressions of a Calvinist ethic have been assimilable by the secular culture is that Calvinism has never rejected too many socially basic functions or posed too utopian an ideal. Without doubt this assimilability has much to do with why aggressive new Sects *can* grow and become large denominations.

The new typology suggests some interesting interpretations among those Sects that do develop along the lines laid down by Niebuhr and Pope. One of the first implications of the new formulation is that the divergence between the actual content of the value systems of the old-line denominations like the Methodists and Presbyterians and that of new aggressive Sects like the Holiness may not be as great as once assumed. The latter already contain the seeds of growth into the former.

The author has strong preliminary indications from his research into Holiness groups of a basic ethical primacy obscured by a more striking emotionalism.[13] The content of this ethic is largely what Weber calls "inner-worldly asceticism"; it is oriented to production rather than to consumption, to achievement for its own sake, to leading consistent, disciplined lives. In short, in many new Sectarian movements the underlying ethical themes are already framed in the same general terms as those of the older denominations.

John Holt noted some years ago that most of the phenomenal growth of the Holiness movement in the South had taken place in those areas characterized by rapid industrial or agricultural development.[14] He saw this as an attempt on the part of new lower-class elements in these areas to cope with the disruption of their traditional rural life patterns. He viewed the resulting upsurge of Holiness religion as "reactionary and [morally] reformist" rather than "constructive."

As an alternative hypothesis, Holiness religion may be a powerful

---

[13] G. Benton Johnson, *A Framework for the Analysis of Religious Action with Special Reference to Holiness and Non-Holiness Groups* (unpublished doctoral dissertation, Harvard University, 1953). The author found nearly unanimous agreement among his Holiness informants that a person cannot be a sincere, converted Christian (despite "spiritual" manifestations such as prayer, testimonials, and even speaking in tongues) without leading a scrupulously moral life. It is possible, however, to lead a moral life, refrain from "spiritual" signs and be considered a Christian so long as commitment to the religious ideals is understood. The author does not assume that all Pentecostal or Holiness groups are ethical Sects.

[14] John B. Holt, "Holiness Religion: Cultural Shock and Social Reorganization," in *American Sociological Review*, 5 (October 1940): 740–747.

agent in socializing lower-class groups in the values and usages of our predominantly middle-class society. Certainly the appearance in any region of industrial or market agriculture developments poses the need for the internalization of a rather specific type of value orientation on the part of those who are to participate in the system. The lack of such internalization is most apparent in lower-class groups. Insofar as Holiness religion, among other things, requires a steady, conscientious involvement in the new system, it is more than just a reactionary coping with a strange new life by an appeal to rural values. This is a problem area in which a good deal of work needs to be done and may lead to better integration of the sociology of religion with other phases of sociology, notably social mobility and stratification.

Although the proposed reformulation of the Church-Sect typology reflects only one range of theoretically important considerations, it is hoped that this paper will provoke renewed interest both in the basic theory of the sociology of religion and in the realm of concrete research problems.

A distinctive feature of Johnson's approach is the assumption that one best understands organizational differences between religious groups by studying intrinsic differences in their theologies. The church is a distinct and identifiable form of religious organization because of its liturgical religious style. Conversely, the ethicalism of its theology distinguishes the sectarian form of religion. In practice, Johnson's essay served to reopen the debate over church-sect rather than to close it. The criteria for definition he suggests here were not widely employed in empirical research and even Johnson later changed his view of things. In his essay "On Church and Sect,"[4] he returned to the more common strategy of asking whether or not the particular religious group could be viewed as supportive of the general social values and norms in its society. Based on this criteria, the church is understood as the type of religious group that reinforces social consensus and order, while the sect is viewed as some form of oppositional or contra-cultural social organization. Today, most sociologists of religion employ the terms "church" and "denomi-

---

[4] Benton Johnson, "On Church and Sect," *American Sociological Review*, 28 (1963): 539–549.

nation" interchangeably to describe the established mainstream (i.e., larger) religious groups in the United States. The term "sect" is employed to describe groups that are at once smaller than denominations and, most importantly, at variance theologically from the mainstream. Perhaps the most intriguing avenue of study growing out of the church-sect distinction has been the scrutiny of differences within the sectarian branch of American religion. For regardless of the criteria employed, once one has distinguished between church and sect, it immediately becomes apparent that there are more differences between the many sects than between church and sect.

In the following essay Bryan Wilson raises a number of essential questions about sectarian religious groups. What types of sects are there? Under what conditions do they emerge? What are their internal structures like? How do these groups relate to the societies in which they are found? While even Wilson has proposed alternative typologies of sects,[5] the types he discusses in the following essay do allow him to devise a number of general theoretical propositions about such groups. His essay consists of a balanced examination of both the different types of sectarian groups and the social processes that characterize them.

[5] See his essay "Typologie des sects dans une perspective dynamique et comparative," Archives de Sociologie des Religions, 8, Number 16 (1963): 49–63. A translation of this essay appears in Roland Robertson (ed.), The Sociology of Religion: Readings (Baltimore: Penguin Books, 1969), pp. 361–383.

An Analysis of Sect Development
by Bryan R. Wilson

The tendency for sects to become denominations has frequently been noted, and on the basis of this tendency the generalization has sometimes been made that a sect-type organization can exist for only one generation, that in the second generation the sect (and the cult in Becker's use of the term) becomes a church or a denomination.[1] Yet, if one surveys existing religious organizations, it is evident that, in both the sociological and the everyday use of the term, some sects persist as such over several generations. In view of the fact that some sects have undeniably gravitated towards a denominational structure, however, we need to know just what factors in the organization and circumstances of sects promote or retard this development.[2] Since sects are not all of a piece, we need

Bryan Wilson is reader in sociology at Oxford and a fellow of All Souls College, England. He is the author of *Sects and Society* (1961), *Religion in Secular Society* (1966), and *Religious Sects* (1970).

Reprinted from *American Sociological Review*, 24 (February 1959): 3–15. Used with permission of the author and publisher.

[1] H. Richard Niebuhr, *The Social Sources of Denominationalism* (New York: Holt, 1929), p. 19; Howard Becker, *Systematic Sociology on the Basis of the Beziehungslehre and Gebildelehre of Leopold von Wiese* (New York: Wiley, 1932); Liston Pope, *Millhands and Preachers* (New Haven: Yale University Press, 1942), pp. 118 ff.

[2] J. M. Yinger, *Religion in the Struggle for Power* (Durham: Duke University Press, 1946), suggested an alternative development for the sect, into an "estab-

to distinguish and delineate certain sub-types which should prove of greater predictive utility than does the grosser concept of the sect, and with which we may pass from crude hypothesis to more fully developed theory. Once these sub-types have been identified we may turn to the elements in sect organization which are focal points of tension. It is here hypothesized that sects experience different types of tension which vary according to their own constellation of values, as well as the circumstances of their origin. In response to such tensions, in the attempt at their management, we may expect to find the genesis of processes which cause some sects to develop into denominations, others to wither, some to be exterminated, some to fragment, and some to remain, over several generations, as sects.[3] This paper considers the following elements: the circumstances of sect emergence, the internal structure of sect organization, the degree of separateness from the external world, the coherence of sect values, and group commitments and relationships.

Characterization of Sect and Denomination

Typically a *sect* may be identified by the following characteristics: it is a voluntary association; membership is by proof to sect authorities of some claim to personal merit—such as knowledge of doctrine, affirmation of a conversion experience, or recommendation of members in good standing; exclusiveness is emphasized, and expulsion exercised against those who contravene doctrinal, moral, or organizational precepts; its self-conception is of an elect, a gathered remnant, possessing special enlightenment; personal perfection is the expected standard of aspiration, in whatever terms this is judged; it accepts, at least as an ideal, the priesthood of all believers; there is a high level of lay participation; there is oppor-

---

lished sect." More recently Yinger has suggested that established sects develop because they emphasize the evil nature of society, while denominationalizing sects are those which stress the reduction of individual anxiety and guilt—a conclusion generally consistent with the analysis proposed here; see Yinger's *Religion, Society and the Individual* (New York: Macmillan, 1957), pp. 151–152. Recognition of the limitations of the Niebuhr hypothesis is offered in the context of a discussion somewhat different from the above by Benton Johnson, "A Critical Appraisal of Church-Sect Typology," *American Sociological Review*, 22 (February 1957): 88–92. For another approach to this process, see Harold W. Pfautz, "The Sociology of Secularization: Religious Groups," *American Journal of Sociology*, 61 (September 1955): 121–128.

[3] The type of analysis to be followed owes much to the work and the suggestions of Philip Selznick; see especially his book, *The Organizational Weapon* (New York: McGraw-Hill, 1952).

tunity for the member spontaneously to express his commitment; the sect is hostile or indifferent to the secular society and to the state.[4]

In elaboration of this general identification of the sect, it might be added that although sects differ among themselves in their characteristic social relationships, the commitment of the sectarian is always more total and more defined than that of the member of other religious organizations. The ideology of the sect is much more clearly crystallized, and the member is much more distinctly characterized than is the adherent of the larger denomination or church. The behavioral correlates of his ideological commitment also serve to set him and keep him apart from "the world." Sects have a totalitarian rather than a segmental hold over their members: they dictate the member's ideological orientation to secular society; or they rigorously specify the necessary standards of moral rectitude; or they compel the member's involvement in group activity. Ideological conformity may be achieved by compulsory participation, but the system of control varies widely.[5] Not only does the sect discipline or expel the member who entertains heretical opinions, or commits a moral misdemeanor, but it regards such defection as betrayal of the cause, unless confession of fault and appeal for forgiveness is forthcoming.

The *denomination*, in contrast, shows the following features: it is formally a voluntary association; it accepts adherents without imposition of traditional prerequisites of entry, and employs purely formalized procedures of admission; breadth and tolerance are emphasized; since membership is laxly enrolled, expulsion is not a common device for dealing with the apathetic and the wayward; its self-conception is unclear and its doctrinal position unstressed; it is content to be one movement among others, all of which are thought to be acceptable in the sight of God; it accepts the standards and values of the prevailing culture and conventional morality; there is a trained professional ministry; lay participation

---

[4] The characterization of the sect here proposed is in many respects more general than the "type-constructs" offered by Becker, Yinger, and Pope in the works cited above, and by E. D. C. Brewer, "Sect and Church in Methodism," *Social Forces,* 30 (May 1952): 400–408. It omits such characteristics as subjectivism, informality, the expression of fervor, and poverty, since these characteristics appear to belong to certain sub-types only.

[5] Thus in Christian Science, for example, doctrinal purity is maintained without members being compelled to participate in an intense round of group activity. Illustrative material is largely from the writer's own research into sects and sect literature in England; for these cases and for cases where the facts are widely known or well established, specific citations are omitted.

occurs but is typically restricted to particular sections of the laity and to particular areas of activity; services are formalized and spontaneity is absent; education of the young is of greater concern than the evangelism of the outsider; additional activities are largely non-religious in character; individual commitment is not very intense; the denomination accepts the values of the secular society and the state; members are drawn from any section of the community, but within one church, or any one region, membership will tend to limit itself to those who are socially compatible.[6]

Characterization of Types of Sect

Given these general types of organization, we need to distinguish the sub-types of sects.[7] The basis of the present classification is the characterization of types of mission which might be discerned among sects. Generally these types of mission rest on the ideological and doctrinal character of sects, and serve as useful indicators of the clusters of other characteristics to be found in each type. For our purposes, within the framework of Protestant Christianity, four broad types may be discerned. Such a classification is not necessarily exhaustive, nor necessarily exclusive of alternative types. It rests essentially on the response of the sect to the values and relationships prevailing in society. This response, in the nature of sectarianism as we have already described it, is necessarily one of greater or lesser rejection. The *Conversionist* sects seek to alter men, and thereby to alter the world; the response is free-will optimism. The *Adventist* sects predict drastic alteration of the world, and seek to prepare for the new dispensation—a pessimistic determinism. The *Introversionists* reject the world's values and replace them with

[6] This characterization of the denomination stresses many points similar to those suggested by Pope, *op. cit.*, pp. 120 ff., but avoids making a direct comparison of sect traits and denominational traits, as well as the implication that sect characteristics automatically undergo mutation and become denominational traits.

[7] An earlier categorization of sects is offered by E. T. Clark in *The Small Sects in America* (Nashville: Abingdon Press, 1937), which uses rather diverse criteria, including attitudinal, doctrinal, and organizational elements. In the classification offered here the distinction advanced by Howard Becker, *op. cit.*, between sects and cults, and more recently employed by W. E. Mann, *Sect, Cult and Church in Alberta* (Toronto: University of Toronto Press, 1955), is abandoned; movements styled as cults by Becker and Mann are here subsumed in a more generalized typification of the sect, and as a sub-type would figure principally among gnostic sects. For an extremely suggestive classification of sects, which has come to my notice since this paper was written, but which shares certain similarities with the categorization here proposed, see Peter L. Berger, "The Sociological Study of Sectarianism," *Social Research*, 21 (Winter 1954): 467–485.

higher inner values, for the realization of which inner resources are cultivated. The *Gnostic* sects accept in large measure the world's goals but seek a new and esoteric means to achieve these ends—a wishful mysticism. This classification is sociological rather than psychological; the responses are built into particular institutions. The implications of these four depictions are elaborated in the following characterizations, and although the empirical correlates of each type are not explored, the implications themselves are not simply logical extensions of the hypothesized types of response. What is here suggested is that, given particular responses *within the context of Christianity*, these further corollaries may be expected.[8]

1. The Conversionist sect is one whose teaching and activity centers on evangelism; in contemporary Christianity it is typically the orthodox fundamentalist or Pentecostal sect. It is typified by extreme bibliolatry: the Bible is taken as the only guide to salvation, and is accepted as literally true. Conversion experience and the acceptance of Jesus as a personal saviour is the test of admission to the fellowship; extreme emphasis is given to individual guilt for sin and the need to obtain redemption through Christ. Despite the theoretical limit on the number who can gain salvation, the sect precludes no one and revivalist techniques are employed in evangelism. It is distrustful of, or indifferent towards, the denominations and churches which at best have diluted, and at worst betrayed, Christianity; it is hostile to clerical learning and especially to modernism; it is opposed to modern science, particularly to geology and to evolutionary theories; it disdains culture and the artistic

---

[8] The basic types of response here proposed may be compared to the typology of modes of individual adaptation in Robert K. Merton's "Social Structure and Anomie" (*Social Theory and Social Structure* [Glencoe, Ill.: Free Press, 1957], pp. 131 ff.). There is some correspondence between introversionist sects and the retreatist response, revolutionist sects and the rebellious response, and gnostic sects and the innovative type. Merton's conformist case is clearly not appropriate to sects, nor is the ritualist, unless one admits some schisms of the Catholic church and even then the case is doubtful. See also, Karen Horney, *The Neurotic Personality of Our Time* (New York: Norton, 1937).

It is clear that a given sect may well shift in its response to the external society, and whilst remaining a protest group, alter the terms of its protest. Our analysis here is primarily concerned with the process of accommodation—the conditions under which sects become denominations or fail to do so. A development unexplored here is the sect which, whilst remaining a sect, changes character by changing its response; frequently the shift will be of emphasis rather than of complete transformation. There is some evidence to show that revolutionist sects, under circumstances of external duress, have altered their response to one of introversion. The processes here involved would require further analysis in the light of the sociological variables underlying such changes, both as internal and external factors.

values accepted in the wider society. Examples are to be found in the Salvation Army and the Pentecostal sects.

2. The Adventist—or revolutionist—sect focuses attention on the coming overturn of the present world order: in contemporary Christianity it is the adventist movement. It is typified by its emphasis on the Bible, and particularly of its exegesis of the allegorical and prophetic books from which the time and circumstances of the second advent of Christ is discerned. The conventional eschatological ideas of heaven and hell are regarded as false, and the resurrection of the dead for judgment is accepted as the principal eschatological event. Christ is regarded as a divine commander, not only as a saviour, and a high moral standard is based on the moral precepts of Jesus. Participation in the new kingdom will be limited and only those who have maintained doctrinal and moral rectitude will be eligible; admission to the fellowship is by thorough understanding of necessary doctrine, and not by affirmation of conversion. Evangelism is undertaken by way of preaching the word but quick conversions are not sought and revivalism is despised as emotional and misguided. The established church is regarded as fulfilling the role of the antichrist: clerical learning is despised (but science is depreciated only in so far is its doctrines conflict with adventist biblical exegesis) and the professional ministry is vigorously opposed. Separation from the world is a more crucial interdiction than are restrictions placed upon certain worldly activities. The sect is hostile towards the wider society and looks forward to its overthrow.[9] Examples are Jehovah's Witnesses and the Christadelphians.

3. The Introversionist—or pietist—sect directs the attention of its followers away from the world and to the community and more particularly to the members' possession of the Spirit; in recent Christianity it is exemplified in the pietist sect. Such a sect is typified by reliance on inner illumination, whether this be regarded as the voice of conscience or the action of the Holy Ghost. The Bible is a source or stimulant of inner inspiration and ethical insight; doctrine is of lesser importance in that the letter has surrendered to the spirit, the deepening of which is a central preoccupation. The sect develops a particular *Weltanschauung* and considers itself an

[9] The similarities of the adventist type sect and the revolutionary political movement have been brought out by Donald G. MacRae in "The Bolshevik Ideology," *The Cambridge Journal*, 3 (December 1954): 164–177, and are also dealt with in Bryan R. Wilson, *Minority Religious Movements in Modern Britain* (forthcoming). See also Werner Cohn, "Jehovah's Witnesses as a Proletarian Movement," *The American Scholar*, 24 (Summer 1955): 281–298.

enlightened elect; inner values may be regarded as incommunicable and eschatological ideas are unarticulated or of little significance. No evangelism is undertaken and a strong ingroup morality is developed; the sect withdraws from the world, or allows its members to be active in the world only for human betterment at the behest of conscience and at the periphery of social concern. It is indifferent to other religious movements. It admits of no spiritual directors or ministers. Examples include some Holiness movements, Quakers, and the Society of the Truly Inspired (Amana Community).

4. The Gnostic sect emphasizes some special body of teaching of an esoteric kind. In contemporary Christianity it is a sect offering a new or revived interpretation of Christian teaching. It accepts the Bible as allegorical and complementary to its own gnosis; conventional Christian eschatology is replaced by a more optimistic and esoteric eschatology; Christ is a wayshower, an exemplar of truth, rather than a saviour. Christian mystical teachings, such as the Trinity, are replaced by other more exclusive mysticism, the significance of which the adherent can hope only gradually to penetrate; doctrine includes teachings which replace secular scientific explanations, and offer a cosmology, an anthropology, and a psychology of their own. The utility of the gnosis for everyday life is emphasized, particularly in the achievement of worldly success, self-realization, health, material well-being and happiness. Conversion is an alien concept to the Gnostic sect, but instruction and guidance is offered to the outsider or the neophyte; there are stages in understanding: enlightenment "unfolds." There is a charismatic leader (or a succession of such leaders) who pronounces wisdom; ministers are usually styled as teachers or guides, and ministerial functions are subdivided among laity with appropriate qualification. Other churches are regarded with indifference as ignorant or backward; secular knowledge is seen as valid and useful relatively, except where it contravenes sect teaching. The cultural standards of the society are accepted and even utilized: the Gnostic sectarian does not withdraw from the world but seeks to use his special knowledge for his own advancement, or that of the movement, in the world. These traits are found, for example, in Christian Science, New Thought sects, Koreshanity, and the Order of the Cross.[10]

[10] The types here hypothesized are primarily Christian, and each type finds some support within Christian scriptures. Whether such a classification could be usefully employed for other major religions is doubtful in that, although revolutionist and intraversionist sects appear to be common to many religions, and the gnostic sects occur in some, conversionism is perhaps less widespread. The situation is sometimes confused with regard to the relative positions of orthodoxy and sectarianism,

Circumstances of Sect Emergence

The conditions under which sects emerge may, for analytical purposes, be divided into three elements: the method by which the sect comes into being, the specific factors of stimulus, and the external social conditions prevailing.

1. The principal methods of sect emergence are by spontaneous development around a local charismatic leader, by schism, and by organized revival. In the case of a sect emerging around a leader much will depend on his teaching and his organizational ability. Some such sects disappear when the leader dies or departs. Others, particularly those in which the leader offers a new gnosis which is consonant with the age, spread and retain their identity. The gnosis may be a new combination of ideas or the retailing of older ideas to a new audience.[11] Thus the optimism, feminism, and success-orientation of the New Thought sects and of Christian Science fitted well with American ideals at the end of the nineteenth century. If the leader offers a variant of traditional Christianity, however, then such a group is likely to remain local and, if persisting, eventually to make common cause with other fundamentalist movements or with the fundamentalist wing of one of the larger denominations, usually the Baptists. Many independent missions of this type joined with the Pentecostal sects in England during the first three decades of this century. But if such sects spread they appear to be particularly likely to become denominationalized, as the distinctive needs of members change—assuming that there is no constant stream of new admissions to keep alive the pristine spirit of the movement.

The schismatic sect tends to be vigorous as long as its protest against the parent body remains significant, and as long as the rival group exists as a challenge; in this period it is likely to grow only by accretions from the parent body. Subsequently, as the issue of disagreement wanes in importance, such a schismatic group may adjust to continuance as a sect, may decay in the absence of opposition, or may partially and gradually rejoin the parent body. Illustrations of such processes are afforded in the history of the

---

and by the difference between the relationship of religion and the state which prevails in many non-Christian countries and the pattern which has generally obtained in the West.

[11] This syncretistic approach is typical of gnostic sects: many such movements have drawn on diverse sources for their teachings. See, for example, Bryan R. Wilson, "The Origins of Christian Science," *The Hibbert Journal*, 57 (January 1959): 161–170.

Plymouth Brethren in England, and of the Christadelphians in England, the United States, Canada, and Australia.

Organized revival is the method of development most usual to fundamentalist sects, and may well begin in a nondenominational spirit. Success, however, tends to impose organizational responsibilities and, if there are distinctive teachings, sects tend to emerge. The Full Gospel Testimony and the Elim Foursquare Gospel Church in England are examples of this development, the teachings being pentecostal. Such groups usually experience rapid growth and high turnover of personnel; since they rely on revivalists for stability and permanence there is, in the nature of the case, an acceptance of trained functionaries, and in this respect a tendency towards denominational development.

2. The specific factors of stimulus of sect emergence are usually found in the stresses and tensions differentially experienced within the total society. Change in the economic position of a particular group (which may be a change only in relative position); disturbance of normal social relations, for instance in the circumstances of industrialization and urbanization; the failure of the social system to accommodate particular age, sex, and status groups—all of these are possible stimuli in the emergence of sects. These are the needs to which sects, to some extent, respond. Particular groups are rendered marginal by some process of social change; there is a sudden need for a new interpretation of their social position or for a transvaluation of their experience. Insecurity, differential status anxiety, cultural neglect, prompt a need for readjustment which sects may, for some, provide. The maladjusted may be communities, or occupational groups, or dispersed individuals in similar marginal positions. The former cases are more typical for the emergence of Conversionist, Adventist, and Introversionist groups, the latter for the Gnostic sects. Sudden social dislocation, as experienced in urbanization and industrialization, appears to be a frequent circumstance in which Conversionist sects emerge, while Adventists and Introversionists have arisen in the midst of longer persisting deprivation.

3. The external social conditions are not easily distinguished from the stimulus factors considered above, but taken in their widest sense it is evident that there are different consequences for sects according to the political and moral character of the society in which they emerge. In feudal, authoritarian, or totalitarian societies, the sect is persecuted; if it persists it will do so only as a clandestine organization. It will tend to be hostile to the world (whether or not

this was its original orientation) and may, in reality or in fantasy, project this hostility upon society. The very early Quakers, the Fifth Monarchy Men, and the numerous pietist and millennial movements in Europe from the thirteenth to the eighteenth centuries, illustrate this reaction.[12] An alternative development in the past has been for the sect to migrate and seek an environment where it could live according to its own standards. The achievement of such isolation has, in itself, consequences for sect organization and promotes communistic arrangements. Examples here are the Rappites, Amana Society, and other movements flourishing in eighteenth and nineteenth century America after migrating from Germany.[13] In such circumstances, to which more specific reference is made below, the sect is unlikely to show marked denominational tendencies.

In democratic or pluralist societies the sect is not pushed into the search for isolation, and although revolutionary type movements (Adventist) may emerge, they are likely to maintain their separation from the world by other methods. Clearly, during rapid social change the various stimulus factors discussed above are more likely to become operative, and it is empirically well established that sects proliferate in periods of social unrest. In this connection, some very general propositions have been offered on the basis of data drawn from the United States in the period from 1800 to the present time. This was a society undergoing almost uninterrupted expansion, rapid social change, high mobility, intense urbanization, and successive waves of immigration (from which its proletariat was continually re-recruited). In face of these developments the original social values were undergoing constant modification through differential acceptance by diverse ethnic and religious groups. In short, this was a highly atypical context from which to make generalizations concerning the development of sects. The absence of tradition and of stable class differences, the promotion of denominational competition, and the expectation of growth and development resulted in extreme accommodation which helped sects rapidly to evolve into denominations—almost as part of a "success-pattern." In this situation even the Quakers could develop a schism which accepted a ministry and became virtually a denomination. The external social circumstances, rather than the intrinsic nature of the

[12] On European millennial movements see Norman Cohn, *The Pursuit of the Millennium* (London: Secker and Warburg, 1957).

[13] For a recent brief account of such movements, see Henri Desroche, "Micro-millenarismes et Communautorismes Utopique en Amérique du Nord du XVII° au XIX° Siècle," *Archives de Sociologie des Religions,* 4 (Juillet–Décembre 1957): 57–92.

sect as such, must here be invoked to explain why sects become denominations.[14]

The Internal Structure of Sect Organization

A feature of sects in contemporary society is that they tend to develop some sort of centralized organization, however minimal. This development has been prompted by the need for communication between dispersed communities, the increase in mobility, and the growing impact of legislation on sects, particularly in wartime. Central organization in itself, however, is not to be equated with a denominational tendency, since central control may be effectively employed to prevent such trends, as with Jehovah's Witnesses.[15] On the other hand, such agencies may be a departure from the original sect ideal—their development may be a response to some external threat to the sect's values, but they also imply the surrender of other values. The most significant question about this development would seem to be whether or not those who acquire responsibilities in the central agencies of the sect become professional *public* functionaries—where functions become institutionally differentiated and specialization of roles occurs.

The initial position of the sect, where there is no local charismatic leader, is the occupation of offices by members in rotation, by lot, or by seniority, and subsequently to institute the lay leader, usually chosen by the group for his particular abilities. Once the concept of special training of such leaders is admitted, then a step to denominationalism has been taken. Training implies lack of parity between leaders and members, it compromises the radical democracy of the sect and the ideal of the priesthood of all believers. Spontaneity disappears, and leaders employ the status symbols of their profession, seeking equal esteem with the pastors of other movements.[16]

Such a radical departure from sect values does not normally occur

[14] For a discussion of internal and external factors in a clinical, as distinct from a typological, examination of sect development, see Bryan R. Wilson, "Apparition et Persistence des Sectes dans un Milieu Social en évolution," *Archives de Sociologie des Religions*, 5 (Janvier–Juin 1958): 140–150.

[15] See H. H. Stroup, *Jehovah's Witnesses* (New York: Columbia University Press, 1945); also E. Royston Pike, *Jehovah's Witnesses* (London: Watts, 1954); Werner Cohn, *op. cit.*

[16] The equivocal position of the ministry emerging within a sect which is undergoing transformation to a denomination, is discussed in Bryan R. Wilson, "Pentecostalist Minister: Role Conflicts and Status Contradictions," *American Journal of Sociology*, 64 (March 1959): 494–504.

abruptly, nor does denominational character rest on this one factor alone. Obviously, different types of sect show a different proclivity to this development. We can fully expect sects highly concerned with exangelism and revivalism to be most prone to evolve in this way. If missionaries and revivalists are being supported by the group, the value of special training is likely to be accepted and will probably be provided within and by the organization itself. The economies of scale may well induce the movement to train more people than can readily be absorbed in the mission field, or than can be supported there, whilst there is also a limit to the number of active revivalists who can operate on behalf of a particular movement. The replacement of local lay pastors by trained ministers is then a likely consequence. Something like this sequence can be seen in the development of pentecostal sects in Britain. Of other groups, the sect known as the Church of God in the British Isles and Overseas has full-time itinerant revivalists who preach in the meeting houses in place of local lay leaders. This development may be regarded as a stage in the same general process, retarded in this instance by the sect's strong anti-ministerial ideology.

This type of development is most probable in the Conversionist sects. The orthodox fundamentalist sect stands nearest to traditional Christianity and may have had its own origins in some larger movement with a ministry, whose organization might be accepted even if its teachings are rejected. The Adventist sect resists organizational change in its confident expectation of an early end to the present dispensation and is, in any case, hostile to any institution associated with the established order. Similarly, the pietist (Introversionist) sect is ideologically resistant to the development of a ministry and, moreover, is not concerned with evangelism. In that the adventists evangelize they do so without the use of revivalist techniques. The Gnostic sect, while usually instituting a system of special instruction, does so for the private and personal benefit of the member and not as a qualification for any particular office in the movement, even though in practice the more highly taught are likely to gain easier admission to leadership positions. Worship is not usually of major importance to the Gnostic sect and when professional functionaries do arise they are more likely to be private counsellors than public ministers.

Elites emerge in sects both at the local level and, once centralized agencies have arisen, also at the center. They may be elected by the generality, but they tend to become self-recruiting both locally and at the center. Central control of local leaders may also occur, and when it does the local elite will be the group which interprets, explains, and rationalizes the activity of the central group. In such movements there is a distinct centripetal tendency of responsibility: allegiance is to "headquarters," "the central board," "the executive." Christian Science and Jehovah's Witnesses both typify this organizational structure. The existence of such elites has no specific implication for the development of the sect into a denomination for the crucial matters are whether the elite is specially trained and whether its function becomes that of a professional ministry. What may be noted, however, is that centralized movements appear to be better able to prevent schism than movements in which the central agencies are less well articulated and in which centripetal responsibility has not developed.

Schism is a feature of sects and of churches more than of denominations (except in the early period of denominational development). (This is partly because sects and churches tend to possess a much more clearly articulated structure of doctrine and organization than do denominations.) Otherwise, schism usually centers on the question of purity of doctrine, and successful schism usually finds its leader in the very inner elite of the movement.[17] Schism of this kind serves to preserve the distinctive sectarian character of the organization since the schismatic groups tend to become the keepers of each other's consciences in relation to the maintenance of traditional values. The two groups compete for the same public, and frequently appeal to the same sources and authorities in legitimation of their position, thus engendering a competitive struggle to prove the purity of their doctrine and social practice. The Plymouth Brethren, the Mennonites, and the Christadelphians provide illustrations of this development.

Degree of Separateness from the World

The relationship which a sect permits itself and its members to the external world is of vital importance to the nature of its continuance. In some measure, and by some methods, the sect is committed to keeping itself "unspotted from the world": its distinctness must be evident both to its own members and to others. To this end there are two principal types of mechanism, *isolation* and *insulation*. Isolation may be consciously designed, or unconsciously accepted. It may be vicinal isolation in which social isolation is necessarily

---

[17] For an excellent illustration of this point, see A. K. Swihart, *Since Mrs. Eddy* (New York: Holt, 1931); for further examples in Christian Science and other movements, see Wilson, "Minority Religious Movements..." *op. cit.*

implied, but this is readily achieved only by groups which accept a communistic type of organization; such organization, in turn, acts as a further isolating device. Sects which have aspired to be self-contained in this way, and have sought to avoid the "alien" even in those spheres where most sects are prepared to treat with him, have usually been of the Introversionist type. Clearly, such a radical mechanism for the achievement of self-maintenance would mean too profound a change in sect character for Conversionist sects, while the expectation of an early overturn of normal social relations makes such action premature for Adventists. Gnostic sects usually lack the community basis for such a venture and seek their separateness from the world in different ways. Isolation may also be linguistic, a condition illustrated by the various bodies of Mennonites, Hutterites, and Doukhobors. Finally, isolation may be simply the injunction to maintain social separateness from the alien; this is urged by most sects, even the evangelical.

Insulation consists of behavioral rules calculated to protect sect values by reducing the influence of the external world when contact necessarily occurs. Of course, insulation may be a latent function of the moral demands of sect teaching, the justification for which is biblical or revealed prescription; the sect leaders and the members themselves, however, often become aware of the real value of such precepts. Distinctive dress is such an insulating device, characteristic of some Mennonites, early Quakers, and Hutterites. Group endogamy is a more widely used method of insulation and is the rule for most Adventist and Introversionist sects, the expectation in many Conversionist sects, and the preferred form, if marriage is approved at all, in Gnostic sects.

The Coherence of Sect Values

Separateness from the world is clearly a part of the general constellation of values embraced by sects. The coherence of such values and the tensions which their acceptance involves are discussed below. However, it is analytically possible to distinguish between tensions arising from the conflict of this particular value and others embraced by the sect and the tensions resulting from the conflict between sect ideals and the ideals of the wider society, and ultimately with those of the state.

The principal tension between the demand for separateness and other sect values arises in the injunction, accepted by many sects, to go out and preach the gospel. Evangelism means exposure to the world and the risk of alienation of the evangelizing agents. It means also the willingness to accept into the sect new members. This throws a particular weight on the standards of admission if, through the impact of recruitment, the sect itself is not to feel the effect of members who are incompletely socialized from the sect's point of view. The more distinctive the sect doctrines and the more emphatic the insistence on strict standards of doctrinal understanding, the less likely it is that the sect will suffer from its evangelism. The Introversionist and Gnostic sects do not experience this type of tension since they do not evangelize the alien, or seek to do so only by formalized procedures. The Adventist sect regards it as one of its responsibilities to preach the kingdom, to forewarn the world of events portending, and to gather a remnant, but it sends its evangelizing agents into the world only after their doctrinal understanding has been thoroughly tested and their allegiance well tried. Equally it does not expect rapid returns, but subjects those who wish to join the movement to examination of their doctrinal knowledge. The Conversionist sects, which are fundamentalists, experience this tension most fully and have evolved least protection for themselves on these vulnerable points. Their agents are young, their doctrine often less sharply distinguished from that of the denominations, and their tests of good faith inadequate, subordinate to conversionist enthusiasm, and easily, if unwittingly, counterfeited by the emotionally overwrought in the revivalist situation.

The recruitment of the second generation is also an aspect of evangelism. There are similar problems of the tests of admission and the process of socializing the in-comers. Niebuhr, and subsequently Pope, pinpointed a key tension for sect organization in recognizing the significance of accepting the second generation.[18] It is an oversimplification to say, however, that the second generation makes the sect into a denomination. As indicated above, such development depends on the standards of admission imposed by the sect, the previous rigor with which children have been kept separate from the world, and on the point at which a balance is struck between the natural desire of parents to have their children included in salvation and their awareness of the community view that any sort of salvation depends on the maintenance of doctrinal and moral standards. Obviously, whether the sect tends to embrace whole families or simply individuals is a significant matter. In general, Gnostic sects, which tend to have an individualistic appeal and do not emphasize the normal type of separation from the world, have more difficulty in winning the allegiance of the second gen-

[18] Niebuhr, *op. cit.*; Pope, *op. cit.*

eration than have other sects. Pietistic and Adventist sects, enjoying both doctrinal distinctiveness and the allegiance of whole families (supported by endogamous injunctions) and also tending to have exacting standards for would-be joiners, are apt to hold their second generation without damage to sect identity. The fundamentalist Conversionist groups—who often appeal to individuals, have a less clearly articulated difference of doctrine from the denominations, and whose standards of admission are simple acceptance of a saviour—are most likely to be affected by the degree of adherence of the second generation.[19]

The sect's desire to be separate from the world and its concerns— and the values which express that separateness—results in certain distinct tensions for the organization and for its members. For each sect there must be a position of optimal tension, where any greater degree of hostility against the world portends direct conflict, and any less suggests accommodation to worldly values. The typical issues of this conflict of values include: divergence of sect and external society on what constitutes true knowledge (which leads to conflict concerning education); the refusal of sects to recognize the legitimacy of society's legal arrangements and the refusal to accept conventionalized sacred practices such as oath-swearing; withdrawal of the sect from the political arrangements of society, refusal to vote, to salute national emblems, and the like; conscientious objection to participation in military activities of the state; the refusal to recognize the marital and familial regulations imposed by the state; objection to state medical regulations; disregard of economic institutions of society, as in the refusal to register land ownership or to join labor unions.

The means used by the sect to cope with these particular tensions is crucial for the persistence of sect organization. The sect may depart from the accepted moral rules of the wider society, but beyond a certain point the sect comes into conflict with even the democratic state in the pluralist society. The state does not always win in such conflicts, as the exemptions from oath-swearing, flag-saluting, military service, and medical regulation all illustrate. But the sect itself, in pursuit of its values, in its search for exemption, may experience change of character. It must, for instance, develop agencies to treat with the state; to preserve its values it may be thrust into new types of social action, new contact with worldly

[19] Both Niebuhr and Pope base their generalizations on the examination of what we have called Conversionist sects; the present classification has thus prevented or decreased errors in prediction.

organization—perhaps even fighting its case in the law courts of "the world," although this conflicts with the desire of most sects to be a law unto themselves. Action to reduce external tensions may in this way generate new internal tensions as the sect departs from older practices and values.

Thus when Christian Scientists joined with other unconventional healing movements to resist state legislation concerning medical care, they appeared, to some members, to compromise their stand that Christian Science alone could really heal. When, in Britain in the First World War, Christadelphians developed an organization to seek exemptions from military service, they allowed the activities of the state to induce them to establish committees at a national level, which conflicted with their ideal of minimal organization and prompted dissension and schism. When the Doukhobors, facing the demand of the state that it regulate its marriages and accept secular schooling, resort to arson and violence, they trespass on their own pacifist ideals.[20] Clearly in such cases of challenge and response there may readily be the beginnings of sect change in that the sect develops agencies more like those of denominations, and admits, by the back door, the values prevalent in the wider society.

If the sect is to persist as an organization it must not only separate its members from the world, but must also maintain the dissimilarity of its own values from those of the secular society. Its members must not normally be allowed to accept the values of the status system of the external world. The sect must see itself as marginal to the wider society, and even when the marginality of extreme poverty, for example, has objectively disappeared, the consciousness of the inapplicability of the standards of the outside world must be retained. Whatever the changes in their material circumstances, the group must persist in the feeling of being a people apart if it is to persist. Status must be status within the sect, and this should be the only group to which the status-conscious individual makes reference. Yet for the proselytizing sect this is often accomplished only with difficulty since the social status of its members may radically affect its prospect of winning recruits. Even the sect of the very poor is usually pleased when a prominent personage is converted and often accords him a place of honor because of his status in the wider society. The classic cases of sects developing into denominations (usually accompanied by schism from the parent body on the part of those poorer members who resist the growth of for-

---

[20] On the Doukhobors, see H. B. Hawthorn (ed.), *The Doukhobors of British Columbia* (University of British Columbia Press, 1955).

mality and other denominational characteristics) illustrate just such a conflict of sect values: between genuine separateness from the world and the desire for social respectability.[21]

As we have seen, the Adventist and Introversionist sects are more fully insulated against this type of value conflict. Nor does this type of tension occur in the Gnostic sects which insulate the two areas ideologically by teaching, in many cases, that the material world is less real. Although the member might gain status in the group if improvement in his material circumstances can be attributed to his special sect-inculcated knowledge, still the two levels of experience are clearly distinguished.

Finally, we may note the significance of exclusiveness in the development of sects. The more fully the sect sees itself as a chosen remnant, the more fully will it offer resistance to the broadening process which is implied in becoming a denomination. Such resistance is more likely to be successful, however, if the sect has an aristocratic ethic concerning salvation—if it sees itself as a chosen elect, limited in size by divine command. Sects which emphasize free will and the availability of Christ to all (even if they accompany such a teaching with an expectation that not many will in fact avail themselves of the opportunity), and which thus accept a general Arminian position theologically, are much more likely to practice evangelism and to seek rapid growth than are the others.[22] The Conversionist sects inherit this theological position and accept this mission, whereas the Adventist sects, who accept the command to preach the truth, nonetheless make truth difficult to obtain. Both

[21] The history of Methodism, the Church of the Nazarene, and some Pentecostal groups illustrate this process. See, for example, E. D. C. Brewer, op. cit.; W. R. Goldschmidt, "Class Denominationalism in Rural California Churches," American Journal of Sociology, 49 (January 1944): 348–355; Oliver R. Whitley, "The Sect to Denomination Process in an American Religious Movement: The Disciples of Christ," Southwestern Social Science Quarterly, 36 (December 1955): 275–282.

[22] Arminian type theology, as distinct from Calvinism, would appear to be a significant factor in promoting the growth of sect to denomination; Benton Johnson's statement (op. cit.), that this development is largely confined to voluntarist Calvinist sects, is in need of clarification. That some Calvinist groups could pass from sect to established church was made possible by the unusual circumstances of the settlement by sectarians of new territories. (It is doubtful whether the establishment of the Calvinist church at Geneva could be described as a sect-to-church process.) Elsewhere the Calvinist sects which developed into denominations did so only as their Calvinism gave way to a more Arminian and less exclusive teaching, as with the Baptists in England. Those groups which have retained Calvinistic teaching in anything like its pristine rigor have not fully experienced denominational development, e.g., the Strict and Particular Baptists whose organization remains essentially sectarian in character.

Introversionist and Gnostic sects emphasize a gradual unfolding of grace or truth to the individual; although, particularly in the Gnostic groups, there is no sense of absolute exclusiveness, in both types there is an emphasis on an elect.

Group Commitments and Relationships

At some level the individual member's commitment to the sect must be total. This may mean the acceptance of a leader's commands, or a general ideological commitment, or a more specific doctrinal commitment, or a commitment to regulate all social and moral affairs entirely as the sect directs. In the Gnostic sect commitment tends to be simply to the leader or to the general ideological position of the movement; the member must acquire the *Weltanschauung* of the sect if benefit of its special gnosis is to be gained. There are few moral correlates of this ideological position, and those which do exist are typically personal aids to self-fulfillment, for example, abstinence in matters of diet and in use of drugs, tobacco, and alcohol. The Introversionist sects (which may or may not have recognized leaders, and whose leaders may or may not claim distinctive charisma) add to the commitment of the member a distinct moral commitment: certain types of behavior are expected, and there is a strong commitment to the fellowship itself. The Adventist group demands commitment to specific doctrine and specific morality, which further implies commitment to the brethren themselves. The Conversionist sects, while expecting doctrinal and moral rectitude, are less sharply exclusive in demands towards the fellowship as such and are even prepared to extend their general idea of community to embrace "all born-again believers."

Introversionist and Adventist sects are distinctly *Gemeinschaften*. Fellowship is an important value for all members: fellow-members are "brethren"; relationships as far as possible are primary; the local meeting is a face-to-face group. The individual is a sect-member before he is anything else, he is expected to find his friends within the group, group endogamy is the rule, and there is expulsion of the wayward and lax. The membership is a membership of families rather than of individuals and sect values are mediated by the kin-group. The Introversionists are sharers of an inner and unseen truth; the Adventists are participants in revolutionary intrigue. The Conversionist sect shares these general characteristics only partially: its concept of brotherhood extends beyond sect boundaries and its standards are less rigorous. It accepts individuals more lightly, socializes them less intensely, and loses them more easily—all of which disturbs the strong sense of community. Its appeal is to the individual seeking salvation, and consequently it is less typically composed of families. The Gnostic sect is much more frankly a *Gesellschaft:* the individual's relationships to other devotees are secondary to his commitment to the ideology and the leadership. Brotherhood is an alien concept. Discipline is for disloyalty, not for specific moral misdemeanor. The impersonality of relationships may even be regarded as ideal, since the gnosis, "the principle," is what matters. Since there are fewer behavioral correlates of sect affiliation, the member, socially, may hide his membership and so avoid the disapproval of the outside world.

Conclusions

Our analysis has brought out a number of items which are subject to variation as between different types of sect and which help to determine the likely development of such movements. Thus it is clear that sects with a general democratic ethic, which stress simple affirmation of intense subjective experience as a criterion of admission, which stand in the orthodox fundamentalist tradition, which emphasize evangelism and use revivalist techniques, and which seek to accommodate groups dislocated by rapid social change are particularly subject to denominationalizing tendencies. These same tendencies are likely to be intensified if the sect is unclear concerning the boundaries of the saved community and extends its rules of endogamy to include any saved person as an eligible spouse; if its moral injunctions are unclearly distinguished from conventional or traditional morality; and if it accepts simple assertion of remorse for sin as sufficient to readmit or to retain a backslidden member. Denominationalization is all the more likely when such a sect inherits, or evolves, any type of preaching order, lay pastors, or itinerant ministers; when revivalism leads to special training for the revivalists themselves (and so leads to a class of professionals who cease to rely on "love-offerings" but are granted a fixed stipend); and when the members are ineffectively separated from the world, a condition enhanced by proselytizing activities.

It is clear that the types of sect which we described as Conversionist are most likely to fulfill the conditions which transform sects into denominations and are least likely to enjoy the circumstances preventing this process. The Adventist and the Introversionist types appear to be best protected from this development, although by different mechanisms: they fulfill few of the conditions supporting this evolution and often enjoy or create the factors which retard it.

The Gnostic sect is in some ways less clearly protected, but its distinctive ideology performs in some measure the functions which social insulating mechanisms perform for other types.

In a broad way, we can see why certain earlier studies of sects fell into errors of prediction, since the conclusions rested on the experience of certain types of sects, sects which existed in very particular social circumstances and accommodated people whose social marginality and sense of anomie were often temporary and a consequence of inadequate readjustment to rapidly changing social conditions. Of course, to predict the development of any given sect requires examination in close detail of its circumstances. Once these are known, however, the foregoing analysis should provide a guide for the interpretation of these facts.

In spite of the large quantity of research that has been guided by the church-sect distinction, these concepts far from exhaust the range of conceptual approaches to the sociological study of religious organizations. The following essay by Thomas O'Dea echoes several important themes that were first contributed by sociology's classical period founders. In the tradition of Durkheim and Otto, he argues that the starting point for the analysis of all religious organizations is the recognition of the unique quality of the "sacred" or "holy." From this vantage point O'Dea argues that all religious groups must cope with the problem of "transforming the religious experience to render it continuously available to the mass of men and to provide for it a stable institutional context." In other words, much like Weber, O'Dea is greatly concerned with the problem of institutionalization and with what Weber called the "routinization of charisma." All religious groups, in order to survive, must communicate the uniqueness of their message or the immediacy of the religious experience from one generation to the next. For O'Dea this fact results in five distinct "dilemmas" for religious organizations.

Five Dilemmas in the Institutionalization of Religion

by Thomas F. O'Dea

I

Although much fruitful research has been done in the sociology of religion, the explicit formulation of an adequate conceptual scheme for observation and interpretation of data still leaves much work to be done. American thinking in this field in recent years has largely been in terms of what may be called a "functional" frame of reference. While helpful in the study of many aspects of religious life, the functional approach does not focus attention squarely upon the problems of the sociology of religion as such. Rather it raises two questions, important in their own right. First of all it concerns itself with what religion does for and to society, seeing religious institutions as one set of institutions among others, and interesting itself in the contribution of religious institutions and religious ideas

Thomas O'Dea is professor of religious studies and sociology at the University of California, Santa Barbara. A collection of his papers appear under the title *Sociology and the Study of Religion* (1970). He is the author of *The Mormons* (1957), *American Catholic Dilemma* (1958), and *The Sociology of Religion* (1966); and is co-author of *Religion and Man* (with Comstock, Baird, Bloom, O'Dea, and Adams, 1971).

Reprinted from *Journal for the Scientific Study of Religion*, 1, no. 1 (1961): 30–39. Used with permission of the author and publisher.

to the maintenance of the ongoing equilibrium of the social system. In a more psychological, but still basically functional frame of reference, it also asks what is the contribution of religion to the preservation and achievement of adequate adaptation and stability for the individual personality.

The first question is not, of course, the sociology of religion in any but a peripheral sense. It is rather the sociology of total social systems, particularly concerned with the contribution of one institutional complex, in this case the religious, to the functioning of society. The second, while directing our understanding to important problems involving religion and stratification, religion and social disorganization, religion and social change, and the general area of problems involved in selfhood and identity, does not aim its sights squarely upon religious phenomena in their own right.[1]

The functional approach sees the importance of religion in that religion gives answers to questions that arise at the point of ultimacy, at those points in human experience that go beyond the everyday attitude toward life with its penultimate norms and goals. The study of religion is an important part of the study of human society because men are cognitively capable of going to the "limit-situation," of proceeding through and transcending the conventional answers to the problem of meaning and of raising fundamental existential questions in terms of their human relevance. Such "breaking points" of routine experience often appear in the context of experienced uncertainty, of adversity and suffering, and in the frustrating but inevitable experience of the limitations of human finitude.[2]

Moreover, the ultimate tends to be apprehended in a special modality all its own. In terms of Durkheim and Otto, man experiences the "sacred" or "holy" as an irreducible category of existence that is drastically other than the ordinary prosaic workaday world.[3] From a functional point of view religion is important because it

---

[1] For example see Kingsley Davis, *Human Society* (New York: Macmillan, 1950), p. 529; Bronislaw Malinowski, *Magic, Science, and Religion and other essays* (Glencoe, Illinois: The Free Press, 1948), among other works. For a worthwhile discussion see "The Sociology of Religion," Charles Y. Glock, in *Sociology Today,* Robert K. Merton, Leonard Broom, and Leonard S. Cottrell, Jr., eds. (New York: Basic Books, 1959).

[2] See Talcott Parsons, "The Theoretical Development of the Sociology of Religion," *Essays in Sociological Theory* (Glencoe, Illinois: The Free Press, 1959), pp. 194–211.

[3] Emile Durkheim, *The Elementary Forms of Religious Life,* J. W. Swain, tr. (Glencoe, Illinois: The Free Press, 1954); and Rudolf Otto, *The Idea of the Holy,* J W. Harvey, tr. (London: Oxford University Press, 1923).

sustains life precisely at these breaking points. From the religious point of view, however, these breaking points are important precisely because they are the occasions of the experience out of which religion arises. Talcott Parsons years ago emphasized the importance in sociological study of taking the point of view of the participators in the social action studied.[4] Since religious institutions arise out of this experience of ultimacy and the sacred, the sociology of religion must begin with considerable empathy precisely at this point.

From the unusual religious experiences of unusual people the founded religions emerge, translating and transforming the insights of founders into institutional structures. Thus there arise the formed and formulated entities of belief-systems, systems of ritual and liturgy, and organization.[5] It is important therefore especially in the study of the founded religions to begin with a phenomenological analysis of the religious experience as such, for out of it emerge the chief dimensions of religious institutions as well as their chief functional problems. Here man is seen neither in terms of the Cartesian "I think, therefore I am" which was the model of 17th century thinking, nor of the "I do, therefore I am," of 19th century thought. Rather he is recognized as a being who is not a dichotomous compartmentalization of "adaptive" and "expressive" needs but one capable of and exhibiting holistic response and commitment to what he experiences as impinging upon his consciousness.[6] It is indeed because man is primarily a responding animal and because his responses in interaction with those of his fellows become crystallized into stabilized expectations and alliegances, that contemporary sociology has proved its greater adequacy for the study of human action over the rationalistic conceptions of the past century. Yet modern sociological theory often reads as though it had not in fact superseded those older partial views of man.

Religion is first of all a response and a response is to something experienced. The religious response is a response to the ultimate and the sacred which are grasped as relevant to human life and its fundamental significance. While the religious response is indeed peripheral and residual to the day-to-day life of men and the

---

[4] Talcott Parsons, *The Structure of Social Action* (Glencoe, Illinois: The Free Press, 1949), *passim*.

[5] Joachim Wach, *Sociology of Religion* (Chicago: University of Chicago Press, 1944), ch. II, pp. 17–34.

[6] For a good discussion see the final chapter, "*Respondeo, ergo sum,*" of *Existentialism and the Modern Predicament*, F. H. Heinemann (New York: Harper Torchbooks, Harper & Brothers, 1958), pp. 190–204.

penultimate ends of that life and related to them only as their ultimate ontological underpinning, it is central to the religious life. It is its constitutive element and out of it proceeds the process of the elaboration and standardization of religious institutions. Since such institutionalization involves the symbolic and organizational embodiment of the experience of the ultimate in less-than-ultimate forms and the concomitant embodiment of the sacred in profane structures, it involves in its very core a basic antinomy that gives rise to severe functional problems for the religious institution. In fact this profound heterogeneity at the center of religious institutionalization constitutes a severe and unavoidable dilemma from which problems arise for religious movements and institutions that recur again and again and can never be finally solved. Moreover, since the religious experience is spontaneous and creative and since institutionalization means precisely reducing these unpredictable elements to established and routine forms, the dilemma is one of great significance for the religious movement.

This view which concentrates upon religious phenomena makes possible an "internal functionalism" of religious institutions themselves since it concentrates attention upon the peculiarly religious problems or more precisely the specific problems of religious institutions qua *religious* institutions.

II

An institutional complex may be viewed as the concrete embodiment of a cultural theme in the on-going life of a society, as the "reduction" of a set of attitudes and orientations to the expected and regularized behavior of men. These institutionalized expectations include definitions of statuses and roles, goals, and prescribed and permitted means, and they articulate with the culture of the society and with the personality structures that the socialization processes have produced in a given society.[7]

It is the great virtue of social institutions from the point of view of the functioning of social systems that they provide stability in a world of inconstancy. The unusual and creative performance of the hero, sage or saint, though of great exemplary and genetic importance, is too unpredictable to become the basis of everyday life. The human world would be an unsteady and incalculable affair indeed were it chiefly dependent upon such phenomena. Yet the achievement of the necessary stability involves a price. It involves

[7] See Talcott Parsons, *The Social System* (Glencoe, Illinois: The Free Press, 1951).

a certain loss of spontaneity and creativity, although these are often found operating in some measure within the expectations of institutional patterns.

The founded religions display this fundamental antinomy in their histories. They begin in "charismatic moments" and proceed in a direction of relative "routinization." This development necessary to give objective form to the religious movement and insure its continuity may in Weber's terms proceed either in a traditional or a rational-legal direction.[8] Such routinization is an unavoidable social process, and as such represents for religious institutions a many-sided and complex paradox.

The charismatic moment is the period of the original religious experience and its corresponding vitality and enthusiasm. Since, as we have seen, this experience involves the deep engagement of the person involved with a "beyond" which is sacred, it is unusual in a special sense. It would remain a fleeting and impermanent element in human life without its embodiment in institutional structures to render it continuously present and available. Yet in bringing together two radically heterogeneous elements, ultimacy and concrete social institutions, the sacred and the profane, this necessary institutionalization involves a fundamental tension in which five functional dilemmas take their origin.

In other words, religion both needs most and suffers most from institutionalization. The subtle, the unusual, the charismatic, the supra-empirical must be given expression in tangible, ordinary, and empirical social forms. Let us now examine the five dilemmas which express this fundamental antinomy inherent in the relation of religion to normal social processes.

1. The Dilemma of Mixed Motivation

In the pre-institutionalized stage of a religious movement, the classical type of which is the circle of disciples gathered about a charismatic leader, the motivation of the followers is characterized by single-mindedness. The religious movement does satisfy complex needs for its adherents, but it focuses their satisfaction upon its values and their embodiment in the charismatic leader. The charismatic call receives a wholehearted response. With the emergence of a stable institutional matrix, there arises a structure of offices—of statuses and roles—capable of eliciting another kind of motiva-

[8] Max Weber, *The Theory of Social and Economic Organization,* Talcott Parsons and A. M. Henderson, tr. (New York: Oxford University Press, 1947), pp. 363ff. Also From Max Weber: *Essays in Sociology,* Hans Gerth and C. Wright Mills, tr. (New York: Oxford University Press, 1946), pp. 53, 54, 262ff, 297, 420.

tion, involving needs for prestige, expression of teaching and leadership abilities, drives for power, aesthetic needs, and the quite prosaic wish for the security of a respectable position in the professional structure of the society.

The contrast we have drawn between the earlier and later stages is not absolute as we can see in the Gospel where we read of the disciples of Jesus concerning themselves with who shall be highest in the kingdom (Matt. 18:1, Mark 10:37). Yet such self-interested motivation is in the charismatic period easily dominated by the disinterested motivation of the charismatic response.[9] Moreover, while the charismatic movement offers security to its adherents, it does so quite differently than do the statuses of well-institutionalized organizations.

It is precisely because of its ability to mobilize self-interested as well as disinterested motivation behind institutionalized patterns that institutionalization contributes stability to human life. Yet if this mobilization of diverse motives is its great strength, it is paradoxically also its great weakness. It may in fact become the Achilles' heel of social institutions. The criteria of selection and promotion within the institutional structure must of necessity reflect the functional needs of the social organization and emphasize performance and therefore will not distinguish very finely between the two types of motivation involved. Thus it may develop that the self-interested motivation will come to prevail. There will then result a slow transformation of the original institutional aims, in many cases amounting to their corruption. When the institution so transformed is suddenly confronted by threat or crisis, the transformed motivation and outlook may reveal itself as impotence. Careerism that is only formally concerned with institutional goals, bureaucratic rigorism of a type that sacrifices institutional goals to the defense or pursuit of vested interests,[10] and official timidity and lethargy are some evidences of the transformation.

Such developments give rise to movements of protest and reform, ever recurring phenomena in the history of the founded religions. The Cluniac reform of the Middle Ages offers a striking example as does the Protestant Reformation of the 16th century.

This dilemma of mixed motivation is found not only among those who occupy important positions in the religious organization. It is

[9] Talcott Parsons has most clearly shown how social structure is a balance of motivation. See his *The Social System* and *Essays in Sociological Theory*, cited above.

[10] Robert K. Merton, *Social Theory and Social Structure* (Glencoe, Illinois: The Free Press, 1957), especially "Social Structure and Anomie," pp. 131–160.

also characteristic of changes in the composition of the membership with the passing of the charismatic movement and the founding generation. The passing of the founding generation means that the religious body now contains people who have not had the original conversion experience. Many are born members and their proportion increases with the years. The selection process which voluntary conversion represented often kept out of the organization precisely the kinds of persons who are now brought up within it. Already in the year 150 A.D., Hermas in *The Shepherd* draws a most unflattering picture of some of the lukewarm "born Christians" in the Church.

2. The Symbolic Dilemma: Objectification versus Alienation

Man's response to the holy finds expression not only in community but also in acts of worship.[11] Worship is the fundamental religious response but in order to survive its charismatic moment worship must become stabilized in established forms and procedures.[12] Thus ritual develops, presenting to the participant an objectified symbolic order of attitude and response to which he is to conform his own interior disposition. Worship becomes something not immediately derivative of individual needs, but rather an objective reality imposing its own patterns upon the participants.

Such objectification is an obvious prerequisite for common and continuous worship, for without it prayer would be individual and ephemeral. The symbolic elements of worship are not simply expressions of individual response, but have an autonomy enabling them to pattern individual response. Yet here too the element of dilemma appears. The process of objectification, which makes it possible for cult to be a genuine social and communal activity, can proceed so far that symbolic and ritual elements become cut off from the subjective experience of the participants. A system of religious liturgy may come to lose its resonance with the interior dispositions of the members of the religious body. In such a case the forms of worship become alienated from personal religiosity, and whereas previously cult had evoked and patterned response

[11] An important book, recently reissued, on this subject is Evelyn Underhill, *Worship* (New York: Harper Torchbook, Harber & Brothers, 1957). There is much modern liturgical research; for example see Louis Bouyer, *Liturgical Piety* (Notre Dame, Indiana: University of Notre Dame Press, 1955). See also *Early Christian Worship,* Oscar Cullman, A. Stewart Todd, and James B. Torrence, tr. (London: SCM Press, 1953).

[12] *Christian Worship: Its Origin and Evolution,* Louis Duchesne, M. L. McClure, tr. (New York: Gorham, 1904).

and molded personal religiosity after its own image,[13] now such an overextension of objectification leads to routinization. Liturgy then becomes a set of counters without symbolic impact upon the worshipers. It may of course retain its element of sacredness through the very fact of its obscurity and mystery, a situation conducive to the development of a semi-magical or magical attitude.

This process may be seen in the Christian history of the Middle Ages when it became necessary for Churchmen to replace the lost correspondence between external act and gesture and interior psychological disposition in the Mass with an elaborate secondary allegorization such as that of Durandus which appears so ridiculous in the light of modern liturgical research. One result of such alienation of symbolic systems is to weaken the social character of worship with a consequent weakening of the solidarity of the religious community. Individual prayer as a concomitant of public rites replaces communal worship.

What we have indicated with respect to cult could also be traced out with respect to graphical and musical expression as well. Here too, overextension of the objectification of symbols can turn them into counters, themes can degenerate into clichés, and at times symbols may become simply objectively manipulatable "things" to be used for achieving ends. In the last case religion becomes semi-magic. Parallels can be made with verbal symbolism where the statements of important religious insights in words suffers routinization and a consequent alienation from interior religiosity and deep understanding occurs. Profound statements then become merely facile formulae.

The alienation of symbolism is one of the most important religious developments and its possibility and likelihood derives from the fact that the religious symbol is in itself an antinomy—an expression *par excellence* of the dilemma of institutionalizing religion.[14] To symbolize the transcendent is to take the inevitable risk of losing the contact with it. To embody the sacred in a vehicle is to run the risk of its secularization. Yet if religious life is to be shared and transmitted down the generations the attempt must be made.

Historians have too often failed to see the importance of this dilemma, although the history of religious protest movements is full of evidence of just how central it is. The symbol—word, gesture,

---

[13] See Dietrich von Hildebrand, *Liturgy and Personality* (New York, London, Toronto: Longmans, Green and Co., 1943).

[14] See Mircea Eliade, *Comparative Patterns of Religion* (New York: Sheed and Ward, 1958).

act, or painting, music and sculpture—provides the medium of genuine communication and sharing and thereby the basis for socializing the religious response. When it is lost a central element in the religious life disappears. Moreover, when the resonance between the external and internal is lost, the symbol often becomes a barrier where previously it had been a structured pathway. It then becomes the object of aggression. Hence it is that the English Reformation concentrated so much of its fire upon the Mass, the priest as the celebrant of the Mass, the destruction of altars, stained glass, statues, etc. The radical anti-symbolism of the Puritans derives from the same experience of lost resonance with the established liturgy. This is one kind of protest that can arise as a response to this dilemma. In the Catholic and Protestant movements for liturgical renascence to be seen in our own day we see another kind of response to these developments.

3. The Dilemma of Administrative Order: Elaboration versus Effectiveness

Max Weber showed that charismatic leadership soon undergoes a process of routinization into a traditional or rational-legal structure made up of a chief and an administrative staff. There is an elaboration and standardization of procedures and the emergence of statuses and roles within a complex of offices. One important aspect is the development in many cases of a distinction between the office and its incumbent, which has become characteristic of the bureaucratic structures of the modern world. The Catholic Church has been the chief prototype in this evolution of the concept of office in European society.

It is characteristic of bureaucratic structure to elaborate new offices and new networks of communication and command in the face of new problems. Precedents are established which lead to the precipitation of new rules and procedures. One result may indeed be that the structure tends to complicate itself. This state of affairs evolves in order to cope with new situations and new problems effectively. Yet such self-complication can overextend itself and produce an unwieldly organization with blocks and breakdowns in communication, overlapping of spheres of competence, and ambiguous definitions of authority and related functions. In short developments to meet functional needs can become dysfunctional in later situations. Weber noted that bureaucracy of the rational-legal type was the most effective means for rational purposeful management of affairs. Yet the word "bureaucracy" has not become a pejorative epithet in the folklore of modern Western societies for nothing. The tendency of organization to complicate itself to meet new situations often transforms it into an awkward and confusing mechanism within whose context it is difficult to accomplish anything.

This dilemma of the necessity of developing a system of administrative order versus the danger of its over-elaboration must be seen in relation to the first dilemma—that of mixed motivation. For the involvement of secondary motivation in bureaucratic vested interests complicates this third dilemma considerably. Genuine organizational reform becomes threatening to the status, security and self-validation of the incumbents of office. The failure of many attempts at religious and ecclesiastical reform in the 14th and 15th centuries is significantly related to this third dilemma and its combination with the first. The Tridentine insistence on organizational reform in the Catholic Counter Reformation as well as the great concern of the Protestant Reformation with the forms of ecclesiastical organization indicates that contemporaries were not unaware of this aspect of their problems.

Certainly such self-complication of procedures and offices is one of the elements involved in Arnold J. Toynbee's observation that an elite seldom solves two major problems challenging its leadership, for successful solution of the first transforms and incapacitates it for meeting the second.

4. The Dilemma of Delimitation: Concrete Definition versus Substitution of Letter for Spirit

In order to affect the lives of men, the import of a religious message must be translated into terms that have relevance with respect to the prosaic course of everyday life. This translation is first of all a process of concretization. It involves the application of the religious insight to the small and prosaic events of ordinary life as lived by quite ordinary people. In that process the religious ideas and ideals themselves may come to appear to be of limited prosaic significance. Concretization may result in finitizing the religious message itself. For example, ethical insights are translated into a set of rules. Since rules, however elaborate, cannot make explicit all that is implied in the original ethical epiphany, the process of evolving a set of rules becomes a process of delimiting the import of the original message. Translation becomes a betraying transformation. Moreover, the more elaborate the rules become in the attempt to meet real complexities and render a profound and manysided ethic tangible and concrete, the greater the chance of transforming the original insight into a complicated set of legalistic formulae and the development of legalistic rigorism. Then, as St. Paul put it, The letter killeth but the spirit giveth life.

Yet the fact is that the ethical insight must be given some institutionalized concretization or it will remain forever beyond the grasp of the ordinary man. The high call of the ethical message may well, however, be reduced to petty conformity to rules in the process. Brahmanic developments of ritual piety, Pharisaic rituals in late classical Judaism, and legalism in Catholicism offer three examples. This fourth dilemma may be compounded with the third and the over-elaboration of administrative machinery may be accompanied by a deadening legalism. It may also become compounded with the second, and the delimitation of the religious and ethical message may contribute to and be affected by the loss of interior resonance of the verbal and other symbols involved.

5. The Dilemma of Power: Conversion versus Coercion

The religious experience exercises a call. In Otto's words, its content "shows itself as something uniquely attractive and *fascinating.*"[15] Moreover, the propagation of the religious message in Christianity has involved an invitation to interior change. This interior "turning" or "conversion" is the classical beginning of the religious life for the individual. With institutionalization of the religious movement, such a conversion may be replaced by the socialization of the young so that a slow process of education and training substitutes for the more dramatic conversion experience. Yet even in this case, the slower socialization in many instances serves as a propaedeutic for conversion. Christians, both Catholic and Protestant, agree that the act of acceptance must be voluntary, involving such interior turning.

However, as religion becomes institutionalized it becomes a repository of many of the values from which much of the life of the society derives its legitimation. Thus the preservance of religious beliefs and even the maintenance of the religious organization can come to be intertwined with societal problems of public order and political loyalty. This tends to become the case whether or not there is a legal separation of church and state.

In addition, since religion is dependent upon interior disposition and since that disposition is subject to numerous unexpected shocks and is always weak among those merely nominally religious, there is always the subtle temptation for religious leaders to avail themselves of the close relation between religion and cultural values in order to reinforce the position of religion itself. A society may find

[15] Rudolf Otto, *op. cit.,* p. 31.

itself unable to tolerate religious dissent, since such dissent is seen as threatening the consensus upon which social solidarity rests. Religious leaders may be tempted to utilize the agencies of a society so disposed to reinforce the position of their own organization.

While such an interpenetration of religious adherence and political loyalty may strengthen the position of religion in the society, it may also weaken it in important respects. It may antagonize members of the religious body who are political oppositionists, and it may antagonize political oppositionists who otherwise might have remained religiously neutral. Second, it may produce an apparent religiosity beneath which lurks a devastating cynicism. History offers many examples of such a coalescing of religious and political interests. Punitive use of the secular arm, the later confessional states in both Catholic and Protestant countries with their "union of throne and altar," and the real though unofficial identification of Protestantism with American nationalism and even nationality in the 19th century offer some cases.

A genuine dilemma is involved. Religion cannot but relate itself to the other institutions of society since religious values must be worked out to have some relation to the other values of a particular cultural complex. Since religion is concerned with ultimate values which legitimate other values and institutions, a relation with established authority and power structures is unavoidable. Such partial identification of basic values in religion and culture tends to strengthen both religious conformity and political loyalty. Yet with the progressive differentiation of society, the confusion of the two soon tends to be detrimental to both. It weakens the bonds of the religious community by weakening voluntary adherence and thereby diluting the religious ethos and substituting external pressures for interior conviction. It weakens the general society by narrowing the possibility of consensus among the population by insisting on a far greater area of value agreement than would in fact be necessary to the continued life of society. Yet some relation between the functionally necessary values in a society and the ultimate sanction of religion is necessary and it necessarily involves a relation between religious institutions and power and authority structures.

Anyone acquainted with the religious wars of the 16th century will readily recognize this dilemma as one important element involved. The long and painful travail of the development of religious freedom was made more difficult by such a confusion of religious and societal interests. Moreover, this confusion caused many men to welcome secularization since it brought a measure of liberation from the fanatical conflicts of the preceding period.

III

These five dilemmas represent five sides of the central dilemma involved in the institutionalization of religion, a dilemma which involves transforming the religious experience to render it continuously available to the mass of men and to provide for it a stable institutionalized context. The nature of the religious experience tends to be in conflict with the requisites and characteristics of the institutionalization process and the resultant social institutions. From this incompatibility there derive the special problems of the functioning of religious institutions delineated in this paper. Some of these antinomies have their analogues in other social institutions. Yet there is reason to suspect that because of the unique character of the religious experience, its elements of incompatibility with institutionalization are more exaggerated than is the case with other areas of human activity. Yet *mutatis mutandis* these dilemmas are applicable to other institutions as well. Indeed the present theoretical formulation represents one way of apprehending general instabilities inherent in social processes or more precisely in the relation between institutionalization and spontaneous creativity.

Such instabilities have been studied—in some cases for a very long time—in terms of other categories of analysis. The first and fifth dilemmas are related to the problem of restraining force and fraud which besets all societies, and which has been a concern of European political philosophy since the Middle Ages. Yet our treatment reveals important new elements. It gets away from an ethical treatment to an analysis of inevitable tendencies in the development of social organizations and their changing relation to their participants. The second, third, and fourth dilemmas are really special forms of that general social process that Weber called "the routinization of charisma." Our formulation has, however, indicated facets of the problem which Weber did not pursue. Actually the fifth dilemma is discussed, in substantially the form presented here, by Talcott Parsons in his book, *The Social System.* He was the first to use the term "dilemma of institutionalization" which he applied to this fifth dilemma.[16]

The present formulation obviously bears a close resemblance to Troeltsch's treatment of the perennial tension between the transcendent call of the New Testament and the world, giving rise to the ecclesiastical tendency to compromise and the sectarian rejec-

[16] Talcott Parsons, *The Social System* (Glencoe, Illinois: The Free Press, 1951), pp. 165–166.

tion of compromise with the world. The present treatment, however, calls attention to other and more subtle aspects of the "world" which need considerable empirical investigation. For example nowhere is the social and psychological problem of the alienation and "wearing out" of symbolism given the kind of investigation it deserves. Nor are the functionally unavoidable elements involved in the dilemma of mixed motivation the object of the kind of research which is needed if we are to understand on both sociological and psychological levels what actually is involved in the day-to-day functional problems of religious institutions.

The present statement does attempt to indicate how we can go beyond all these previous formulations and tries to gather their insights into a consistent scheme dealing with one important dynamic set of factors internal to the functioning of religious movements and bodies. It is a conceptual scheme derived chiefly from the history of Christianity, and particularly of Catholicism. In no way does it pretend to be an overall framework for the sociology or religion, but rather to be what Merton called theory of the middle range dealing with one side or aspect of the complex phenomenon of institutionalized religion. A further examination of the meaning of ultimacy in the religious experience, for example, would throw meaningful light on the element of authoritarianism in much of the history of institutionalized religion in the West. For it is precisely this recognition of and response to the ultimate which, when objectified in institutionalized forms, has in the past led to ecclesiastical imperialism and authoritarian rigor.

In the present paper we have simply attempted to indicate the importance of an internal functional analysis of religious institutions based upon their own peculiar inner structure which derives from the particular religious experience upon which they happen to have arisen. Then we turned to follow out such an analysis with respect to one aspect of the founded religions, that derived from the basic antinomy involved in an institutionalization of religion. The present statement has the advantage of articulating with other theoretical developments in sociology today. It is consistent with theory in the field of the analysis of social systems, and with much theory and research upon bureaucratic structure. Its emphasis upon emergence relates it to work done by both sociologists and social psychologists on small groups. Moreover, it introduces the historical dimension into the heart of sociological analysis. The understanding of behavior in old established religious bodies requires some knowledge of the transformations which the group has undergone in its past history.[17] Finally it indicates the relation of certain of these historical processes to human motivation and its transformation and expression in institutional forms.

While specific to the field of the study of religious institutions the present analytical scheme points to a fundamental dilemma involved in all institutionalization. It may be stated with stark economy as follows: what problems are involved for social systems in their attempt to evolve workable compromises between spontaneity and creativity on the one hand and a defined and stable institutionalized context for human activity on the other? Spontaneity and creativity are the very stuff of human vitality and the source of necessary innovation. Yet social institutions are necessary as the context for action for without them life would dissolve into chaos. Moreover, men inevitably evolve stable institutionalized forms. The present emphasis provides some element of corrective to the kind of "sociologism" which sees the ready-made, the emerged, the products of past interaction as so important that the importance of the new, the emergent, the coming-to-be, is missed.

[17] *The Social Teachings of the Christian Churches,* Ernst Troeltsch, Olive Wyon, tr. (New York and London: Macmillan, 1931), Vols. I and II.

O'Dea's essay provides a number of interesting contrasts to those of Johnson and Wilson. In place of the general strategy of church-sect analysis, wherein the differences between religious groups are stressed, O'Dea provides a deeper understanding of the nature of religious groups per se. His focus is upon what they have in common. While Johnson, and more so Wilson, places significant emphasis upon the relationship between the religious group and the society in which it is located, O'Dea is exclusively concerned with the internal problems of the group. J. Milton Yinger has criticized O'Dea for this very aspect of his essay. Yinger contends that the "internal functionalism" of O'Dea's analysis provides very little information about the broader sociocultural meanings of the religious group.[6] It is clear that even after it is agreed that the study of religious organizations is worthy of

[6] J. Milton Yinger, "Comment," *Journal for the Scientific Study of Religion,* 1 (1961): 40–41.

sociological investigation, different scholars will ask very different questions about them.

Perhaps a more salient criticism offered by Yinger is his observation that O'Dea's "five dilemmas" pertain not just to religious groups but to all human institutions. O'Dea eludes to this idea himself in his concluding remarks. From this standpoint O'Dea's essay points implicitly to one of the fundamental ideas of the sociology of religion—that whatever else religious institutions may be, they are social institutions and experience problems common to all social institutions.

The final essay in this section provides a perspective that is again different from those presented thus far. The three preceding essays examine religion to the extent that it is embodied in so-called formal organizations. Each author is concerned with groups that have well defined organizational structures, a regular membership, stated goals and purposes, and the like. The realm of social movements provides an equally important assortment of religious phenomena. Social movements are defined as human associations that are larger than a specific formal organization and may in fact encompass several of them. Typically, a social movement exhibits a distinctive ideology that is the focal point for those who join or follow the movement. Moreover, most social movements are aimed at achieving some form of social change in society.[7]

Ernest Sandeen's essay on American Fundamentalism examines one of the most significant movements in American Protestantism. As Sandeen notes, while many people associate the term Fundamentalism with an earlier period in American history, the movement is "alive and well" today. It encompasses easily half of the so-called mainstream groups in American Protestantism.

[7] An extensive discussion of social movements, as well as different types of social movements will be found in the *International Encyclopedia of the Social Sciences,* ed. David L. Sills (New York: Macmillan, 1968), Volume 14, pp. 438–452.

Fundamentalism
and American Identity

by Ernest R. Sandeen

Fundamentalism, a movement most commonly described as last-ditch reaction and anachronistic, rural anti-intellectualism, has refused to die. Instead of disappearing as predicted, one finds Fundamentalist leader Billy Graham named in public opinion polls as one of the most admired men in the United States and chosen as spiritual advisor and friend by President Richard Nixon. Of course, neither Mr. Nixon's faith nor Dr. Graham's popularity can be expected to persuade theologians to accept the inerrancy of the Scriptures, or historians to applaud William Jennings Bryan's attacks upon evolution. This is the enigma of contemporary Fundamentalism: although it is described as a lost cause and a hopeless crusade in every scholarly analysis, it continues to flourish in defiance of the experts. Within this paradox lies a world of significance for the understanding of the Fundamentalist as Christian and American, and for the understanding of American identity in the 1960s.

Ernest R. Sandeen is associate professor of history and director of the American Studies Institute at Macalester College in Minnesota. He is author of *Roots of Fundamentalism* (1970) and *Millenarianism* (1970).

Reprinted from *The Annals of the American Academy of Political and Social Science*, 387 (January 1970): 57–65. Used with permission of the author and publisher.

Origin and Basic Doctrines of Fundamentalism

Most discussions of Fundamentalism never escape from the semantic muddle which was created during the 1920s by the description of every foe of evolution as a Fundamentalist. The absurdity of arguing that everyone who supported prohibition was a Fundamentalist, or that everyone who wished to impeach Earl Warren was a Fundamentalist, is obvious to all. But the word "Fundamentalism" was invented just at the opening of the antievolution controversy, creating the mistaken impression that Fundamentalism was simply the name of a party opposing modernism in its many manifestations, a party created purely out of reaction to contemporary issues. In a study published elsewhere, I have argued another thesis: Fundamentalism has existed as a religious movement, possessing structure and identity, from about 1875 up to the present day.[1] The movement was rooted in concern with two doctrines—the personal, imminent return of Christ (millenarianism), and the verbal, inerrant inspiration of the Bible (literalism). These two concerns have remained definitive for Fundamentalists.

Most nineteenth-century American Protestants were millennialists. They believed that the Bible had foretold a thousand-year period of earthly blessedness. They expected that the beginning of the millennium was imminent and that its final years would be climaxed by the appearance of Christ as king. They were convinced that the course of history was progressive and that the forces now working toward the world's betterment—pre-eminently the Christian Gospel —would soon succeed in creating this near-perfect society. However, during the last quarter of the century, many responsible and respectable clergymen found themselves drawn toward a more apocalyptic doctrine of Christ's second advent. Through periodicals, books, and regular conferences, this millenarian message was spread: the world is rushing toward judgment, not perfection; man's wickedness is beyond remedy; man's government, philosophy, art, and science are only serving to amplify his degeneracy. To the sinner who repented, there remained an escape, however, for Christ would return to this world to rescue his Church and snatch it from the destruction which the world would soon suffer. Only after Christ's coming would the millennium be inaugurated, and thus the millenarian position was sometimes called premillennialism. This variant

---

[1] Ernest R. Sandeen, *Toward a Historical Interpretation of the Origins of Fundamentalism* (Philadelphia: Fortress Press, 1968), reprinted from *Church History*, 36 (March 1967).

view proved appealing to those whose faith in progress was being undermined by labor unrest, threats of socialism and anarchism, the flood tide of predominantly Catholic immigrants, and a series of financial panics. But it should be emphasized that the leaders of the millenarian movement at this time were far from being cranks or fanatics. Drawn primarily from the Episcopal, Presbyterian, and Baptist denominations, they were respected by those who did not agree with them, and often served in positions of responsibility. The Reverend Adoniram J. Gordon, at the time of his death in 1895, was a leader in Boston's religious life and was certainly one of the most prominent Baptists in New England. The Reverend James Hall Brookes held a similar position of influence in St. Louis and played an active role in the work of the General Assembly of the Presbyterian Church.

The unrest of the time, in the minds of the millenarians, played a distinctly secondary role to the authority of the Scriptures in convincing them of the truth of Christ's Second Coming. Millenarian insistence upon literalistic interpretation seemed excessive even to some who had no questions about the divine inspiration of the Bible, but the millenarian insisted that each detail of the prophetic panorama would be literally fulfilled, and he found in any challenge to verbal, inerrant inspiration of the Bible an attack upon the heart of his faith. By 1875, the millenarians had bonded the doctrine of inspiration onto expectations of the Second Coming of Christ—and they remain as indissolubly linked for the Fundamentalist of the 1960s as they were for the millenarian of the 1870s. During the last decades of the nineteenth century, millenarianism developed enough structure to justify calling it a movement. This is manifested, on the one hand, by the growth of group spirit behind the leadership of men like Brookes and Gordon. Converts to the cause were nurtured through one or another of the millenarian periodicals and were encouraged to attend one of the dozen conferences that were springing up across the country. On the other hand, millenarian teachers, without in the least de-emphasizing the doctrine of Christ's Second Coming, began to branch out into other spheres; they began to transform millenarianism from a special-interest group within certain denominations into an embryonic sect with well-articulated teachings on all aspects of the Christian faith. Millenarians developed special teachings concerning the work of the Holy Spirit, constructed a significant theology of missionary evangelism, and continued to emphasize the plenary, verbal, inerrant inspiration of the Scriptures.

This development took place, it should be noted, precisely at the time when the advocates of the New Theology, such as Washington Gladden, and the first proponents of higher criticism, such as Charles A. Briggs, were, in millenarian eyes at least, assaulting the foundations of Christian faith. Millenarianism, though a theology with no more seniority than modernism, and, in a real sense, the product of the same cultural complex, defended its position in the name of the historic Christian faith. Modernism did not perceive its role any more clearly. Though both groups had come into existence as the offspring of a sectarian brand of Protestant revivalistic evangelicalism, they squared off against each other in apologetic uniform as the conservative defender of the apostolic faith and the emancipated prophet of truth authenticated by science. Historians accepted these labels much too tamely and for far too long.

The Evolution Controversy

When the storm of controversy broke out in the 1920s, Fundamentalism, though newly christened, was scarcely a fledgling movement. While admitting that not everyone who participated in the fight against modernism was a millenarian, I am prepared to argue that the Fundamentalist movement of the 1920s was only the millenarian movement renamed. During the excitement of World War I, many millenarian conferences were held, particularly during 1918, when the British occupation of Palestine stirred hopes that prophecies relating to the return of the Jews to the Holy Land would soon be fulfilled. The one organization with an undisputed claim to leadership in the Fundamentalist movement—the World's Christian Fundamentals Association—was organized in 1919 as the result of those wartime conferences and was established and directed entirely by millenarians—men like Reuben A. Torrey, Amzi C. Dixon, and William Bell Riley. The struggle over modernism in the mission fields, especially in China, was instigated by millenarians Charles G. Trumbull and W. H. Griffith Thomas. And the battles within the Baptist and Presbyterian denominations, the two most severely affected by the Fundamentalist controversy, were fought principally, though not exclusively, by millenarians.

The grand cause of the 1920s, the antievolution crusade, would have existed without any aid or comfort from millenarianism, and it certainly received the greater part of its support from nonmillenarians. Some millenarian-Fundamentalist leaders, for example, William Bell Riley, plunged furiously into the battle to save the innocent from Darwin's dragon, but that was not true of all millenarians. More significantly, the antievolution crusade won thousands of followers, and many of its leaders, from nonmillenarian ranks. The great commoner, W. J. Bryan, though he spoke in defense of Christianity as he understood it, did not understand what he defended at all well, and seems to have had no acquaintance with millenarian teachings. With the exception of Minnesota, where Riley managed the campaign, the greatest part of the agitation over anti-evolution legislation took place in the South and Southwest, where, by the 1920s, millenarianism had scarcely penetrated, and where the churches were not yet troubled by doctrinal controversy. The antievolution crusade remains a significant episode in the history of millenarian-Fundamentalism, but it was not a definitive one.

Much like the threat of modernist subversion in that day and the threat of Communist subversion in our own, evolution was looked upon as an issue that focused popular discontent. Uneasiness with the new science provided millenarians with an opportunity for alerting a sleeping world to the peril it faced. But to plunge into a struggle to prohibit the teaching of evolution in the public schools violated the theological principles upon which millenarianism had been founded. Millenarians have consistently taught that nothing can save this world from destruction, and that attempts to ameliorate the condition of man, protect the schools, censor the theater, or save the republic are all doomed. The one activity to which Christians are called is the salvation of souls. One who held these views could hardly justify co-operation in the campaign against evolution. Perhaps this explains why no more millenarians joined Riley in his campaigns. That so many did participate in the crusade would seem to indicate an unresolved tension within the membership of the movement—a tension which has remained alive through the 1960s.

Changes in Fundamentalist Leadership

By the early 1930s, Fundamentalist leaders had been forced to accept the fact that they were powerless to drive modernism from its entrenchment in the major denominations. They either had to accept a broad church policy of accommodation or split off from the parent body. After the market collapse in 1929, public attention could no longer be concentrated on denominational squabbles. Fundamentalism dropped out of prominence and was forgotten. But while the movement survived, it did not remain unchanged. Even during the 1920s, Fundamentalist leadership profiles reflect a significant shift in the movement's center of gravity. In the 1870s, millenarianism had been dominated by Presbyterians, Episcopalians,

Congregationalists, and Baptists. By 1900, Episcopal and Congregational support had diminished considerably. At the turn of the century, the Baptists were most numerous and the Presbyterians most prominent. By the 1920s, another shift had taken place. Presbyterian support greatly diminished, and a new element, composed of virtually nondenominational Bible institute professors, shared the conference platforms with the continuing ranks of Baptist ministers. In the 1950s and 1960s, leadership in the Fundamentalist movement has not changed substantially, but the Pentecostalists have been drawn into much closer alliance with the older membership.

The events of the 1920s made it essential for Fundamentalism to secure its existence outside the old-line denominations where its members could hope for no more than tolerance. Happily for them, this institutionalization was virtually complete before it became necessary to transfer allegiance. By 1910, several dozen Bible institutes, the most important of which were Moody Bible Institute in Chicago and the Bible Institute of Los Angeles, had been founded; and an association of colleges and academies, known for their continued fidelity to standards of biblical authority, had been organized, in 1919, at the first meeting of the World's Christian Fundamentals Association. Although not designed for this purpose, the Bible institutes soon began to function as ministerial training schools for the large number of churches—whether technically nondenominational or not—which looked to such institutes as, virtually, denominational headquarters.

Internal relationships among Fundamentalist leaders during the 1930s were hardly more friendly than had been the relationship between modernists and Fundamentalists. Schisms occurred in newly established Fundamentalist denominations, such as the Presbyterian church in America, established in 1936 chiefly through the efforts of J. Gresham Machen. This tendency toward infinite division and inextinguishable suspicion has never been resolved, but Fundamentalists have ordinarily lined up in one of two large blocs, the American Council of Christian Churches (ACCC), founded in 1941, or the National Association of Evangelicals (NAE), founded in 1942. The former body is flamboyant, militant, and negative. The NAE operates more as a holding corporation or accrediting agency. Fundamentalist faith in individualism and jealousy of doctrinal freedom prevent members from delegating any significant amount of authority to the NAE. The NAE and the ACCC are, quite transparently, the Fundamentalist counterpart of the National Council of Churches (NCC). The NAE conducts its business without consciously mimicking the National Council, but the ACCC carries on operations in virtual parody of the NCC, meeting at the same time and place, picketing, and protesting.

Within the context of the ecumenical movement, this phenomenon of parallel institutionalism has been a matter of common knowledge, but the extent to which the parallelism has dominated and shaped the character of the Fundamentalist movement has not, I believe, been adequately recognized. For virtually every professional and scholarly group in the United States, there exists a Fundamentalist equivalent. When the Society of Biblical Exegesis meets, not far away one will find the Evangelical Theological Society. Fundamentalist scientists can join the American Scientific Affiliation. At meetings of the American Historical Association, the Evangelical Historians hold a breakfast. There exist a Christian Businessmen's Association, a Christian Medical Association, an Intervarsity Christian Fellowship for students, an Evangelical Press Association, a Fellowship of Christian Athletes, and even a Christian Women's Group for housewives. These and dozens of other parallel institutions, along with Fundamentalist colleges and Bible institutes, provide the structure for the Fundamentalist movement. Research in this field ought to prove intriguing to either historians or sociologists, and might provide a much better insight than we now possess into the potentialities of the movement. At this point, it is possible only to suggest a hypothesis about the function and meaning of this parallelism.

Fundamentalism and Its Adversaries: A Symbiotic Relationship

From reading the polemical literature of the movement, one might conclude that Fundamentalists would like nothing better than to be rid of the National Council of Churches and the whole liberal establishment. In reading the liberal academicians' interpretations of Fundamentalism, one detects a similarly negative mood. One might conclude that they would like nothing better than to be rid of the movement, their attitude appearing as little more than a ritualized death wish directed against it.

In fact, Fundamentalism lives in symbiotic relationship with its adversaries. In the cases of the ACCC and leaders like Billy James Hargis or Carl McIntire, this relationship can probably be described as parasitic symbiosis, but for moderate Fundamentalists and their foes, it appears to be—in defiance of their rhetoric—a complex and mutually advantageous relationship. The very breath of life seems to be provided for the Fundamentalist by those whom he opposes, each of his positions and opinions being conceived through opposition to a liberal stance or utterance. In their annoyance over this behavior, the critics of Fundamentalism have failed to notice that they are themselves benefiting from the vitality of the movement.

How does this relationship affect Fundamentalism? Though it might be argued that Fundamentalism functions like a shadow cabinet, preparing for the day when it will come to power and substitute its positions for those of the present majority, I find that thesis difficult to accept. Rather, Fundamentalists have continued to operate within the same paradoxical position that created so much tension in the 1920s. On the one hand, they accept and teach a theology which allows no room for hopes of eventual peace or victory in this world. They cannot, without rejecting the foundation stone of their creed, lend their support to institutions and organizations whose aim is social betterment. Their theology states unequivocally that this world cannot be wrestled from the grip of Satan except by the coming Messiah, and that attempts to ameliorate the effects of sin and evil will eventually play into the hands of him whose world this is. The Christian's present task must be only to preach the Gospel, so that some may escape the inevitable judgment. On the other hand, individual Fundamentalists are overwhelmingly drawn from the white, relatively affluent, middle class, and only rarely seem to feel any personal alienation from contemporary society. Fundamentalists as a group have shown very little sympathy with student revolts and black despair, though one would have thought that the similarity in their ideologies might have drawn such groups together. And, given the Fundamentalist's position on the fallibility and seductiveness of man's works, there seems to be some incongruity in his contemporary receptivity to the propaganda of superpatriotism.

Without realizing it, the Fundamentalist has become trapped. He does not want to hate his country. Like most other Americans, he enjoys his creature comforts—watches too much television, overeats, and works crossword puzzles. He really believes that America is beautiful, and that someone ought to do something about water and air pollution, and especially about beer-can clutter on the roadside. At the same time, he cannot contemplate throwing over the millenarian theology of apocalypticism and alienation. To drop these beliefs would be to lose one's identity as a Fundamentalist. Institutionally, it is obvious that the decision to surrender the dogma is unthinkable. The solution to this dilemma has been found in the creation of these parallel institutions through which one can work to benefit society without actually identifying with it.

On the other side of the symbiosis, the non-Fundamentalist forces —the old terms "liberal" and "modernist" mean virtually nothing in contemporary society—continue to benefit from Fundamentalism. As seminary enrollments have dropped during the 1960s, the Fundamentalist colleges and Bible schools have continued to supply a surprising number of students, not only to their own schools, but also to institutions such as Union Theological Seminary and the University of Chicago Divinity School, even though the faculties are reputed to be a pack of lions whose regular diet is Christian flesh. Without the continuous transfusion of Fundamentalist vitality, there is reason to doubt whether Protestantism could have survived into the 1960s with as much resiliency as it now displays.

Contemporary Fundamentalism

Fundamentalism has passed through the 1960s without altering any of its essential doctrinal or organizational positions. Once again, the movement dropped one name for another, preferring to be known, at this point in history, as Evangelicalism. Billy Graham, whose surprising success in the 1950s demonstrated the continuing appeal of the message of biblical literalism and whose style mirrored the postwar Fundamentalist drive for respectability and conformity mixed with godliness, continued to function as the spokesman for the Evangelical-Fundamentalists, although his associations with representatives of the National Council of Churches proved too compromising to Fundamentalist extremists like McIntire. Since World War II, Fundamentalism has faced no external threat to its existence. The affluence of the past quarter of a century has been appropriated as much by the Fundamentalists as by any other segment of the population. During the first years of Graham's fame, Fundamentalists continually asked each other a question that reflected doubts about themselves and about the movement as a whole: Would success spoil Billy Graham? Despite the grumping of the ACCC, it seems to me that Graham's stability, strength, and adaptability correctly reflect qualities in the movement from which he sprang to prominence, and which he still serves as spokesman and demigod.

Perhaps it was because so little remained in America to trouble the souls of contemporary Fundamentalists that the anti-Communist crusade of the 1950s and 1960s, for the first time since the anti-evolution campaigns of the 1920s, threatened to become an issue which might swamp the movement. The absence of serious tension between Fundamentalism and contemporary American society, and the Fundamentalists' growing prosperity, created a situation in which the antagonist (Russian communism, instead of German theories of higher criticism) might better be located somewhere other than within America, though its effects could be fought here. For a time, I believe, there was serious danger that anti-Communist hysteria might actually sweep Fundamentalism off its feet. Though the movement of the Radical Right has not evaporated, and still appeals to many Fundamentalists, the identification of the two movements now seems unlikely. As in the 1920s, there are those leaders, for example, Billy James Hargis and Carl McIntire, for whom anti-Communist subversion has become virtually the only topic of discourse. But other leading Fundamentalist institutions have maintained their balance. Moody Bible Institute, for example, devoted one of its main sessions at an annual Founder's Day Conference in the early 1960s to the menace of Communist subversion, but then, in the face of criticism, backed away from such topics.

When one looks at Fundamentalism from the perspective of the 1960s, there is much about the movement that would appear to be significant. Their antagonists accused the Fundamentalists of obscurantism and anti-intellectualism because they refused to accept the scholars' arguments concerning the authorship of the Pentateuch or the date of Daniel. The Fundamentalist's response was often anti-intellectual, but it was also classically American. He claimed his God-given, democratic birthright to believe whatever he pleased. As observers from the time of Tocqueville have noticed, Americans place little restraint upon the right of a majority—often in defiance of minority rights and in spite of the weight of evidence on the other side, to decide—to accept, to do, or to believe what they please. Lawrence Levine, in his recent study of W. J. Bryan's last years, has given a brilliant exposition of this side of Bryan's character, depicting, for example, a Bryan who believed that if only enough people joined in signing declarations against war, nothing could prevent the triumph of peace. No refutation of this concept is necessary, of course, but it does seem necessary, especially in the face of the derision which has been heaped upon the Fundamentalists for responding in this fashion, to emphasize that, though they may have been wrong, they were mistaken in the true-blue American way.

Fundamentalism as an Authentic Conservative Tradition

Their significance also arises from the fact that Fundamentalism can lay claim to representing one of the few authentic conservative traditions in American history. During the past few decades, there has been considerable interest by historians in the quest for an American conservative tradition, though the search has proved unsuccessful to this date. None of the likely candidates, like Calhoun or the theorists of the American Revolution, possessed the integrity, consistency, and sense of tradition necessary to fill the role. My nomination of Fundamentalism to play this part may, at first, seem ludicrous to many readers, but I believe it deserves serious consideration. I have already denied to Fundamentalism what might seem to be the one essential ingredient in any conservative tradition —a clear and accurate understanding of the past. Fundamentalists claimed that they were fighting to defend the doctrine and discipline of the Apostles, whereas it has been my contention that they were, rather, defending weak points in a quite sectarian variant of nineteenth-century evangelical theology. The fallacy in this objection lies in the mistaken premise. Conservative traditions seem to flourish best where the leaders' memories are selective or faulty, and no probing historical inquiries interrupt the defense of the cause. This was certainly true of the Roman, Papal, and British traditions. Fundamentalism appears to possess every other requisite of a viable conservative tradition as well. The movement has been built out of grass-roots support, its values and truths are well articulated and consistently maintained, the connection with an appealing and vital past is never forgotten, and it survives.

There could be no conservative tradition at all in America if the arguments of the historians of consensus were valid. Each conflict in American history, these scholars argue, has concluded with a resolution of the issue and the emergence of a new consensus to which everyone pledges his allegiance. The losers either pack up and leave, like the Tories in the American Revolution, or swallow their pride, abandon their views, and join in the celebration of victory. That historians such as Richard Hofstadter and William G. McLoughlin can offer this interpretation of the fate of Fundamentalism during the 1960s strikes me as not only mistaken but perverse.[2] By pretending that Fundamentalism is quietly fading away, these scholars are obscuring that perspective on the Fundamentalist movement which might provide the most helpful insight into the nature of the contemporary American dilemma. We exist

---

[2] Richard Hofstadter, *Anti-Intellectualism in American Life* (New York: Alfred A. Knopf, 1963); Wm. G. McLoughlin, "Is There a Third Force in Christendom?," *Daedalus* (Winter 1967): 43–68.

in a fragmented and divided culture, not in one pervaded by consensus. We live in a society in which most of the problems are created by subgroups whose values and ideals are threatened by changes in technological, economic, or political practices, and who doggedly refuse to drop their claims or change their attitudes as the result of a little more education or the passage of a little more time. Prayer in the public schools, Negroes living in white neighborhoods, the guaranteed annual wage, the new morality, Communist infiltration of government agencies, deficit spending—the list of issues seems almost infinitely expansible. It seems very much to the point, in the face of such a catalogue of grievances—each with its own organization dedicated to maintaining that particular truth and defeating the agents of innovation—to challenge the pollyanna of progress, and to recognize that this century is seeing American culture in a new context. The era of consensus is past, and the millenarian-Fundamentalist movement—now nearly one hundred years old—provides us with a model for the study of conservative survival and vitality.

Conclusion

Thus, Fundamentalism, which, in the 1920s, was given very little chance for survival, much less development, continues to exist, to grow, and, one might almost say, to flourish. The closely related nineteenth-century doctrines of the imminent Second Coming of Christ and the verbal, inerrant inspiration of the Bible had not seemed to be the kind of base upon which to build such an institutional structure. The maintenance of a conservative tradition founded essentially upon ideas unsupported by the intellectual and scientific authorities in the society, and possessed of no clear or direct commitment from any of the powerful vested interests in the nation, seemed to hold little promise of longevity. But what has seemed an enigma now begins to look like a model. Ninteenth-century culture apparently developed more than one idea endowed with conservative potential. The process of rapid, technologically induced change seems destined to succeed where poets and historians have previously failed. By stripping every sector of American society to its bare essentials, to its irreducible commitments, this giant change machine is defining the American character. Everyone today seems faced with a choice between a role as modern man or as American. Modern man must be the man who can adapt to anything, who can live in any surroundings with a set of functional values designed to help him survive in that environment. But the American is emerging as the man who has something to remember and something to protect. At this point in the twentieth century, the Fundamentalist continues to insist that he is the inheritor, guardian, and advocate of the central truths of the Christian faith. And at this point in the twentieth century, one might ask if he does not also represent the archetypal and modal American—the man who while losing his country has found it.

Sandeen's essay shows that some of the characteristics usually attributed to highly sectarian groups also flourish within the mainstream. Consider, for instance, the way in which Fundamentalism thrives upon its opposition to the National Council of Churches and other religious organizations that it views as excessively liberal in matters of both theology and social policy. Moreover, it should not be assumed that as a historian Sandeen's emphasis upon the internal diversity of American Protestantism contradicts the work of sociologists in this area. Both Glock and Stark[8] and Hadden[9] have drawn attention to both the differences between the various major Protestant denominations as well as the degree of variation of individual beliefs and opinions within each denomination. While these sociologists have not dealt with Fundamentalism per se as a movement, they have stressed the importance of understanding the different types of denominations within the mainstream.

One of the most serious inferences to be drawn from Sandeen's essay is that the notion of an American religious "mainstream" may well be a convenient sociological fiction. Herberg, Bellah, and others have argued that America's three-religion pluralism (Protestant-Catholic-Jew) stands united upon the foundation of

---

[8] Glock and Stark, in *Religion and Society in Tension* (Chicago: Rand McNally, 1965), call attention to these denominational differences and continue to employ a typology of denominations in their later work, *American Piety: The Nature of Religious Commitment* (Berkeley: The University of California Press, 1970). Yet ironically, they overlook these important differences between Protestant denominations in their most controversial work *Christian Beliefs and Anti-Semitism* (New York: Harper and Row, 1966).

[9] Jeffrey K. Hadden, *The Gathering Storm in the Churches* (Garden City: Doubleday, 1969).

a general "civil religion."[10] It is argued that minor theological differences count for little when contrasted with what the major three faiths have in common. Yet, Sandeen's essay suggests that even within the Protestant fold there are at least two "civil religions" divided along both political and religious liberal and conservative poles. These broader differences may well be more significant for the social order than such smaller distinctions as church-sect and the like.

[10] See Will Herberg, *Protestant-Catholic-Jew* (Garden City: Doubleday, 1955); and Robert Bellah, "Civil Religion in America," *Deadalus*, 96 (1967): 1–21. Bellah's essay is contained in this book, pp. 111–121.

Patterns of Religious Change

Part VI

Patterns of Religious Change

One of the most difficult and intriguing questions in any branch of science is, What will the future bring? Regarding religion, answers to this question have traditionally involved the concept of secularization. Like the sociology of religion itself, the concept of secularization is a major theme that emerges from the European classical tradition. Like the other trends that the classical theorists observed—urbanization, industrialization, rationalization, and bureaucracy—secularization became an assumption of contemporary sociology. Yet, if the alleged religious revival of the 1950s stimulated a revival of interest in the sociology of religion, it also called into question this major assumption of the field. Since the mid-1950s, the subject of secularization, rather than being an assumed fact, has become a source of controversy and debate among sociologists of religion.

A useful cautionary note on these debates has been provided by Richard K. Fenn. He contends, quite correctly, that:

> Debates on the issue of secularization tend to be a confusing mixture of statements of faith, functionalist axioms about the general importance of religion to societies and specific theories in the sociology of religion.[1]

[1] Richard K. Fenn, "Talking Past One Another: Notes on the Debate," *Journal for the Scientific Study of Religion,* 12, no. 3 (1973): 353.

Before facing the problem of distinguishing statements of faith from testable scientific hypothesis, it is necessary to distinguish the different definitions of the term "secularization" employed by different investigators. Larry E. Shiner's essay, "The Concept of Secularization in Empirical Research," provides a starting point. Shiner considers both the historical development of the concept as well as a survey of the different ways it has been used by contemporary sociologists. He is realistic in recognizing the improbability of everyone agreeing upon a single definition of the term. Yet, he does offer some suggestions for clarifying the term's meaning as well as some avenues of research that would allow sociologists to answer the question, Is secularization occurring? While one may not necessarily agree with Shiner's suggestions, he does provide the best definition of the problem yet to appear in the literature on the subject.

The Concept of Secularization in Empirical Research*
by Larry E. Shiner

Secularization, once branded *the* enemy, has suddenly become the darling of Protestant theology, and there are strong indications that some Roman Catholic theologians are softening. But why should such theological conundrums as "the secular meaning of the Gospel" or "secular Christianity" be relevant to the scientific analysis of religion? At the least, this recent theological attack on the received interpretation of secularization should inspire the analyst to reconsider the customary definitions and measures used in research. What *is* an index of secularization? Is it church attendance? Belief in immortality? The amount of private prayer? The number of scientists who believe in God? Or could it be that the indicators are

Larry E. Shiner is associate professor of philosophy at Sangamon State University, Illinois, and is the author of *The Secularization of History* (1966).

Reprinted from *Journal for the Scientific Study of Religion*, 6, no. 2 (1967): 207–220. Used with permission of the author and publisher.

*A revision of a paper presented at the Annual Meeting of the Society for the Scientific Study of Religion in Chicago, October 27–29, 1966.

more subtle, so much so that secularization could even permeate what on the surface appears to be religious fervor? Is secularization a low score on a conventional index of religiosity? Or is it another form of religiosity? Or is it an independent process quite uncorrelated with religiosity? In both the empirical and interpretive work on secularization today, the lack of agreement on what secularization is and how to measure it stands out above everything else.

The following analysis is an attempt to bring the concept of secularization at least partially into focus by considering (1) its history, (2) its current definitions, (3) its use in empirical research, and (4) its weakness as an analytical tool and some possible alternatives.

An Historical Overview[1]

The English term "secular" comes from the Latin *saeculum,* which means a generation, or an age, or the spirit of an age, and could also signify the span of a century. By the time of the Vulgate the Latin *saeculum* had already achieved considerable ambiguity, bearing both the religiously neutral sense of an immeasurably great span of time (e.g., *in saecula saeculorum,* I Tim. 1:17) and the religiously negative sense of "this world" which is under the power of Satan (e.g., *Et nolite confirmari huic saeculo,* Rom. 12:2). In the Middle Ages the idea of "this world" had itself been neutralized to some extent so that such concepts as "secular clergy" or the "secular arm" did not connote hostility to religion.

The first appearance of the form "secularization" *(saecularizatio)* in a sense approximating its present connotations was not until the negotiations for the Peace of Westphalia. Here the French representative introduced the term to signify lands and possessions transferred from ecclesiastical to civil control. Although most subsequent Roman Catholic discussions of secularization in this sense have regarded it as an unmitigated evil, not all the transfers in the 17th century were opposed by the Church, and the word retained in general a neutral and descriptive connotation.[2] By the 18th century, however, there were those who claimed that all ecclesiastical property should be at the disposition of the state as a matter of principle.[3] During the French Revolution, of course, this principle began to be carried out and expanded to all areas of life.

[1] There are two discussions of the history of the concept of secularization available. Martin Stallmann, *Was ist Säkularisierung?* (Tübingen: J. C. B. Mohr, 1960), Chapt. I. Hermann Lübbe, *Säkularisierung, Geschichte eines ideenpolitischen Begriffs* (Freiburg: Karl Alber, 1965).

[2] Stallmann, *op. cit.,* pp. 5–7.

[3] *Ibid.,* p. 8.

The best known use of the secularization terminology in a militant sense during the 19th century was by G. J. Holyoake and his free-thinker's organization known as the "Secular Society." Holyoake called his program "Secularism," by which he meant "a practical philosophy for the people" intended to interpret and organize life without recourse to the supernatural.[4] Side by side with this aggressively programmatic meaning of "secularism" there has also grown up a usage which defines "secularism" as an attitude of indifference to religious institutions and practices or even to religious questions as such.

The historical sediment of most of these past meanings still clings to "secularism" and "secularization" as they are employed today in ordinary discourse. However, the dominant connotations, reflecting the long struggle against the tutelary function of the Churches and the Christian world view, are indifference, anticlericalism, and irreligion. Beginning with Max Weber and Ernst Troeltsch, "secularization" was used as a descriptive and analytical term, and it was soon picked up by historians. Despite the relative neutrality attached to it in history and sociology during the first decades of the century, in theology it still designated a militant force to be combatted.

Since the Second World War, however, there has been an about-face among an increasing number of theologians. Dietrich Bonhoeffer and Friedrich Gogarten are the most significant of those who have argued that secularization is not only in part a result of Christian faith, but is also actually demanded and fostered in all areas of life by the freedom and responsibility laid on the man of faith. According to Gogarten, the independence of science and culture from the supposedly "Christian" world view is the logical and appropriate outcome of God's having turned the world over to man's responsibility.[5]

Many other theologians who are not ready to go as far as Bonhoeffer and Gogarten in celebrating the autonomy of man accept secularization as a positive development. This includes Catholic progressives who speak appreciatively of a secular society and look upon the medieval sacral society as an historical development

---

[4] For a short discussion of the background and principles of the movement see Eric S. Waterhouse's article on Secularism in the *Encyclopedia of Religion and Ethics,* Vol. XI (New York: Charles Scribner's Sons, 1921), pp. 347–350.

[5] Gogarten's fullest statement of this position is to be found in *Verhängnis und Hoffnung der Neuzeit* (Stuttgart: Friedrich Vorwerk, 1953). Bonhoeffer's comments are found in *Prisoner for God* (New York: Macmillan, 1953), and *Ethics* (New York: Macmillan, 1955).

necessitated by the Constantinian triumph but not as a phenomenon integral to the Christian faith. Although many of these more moderate Catholic and Protestant thinkers are "transformationists" who believe that secular society ought to be graced with the leaven of the sacred, it is clear that for them "secularization" is no longer a term of opprobrium but rather, an instrument of description and analysis.[6]

Types of Secularization Concept

If we put aside the special usage of economics and the legal definition derived from Westphalia, there appear to be six types of secularization concept in use today. Since what we are about to delineate are *types*, most of the actual definitions or usages one encounters in the literature will deviate to some degree or else represent combinations. Each is presented in terms of a brief definition which describes the kind of process involved and its theoretical culmination. Then a few examples are given before a critical assessment is attempted.

1. Decline of Religion

The previously accepted symbols, doctrines, and institutions lose their prestige and influence. The culmination of secularization would be a religionless society. J. Milton Yinger, for example, terms secularization the process "in which traditional religious symbols and forms have lost force and appeal."[7]

Examples in research. One of the most significant general studies of American religion in the last few years, Glock and Stark's *Religion and Society in Tension*, makes use of a doctrinal version of the decline theory. The authors accept a definition of secularization as the replacement of "mystical and supernatural elements of traditional Christianity" by a "demythologized, ethical rather than theological religion."[8] They claim that some denominations are becoming relatively secularized in terms of the substantial percentage

---

[6] For a discussion of the main theological attempts to come to grips with the problem of secularization, see Larry Shiner, "Towards a Theology of Secularization," *Journal of Religion*, October 1965, pp. 279–295.

[7] J. Milton Yinger, *Religion, Society and the Individual* (New York: Macmillan, 1957), p. 119.

[8] Charles Y. Glock and Rodney Stark, *Religion and Society in Tension* (Chicago: Rand McNally, 1965), p. 116.

of members who either deny or are doubtful about many elements of their Church's historic creed.[9] Other studies have measured the decrease in clerical prestige, the number of marriages before clergymen, the amount of prayer or Church attendance, or the number of paintings with "religious" as opposed to "secular" themes.[10] Some, like Pitirim A. Sorokin, have put together a collection of such variables relating to belief and practice and developed a general theory of decline.[11]

Assessment. There are two major difficulties with the decline thesis. One is the problem of determining when and where we are to find the supposedly "religious" age from which decline has commenced. David Martin has noted that even secularists tend to take a utopian view of medieval religious life.[12] And as Gabriel Le Bras says of the term "dechristianization" which is widely used in France, such language presupposes a "christianized" France which never was. Moreover, although there has been a decrease in conventional forms of religious practice in France, Le Bras points out that there were in former times built-in premiums and liabilities relating to practice which may have produced large scale conventional acceptance of Christianity but little depth. Le Bras argues that in "dechristianized" France today there are, among practicing Catholics, probably more who participate voluntarily, faithfully and with an understanding of what they are doing than there were before 1789.[13]

Le Bras' suggestion regarding the seriousness of contemporary religious practice points to the other problems with the decline thesis: the ambiguity of most measures which are used. The easily measurable variables—church attendance, replies to belief questionnaires, proportion of contributions—are notoriously difficult to

---

[9] *Ibid.,* pp. 116–120.

[10] Some examples may be found in Robert S. Lynd and Helen Merrell Lynd, *Middletown* (New York: Harcourt, Brace and Company, 1929), pp. 112, 120–121, 462; Daniel Lerner, *The Passing of Traditional Society* (Glencoe: The Free Press, 1958), p. 230; John T. Flint, "The Secularization of Norwegian Society," *Comparative Studies in Society and History,* VI, 1964, pp. 325–344.

[11] Pitirim A. Sorokin, "The Western Religion and Morality of Today," *International Yearbook for the Sociology of Religion,* Vol. II (Köln und Opladen: Westdeutscher Verlag, 1966), pp. 9–43.

[12] David A. Martin, "Utopian Aspects of the Concept of Secularization," *International Yearbook for the Sociology of Religion,* Vol. II (Köln und Opladen: Westdeutscher Verlag, 1966), p. 92.

[13] Gabriel Le Bras, "Déchristianisation: mot fallacieux," *Social Compass,* X, 1963, pp. 448, 451.

assess. Although the Glock and Stark study was a considerable improvement over past measures of belief, and although the refinements developed by Fichter, Lenski, and Fukuyama have contributed much, the problem of the norm for doctrinal or practical deviation remains, as well as the question of whether such deviation from tradition is necessarily a decline.

Glock and Stark seem to accept the religious conservative's tendency to make "liberal theologically" the equivalent of "secularized." But is "liberal" theology really an adulteration of the historical faith? Or may it not be, as the best liberal theologians have always insisted, an interpretation of the essence of the tradition in the thought forms and language of today? Bultmann and others have even suggested that to repeat the old language and thought forms actually points men away from the genuine core of faith to peripheral matters and may demand an entirely unnecessary *sacrificium intellectus.* Moreover, far from being a mere capitulation or conformity to the reigning opinion of "this world," such an approach is viewed by its creators as the *only* way to face men with the real stumbling block of Christianity.[14] What can be the social scientist's justification for calling this effort to make a religious tradition more vital a "secularization" in the sense of a decline or subversion?

It is evident that part of the difficulty in measuring the decline of religion is the definition of religion itself.[15] As we proceed to examine other types of the secularization concept, the issue of the nature of religion will come up again and will finally have to be dealt with explicitly.

2. Conformity with "This World"

The religious group or the religiously informed society turns its attention from the supernatural and becomes more and more interested in "this world." In ethics there is a corresponding tendency away from an ethic motivated by the desire to prepare for the future life or to conform to the group's ethical tradition toward an ethic adapted to the present exigencies of the surrounding society. *The culmination of secularization would be a society totally absorbed with the pragmatic tasks of the present and a religious group in-*

[14] Rudolf Bultmann, "The New Testament and Mythology," in *Kerygma and Myth,* ed. H. W. Bartsch (London: S. P. C. K., 1953), pp. 1–6. See also pp. 120–123 on the "real skandalon" of Christian faith.

[15] Paul Tillich, "Existentialist Aspects of Modern Art," in *Christianity and the Existentialists,* ed. Carl Michalson (New York: Charles Scribner's Sons, 1956), pp. 133–138.

distinguishable from the rest of society. Harold W. Pfautz has defined secularization as "the tendency of sectarian religious movements to become both part of and like 'the world.' "[16]

Examples in research. The classic statement of this position is Adolf Harnack's characterization of the early Church's growth in numbers and wealth, its emerging hierarchical organization, and its involvement with Greek thought as a "secularization."[17] Pfautz's analysis of Christian Science measures conformity to the world in terms of an "increasing traditional and purposeful-rational motivation, and decreasing affectual motivation."[18] In an important study of the general sect-church spectrum, Pfautz develops a more complex set of variables for measuring secularization in terms of demography, ecology, associational character, structural differentiation, and social-psychological texture. The movement across this typology is termed a "secularization" because it involves a constant increase in size, complexity, and rationalization of structures and modes of participation.[19]

By far the most provocative investigation of this type of secularization in America has been Will Herberg's *Protestant-Catholic-Jew.*[20] In his more recent Harlan Paul Douglas lectures he distinguishes between *conventional* religions (e.g., Judaism, Islam, Protestant denominations) and the *operative* religion of a society which actually provides its own "ultimate context of meaning and value."[21] Then he defines a secularized culture as one in which "conventional religion is no longer the operative religion in the sociological sense."[22] In his earlier book Herberg measured secularization by the degree to which nominal believers who belong to conventional religions actually reflect the outlook of the operative religion of American society.[23] In the second of his Douglas lectures, he modified Pfautz's typology of religious groups and con-

---

[16] Harold Pfautz, "Christian Science: A Case Study of the Social Psychological Aspect of Secularization," *Social Forces,* 34 (1956): 246.

[17] Adolf von Harnack, *Monasticism: Its Ideals and History* (London: Williams Norgate, 1901), p. 112.

[18] Harold W. Pfautz, *op. cit.,* p. 247.

[19] Harold W. Pfautz, "The Sociology of Secularization: Religious Groups," *American Journal of Sociology,* 61 (1955): 121–128.

[20] Will Herberg, *Protestant-Catholic-Jew* (New York: Anchor Books, 1960).

[21] Will Herberg, "Religion in a Secularized Society: The New Shape of Religion in America," *Review of Religious Research,* 3 (1961–62): 146.

[22] *Ibid.,* p. 148.

[23] Herberg, *op. cit.,* pp. 74–79, 82–83.

cluded: "The series can now be completed: *cult—sect—denomi-nation—socio-religious community—tri-faith system*. Beyond this, secularization cannot go."[24]

Assessment. As in the case of the decline thesis, the main difficulty with the idea of secularization as conformity to the world is the ambiguity of the measures applied. Moreover, simply by employing the Church/world or "this world/other world" dichotomy, the social scientist has taken over a particular theological framework as his own. In any given case we must ask whether something *integral* to a religious tradition is being surrendered in favor of "this world" or whether the change which is taking place may not be quite compatible with the main stream of the tradition. Is it a subversion of Islam or Christianity that one becomes increasingly concerned with the good life in "this world," or is it perhaps as much a shift of emphasis from certain elements in these traditions to other elements no less integral? And may not an apparent compromise with the world on the part of a religious group be part of a necessary differentiation within the group which leaves behind the affectional relationships of the "good old days" without breaking down the core of the tradition?

These observations are not meant to depreciate the usefulness of Pfautz's typology, but rather to question the value of terming the process one of "increasing secularization" when this implies a deviation or subversion from a more genuinely religious position. A similar objection may be made to Herberg's thesis, since what looks like secularization to Herberg appears to some religious liberals as the triumph of the "common faith" of America. The latter may be in some respects false or shallow, but it is a misleading (if not simply pejorative) use of the word to term the one religion "secularized" and treat the other as "authentic."

Although the three types of concept we will consider next have not been used as widely in empirical research as the two above, they are worth delineating in equal detail since they are more descriptive and also more suggestive in terms of the relationship between religious change and other variables.

3. Disengagement of Society from Religion

Society separates itself from the religious understanding which has previously informed it in order to constitute itself an autonomous

[24] Will Herberg, "The New Shape of American Religion: Some Aspects of America's Three-Religion Pluralism," *Review of Religious Research*, 4 (1962–63): 39.

reality and consequently to limit religion to the sphere of private life. The culmination of this kind of secularization would be a religion of a purely inward character, influencing neither institutions nor corporate action, and a society in which religion made no appearance outside the sphere of the religious group. Hannah Arendt defines secularization in one place as "first of all simply the separation of religion and politics."[25] The French theologian and social analyst Roger Mehl has described secularization as the "historical process which tends to contest the public role of religion, to substitute other forms of authority for religious authority, and finally to relegate religion to the private sector of human existence."[26]

Examples in research. This understanding of secularization has been extensively investigated by historians, who see it as taking two forms, one intellectual-existential, the other institutional-social. Institutional secularization is usually traced in terms of the rise of the "secular" state and its gradual assumption of the educational and welfare functions once performed by the churches. A recent non-Western example of this is given in Donald E. Smith's *India as a Secular State,* where it is argued that the Indian government has been secularized in the sense that it has adopted an attitude of neutrality toward both individual and group religious belief and practice.[27] The social transformation which usually accompanies the secularization of the state has been analyzed in a variety of ways and has produced studies of the secularization of work, welfare, family life, etc. The intellectual-existential aspect of disengagement has probably been as extensively explored as any phenomenon of secularization. Bernhard Grotheuysen aptly describes the process as "the attempt to establish an autonomous sphere of knowledge purged of supernatural, fideistic presuppositions."[28] Concretely, one speaks of the secularization of science or ethics or art insofar as they are separated from ecclesiastical control or from the context of a particular version of the Christian world view.

Assessment. Although more specific than the thesis of decline or conformity with the world, the concept of secularization as dis-

[25] Hannah Arendt, *Between Past and Future* (Cleveland: Meridian Books, 1963), p. 69.

[26] Roger Mehl, "De la sécularisation à l'atheism," *Foi et Vie,* 65 (1966): 70.

[27] Donald E. Smith, *India as a Secular State* (Princeton: Princeton University Press, 1963).

[28] Bernhard Grotheuysen, "Secularism," *Encyclopedia of the Social Sciences,* 1934, XIII, p. 631.

engagement suffers from parallel handicaps. Smith's argument that the Indian state is secularized because it is neutral on religious beliefs and practices has been criticized as overlooking the fact that the Hindu and Islamic faiths have never been a matter of purely private beliefs and practices. Smith's critics suggest that Indian secularity involves a strong dose of secularism, by which they mean a commitment to an ideology which seeks to embrace the whole of life and to replace the role once held by the religious communities.[29] A number of Christian thinkers have made a similar distinction between "secularization" or "secularity," which they take as signifying the rejection of religious or ecclesiastical tutelage of society, and "secularism" as signifying an all-embracing ideology which seeks to deny religious institutions or viewpoints any formative role in society. In reply, Smith acknowledges that the same sort of distinction is actually accepted by many Hindus and Moslems who find the relative restriction of their religious life to the private sphere fully consonant with the integrity of the faith.[30]

By its careful attention to the conceptual problem, Smith's work illustrates the pitfalls of defining secularization as disengagement. His work has also clearly raised the important question of how one decides when secularization in this sense has taken place and when we should speak rather of an internal adjustment within the religious tradition, or even of the triumph of one religion or religiously colored ideology over another.

One way of remedying the defects in the disengagement thesis is to substitute the more descriptive and neutral concept of *"differentiation"* that has been developed by Parsons and Bellah.

Parsons proposes "differentiation" as an alternative to the interpretation of modern society as undergoing a process of secularization in the sense of a "decline" of religion.[31] In an argument strikingly similar to that proposed by Gogarten, he points out that Christianity contains within itself the principle of differentiation between the community of faith and the social community as well as the differentiation within the religious community between faith and ethics. Similarly, in speaking of the Reformation's extension of the autonomy of the social and economic community and the Re-

[29] Marc Galanter, "Secularism, East and West," *Comparative Studies in Society and History,* 7 (1965): 148–153.

[30] Donald E. Smith, "Secularism in India," *Comparative Studies in Society and History,* 7 (1965): 169–170.

[31] Talcott Parsons, "Christianity and Modern Industrial Society," in *Sociological Theory, Values and Sociocultural Change,* ed. Edward A. Tiryakian (Glencoe: Free Press, 1963), pp. 33–70.

formers' religious enfranchisement of the individual, Parsons notes that the Lutheran concept of the calling could be termed a secularization, but he prefers to see it as the "endowment of secular life with a new order of religious legitimation."[32] It is indeed true that many of the functions performed by the Churches and religious communities and many of the values of the Christian ethical tradition have been taken over by society at large and generalized. But this is not a sign that the Western religious tradition has collapsed; it is, rather, that the religious community plays an altered role in keeping with the general differentiation of society. Parsons is quite aware, of course, that Christianity has been facing a serious challenge to its understanding of man and the world.[33]

Bellah's version of the concept is intended as an overall framework for understanding religious evolution in general. He makes use of Voegelin's notion of the movement from compact to differentiated symbols, as well as describing differentiation within religious groups and between religion and other facets of society.[34] He refuses to consider even the rejection of the natural-supernatural schema and the gradual loss of concern for doctrinal orthodoxy a sign of "indifference or secularization," seeing it as simply a reflection of a new way of conceiving and practicing religion.[35] In this he would be supported by a good number of contemporary theologians. At the least, the concept of differentiation suggests that the idea of secularization as a disengagement of society from religion which reduces religion to insignificance may be a somewhat crude and value-charged designation of a much more complex and subtle phenomenon.

4. Transposition of Religious Beliefs and Institutions

Knowledge, patterns of behavior, and institutional arrangements which were once understood as grounded in divine power are transformed into phenomena of purely human creation and responsibility. In the case of disengagement, the institutions or social arrangements which are secularized are seen as something which did not necessarily belong to the sphere of religion, whereas in the case of transposition it is aspects of religious belief or experience themselves which are shifted from their sacral context to a purely human

[32] *Ibid.*, p. 50.

[33] *Ibid.*, p. 69.

[34] Robert N. Bellah, "Religious Evolution, *American Sociological Review*," 29 (1964): 358–359.

[35] Bellah, *op. cit.*, p. 73.

context. *The culmination of this kind of secularization process would be a totally anthropologized religion and a society which had taken over all the functions previously accruing to the religious institutions.* Writing of the secularization of historical interpretation, Adalbert Klempt speaks of secularization as the "transformation of conceptions and modes of thought which were originally developed by the Christian salvation belief and its theology into ones of a world-based outlook."[36]

Examples in research. Although it is difficult to find examples of "pure" transpositions with no admixture of other ideas or experience, some well-known theses have proposed the "spirit of capitalism" as a secularization of the Calvinist ethic, the Marxist version of the consummation of the revolution as coming from Jewish-Christian eschatology, psychotherapy as a secular outgrowth of confession and the cure of souls, etc. The classical treatment of transposition comes from Ernst Troeltsch, who spoke, for example, of "the complete severance of sexual feelings from the thought of original sin" which has been effected "by modern art and poetry" as "nothing else than the secularization of the intense religious emotions."[37] In another work he writes of the belief in progress as a "secularization of Christian eschatology."[38]

Assessment. The difficulty with the transposition thesis, of course, is the problem of identifying survivals or transmigrations. Is a supposed transposition really a Jewish or Christian belief or practice now appearing under the guise of a more generalized rationale, or is it something of separate origin and conception which has taken over some of the functions of the former religious phenomenon? We need only call to mind the sharp debate over the Weber thesis to envisage the kind of disagreements which can beset any particular thesis regarding a transposition. The widespread view that Marxism contains a transposition of some Jewish-Christian elements has also come under heavy attack.[39]

The German philosopher Hans Blumenberg has offered what is

[36] Adalbert Klempt, *Die Säkularisierung der Universalhistorischen Auffassung* (Gottingen: Musterschmidt, 1960), p. 7.

[37] Ernst Troeltsch, *Protestantism and Progress* (Boston: Beacon Press, 1958), p. 96.

[38] Ernst Troeltsch, *Der Historismus und seine Probleme* (Tübingen: M. C. B. Mohr, 1922), p. 57.

[39] Reinhard Wittram, "Möglichkeiten und Grenzen der Geschichtswissenschaft in der Gegenwart," *Zeitschrift für Theologie und Kirche,* 62 (1965): 430–457. Henri Desroche, *Marxisme et Religions* (Paris: Presses Universitaires de France, 1962).

perhaps the most complete and also the most perceptive critique of the concept of secularization as transposition. Using as his test case the theory that the idea of progress is a secularization of Christian eschatology, he points out that neither is there proof of causal dependence, nor are the two ideas really the same in content; the parallel, rather, is one of function.[40]

Another fallacy implicit in the transposition thesis derives from its origin in the use of the term "secularization" for the transfer of ecclesiastical possessions from the Church to the princes. Is the vision of an ultimate consummation of history, for example, really the "possession" of Judaism or Christianity so that its later use by other movements must be regarded as a usurpation?[41] Blumenberg goes so far as to suggest that this way of conceiving secularization functions simply as a weapon of the theologians in their attack on the legitimacy of the modern world, and that its use by historians and sociologists reflects a fundamental uncertainty on their part as to the rightful place of the modern outlook. Whether or not one is willing to go that far, it must be admitted that Blumenberg has given us grounds for demanding that any reputed transposition theory pass strict methodological criteria.

5. Desacralization of the World

The world is gradually deprived of its sacral character as man and nature become the object of rational-causal explanation and manipulation. The culmination of secularization would be a completely "rational" world society in which the phenomenon of the supernatural or even of "mystery" would play no part. Historian Eric Kahler writes that secularization means "that man became independent of religion and lived by reason, face to face with objectified, physical nature."[42]

Examples in research. The classical statement of this view is Max Weber's concept of "disenchantment" *(Entzauberung)* which signifies an irreversible trend of rationalization leading to a view of the world as a self-contained causal nexus.[43] Among contemporary writers, Mircea Eliade has given us the most sensitive evocation of

[40] Hans Blumenberg, "Säkularisation: Kritik einer Kategorie Historischer Illegitimität," in *Die Philosophie und die Frage nach dem Fortschritt,* ed. Helmut Kuhn and Franz Wiedmann (München: Anton Pustet, 1964), pp. 249–250.

[41] *Ibid.,* pp. 247–248.

[42] Eric Kahler, *Man the Measure* (New York: Pantheon Books, 1943), p. 333.

[43] Max Weber, "Science as a Vocation," in *From Max Weber, Essays in Sociology,* ed. and trans. H. H. Gerth and C. Wright Mills (New York: Oxford University Press, 1946), p. 139.

the loss (or suppression) of the sense of the sacred. Eliade too finds the root of desacralization in science, which has so neutralized nature and human life that no point can have "a unique ontological status" which integrates the whole.[44]

The proponents of the desacralization thesis do not agree as to how far this process can go. Some apparently feel that it will one day complete itself and religion, insofar as it is bound to an acknowledgement of the "sacred" or "holy," will disappear. Others hold that man is "incurably religious" and believe either that the sense of the sacred has been pushed into the unconscious for the time being or that it is in the process of finding new forms of expression.

Assessment. Although less global and simplistic than the decline thesis, the desacralization concept bears certain similarities to it. The inherent problem with the desacralization view is its assumption that religion is inextricably bound up with an understanding of the world as permeated by sacred powers. There is in the Hebraic faith, however, a definite desacralization of the world through the radical transcendence of the Creator, who alone is eminently holy and who has, moreover, given the world over to the dominion of man (Gen. 1:24). In Christianity the process is carried further through the separation of religion and politics and the notion of sonship through Christ in which man is free from the elemental spirits of the universe (Mk. 12:17 and Gal. 4:1 ff). This phenomenon of a religious tradition which itself desacralizes the world suggests that the desacralization view of secularization is not applicable to at least the Western tradition, without qualification.

6. Movement from a "Sacred" to a "Secular" Society

This is a general concept of *social change,* emphasizing multiple variables through several stages. According to Howard Becker, its chief developer, the main variable is resistance or openness to change. Accordingly, *the culmination of secularization would be a society in which all decisions are based on rational and utilitarian considerations and there is complete acceptance of change.*[45] A

---

[44] Mircea Eliade, *The Sacred and the Profane* (New York: Harper Torchbooks, 1961), p. 17.

[45] Howard Becker, "Current Secular-Sacred Theory and Its Development," in *Modern Sociological Theory in Continuity and Change,* ed. Howard Becker and Alvin Boskoff (New York: Dryden Press, 1957), pp. 133–186. The most recent statement is contained in Becker's articles "Sacred Society" and "Secular Society" in *A Dictionary of the Social Sciences,* ed. Julius Gould and William L. Kolb (New York: Free Press of Glencoe, 1964), pp. 613, 626.

theological version of this type of secularization concept has been developed by Bernard Meland, who defines secularization as "the movement away from traditionally accepted norms and sensibilities in the life interests and habits of a people."[46] Since Meland means by "sensibilities" a capacity to "respond appreciatively and with restraint to accepted ways of feeling or behavior," secularization does not refer merely to religious phenomena but to any traditional norms and perceptions.[47] Since this type of secularization concept is a general theory of social change rather than a theory of specifically religious change, it would take us well beyond the limits of the present inquiry if we were to examine the vast empirical literature that has grown out of it.

The Secular-Religious Polarity

Criticism of "Religion" Concept

Because the concept of secularization usually refers back to a secular-religious or sacred-profane polarity, our critique of it has often implied a parallel critique in certain definitions of "religion." It is evident that the criticisms made above were aimed at a view of religious phenomena which narrowly restricts them to certain external elements in the Western tradition, e.g., church attendance and financial support, conventional forms of public and private devotional practice, belief scales based on traditional creeds. The suggestion was also made that belief in the supernatural or in sacral powers pervading man and nature is not essential to all the kinds of phenomena we characterize as religious. My reasons for refusing to restrict the understanding of religion in any of these ways is twofold.

In the first place, the range of phenomena which have been considered religious is so varied that no single definition of the "essence" of religion can embrace them all. Consequently, it would be extremely difficult to discover a list of measurable indices of decline, subversion, transposition or other radical shift away from the "religious" toward the "secular." After examining some of the various ways of defining the polarity, David Martin concludes that it is impossible to develop criteria for distinguishing between the religious and the secular since it would be "an obvious absurdity"

---

[46] Bernard E. Meland, *The Secularization of Modern Cultures* (New York: Oxford University Press, 1966), p. 3.

[47] *Ibid.*, p. 9.

to combine "the metaphysical and mythopoetic modes of thought, the acceptance of miracle, belief in historical purpose, rejection of material benefits, and lack of confidence towards the world under the common rubric of religion."[48]

Secondly, most definitions of the essence of religion, even when they have not been crude combinations of practice and belief, have assumed that there exists an *entity* called "religion." This reification, as Wilfred Cantwell Smith has pointed out, is of recent origin even in the West, and many of its current connotations represent a polemical situation growing out of the Enlightenment.[49] This is perhaps why we not only have numerous Christian theologians denying that Christian faith is a religion (although Christianity may be), but we also have Jewish, Buddhist, Hindu, and Muslim thinkers who refuse to consider their faith one of the "religions."

Paul Tillich has even suggested that the existence of a religious as opposed to a secular realm in human experience is an expression of "the tragic estrangement of man's spiritual life from its own ground and depth."[50] Thus, the notion of a religion as a separate part of culture presupposes an advanced stage of differentiation and reflects an attitude contrary to the way at least some of the adherents understand their own tradition. Therefore, I can sympathize with Smith's suggestion that we drop the substantive form "religion" altogether and use the concepts "faith" and "tradition" to convey respectively the interior and external aspects of what have been called "the religions."[51] This does not mean, of course, that we should give up the attempt to describe the quality or qualities which may be designated "religious," e.g., "ultimate concern," "openness for mystery," "apprehension of harmony," "commitment to creativity." But unfortunately, even the term "religious" continues to retain many connotations which would lead sensitive persons to hesitate to apply it to themselves or to their tradition.

Criticism of Polarity

Before leaving the problem of the definition of "religion" and the "religious" one further critical question needs to be raised. Must

[48] David Martin, "Towards Eliminating the Concept of Secularization," in *Penguin Survey of the Social Sciences,* ed. Julius Gould (Baltimore: Penguin Books, 1965), p. 173.

[49] Wilfred Cantwell Smith, *The Meaning and End of Religion* (New York: The New American Library, 1964), pp. 43 ff.

[50] Paul Tillich, *Theology of Culture* (New York: Oxford University Press, 1959), p. 8.

[51] Smith, *op. cit.,* pp. 139–181.

we think in polar terms at all? There are three disadvantages to a polar concept of the secular-religious type.

First, it tends to deceive us into taking a particular form of differentiation in the West as normative. Niyazi Berkes has pointed out that the usual dichotomy is based on the Western model of "church" and "state," which presupposes an institutionalized religion distinct from the political order. When we apply this "spiritual-temporal" polarity to non-Western situations where such differentiations did not originally exist, we falsify the data.[52]

Second, the secular-religious polarity easily encourages the assumption that an increase of activity in the so-called secular sphere must mean a corresponding decline in the religious area. But, as J. H. Hexter has remarked of this particular intellectual trap, there is considerable evidence that in some periods of history—the sixteenth century is one—*both* aspects of society rose to higher levels of intensity.[53]

Finally, the secular-religious polarity simply compounds the deception in the idea that religion is an entity of some kind. For if one does not begin by defining religion or the religious in terms of institutional or behavioral traits there will be no need to find a polar opposite. When "religious" is used to designate a certain quality of life or dimension of individual and social experience which concerns the whole man and the whole of society, this dimension may be as much in play in certain activities conventionally labeled "secular" as it is not in play in some that are conventionally labeled "religious."

Conclusion

During its long development the term "secularization" has often served the partisans of controversy and has constantly taken on new meanings without completely losing old ones. As a result it is swollen with overtones and implications, especially those associated with indifference or hostility to whatever is considered "religious."

On one hand, Martin has gone so far as to suggest that it has been a "tool of counter-religious ideologies," which define the "real" basis of religion and claim that religion so defined is in a process of irreversible decline. Martin believes the motives behind this are partly "the aesthetic satisfactions found in such notions and

---

[52] Niyazi Berkes, "Religious and Secular Institutions in Comparative Perspective," *Archives de Sociologie des Religions,* 8 (1963): 65–72.

[53] J. H. Hexter, *Reappraisals in History* (New York: Harper Torchbooks, 1961), pp. 40–43.

partly as a psychological boost to the movements with which they are associated."[54]

At the other end of the spectrum are the all too familiar clerical lamentations over the increase of "secularism." Blumenberg, as we have seen, even suggests that the concept of secularization has been a tool of those theologians and clerics who want to impugn the legitimacy of the modern world.

As if the conceptual situation were not confusing enough, the current enthusiasm in theology for styling one's version of Christianity "secular" muddies the conceptual waters almost to the point of hopelessness. As noted above, behind the present secular theology fad lies the work of several more sober theologians (Bonhoeffer, Gogarten, Michalson) who have worked out a sophisticated defense of secularization conceived in terms of man's coming into responsibility for his own destiny. To them, what Herberg calls a secularization of society is actually the triumph of "religion," whereas the legitimate outcome of faith would be the secularization of society in the sense of neutralizing conventional religiosity. Although Bonhoeffer and Gogarten do not style themselves "secular" theologians, the recent rash of books proclaiming "the secular meaning of the Gospel" or a "secular Christianity," or praising the "secular city" as the solely authentic place of Christian existence have made "secularization" once again an ecclesiastical battle slogan by stinging traditionalists and conservatives into a counter attack on this "secularization of Christianity."[55]

This accumulation of contradictory connotations would be enough of a handicap, but there is an even more serious one in the fact that so many different processes and phenomena are designated by the term "secularization." Often the same writer will use it in two or more senses without acknowledging the shift of meaning. Thus Weber could employ it not only for "disenchantment" but also for transpositions (spirit of capitalism), and at times even in the sense of becoming "worldly," as when he speaks of the "secularizing influence of wealth" on monasticism.[56]

The appropriate conclusion to draw from the confusing connotations and the multitude of phenomena covered by the term secu-

[54] David Martin, *op. cit.*, p. 176.

[55] E. L. Mascall, *The Secularization of Christianity* (London: Darton, Longman & Todd, 1965). The other books alluded to are Paul Van Buren, *The Secular Meaning of the Gospel* (New York: Macmillan, 1963); Ronald Gregor Smith, *Secular Christianity* (New York: Harper & Row, 1966); Harvey Cox, *The Secular City* (New York: Macmillan, 1965).

[56] Max Weber, *The Protestant Ethic and the Spirit of Capitalism* (New York: Charles Scribner's Sons, 1958), p. 174.

larization would seem to be that we drop the word entirely and employ instead terms such as "transposition" or "differentiation" which are both more descriptive and neutral.

Since a moratorium on any widely used term is unlikely to be effected, however, there are two ways of salvaging "secularization" as a useful concept in empirical research. One, of course, is for everyone who employs it to state carefully his intended meaning and to stick to it.

The other is for researchers to agree on the term as a general designation or large scale concept covering certain subsumed aspects of religious change.

Three of the processes discussed above could be embraced significantly by the term "secularization" since they are not contradictory but complementary: desacralization, differentiation and transposition. To a certain degree they can also be seen as representing successive and overlapping emphases in Western religious history. Although the desacralization of nature and history, for example, seems to have generally preceded political and social differentiation, the former was not accomplished all at once. And it is evident that transposition cannot take place without the prior or concomitant occurrence of differentiation. To work out the exact bearing of and the measurement criteria for these subconcepts is a task that still requires considerable reflection. I am afraid, however, that the careless and partisan use of "secularization" is so general that its polemical connotations will continue to cling to it despite the social scientist's efforts to neutralize it.

Whether one would opt for the particular use of the term "secularization" suggested by Shiner is very much a matter of individual taste and research interest. Yet it should be recognized that just as different definitions of the term "religion" imply different theoretical perspectives, so different definitions of the term "secularization" imply different theoretical perspectives. Shiner's contention that secularization may be understood as a specific instance of social differentiation appears to imply a functionalist theory of religion. Secularization means that in the face of an ever-increasing process of differentiation (specialization), religious institutions are experiencing a loss of some of their previous functions.

As was previously shown in Allan Eister's essay,[2] the functional theory of religion is highly problematic. Theorists have frequently disagreed over which social functions are fulfilled by which social institutions. In Eister's view, religion is one of the most difficult institutions to which specific functional categories can be assigned. Beyond this problem is the additional dilemma that if one defines religion according to its functions, anything that replaces religion functionally must be viewed as religion. This tautology of definition—religion is what religion does, and anything that does what religion once did is also religion—means that sociologists of religion will spend much of their time studying various types of social and political groups. The term "religion" becomes meaningless if it is synonymous with any form of social doctrine that provides certain kinds of services to society. In summary, the idea that secularization means differentiation opens the door to a host of related conceptual and theoretical difficulties.

The first definition of the term "secularization" examined by Shiner—a decline in religious belief and practice—is probably the most frequently encountered and the least complicated definition of the term. It was this understanding of secularization that was most often called into question during the alleged religious revival of the mid-1950s.

Even though the evidence for documenting the return to religion in the mid-1950s (church membership statistics and the like) is not the most plausible or reliable kind of quantitative data, few sociologists would challenge the fact that the *relative* numbers of church members increased between the mid-1950s and early 1960s. In other words, while most sociologists believe that the church membership statistics reported by religious groups themselves are overinflated and are difficult to equate from group to group because of the different ways in which these groups define membership, few sociologists would argue with the fact that these numbers did increase during this period. This relative increase in church membership cast serious doubt upon the idea that the traditional religious groups in America are undergoing a process of decline—i.e., secularization.

Dennison Nash's study represents a creative attempt to answer the question, Are we undergoing secularization or a religious revival? In Nash's view the religious revival is not a dramatic reversal of secularizing trends nor are its sources purely religious. Employing United States Census data and National Council of Churches *Yearbook* data, he shows that there is a direct relation-

[2] Reprinted in this anthology, pp. 71–79.

ship between the number of families with children under age 18 and the size of church membership statistics in the United States between 1950 and 1966. Church membership rises and falls in direct relationship to the number of families with children. The religious revival, then, was nothing more than an understandable result of the increase in the number of educable children in a society in which religious education is highly valued. This need not mean that the adult population is getting any more or less religious. Nor does it suggest that there actually was a religious revival. It simply attributes the apparent religious revival to some important population changes in the United States.

A Little Child Shall Lead Them: A Statistical Test of an Hypothesis That Children Were the Source of the American "Religious Revival"[*]
by Dennison Nash

In attempting to explain the postwar "Religious Revival" in America, Nash and Berger questioned a sample of recent joiners of the Congregational-Christian churches in a middle-class New England suburb.[1] They found that in the vast majority of instances "it was the prospect or the presence of children which wholly or partly occasioned the act of joining by their parents."[2]

Dennison Nash is professor of anthropology and sociology at The University of Connecticut and is the author of *Community in Limbo* (1970).

Reprinted from *Journal for the Scientific Study of Religion*, 7, no. 2 (1968): 238–240. Used with permission of the author and publisher.

[*] I wish to thank my colleagues, Herbert Kaufman, Edward Stockwell, and Jerold Heiss for technical and editorial assistance.

[1] See Dennison Nash and Peter Berger, "Church Commitment in an American Suburb: An Analysis of the Decision to Join," *Archives de Sociologie des Religions*, 13 (June 1962): 105–120; "The Child, the Family, and the Religious Revival in Suburbia," *Journal for the Scientific Study of Religion*, 2 (October 1962): 85–93.

[2] Nash and Berger, "The Child, the Family, and the Religious Revival in Suburbia," *op. cit.*, p. 89.

Going beyond their sample, the authors offered a demographic hypothesis to account for the increase in the number (and percentage) of church members in America. They say:

"If what has happened in our churches is representative of America during the period of the "Religious Revival," we suggest that the upsurge in church membership is due at least partly to an increase in the number of children who enter the church *and* parents who follow."[3] Nash and Berger went on to speculate that if motivations related to joining remained constant, variation in church membership would follow the rise and fall in the number of American families with children.

This paper offers a statistical test of this predicted correlation between church membership and the number of families with children.

The year-by-year measures for the variables relevant to the hypothesis now exist from 1950 (at a point in time close to the beginning of the "Revival") through 1966 (close to the end). The *Yearbook of American Churches*,[4] reports church membership (which rose from approximately 57 percent of the American population in 1950 to 64.4 percent in 1964 and declined to 63.9 percent in 1966). U.S. census figures for gross population, number of families, and families with children under 18 are available for almost all of this period.[5] These data are presented in Table 1.

The product-moment correlation between church membership and number of families with own children under 18 for yearly data from 1951 through 1966 is .99, but the coefficient is inflated by the fact that both variables are related to size of population and number of families.[6]

With population held constant, the partial correlation between

---

[3] *Ibid*, 91.

[4] *Yearbook of American Churches* (New York Council Press).

[5] Department of Commerce, U.S. Bureau of the Census, *Current Population Reports*, Series P-20. 1954 data for families with children under 18 are not available. 1950 data are not included in the present analysis because data for numbers of families with children under 6 are not available for that year; this variable was included in the original analysis to test whether effects could be due to some artifact associated with having young children, rather than having children of educable age. However, association of church membership with number of families with children under 6 proved weaker than with children under 18. If 1950 data were included, the coefficients of correlation would be slightly higher.

[6] Product-Monument Correlations:

	Population Size	Number of Families
Number of Church Members	.994	.994
Number of Families with Own Children under 18	.997	.984

Table 1. Number (in thousands) of Church Members, Families with Children under 18, Families, and Size of Population in the United States 1950–66

Year	Church Membership	Families with Children under 18	Families	Population
1950	86,830	19,846	39,193	151,326
1951	88,673	21,224	39,303	154,353
1952	92,277	21,266	40,578	156,981
1953	94,843	21,794	40,832	159,696
1954	97,483		41,202	162,414
1955	100,163	23,181	41,934	165,248
1956	103,225	23,718	42,843	167,181
1957	104,190	24,231	43,445	170,270
1958	109,558	24,551	43,714	173,210
1959	112,227	25,052	44,202	176,213
1960	114,449	25,660	45,062	179,323
1961	116,110	25,820	45,435	182,714
1962	117,946	26,227	46,341	185,708
1963	120,965	26,876	46,998	188,447
1964	123,307	27,008	47,436	191,226
1965	124,682	27,072	47,836	193,848
1966	125,779	26,876	48,278	196,502

church membership and number of families with children under 18 is .78. When both population and number of families are held constant, the second-order partial correlation coefficient between these variables becomes .74, still an extremely high value which indicates a strong association between church membership and families with children under 18.

Thus, the statistical test of the hypothesis suggested by Nash and Berger has produced positive results. For the period of the "Religious Revival" church affiliation does rise (and fall) in association with the number of American families with children.

Is it possible now to put this relationship into cause-effect terms? Nash and Berger found that church commitment by parents in their sample was almost entirely for the sake of their children who were going to Sunday School, and they concluded that this act by the then increasingly numerous families with children (each of which usually added two parents to church rolls)[7] tended to cause the

---

[7] Only the very oldest children in Congregational-Christian churches appear on church rolls; in some other churches younger children, who in Congregational churches would be listed as members of the Sunday School, are considered to be church members.

increase in church membership which constituted the "Religious Revival."

It would be difficult to maintain that this specific reason for affiliation (or the number of affiliates in families) prevails in all—or even most—religions. But it does seem possible to suggest that during the period in question there is something about American families with children which has affected church membership. To the extent that the presence of children has prompted (for whatever reason) familial commitment to religious institutions, it has given us a modern American version of the old adage, "A Little Child Shall Lead Them."

While quantitative research and statistical indices provide one method of gauging the pulse of a society, historical scholarship is yet another. In his widely-read historical essay, *Protestant-Catholic-Jew,*[3] Will Herberg attempts to explain the simultaneous occurrence of secularization and a religious resurgence. While arguing that religious belief is becoming more and more secularized, Herberg predicts a healthy future for religious institutions in the United States. He contends that in the setting of American religious pluralism, it does not matter which religion to which one belongs—as long as one belongs. Church membership is at once a form of social identity as well as a way of participating in a generalized religious ideology that unites the different faiths. America's religion is the doctrine that religion per se is a good thing.

Numerous scholars have offered variations on Herberg's theme. One of the most articulate developments of these ideas is Robert Bellah's "civil religion" hypothesis. Bellah examines some major events in American political history to demonstrate the always-present intermingling of religious and political symbolism. He labels the common core religion a "civil religion." While Herberg saw this common or civil religion as contributing to increasing church membership roles, Bellah emphasizes its contribution to a broad cultural consensus in the United States.

[3] Will Herberg, *Protestant-Catholic-Jew* (Garden City: Doubleday and Company, 1955).

Civil Religion in America
by Robert N. Bellah

While some have argued that Christianity is the national faith, and others that church and synagogue celebrate only the generalized religion of "the American Way of Life," few have realized that there actually exists alongside of and rather clearly differentiated from the churches an elaborate and well-institutionalized civil religion in America. This article argues not only that there is such a thing, but also that this religion—or perhaps better, this religious dimension—has its own seriousness and integrity and requires the same care in understanding that any other religion does.[1]

A biographical note on Robert N. Bellah appears on page 111 of this book.
Reprinted from *Daedalus*, 96 (1967): 1–21. Used with permission of the author and publisher.

[1] Why something so obvious should have escaped serious analytical attention is in itself an interesting problem. Part of the reason is probably the controversial nature of the subject. From the earliest years of the nineteenth century, conservative religious and political groups have argued that Christianity is, in fact, the national religion. Some of them have from time to time and as recently as the 1950s proposed constitutional amendments that would explicitly recognize the sovereignty of Christ. In defending the doctrine of separation of church and state, opponents of such groups have denied that the national polity has, intrinsically, anything to do with religion at all. The moderates on this issue have insisted that the American state has taken a permissive and indeed supportive attitude toward religious groups (tax exemption, et cetera), thus favoring religion but still missing the positive institutionalization with which I am concerned. But part of the reason this issue has been left in obscurity is certainly due to the peculiarly Western

The Kennedy Inaugural

Kennedy's inaugural address of 20 January 1961 serves as an example and a clue with which to introduce this complex subject. That address began:

> We observe today not a victory of party but a celebration of freedom —symbolizing an end as well as a beginning—signifying renewal as well as change. For I have sworn before you and Almighty God the same solemn oath our forebears prescribed nearly a century and three quarters ago.
>
> The world is very different now. For man holds in his mortal hands the power to abolish all forms of human poverty and to abolish all forms of human life. And yet the same revolutionary beliefs for which our forebears fought are still at issue around the globe—the belief that the rights of man come not from the generosity of the state but from the hand of God.

And it concluded:

> Finally, whether you are citizens of America or of the world, ask of us the same high standards of strength and sacrifice that we shall ask of you. With a good conscience our only sure reward, with history the final judge of our deeds, let us go forth to lead the land we love, asking His blessing and His help, but knowing that here on earth God's work must truly be our own.

These are the three places in this brief address in which Kennedy mentioned the name of God. If we could understand why he mentioned God, the way in which he did it, and what he meant to say in those three references, we would understand much about American civil religion. But this is not a simple or obvious task, and American students of religion would probably differ widely in their interpretation of these passages.

Let us consider first the placing of the three references. They occur in the two opening paragraphs and in the closing paragraph, thus providing a sort of frame for the more concrete remarks that form the middle part of the speech. Looking beyond this particular speech, we would find that similar references to God are almost invariably to be found in the pronouncements of American presi-

---

concept of "religion" as denoting a single type of collectivity of which an individual can be a member of one and only one at a time. The Durkheimian notion that every group has a religious dimension, which would be seen as obvious in southern or eastern Asia, is foreign to us. This obscures the recognition of such dimensions in our society.

dents on solemn occasions, though usually not in the working messages that the president sends to Congress on various concrete issues. How, then, are we to interpret this placing of references to God?

It might be argued that the passages quoted reveal the essentially irrelevant role of religion in the very secular society that is America. The placing of the references in this speech as well as in public life generally indicates that religion has "only a ceremonial significance"; it gets only a sentimental nod which serves largely to placate the more unenlightened members of the community, before a discussion of the really serious business with which religion has nothing whatever to do. A cynical observer might even say that an American president has to mention God or risk losing votes. A semblance of piety is merely one of the unwritten qualifications for the office, a bit more traditional than but not essentially different from the present-day requirement of a pleasing television personality.

But we know enough about the function of ceremonial and ritual in various societies to make us suspicious of dismissing something as unimportant because it is "only a ritual." What people say on solemn occasions need not be taken at face value, but it is often indicative of deep-seated values and commitments that are not made explicit in the course of everyday life. Following this line of argument, it is worth considering whether the very special placing of the references to God in Kennedy's address may not reveal something rather important and serious about religion in American life.

It might be countered that the very way in which Kennedy made his references reveals the essentially vestigial place of religion today. He did not refer to any religion in particular. He did not refer to Jesus Christ, or to Moses, or to the Christian church; certainly he did not refer to the Catholic Church. In fact, his only reference was to the concept of God, a word which almost all Americans can accept but which means so many different things to so many different people that it is almost an empty sign. Is this not just another indication that in America religion is considered vaguely to be a good thing, but that people care so little about it that it has lost any content whatever? Isn't Eisenhower reported to have said, "Our government makes no sense unless it is founded in a deeply felt religious faith—and I don't care what it is,"[2] and isn't that a complete negation of any real religion?

These questions are worth pursuing because they raise the issue of how civil religion relates to the political society, on the one

---

[2] Quoted in Will Herberg, *Protestant-Catholic-Jew* (New York, 1955), p. 97.

hand, and to private religious organization, on the other. President Kennedy was a Christian, more specifically a Catholic Christian. Thus, his general references to God do not mean that he lacked a specific religious commitment. But why, then, did he not include some remark to the effect that Christ is the Lord of the world or some indication of respect for the Catholic Church? He did not because these are matters of his own private religious belief and of his relation to his own particular church; they are not matters relevant in any direct way to the conduct of his public office. Others with different religious views and commitments to different churches or denominations are equally qualified participants in the political process. The principle of separation of church and state guarantees the freedom of religious belief and association, but at the same time clearly segregates the religious sphere, which is considered to be essentially private, from the political one.

Considering the separation of church and state, how is a president justified in using the word *God* at all? The answer is that the separation of church and state has not denied the political realm a religious dimension. Although matters of personal religious belief, worship, and association are considered to be strictly private affairs, there are, at the same time, certain common elements of religious orientation that the great majority of Americans share. These have played a crucial role in the development of American institutions and still provide a religious dimension for the whole fabric of American life, including the political sphere. This public religious dimension is expressed in a set of beliefs, symbols, and rituals that I am calling the American civil religion. The inauguration of a president is an important ceremonial event in this religion. It reaffirms, among other things, the religious legitimation of the highest political authority.

Let us look more closely at what Kennedy actually said. First he said, "I have sworn before you and Almighty God the same solemn oath our forebears prescribed nearly a century and three quarters ago." The oath is the oath of office, including the acceptance of the obligation to uphold the Constitution. He swears it before the people (you) and God. Beyond the Constitution, then, the president's obligation extends not only to the people but to God. In American political theory, sovereignty rests, of course, with the people, but implicitly, and often explicitly, the ultimate sovereignty has been attributed to God. This is the meaning of the motto, "In God we trust," as well as the inclusion of the phrase "under God" in the pledge to the flag. What difference does it make that sovereignty belongs to God? Though the will of the people as expressed in majority vote is carefully institutionalized as the operative source of political authority, it is deprived of an ultimate significance. The will of the people is not itself the criterion of right and wrong. There is a higher criterion in terms of which this will can be judged; it is possible that the people may be wrong. The president's obligation extends to the higher criterion.

When Kennedy says that "the rights of man come not from the generosity of the state but from the hand of God," he is stressing this point again. It does not matter whether the state is the expression of the will of an autocratic monarch or of the "people"; the rights of man are more basic than any political structure and provide a point of revolutionary leverage from which any state structure may be radically altered. That is the basis for his reassertion of the revolutionary significance of America.

But the religious dimension in political life as recognized by Kennedy not only provides a grounding for the rights of man which makes any form of political absolutism illegitimate, it also provides a transcendent goal for the political process. This is implied in his final words that "here on earth God's work must truly be our own." What he means here is, I think, more clearly spelled out in a previous paragraph, the wording of which, incidentally, has a distinctly Biblical ring:

> Now the trumpet summons us again—not as a call to bear arms, though arms we need—not as a call to battle, though embattled we are—but a call to bear the burden of a long twilight struggle, year in and year out, "rejoicing in hope, patient in tribulation"—a struggle against the common enemies of man: tyranny, poverty, disease and war itself.

The whole address can be understood as only the most recent statement of a theme that lies very deep in the American tradition, namely the obligation, both collective and individual, to carry out God's will on earth. This was the motivating spirit of those who founded America, and it has been present in every generation since. Just below the surface throughout Kennedy's inaugural address, it becomes explicit in the closing statement that God's work must be our own. That this very activist and non-contemplative conception of the fundamental religious obligation, which has been historically associated with the Protestant position, should be enunciated so clearly in the first major statement of the first Catholic president seems to underline how deeply established it is in the American outlook. Let us now consider the form and history of the civil religious tradition in which Kennedy was speaking.

The Idea of a Civil Religion

The phrase *civil religion* is, of course, Rousseau's. In Chapter 8, Book 4, of *The Social Contract,* he outlines the simple dogmas of the civil religion: the existence of God, the life to come, the reward of virtue and the punishment of vice, and the exclusion of religious intolerance. All other religious opinions are outside the cognizance of the state and may be freely held by citizens. While the phrase *civil religion* was not used, to the best of my knowledge, by the founding fathers, and I am certainly not arguing for the particular influence of Rousseau, it is clear that similar ideas, as part of the cultural climate of the late-eighteenth century, were to be found among the Americans. For example, Franklin writes in his autobiography,

> I never was without some religious principles. I never doubted, for instance, the existence of the Deity; that he made the world and gov-ern'd it by his Providence; that the most acceptable service of God was the doing of good to men; that our souls are immortal; and that all crime will be punished and virtue rewarded, either here or here-after. These I esteemed the essentials of every religion; and, being to be found in all the religions we had in our country, I respected them all, tho' with different degrees of respect, as I found them more or less mix'd with other articles, which, without any tendency to inspire, promote or confirm morality, serv'd principally to divide us, and make us unfriendly to one another.

It is easy to dispose of this sort of position as essentially utilitarian in relation to religion. In Washington's Farewell Address (though the words may be Hamilton's) the utilitarian aspect is quite explicit:

> Of all the dispositions and habits which lead to political prosperity, Religion and Morality are indispensable supports. In vain would that man claim the tribute of Patriotism, who should labour to subvert these great Pillars of human happiness, these firmest props of the duties of men and citizens. The mere politician, equally with the pious man, ought to respect and cherish them. A volume could not trace all their connections with private and public felicity. Let it sim-ply be asked, where is the security for property, for reputation, for life, if the sense of religious obligation *desert* the oaths, which are the instruments of investigation in Courts of Justice? And let us with caution indulge the supposition that morality can be maintained

without religion. Whatever may be conceded to the influence of refined education on minds of peculiar structure, reason and experience both forbid us to expect that National morality can prevail in exclusion of religious principle.

But there is every reason to believe that religion, particularly the idea of God, played a constitutive role in the thought of the early American statesmen.

Kennedy's inaugural pointed to the religious aspect of the Declaration of Independence, and it might be well to look at that document a bit more closely. There are four references to God. The first speaks of the "Laws of Nature and of Nature's God" which entitle any people to be independent. The second is the famous statement that all men "are endowed by their Creator with certain inalienable Rights." Here Jefferson is locating the fundamental legitimacy of the new nation in a conception of "higher law" that is itself based on both classical natural law and Biblical religion. The third is an appeal to "the Supreme Judge of the world for the rectitude of our intentions," and the last indicates "a firm reliance on the protection of divine Providence." In these last two references, a Biblical God of history who stands in judgment over the world is indicated.

The intimate relation of these religious notions with the self-conception of the new republic is indicated by the frequency of their appearance in early official documents. For example, we find in Washington's first inaugural address of 30 April 1789:

It would be peculiarly improper to omit in this first official act my fervent supplications to that Almighty Being who rules over the universe, who presides in the councils of nations, and whose providential aids can supply every defect, that His benediction may consecrate to the liberties and happiness of the people of the United States a Government instituted by themselves for these essential purposes, and may enable every instrument employed in its administration to execute with success the functions allotted to his charge.

No people can be bound to acknowledge and adore the Invisible Hand which conducts the affairs of man more than those of the United States. Every step by which we have advanced to the character of an independent nation seems to have been distinguished by some token if providential agency. . . .

The propitious smiles of Heaven can never be expected on a nation that disregards the eternal rules of order and right which Heaven itself has ordained. . . . The preservation of the sacred fire of liberty and the destiny of the republican model of government are justly considered, perhaps, as *deeply*, as *finally*, staked on the experiment intrusted to the hands of the American people.

Nor did these religious sentiments remain merely the personal expression of the president. At the request of both Houses of Congress, Washington proclaimed on October 3 of that same first year as president that November 26 should be "a day of public thanksgiving and prayer," the first Thanksgiving Day under the Constitution.

The words and acts of the founding fathers, especially the first few presidents, shaped the form and tone of the civil religion as it has been maintained ever since. Though much is selectively derived from Christianity, this religion is clearly not itself Christianity. For one thing, neither Washington nor Adams nor Jefferson mentions Christ in his inaugural address; nor do any of the subsequent presidents, although not one of them fails to mention God.[3] The God of the civil religion is not only rather "unitarian," he is also on the austere side, much more related to order, law, and right than to salvation and love. Even though he is somewhat deist in cast, he is by no means simply a watchmaker God. He is actively interested and involved in history, with a special concern for America. Here the analogy has much less to do with natural law than with ancient Israel; the equation of America with Israel in the idea of the "American Israel" is not infrequent.[4] What was implicit in the words of Washington already quoted becomes explicit in Jefferson's second inaugural when he said: "I shall need, too, the favor of that Being in whose hands we are, who led our fathers, as Israel of old, from their native land and planted them in a country flowing with all the nec-

[3] God is mentioned or referred to in all inaugural addresses but Washington's second, which is a very brief (two paragraphs) and perfunctory acknowledgment. It is not without interest that the actual word *God* does not appear until Monroe's second inaugural, 5 March 1821. In his first inaugural, Washington refers to God as "that Almighty Being who rules the universe," "Great Author of every public and private good," "Invisible Hand," and "benign Parent of the Human Race." John Adams refers to God as "Providence," "Being who is supreme over all," "Patron of Order," "Fountain of Justice," and "Protector in all ages of the world of virtuous liberty." Jefferson speaks of "that Infinite Power which rules the destinies of the universe," and "that Being in whose hands we are." Madison speaks of "that Almighty Being whose power regulates the destiny of nations," and "Heaven." Monroe uses "Providence" and "the Almighty" in his first inaugural and finally "Almighty God" in his second. See *Inaugural Addresses of the Presidents of the United States from George Washington 1789 to Harry S. Truman 1949*, 82d Congress, 2d Session, House Document No. 540, 1952.

[4] For example, Abiel Abbot, pastor of the First Church in Haverhill, Massachusetts, delivered a Thanksgiving sermon in 1799, *Traits of Resemblance in the People of the United States of America to Ancient Israel*, in which he said, "It has been often remarked that the people of the United States come nearer to a parallel with Ancient Israel than any other nation upon the globe. Hence OUR AMERICAN ISRAEL is a term frequently used; and common consent allows it apt and proper." Cited in Hans Kohn, *The Idea of Nationalism* (New York, 1961), p. 665.

essaries and comforts of life." Europe is Egypt; America, the prom-·ised land. God has led his people to establish a new sort of social order that shall be a light unto all the nations.[5]

This theme, too, has been a continuous one in the civil religion. We have already alluded to it in the case of the Kennedy inaugural. We find it again in President Johnson's inaugural address:

> They came here—the exile and the stranger, brave but frightened— to find a place where a man could be his own man. They made a covenant with this land. Conceived in justice, written in liberty, bound in union, it was meant one day to inspire the hopes of all mankind; and it binds us still. If we keep its terms, we shall flourish.

What we have, then, from the earliest years of the republic is a collection of beliefs, symbols, and rituals with respect to sacred things and institutionalized in a collectivity. This religion—there seems no other word for it—while not antithetical to and indeed sharing much in common with Christianity, was neither sectarian nor in any specific sense Christian. At a time when the society was overwhelmingly Christian, it seems unlikely that this lack of Christian reference was meant to spare the feelings of the tiny non-Christian minority. Rather, the civil religion expressed what those who set the precedents felt was appropriate under the circumstances. It reflected their private as well as public views. Nor was the civil religion simply "religion in general." While generality was undoubtedly seen as a virtue by some, as in the quotation from Franklin above, the civil religion was specific enough when it came to the topic of America. Precisely because of this specificity, the civil religion was saved from empty formalism and served as a genuine vehicle of national religious self-understanding.

But the civil religion was not, in the minds of Franklin, Washington, Jefferson, or other leaders, with the exception of a few radicals like Tom Paine, ever felt to be a substitute for Christianity. There was an implicit but quite clear division of function between the civil

---

[5] That the Mosaic analogy was present in the minds of leaders at the very moment of the birth of the republic is indicated in the designs proposed by Franklin and Jefferson for a seal of the United States of America. Together with Adams, they formed a committee of three delegated by the Continental Congress on July 4, 1776, to draw up the new device. "Franklin proposed as the device Moses lifting up his wand and dividing the Red Sea while Pharaoh was overwhelmed by its waters, with the motto 'Rebellion to tyrants is obedience to God.' Jefferson proposed the children of Israel in the wilderness 'led by a cloud by day and a pillar of fire at night.' " Anson Phelps Stokes, *Church and State in the United States*, Vol. 1 (New York, 1950), pp. 467–468.

religion and Christianity. Under the doctrine of religious liberty, an exceptionally wide sphere of personal piety and voluntary social action was left to the churches. But the churches were neither to control the state nor to be controlled by it. The national magistrate, whatever his private religious views, operates under the rubrics of the civil religion as long as he is in his official capacity, as we have already seen in the case of Kennedy. This accommodation was undoubtedly the product of a particular historical moment and of a cultural background dominated by Protestantism of several varieties and by the Enlightenment, but it has survived despite subsequent changes in the cultural and religious climate.

Civil War and Civil Religion

Until the Civil War, the American civil religion focused above all on the event of the Revolution, which was seen as the final act of the Exodus from the old lands across the waters. The Declaration of Independence and the Constitution were the sacred scriptures and Washington the divinely appointed Moses who led his people out of the hands of tyranny. The Civil War, which Sidney Mead calls "the center of American history,"[6] was the second great event that involved the national self-understanding so deeply as to require expression in the civil religion. In 1835, de Tocqueville wrote that the American republic had never really been tried, that victory in the Revolutionary War was more the result of British preoccupation elsewhere and the presence of a powerful ally than of any great military success of the Americans. But in 1861 the time of testing had indeed come. Not only did the Civil War have the tragic intensity of fratricidal strife, but it was one of the bloodiest wars of the nineteenth century; the loss of life was far greater than any previously suffered by Americans.

The Civil War raised the deepest questions of national meaning. The man who not only formulated but in his own person embodied its meaning for Americans was Abraham Lincoln. For him the issue was not in the first instance slavery but "whether that nation, or any nation so conceived, and so dedicated, can long endure." He had said in Independence Hall in Philadelphia on 22 February 1861:

> All the political sentiments I entertain have been drawn, so far as I have been able to draw them, from the sentiments which originated in and were given to the world from this Hall. I have never had a

[6] Sidney Mead, *The Lively Experiment* (New York, 1963), p. 12.

feeling, politically, that did not spring from the sentiments embodied in the Declaration of Independence.[7]

The phrases of Jefferson constantly echo in Lincoln's speeches. His task was, first of all, to save the Union—not for America alone but for the meaning of America to the whole world so unforgettably etched in the last phrase of the Gettysburg Address.

But inevitably the issue of slavery as the deeper cause of the conflict had to be faced. In the second inaugural, Lincoln related slavery and the war in an ultimate perspective:

> If we shall suppose that American slavery is one of those offenses which, in the providence of God, must needs come, but which, having continued through His appointed time, He now wills to remove, and that He gives to both North and South this terrible war as the woe due to those by whom the offense came, shall we discern therein any departure from those divine attributes which the believers in a living God always ascribe to Him? Fondly do we hope, fervently do we pray, that this mighty scourge of war may speedily pass away. Yet, if God wills that it continue until all the wealth piled by the bondsman's two hundred and fifty years of unrequited toil shall be sunk, and until every drop of blood drawn with the lash shall be paid by another drawn with the sword, as was said three thousand years ago, so still it must be said "the judgements of the Lord are true and righteous altogether."

But he closes on a note if not of redemption then of reconciliation— "With malice toward none, with charity for all."

With the Civil War, a new theme of death, sacrifice, and rebirth enters the civil religion. It is symbolized in the life and death of Lincoln. Nowhere is it stated more vividly than in the Gettysburg Address, itself part of the Lincolnian "New Testament" among the civil scriptures. Robert Lowell has recently pointed out the "insistent use of birth images" in this speech explicitly devoted to "these honored dead": "brought forth," "conceived," "created," "a new birth of freedom." He goes on to say:

> The Gettysburg Address is a symbolic and sacramental act. Its verbal quality is resonance combined with a logical, matter of fact, prosaic brevity. . . . In his words, Lincoln symbolically died, just as the Union soldiers really died—and as he himself was soon really to die. By his words, he gave the field of battle a symbolic significance that it had

[7] Quoted by Arthur Lehman Goodhart in Allan Nevins (ed.), *Lincoln and the Gettysburg Address* (Urbana, Ill., 1964), p. 39.

lacked. For us and our country, he left Jefferson's ideals of freedom and equality joined to the Christian sacrificial act of death and rebirth. I believe this is a meaning that goes beyond sect or religion and beyond peace and war, and is now part of our lives as a challenge, obstacle and hope.[8]

Lowell is certainly right in pointing out the Christian quality of the symbolism here, but he is also right in quickly disavowing any sectarian implication. The earlier symbolism of the civil religion had been Hebraic without being in any specific sense Jewish. The Gettysburg symbolism (". . . those who here gave their lives, that that nation might live") is Christian without having anything to do with the Christian church.

The symbolic equation of Lincoln with Jesus was made relatively early. Herndon, who had been Lincoln's law partner, wrote:

> For fifty years God rolled Abraham Lincoln through his fiery furnace. He did it to try Abraham and to purify him for his purposes. This made Mr. Lincoln humble, tender, forbearing, sympathetic to suffering, kind, sensitive, tolerant; broadening, deepening and widening his whole nature; making him the noblest and loveliest character since Jesus Christ. . . . I believe that Lincoln was God's chosen one.[9]

With the Christian archetype in the background, Lincoln, "our martyred president," was linked to the war dead, those who "gave the last full measure of devotion." The theme of sacrifice was indelibly written into the civil religion.

The new symbolism soon found both physical and ritualistic expression. The great number of the war dead required the establishment of a number of national cemeteries. Of these, the Gettysburg National Cemetery, which Lincoln's famous address served to dedicate, has been overshadowed only by the Arlington National Cemetery. Begun somewhat vindictively on the Lee estate across the river from Washington, partly with the end that the Lee family could never reclaim it,[10] it has subsequently become the most hallowed monument of the civil religion. Not only was a section set aside for the Confederate dead, but it has received the dead of each succeeding American war. It is the site of the one important new symbol to

---

[8] *Ibid.*, "On the Gettysburg Address," pp. 88–89.

[9] Quoted in Sherwood Eddy, *The Kingdom of God and the American Dream* (New York, 1941), p. 162

[10] Karl Decker and Angus McSween, *Historic Arlington* (Washington, D.C., 1892), pp. 60–67.

come out of World War I, the Tomb of the Unknown Soldier; more recently it has become the site of the tomb of another martyred president and its symbolic eternal flame.

Memorial Day, which grew out of the Civil War, gave ritual expression to the themes we have been discussing. As Lloyd Warner has so brilliantly analyzed it, the Memorial Day observance, especially in the towns and smaller cities of America, is a major event for the whole community involving a rededication to the martyred dead, to the spirit of sacrifice, and to the American vision.[11] Just as Thanksgiving Day, which incidentally was securely institutionalized as an annual national holiday only under the presidency of Lincoln, serves to integrate the family into the civil religion, so Memorial Day has acted to integrate the local community into the national cult. Together with the less overtly religious Fourth of July and the more minor celebrations of Veterans Day and the birthdays of Washington and Lincoln, these two holidays provide an annual ritual calendar for the civil religion. The public-school system serves as a particularly important context for the cultic celebration of the civil rituals.

The Civil Religion Today

In reifying and giving a name to something that, though pervasive enough when you look at it, has gone on only semiconsciously, there is risk of severely distorting the data. But the reification and the naming have already begun. The religious critics of "religion in general," or of the "religion of the 'American Way of Life,'" or of "American Shinto" have really been talking about the civil religion.

---

[11] How extensive the activity associated with Memorial Day can be is indicated by Warner: "The sacred symbolic behavior of Memorial Day, in which scores of the town's organizations are involved, is ordinarily divided into four periods. During the year separate rituals are held by many of the associations for their dead, and many of these activities are connected with later Memorial Day events. In the second phase, preparations are made during the last three or four weeks for the ceremony itself, and some of the associations perform public rituals. The third phase consists of scores of rituals held in all the cemeteries, churches, and halls of the associations. These rituals consist of speeches and highly ritualized behavior. They last for two days and are climaxed by the fourth and last phase, in which all the separate celebrants gather in the center of the business district on the afternoon of Memorial Day. The separate organizations, with their members in uniform or with fitting insignia, march through the town, visit the shrines and monuments of the hero dead, and, finally, enter the cemetery. Here dozens of ceremonies are held, most of them highly symbolic and formalized." During these various ceremonies Lincoln is continually referred to and the Gettysburg Address recited many times. W. Lloyd Warner, *American Life* (Chicago, 1962), pp. 8–9.

As usual in religious polemic, they take as criteria the best in their own religious tradition and as typical the worst in the tradition of the civil religion. Against these critics, I would argue that the civil religion at its best is a genuine apprehension of universal and transcendent religious reality as seen in or, one could almost say, as revealed through the experience of the American people. Like all religions, it has suffered various deformations and demonic distortions. At its best, it has neither been so general that it has lacked incisive relevance to the American scene nor so particular that it has placed American society above universal human values. I am not at all convinced that the leaders of the churches have consistently represented a higher level of religious insight than the spokesmen of the civil religion. Reinhold Niebuhr has this to say of Lincoln, who never joined a church and who certainly represents civil religion at its best:

> An analysis of the religion of Abraham Lincoln in the context of the traditional religion of his time and place and of its polemical use on the slavery issue, which corrupted religious life in the days before and during the Civil War, must lead to the conclusion that Lincoln's religious convictions were superior in depth and purity to those, not only of the political leaders of his day, but of the religious leaders of the era.[12]

Perhaps the real animus of the religious critics has been not so much against the civil religion in itself but against its pervasive and dominating influence within the sphere of church religion. As S. M. Lipset has recently shown, American religion at least since the early nineteenth century has been predominantly activist, moralistic, and social rather than contemplative, theological, or innerly spiritual.[13] De Tocqueville spoke of American church religion as "a political institution which powerfully contributes to the maintenance of a democratic republic among the Americans"[14] by supplying a strong

---

[12] Reinhold Niebuhr, "The Religion of Abraham Lincoln," in Nevins (ed.), *op. cit.*, p. 72. William J. Wolfe of the Episcopal Theological School in Cambridge, Massachusetts, has written: "Lincoln is one of the greatest theologians of America —not in the technical meaning of producing a system of doctrine, certainly not as the defender of some one denomination, but in the sense of seeing the hand of God intimately in the affairs of nations. Just so the prophets of Israel criticized the events of their day from the perspective of the God who is concerned for history and who reveals His will within it. Lincoln now stands among God's latter-day prophets." *The Religion of Abraham Lincoln* (New York, 1963), p. 24.

[13] Seymour Martin Lipset, "Religion and American Values," Chapter 4, *The First New Nation* (New York, 1964).

[14] Alexis de Tocqueville, *Democracy in America*, Vol. 1 (New York, 1954), p. 310.

moral consensus amidst continuous political change. Henry Bargy in 1902 spoke of American church religion as "la poésie du civisme."[15]

It is certainly true that the relation between religion and politics in America has been singularly smooth. This is in large part due to the dominant tradition. As de Tocqueville wrote:

> The greatest part of British America was peopled by men who, after having shaken off the authority of the Pope, acknowledged no other religious supremacy: they brought with them into the New World a form of Christianity which I cannot better describe than by styling it a democratic and republican religion.[16]

The churches opposed neither the Revolution nor the establishment of democratic institutions. Even when some of them opposed the full institutionalization of religious liberty, they accepted the final outcome with good grace and without nostalgia for an *ancien régime*. The American civil religion was never anticlerical or militantly secular. On the contrary, it borrowed selectively from the religious tradition in such a way that the average American saw no conflict between the two. In this way, the civil religion was able to build up without any bitter struggle with the church powerful symbols of national solidarity and to mobilize deep levels of personal motivation for the attainment of national goals.

Such an achievement is by no means to be taken for granted. It would seem that the problem of a civil religion is quite general in modern societies and that the way it is solved or not solved will have repercussions in many spheres. One needs only to think of France to see how differently things can go. The French Revolution was anticlerical to the core and attempted to set up an anti-Christian civil religion. Throughout modern French history, the chasm between traditional Catholic symbols and the symbolism of 1789 has been immense.

American civil religion is still very much alive. Just three years ago we participated in a vivid re-enactment of the sacrifice theme in connection with the funeral of our assassinated president. The American Israel theme is clearly behind both Kennedy's New Fron-

[15] Henry Bargy, *La Religion dans la Société aux États-Unis* (Paris, 1902), p. 31.

[16] De Tocqueville, *op. cit.,* p. 311. Later he says, "In the United States even the religion of most of the citizens is republican, since it submits the truths of the other world to private judgment, as in politics the care of their temporal interests is abandoned to the good sense of the people. Thus every man is allowed freely to take that road which he thinks will lead him to heaven, just as the law permits every citizen to have the right of choosing his own government" (p. 436).

tier and Johnson's Great Society. Let me give just one recent illustration of how the civil religion serves to mobilize support for the attainment of national goals. On 15 March 1965 President Johnson went before Congress to ask for a strong voting-rights bill. Early in the speech he said:

> Rarely are we met with the challenge, not to our growth or abundance, or our welfare or our security—but rather to the values and the purposes and the meaning of our beloved nation.
> The issue of equal rights for American Negroes is such an issue. And should we defeat every enemy, and should we double our wealth and conquer the stars and still be unequal to this issue, then we will have failed as a people and as a nation.
> For with a country as with a person, "What is a man profited, if he shall gain the whole world, and lose his own soul?"

And in conclusion he said:

> Above the pyramid on the great seal of the United States it says in Latin, "God has favored our undertaking."
> God will not favor everything that we do. It is rather our duty to divine his will. I cannot help but believe that He truly understands and that He really favors the undertaking that we begin here tonight.[17]

The civil religion has not always been invoked in favor of worthy causes. On the domestic scene, an American-Legion type of ideology that fuses God, country, and flag has been used to attack nonconformist and liberal ideas and groups of all kinds. Still, it has been difficult to use the words of Jefferson and Lincoln to support special interests and undermine personal freedom. The defenders of slavery before the Civil War came to reject the thinking of the Declaration of Independence. Some of the most consistent of them turned against not only Jeffersonian democracy but Reformation religion; they dreamed of a South dominated by medieval chivalry and divine-right monarchy.[18] For all the overt religiosity of the radical right today, their relation to the civil religious consensus is tenuous, as when the John Birch Society attacks the central American symbol of Democracy itself.

With respect to America's role in the world, the dangers of dis-

---

[17] U.S., *Congressional Record,* House, 15 March 1965, pp. 4924, 4926.
[18] See Louis Hartz, "The Feudal Dream of the South," Part 4, *The Liberal Tradition in America* (New York, 1955).

tortion are greater and the built-in safeguards of the tradition weaker. The theme of the American Israel was used, almost from the beginning, as a justification for the shameful treatment of the Indians so characteristic of our history. It can be overtly or implicitly linked to the idea of manifest destiny which has been used to legitimate several adventures in imperialism since the early nineteenth century. Never has the danger been greater than today. The issue is not so much one of imperial expansion, of which we are accused, as of the tendency to assimilate all governments or parties in the world which support our immediate policies or call upon our help by invoking the notion of free institutions and democratic values. Those nations that are for the moment "on our side" become "the free world." A repressive and unstable military dictatorship in South Vietnam becomes "the free people of South Vietnam and their government." It is then part of the role of America as the New Jerusalem and "the last hope of earth" to defend such governments with treasure and eventually with blood. When our soldiers are actually dying, it becomes possible to consecrate the struggle further by invoking the great theme of sacrifice. For the majority of the American people who are unable to judge whether the people in South Vietnam (or wherever) are "free like us," such arguments are convincing. Fortunately President Johnson has been less ready to assert that "God has favored our undertaking" in the case of Vietnam than with respect to civil rights. But others are not so hesitant. The civil religion has exercised long-term pressure for the humane solution of our greatest domestic problem, the treatment of the Negro American. It remains to be seen how relevant it can become for our role in the world at large, and whether we can effectually stand for "the revolutionary beliefs for which our forebears fought," in John F. Kennedy's words.

The civil religion is obviously involved in the most pressing moral and political issues of the day. But it is also caught in another kind of crisis, theoretical and theological, of which it is at the moment largely unaware. "God" has clearly been a central symbol in the civil religion from the beginning and remains so today. This symbol is just as central to the civil religion as it is to Judaism or Christianity. In the late eighteenth century this posed no problem; even Tom Paine, contrary to his detractors, was not an atheist. From left to right and regardless of church or sect, all could accept the idea of God. But today, as even *Time* has recognized, the meaning of the word *God* is by no means so clear or so obvious. There is no formal creed in the civil religion. We have had a Catholic president; it is conceivable that we could have a Jewish one. But could we have an agnostic president? Could a man with conscientious scruples about using the word *God* the way Kennedy and Johnson have used it be elected chief magistrate of our country? If the whole God symbolism requires reformulation, there will be obvious consequences for the civil religion, consequences perhaps of liberal alienation and of fundamentalist ossification that have not so far been prominent in this realm. The civil religion has been a point of articulation between the profoundest commitments of the Western religious and philosophical tradition and the common beliefs of ordinary Americans. It is not too soon to consider how the deepening theological crisis may affect the future of this articulation.

The Third Time of Trial

In conclusion it may be worthwhile to relate the civil religion to the most serious situation that we as Americans now face, what I call the third time of trial. The first time of trial had to do with the question of independence, whether we should or could run our own affairs in our own way. The second time of trial was over the issue of slavery, which in turn was only the most salient aspect of the more general problem of the full institutionalization of democracy within our country. This second problem we are still far from solving though we have some notable successes to our credit. But we have been overtaken by a third great problem which has led to a third great crisis, in the midst of which we stand. This is the problem of responsible action in a revolutionary world, a world seeking to attain many of the things, material and spiritual, that we have already attained. Americans have, from the beginning, been aware of the responsibility and the significance our republican experiment has for the whole world. The first internal political polarization in the new nation to do with our attitude toward the French Revolution. But we were small and weak then, and "foreign entanglements" seemed to threaten our very survival. During the last century, our relevance for the world was not forgotten, but our role was seen as purely exemplary. Our democratic republic rebuked tyranny by merely existing. Just after World War I we were on the brink of taking a different role in the world, but once again we turned our back.

Since World War II the old pattern has become impossible. Every president since Roosevelt has been groping toward a new pattern of action in the world, one that would be consonant with our power and our responsibilities. For Truman and for the period dominated by John Foster Dulles that pattern was seen to be the great Manichaean confrontation of East and West, the confrontation of democracy and "the false philosophy of Communism" that provided the structure of Truman's inaugural address. But with the last years of

Eisenhower and with the successive two presidents, the pattern began to shift. The great problems came to be seen as caused not solely by the evil intent of any one group of men, but as stemming from much more complex and multiple sources. For Kennedy, it was not so much a struggle against particular men as against "the common enemies of man: tyranny, poverty, disease and war itself."

But in the midst of this trend toward a less primitive conception of ourselves and our world, we have somehow, without anyone really intending it, stumbled into a military confrontation where we have come to feel that our honor is at stake. We have in a moment of uncertainty been tempted to rely on our overwhelming physical power rather than on our intelligence, and we have, in part, succumbed to this temptation. Bewildered and unnerved when our terrible power fails to bring immediate success, we are at the edge of a chasm the depth of which no man knows.

I cannot help but think of Robinson Jeffers, whose poetry seems more apt now than when it was written, when he said:

> Unhappy country, what wings you have! . . .
> Weep (it is frequent in human affairs), weep for
>   the terrible magnificence of the means,
> The ridiculous incompetence of the reasons, the
>   bloody and shabby
> Pathos of the result.

But as so often before in similar times, we have a man of prophetic stature, without the bitterness or misanthropy of Jeffers, who, as Lincoln before him, calls this nation to its judgment:

> When a nation is very powerful but lacking in self-confidence, it is likely to behave in a manner that is dangerous both to itself and to others.
>
> Gradually but unmistakably, America is succumbing to that arrogance of power which has afflicted, weakened and in some cases destroyed great nations in the past.
>
> If the war goes on and expands, if that fatal process continues to accelerate until America becomes what it is not now and never has been, a seeker after unlimited power and empire, then Vietnam will have had a mighty and tragic fallout indeed.
>
> I do not believe that will happen. I am very apprehensive but I still remain hopeful, and even confident, that America, with its humane and democratic traditions, will find the wisdom to match its power.[19]

[19] Speech of Senator J. William Fulbright of 28 April 1966, as reported in *The New York Times*, 29 April 1966.

Without an awareness that our nation stands under higher judgment, the tradition of the civil religion would be dangerous indeed. Fortunately, the prophetic voices have never been lacking. Our present situation brings to mind the Mexican-American war that Lincoln, among so many others, opposed. The spirit of civil disobedience that is alive today in the civil rights movement and the opposition to the Vietnam War was already clearly outlined by Henry David Thoreau when he wrote, "If the law is of such a nature that it requires you to be an agent of injustice to another, then I say, break the law." Thoreau's words, "I would remind my countrymen that they are men first, and Americans at a late and convenient hour,"[20] provide an essential standard for any adequate thought and action in our third time of trial. As Americans, we have been well favored in the world, but it is as men that we will be judged.

Out of the first and second times of trial have come, as we have seen, the major symbols of the American civil religion. There seems little doubt that a successful negotiation of this third time of trial—the attainment of some kind of viable and coherent world order—would precipitate a major new set of symbolic forms. So far the flickering flame of the United Nations burns too low to be the focus of a cult, but the emergence of a genuine trans-national sovereignty would certainly change this. It would necessitate the incorporation of vital international symbolism into our civil religion, or, perhaps a better way of putting it, it would result in American civil religion becoming simply one part of a new civil religion of the world. It is useless to speculate on the form such a civil religion might take, though it obviously would draw on religious traditions beyond the sphere of Biblical religion alone. Fortunately, since the American civil religion is not the worship of the American nation but an understanding of the American experience in the light of ultimate and universal reality, the reorganization entailed by such a new situation need not disrupt the American civil religion's continuity. A world civil religion could be accepted as a fulfillment and not a denial of American civil religion. Indeed, such an outcome has been the eschatological hope of American civil religion from the beginning. To deny such an outcome would be to deny the meaning of America itself.

Behind the civil religion at every point lie Biblical archetypes: Exodus, Chosen People, Promised Land, New Jerusalem, Sacrificial Death and Rebirth. But it is also genuinely American and genuinely

---

[20] Quoted in Yehoshua Arieli, *Individualism and Nationalism in American Ideology* (Cambridge, Mass., 1964), p. 274.

new. It has its own prophets and its own martyrs, its own sacred events and sacred places, its own solemn rituals and symbols. It is concerned that America be a society as perfectly in accord with the will of God as men can make it, and a light to all the nations.

It has often been used and is being used today as a cloak for petty interests and ugly passions. It is in need—as is any living faith —of continual reformation, of being measured by universal standards. But it is not evident that it is incapable of growth and new insight.

It does not make any decision for us. It does not remove us from moral ambiguity, from being, in Lincoln's fine phrase, an "almost chosen people." But it is a heritage of moral and religious experience from which we still have much to learn as we formulate the decisions that lie ahead.

Bellah's approach is clearly Durkheimian. He stresses the cultural contribution of religion to the establishment of moral values and social order in society. He seems to imply that in spite of temporary numerical ups and downs in religious institutional memberships, a society without some basic civil-religious values is unthinkable. Bellah's argument is indeed appealing to those theologians who maintain that people are essentially religious and that their religiosity is always evident in some way in the "ultimate meanings" of cultural life. Those sociologists who have criticized the sociology of religion for focusing too much upon the established religious institutions also see in Bellah's work an important alternative way of interpreting American religion. Perhaps the most serious problem in Bellah's "civil religion" hypothesis is the question of whether such a common value consensus really exists in the United States. In the context of a decade that has seen involvement in a divisive foreign war, as well as numerous domestic social problems, it is hard to depict the common political values, not to mention common religious values, of America's strife-ridden social fabric.

While it is obviously important to observe changes in the established religious institutions in a society, it is equally important to keep track of new religious phenomena. Only by examining both ends of the religious spectrum can one hope to grasp the nature of the religious situation. Martin Marty's essay "The Occult

Establishment" provides a survey of the many non-mainstream religious phenomena that appeared to be growing in the early 1970s. His method of data collection is neither historical nor statistical. Rather, in an attempt to gain some impressions of these movements at the very time when they were emerging, he undertook a content analysis of the literature they produce. From these documents he is able to make some preliminary inferences about the social and religious values of the people joining these diverse religious movements.

The Occult Establishment
by Martin Marty

No one has difficulty recognizing as religion the "high religions" of the world—Buddhism, Islam, Hinduism, Judaism, Christianity, and others. At the same time, sophisticated analysts have trained a large element of the public to recognize as quasi-religions a number of ideologies or forces which make religious claims and demands: Fascism, Marxism, cults of success or sex, modern nationalism may be cited. Between these is a no-gods-land filled with a bewildering variety of options that are less recognized than the high religions but more formal in their religious symbolism than are the ideologies. Outsiders often speak of them as "magic" or "superstition," but to their adherents they serve as integrating elements in a spiritual quest.

No name is acceptable to all adherents or practitioners, but most of these beliefs are associated in their minds with "the occult" or "the metaphysical." In metropolitan areas bookstores specializing in this field are rather commonplace, and in large book or magazine establishments, these titles regularly appear above sections

Martin Marty is professor of modern church history and associate dean at the University of Chicago Divinity School. He is the author of many books, including *The Fire We Can Light: The Role of Religion in a Suddenly Different World* (1973); *Righteous Empire: The Protestant Experience in America* (1970); and *Search for a Usable Future* (1969).

Reprinted from *Social Research*, 37, no. 2 (1970): 212–230. Used with permission of the author and publisher.

placed between sections "For Men Only" or "Home and Garden" and "Photography and Hobbies." Thus *Search* magazine (March, 1970, p. 3) speaks to all who have interests "concerning the occult, the unknown, the metaphysical, the controversial, the suppressed, and allied subjects," presumably in descending order of importance, if the performance of editors is observed.

Some would object to both titles, occult and metaphysical, just as some Anglicans resent being called "Protestant," even though they seem to have to be classified thus by sociologists and statisticians. In this article the terms are not used pejoratively. In the occult-metaphysical circle, of course, many "sects" or schools of thought are to be found, and they are not fully ecumenical in orientation. They struggle to be regarded as serious ventures, sometimes at the expense of one another. It is not our purpose to classify them according to varying degrees of respectability. Remembering that they are located at the "fringe" of conventional religion, it is probably advisable for us for heuristic purposes to keep Gardner Murphy's catholic attitude in mind: "I am interested in all the fringes, whether they're so-called lunatic fringes or normal fringes" (*Psychic*, February, 1970, p. 6).

Many treatments of the fringe phenomena stress their ominous character; an issue of *Esquire* in the winter of 1970 accented "Satanism" and other threatening cults. *McCall's* (March, 1970), in an issue on "The Occult Explosion," featured, as the cover blurbed, "Astrology, Magic, Tarot, Seances, and Satan Worship"; but even its particular brand of satanology looked rather benign and respectable, despite the efforts of the editors to suggest the ominous and the scary. It is possible to discern many layers and levels in this particular sub-culture; in this article, the respectable and established public versions will be stressed.

The occult and metaphysical groups are not new on the American scene. By mid-nineteenth century the Spiritualist churches established by the Fox sisters in western New York had alerted many Americans to a new range of religious experiences, and decades later Madame Blavatsky introduced Theosophy to these shores. To many, groups in the New Thought range and Christian Science were also part of the "fringe" cluster. Through recent decades groups like the Rosicrucians and Astara helped familiarize others with the spiritualist and metaphysical life through their advertisements in mass-circulation magazines. The last two organizations' appeals are also regularly located in the Occult and Metaphysical sections of bookstores; they issue their own periodicals (e.g., *The Rosicrucian Fellowship Magazine* and *Rosicrucian Digest*). Significantly, these are seldom placed among the religious books or magazines by the book sellers.

Astara advertises in the popular occult magazines, and horoscope readers seem to be a promising market (*Horoscope Guide*, March, 1970, page 5, advertisement): "Astara is a world-wide, nonprofit organization . . . [offering] answers . . . gleaned from many sources including the world's great Scriptures, ancient Mystery Schools and their modern counterparts." The Astara claims respond to questions that are so basic to the whole fringe area of belief that they merit citation here:

Do you possess inner powers as yet unused?
Do unseen powers influence your life?
Is your life the success you had hoped for?
Are there other worlds about you?
Can you part the veil to higher worlds?
Can you intuitively tune in to inspiration?
Where did you come from and where will you go from here?
Have you lived before?
Are you afraid to die?
Do the dead ever contact the living?
Is it possible for living man to become immortal?

Questions like these have animated religions for many millennia, and not a few of them are addressed in conventionally respectable religions, where their (to secular eyes) almost scandalous import has been blunted or obscured by the passing of time. That they are offered as options by new groups and in countless periodicals in late twentieth-century America suggests one more instance in which the claims of analysts, both theological and historical, that the world is becoming mainly or utterly secular should be called into question. In the Protestant "secular theology" of the mid-1960s the eclipse of astrology, the atrophy of spiritualism, the collapse of metaphysics, and the absence of alchemy were regularly cited as elements of the long-ago, part of the advance guard of the more sophisticated secularity that was to serve as the model of man and culture for the ages to come. In the 1970s all these options are available to hundreds of thousands if not millions of Americans.

For this article research has been isolated and informal. The current phase or fad having to do with astrology and the psychic has been so sudden and so sweeping that earlier literature is of little use. Most of the standard texts on what Americans believe and how they worship, on the faiths for the few, on strange sects and curious cults, set aside only a few pages for occasional and casual reference to these phenomena. The bibliographies on religion in America suggest that very few research designs and almost no extensive scientific research projects have been undertaken in this particular area of belief.

Against this background it seemed profitable to begin by producing a report on the "presentation of the self" of occult and metaphysical groups and individuals. I have restricted comment here to the advocacies of adherents, as they are communicated to a general public, in a single season. A visit to an airport newsstand will reveal that many more paperback books on astrology and the psychic are available for mass circulation than books that grow consciously out of the Western (Jewish and Christian) "high" religious traditions. A survey of current offerings on such counters would amplify but would not contradict the imagery of the occult movements that is described in this analysis which is based on some of the periodicals available on magazine counters. Needless to say, the journals cited do not make up an exhaustive list. I have worked with about forty magazines and will cite approximately a dozen. To extend the number would have been unprofitable; astrology and horoscope publications are routine, predictable, duplicative. The material on which I have drawn for this article is a representation, a sample.

Having been involved for years with the professional study of the history of religion, and having been alerted to what was purportedly an "Occult Underground" several years ago, I was not prepared for many surprises. At the time of the reports of seances involving the late Bishop James Pike and his son, it had been my assignment to see how the event was covered in occult and metaphysical literature (it was almost entirely overlooked in the literature of the religious establishment), and since that time this literature has continued to interest me. But if there were not many surprises, there was one, at least.

The unexpected element resulted from my sudden awareness that while I was dealing with what many called "fringe" phenomena, much of the reporting to date had given the impression that there existed only an occult underground. The "invasion of the centaurs," the drunken and erotic dionysian types who have threatened orthodox culture, as reported on by Theodore Roszak, or the death-of-God drug-experimenters adrift on what William Braden has described as "the private sea"; the satanologists of *Esquire* and *McCall's;* the W.I.T.C.H. conspiracy so publicized when radical leftist groups demonstrate—all these exist, in impressive numbers and often with violent implications for the society. But they do not have the fringe field to themselves. Instead, most of the energies of the occult and metaphysical exponents go into what I shall call the "Occult Establishment," a safe and often sane "aboveground" expression, whose literature gives every sign of being beamed at what is now usually called "middle America," "the silent majority," or "consensus-U.S.A."

The underground and the establishment interact, and the latter often lives off the relevance supplied by the former. Both are aware that, as they see it, a new era is dawning. Sybil Leek's very respectable *Astrology Journal* (April, 1970, p. 1) headlines the fact that "the publishers, editors and contributing writers of this journal are confident that astrology is valid today as a serious science in a world on the brink of the Aquarian Age." Much is made of this hippie symbol, though little else is made of hippie culture. As a general rule, it is my observation that the higher the level of scientific pretension or sophistication, and thus the higher the level of intellectual and esthetic perception of the presumed audience, the freer are the editors to risk intercourse between underground and establishment on the fringe, and the more likely they are to stress a common pool of symbols between the two. Thus *Psychic* (February, 1970, pp. 9 ff.) features a comprehensive article by Robert W. Neubert, "Age of Aquarius."

Neubert begins by citing lines from the Broadway musical *Hair*, an entertainment obviously not designed to attract the favor of the middle Americans who read most of the other occult and psychic periodicals. Neubert quotes heads of astrology associations, glories in *Time* magazine's cover story treatment of astrologist Carroll Righter, works his way past citations of geologists and archaeologists who have discovered epochal shifts in the world of the past, and relishes Peter Henry Liederman ("a political scientist and self-styled 'contemporary gadfly'") as he describes the change "from the Dialectic Age to the Ecological or Global Age." Alan Watts, a religious scholar; the Rosicrucian Fellowship; Sybil Leek, and other respectable individuals and groups are all referred to in the context of the culturally unsettling anti-establishment ethos of *Hair*. Such treatment is rare; usually references to "the Aquarian Age" are shy about the sources that have made them relevant.

Similar ambivalences are present in most treatments of youth. Except where horoscope magazines or columns are specifically directed to youth (or to the would-be young, as in the women's *Playboy, Cosmopolitan*), the youth culture is ordinarily recognized as an agent giving birth to the occult establishment, but its details are seldom acknowledged. One major exception is Dane Rudhyar,

"The Turned-On Generation" (in *Astroview,* April, 1970, pp. 44 ff.).
Rudhyar reminds readers of the way adult culture is off balance
because of the erraticism and drug-taking of the turned-on "under
thirties," and suggests that their malaise is the result of deeper
psychological disturbances. Throughout he is careful to expound
to an obviously anti-turned-on audience the reasons for cultural
abrasion, and cautions against "quick crystallization and dogmatism," a warning hardly necessary were *Astroview* beamed to the
turned-on. If there is one devastating aspect to the documentation
that lies behind my "establishmentarian" thesis about the purportedly ominous underground, it is this: the turned-on, black
magical, satanist, and otherwise disturbing sector of the population
is always written about and *never* written to! It should be noted
that even moderate apologist Rudhyar reassures his audience that
"there are already 'communes' in which the use of any drug, alcohol
included, is not allowed—and where a discipline of work is enforced." Shades of the reappearance of the Protestant ethic! Did it,
indeed, ever disappear in this version of the occult world? At one
point Rudhyar sounds almost like the Vice-President of the United
States:

> If so much publicity had not been given to [Timothy Learyism] in all
> the media,... it probably would not have spread so much and so
> fast.

Then comes the giveaway, the revelation concerning the market:
"Can we, their elders, help them to feel [a] unitive state.... This is
a very difficult thing to do. Yet this must be done. The only other
solution would be the appearance of some great spiritual personage
who would be able to fascinate this turned-on youth and to draw
into constructive channels their great intelligence, their open sensitivity, and their vital energies."

Contrast Rudhyar's rhetoric and sense of audience with that presumed by editors of any of the underground newspapers (as in Ethel
Grodzins Romm, *The Open Conspiracy*) and it will be clear that
in the latter the spiritual personages are already on the scene (Leary
himself, Allen Ginsberg *et al.*), and the energies they put into drugs,
violence, or obscenity—as Rudhyar's audience would see them—
are already constructive and do not need rechanneling.

As another example of middle America's rejection of the youth
culture, we may cite Albert Fast, "Predictions of Continued Unrest
in the Year 1970" in *Beyond* (March, 1970, pp. 14 ff.). Fast's "cards

warn public figures that 1970 is [a] critical period," and he banners the headline "Student Unrest is Serious Menace to National Welfare." Student life is constantly seen as a "continuing menace." Drugs are consistently criticized, even if so gently as in *The Rosicrucian Digest* (February, 1970, pp. 44 ff.) by "The Imperator" who suggests a more excellent way than that chosen in the ominous occult underground. The drug-taker may even be well-motivated.

> However, his *modus operandi,* or use of drugs, is quite wrong. He is impatient; he is not willing to resort to the *technique* of meditation to find illumination and inspiration.
>
> We may say that he is like a man who finds a door to a room which he wishes to enter to be difficult to open. Instead of taking sufficient time to properly open the door, he blasts it open with an explosive, thereby not only ruining the door but the contents of the room as well.

The violent imagery exposes the thinness of the genteel philosophical veneer used by "The Imperator" in what was the most gentle dismissal of the drug-culture in the periodicals under study.

Similar ambivalences concerning sexuality are also revelatory of the "silent majoritarian" outlook in this large network of publications. If conventionally orthodox Christians and their kind are nervous about the occult establishment, they need have no fears that people who celebrate this version of the psychic-metaphysical life carry on in orgies the way their underground counterparts, to whom so much publicity has been given by the mass media, purportedly do. There is constantly a hint of sexual titillation, but this rarely moves beyond the middle American zones set years ago by the Doris Day movies. It is clear that the astrology and horoscope magazines have to be full of the promise of sexual fulfillment, but they are rather guarded and *The Ladies' Home Journal* and *Good Housekeeping* are more given to "the new morality" than are the occult magazines.

Sybil Leek in her *Astrology Journal* (April, 1970, pp. 6 ff.) goes about as far as anyone in general terms as she criticizes religious repression:

> The vicious circle of love versus sex, instead of the lyric reality of love allied to sex, has been set in motion by the erroneous religious philosophies of the past and today all mankind suffers from a set of problems based on sexual inhibition that range from individual frustration to the great sociological problems of the Universe.

But she does not prescribe orgies, and even the nude human figure almost never appears in any of these magazines, except in occasional advertisements.

H. J. D. Murton in his monthly column, "Matters Arising," takes a typical attitude in the widely available British slick magazine, *Prediction* (February, 1970, pp. 13 ff.). There he reports critically on the attitude of England's *Playboy, Penthouse,* toward psychic and paranormal or spiritual phenomena. The Ghost Club and *Penthouse* had offered £25,000 to anyone producing paranormal phenomena under test conditions. But four distinguished psychic judges, Sir George Joy, Professor H. H. Price, Canon J. Pearce-Higgins and Mrs. K. M. Goldney resigned when they saw how unrespectable the type of magazine in which their names appeared was. "*Penthouse* specialises in luxuriant, but to my mind hardly alluring, nude photographs in glorious something-colour, and much of its reading matter appears to be concerned with a kind of free-for-all 'permissiveness' (euphemism for sex with everything)." Murton is convinced that the paranormal crowd is normal while *Penthouse* shows perverted interest. The occult underground celebrates a kind of sexuality far less respectable and far to the "left" of that which Murton condemns, and would find *Penthouse* as stuffy and capitalist as it finds *Playboy*; in other words, occult establishment and underground approach sexual phenomena from opposite points of view and attack the conventionally "liberated" sexual expressions from opposing angles.

A further indicator of the middle American aspect of the audience is revealed in its racial attitudes. Of course, many Orientals are depicted favorably in journals that for the most part turn their back on Occidental pieties and seek new sustenance from the East. But to my memory not one of the two-score periodicals I have studied portrayed a single black American; few made references to anything but racial unrest in their predictions of the year, and the audience was uniformly and unconsciously presumed to be white— much as the audience in white American denominations is pictured to be always and only white; black Americans are always "they," even in articles that regard them with favor.

The unconscious identification of the occult establishment with the white world appears typically in Ray Palmer, "I Believe in Reincarnation—Sometimes" (*Search*, March, 1970, pp. 12 ff.), in an article that reminds one of the protested use of the term "flesh-colored" by the Band-Aid people when they marketed the pinkish-white bandages. Palmer reminds readers that "the creator initially took a character of a principle and embodied it in special flesh form, the rosy human form. That's us. We are human. Our 'hue' is rosy red. We are also 'man.' " Later the divine spirit decides "what the next embodiment in rosy flesh will be." There seems to be no possibility that black-hued people were created or are in prospect, and Palmer does not seem to want to worry his readers at all with the prospect of what they might become. Surely they will in time be rosy-pink-hued whites. (As a matter of fact, he withholds consent from reincarnation as the rule—it is "the exception, we repeat, not the rule." Enjoy the pink and white-hued existence while ye may!)

Consistently there are efforts to link occultism with mainline culture, often by reference to its prevalence in respectable media. Sybil Leek, the witch, begins her *Astrology Journal* (April, 1970, p. 1) by reminding readers that they are part of an expanding cloud of witnesses: "Of America's 1,750 newspapers, more than 1,200 now carry a regular astrology column, and most national magazines have their own astrologers. Twenty years ago, the total number of newspapers and magazines interested in astrology was scarcely more than a hundred. Today the astrology magazines, monthlies, quarterlies, and annuals have a prominent place on newsstands throughout the country."

The choice of heroes is also middle Americans' choices. Jeanne Dixon is a patron saint, and Edgar Cayce a prophet. Mrs. Spiro T. Agnew is pictured in the company of an astrologer who gives advice on how to throw parties (*Astrology Journal,* April, 1970, p. 30). There is the typical Silent Majority view of the Kennedys: a love-hate relation. (The wards in Gary, Indiana, that voted for George Wallace in 1968 had given signs of being prepared to vote for Robert F. Kennedy that autumn.) Now and again the fascination with a star-crossed family impels editors and authors to treat them favorably. President John and Senator Robert Kennedy are regularly offered in double portraits by artist Alton S. Tobey, in hagiographical guise. But since her second marriage the President's widow is often treated negatively, and Senator Edward Kennedy is consistently seen to be heading for a worse fate and advised to get out of politics. Walter Breen in *Astrology Journal* (April, 1970, p. 10) reminds readers: "In studying Senator Edward Kennedy's horoscope, I am not deliberately indulging in the kick-him-again game. Like any astrologer of integrity, I can only present the traits—and the planetary transits—as I find them." Dr. Olof S. Sandburg in *Beyond* (March, 1970, pp. 7 ff.) proclaims, "Ted Kennedy Could Bring Disaster to America if Elected President," in an article which has Jeanne Dixonian rightist overtones. Sandburg criticizes John Kennedy for events like the Bay of Pigs disaster, and reminds us that the fate of a leader embraces the fate of his people. "It is therefore better to have a lucky head of state, even with personal shortcomings, than a more competent one with an unfortunate destiny." Edward Kennedy's chart "shows that if elected he could bring about a death of a nation." It would be incredible for the journals in question to find such chart-readings for acceptable conservatives like the current President and Vice-President, whose paths are constantly being blocked by restless and menacing students and other disruptive elements.

After having read thousands of pages of occult periodicals, it is necessary for me to report that they are humorless. Even crabby denominational magazines often have cartoons or quotable quotes or even jokes, but the occult and metaphysical people almost never engage in conscious attempts at humor. It was refreshing to find (in *Beyond,* March, 1970, p. 44), an advertisement for a bumper sticker: "Flying Saucers Are Real, The Air Force Doesn't Exist." The grotesque and fantastic assays at the comic in the occult underground are absent in the newsstand sanctuaries.

Is the occult underground religious in its orientation? If by this is meant, is it attempting to develop a worldwide Church in the institutional sense, the answer would be, in most cases, no. Is it setting out to displace all existing religions? Hardly; it can live with many and shares elements of most. But it is clear that it attempts to supply the answers historic high religions once offered, and it duplicates many of the attempts they made to fill needs. In my definition, religion somehow involves men's "ultimate concern"; ordinarily it will make some metaphysical or quasi-metaphysical claims about a kind of transcendent order (thus the title, *Beyond*), and will seek to integrate people into a system of meanings, often through the use of myth and symbol. There will ordinarily be some ceremonial reinforcement of these efforts and, though not always (in the era of "privatized" or "invisible" religions) it will have a communal intention. And religions will seek to encompass the scope, the wholeness of life. If these elements make up conventional definitions of religion, then it is clear that the occult and metaphysical offerings are somehow to be seen as religions—with far less straining than that required of those who "convert by defining" when they speak, say, of nationalism as a religion. It is true that the ideologies, especially when attached to politics, have more power to make totalistic claims; but the occult establishment and underground, while less ambitious and more genteel, ask for greater suspensions of disbelief.

Space does not permit here more than a brief citation of some of the phenomena that make up the occult establishment.

At the base of it all is astrology, some sense that men's lives are determined and guided by cosmic signs and constellations. This feature is so obvious it need not be documented: it appears on almost every page and runs through as a *Grundmotif,* the way a doctrine of God provided substructure for theistic religions and a doctrine of providence served as his expression in the affairs of men. But a doctrine of God and providence needs corollaries, parallels, and supports, and so does astrology.

Theosophy is one version, and *Quest Books,* a theosophical publisher, regularly advertises titles like *The Future is Now: The Significance of Precognition; Man Visible and Invisible; The Etheric Double; This World and That: An Analysis of Psychic Communication; The Meaning of Personal Existence in the Light of Paranormal Phenomena, the Doctrine of Reincarnation,* and *Mystical States of Consciousness.* (See *Psychic,* February, 1970, p. 3.)

Telepathy *(Fate,* April, 1970, pp. 94 ff.) and extrasensory perception are regularly featured as semi-religious and thoroughly scientific phenomena. Katherine Q. Spencer in *Astroview* (April, 1970, pp. 18 ff.), tells "How Dr. Rhine Harnessed ESP" in a generally reportorial article which ends with the suggestion that in the future, through ESP, man will conquer time itself. When laboratory experiments are cited, the authors often move from the controlled to the speculative. Hypnosis provides continual fascination for its paranormal suggestions and the implication that unseen forces are at work behind the processes.

Obsession with illness, old age, and the promise of after-life is pervasive, in the midst of a "secular" world where historic religions have been slighting these elements in their creeds. Reincarnation is the conventional form, but various kinds of survival are proffered or described. Thus Joan Merrill Harmon writes that "Death is a New Beginning" in *Search* (March, 1970, pp. 56 ff.): "Individual spiritual survival of bodily death happens as part of a continuous process." *Search* also carries advertisements (March, 1970, p. 77) of "Dead Man Speaks, Conclusive proof that life continues after death. His words, recorded automatically, explain life in the Heavens and Hells, E.S.P., psychic phenomena, healing, levitation, clairvoyance, UFOs, and prophecies of what is in store for the world. Spirits have shown themselves so that they could be recognized and have their pictures drawn." In the same issue (p. 83) M. R. Keith of Amherst Press, a regular advertiser, offers a book, *What Everybody Ought to Know about Heaven.* Contact with the spiritual world is a common feature; thus the interest in Bishop James Pike, the most widely accepted transfer from the Christian environment to this establishment. *Prediction* includes three pages of want-ad size announcements of the services of mediums ("If you would like a 'postal reading' with Evidence of the Survival of your Loved One . . ." p. 57).

Clairvoyance is advertised by The Gnostic Institute (*Fate*, April, 1970, p. 131) and through it one can "contact the gods' forces." A Spirit Healing Workshop will be held in Arkansas on May 21, 22, and 23, says an advertisement in the same issue (p. 105). You may experience "spirit existence beyond the physical." "Numerology is a guide to the cosmos," and lessons are offered in *Dreams* (1970, pp. 78 ff.). "Handwriting: Clues to Your Character Traits," by Jerome S. Meyer *(Astroview*, April, 1970, pp. 64 ff.), is another common element on the less controversial side. Of course, there is also palmistry as a guide to the cosmos: "Your Hands Reveal Your Destiny," by Mir Bashir (*Astroview*, April, 1970, pp. 37 ff.). Your hands suggest contact with "the Oracles." Water-witching and dowsing are staple elements (George Butler, "Gadsden's Official Dowser," *Fate*, April, 1970, pp. 92 ff.).

It goes without saying that dreams reveal the astral, spectral, and spiritual worlds. They may be treated scientifically (as in Alan Vaughan, "A Dream Grows in Brooklyn," in *Psychic*, February, 1970, pp. 40 ff., a report on "The William C. Menninger Dream Laboratory"), or with the suggestion of promise for the individual as in the whole magazine devoted to *Dreams,* but most frequently dreams are more than expressions of the subconscious, more than relating to Jungian archetypal life: they help man transcend bodily existence. So does astral projection, the highest form of clairvoyance. Cathleen Beara O'Connell in "A Visit to the Land of the Golden Light" (*Search,* March, 1970, pp. 32 ff.) tells that "the purpose of our life on Earth—that our Overself or Soul can gain from the sufferings and trials we have to face here" was a teaching tested in her astral travels, in which she has met the Child Jesus and has a Guardian Angel moving about her. In *Beyond* (March, 1970, pp. 38 ff.), "Three Women Tell of Successful Astral Travel." One of the three is a pastor of Brooklyn's Temple of Divine Guidance; the author makes every effort to connect their experiences with ancient Egyptian or Hindu religious phenomena. Even the effect of prayer on plants as a laboratory experiment is a frequent subject of reports and we learn (*Search,* March, 1970, p. 37) that Rama Singh in India found that plants grow most successfully while listening to female singers like Peggy Lee and Ella Fitzgerald.

All of these semi-scientific, semi-spiritual occurrences appear in a framework of astral beings and deities. The reappearance of the discussion of angels in formal theology cheers the occult establishment, and its editors and authors revisit nineteenth century and early twentieth century divines like the famous Russell Conwell (*Fate,* April, 1970, pp. 73 ff.) who found contact with the angelic world. Conwell's angel was none other than his dead wife, who appeared on his bed in 1920. Conwell was a bit cautious about interpreting the experience; the author concludes the article: "Obviously he saw *something.* Was it his wife?"

The Rosicrucian Fellowship Magazine (April, 1970, pp. 147 ff.) reports with joy on "Renaissance for Angels." Ghosts are omnipresent, and poltergeist stories are treated with great fascination. *Beyond* editors (March, 1970, p. 21) report on English ministers who resorted to exorcism to purge a house of ghosts. Much is made of Erich von Däniken's *Chariots of the Gods,* a book which argues that the ancient world was repeatedly visited by gods who left their trails (as in *Prediction,* February, 1970, p. 10).

The literature on UFOs, unidentified flying objects, is so extensive that it need not be cited: the consistent complaint is that the scientific and governmental communities have deliberately suppressed information about astral and spectral contacts. The Loch Ness monster casts a spell (*Beyond,* March, 1970, pp. 55 ff.). Voodoo is big (*Fate,* April, 1970, pp. 85 ff.). Instruments for making contact with the spirit world or its forces are advertised in all the magazines; Tarot cards and Ouija boards are being revived.

The editors take pains to educate their readers on these mysteries, and the pedagogical dimensions of these "religions" are patiently attended to. Sometimes these teaching tasks go no deeper than "how to" with horoscope charting ("Basic Astrology," by James Raymond Wolfe, in *Your Horoscope Secrets,* March, 1970, pp. 31 ff.), and offer "the heart of astrological lore . . . in one easy lesson." But many efforts are more pretentious or portentous. These have to do with "cosmic law" or "instant evolution" or "soul."

That these religions have been reborn and redeveloped in a scientific-secular world is clear from the efforts many authors and editors make to have things both ways. They want the occult, the metaphysical, the magical, the mysterious—but they want to demonstrate a scientific base. *Psychic* magazine is largely given over to men like Gardner Murphy, who bring scientific respectability to the topics. There is a fascination with the part computers might play in the world of horoscope casting and some editors even offer amusing parallels to historic religious worries in a scientific age.

Thus Walter Breen asks (*Astrology Journal,* April, 1970, p. 9), "Can a computer replace a human astrologer?" (Probably not. One needs the personal, human touch.) Some editors even criticize magic and black magic and superstition. Zolar, in *Dreams* (1970, p. 81), takes an ambiguous attitude:

> Superstition, in this day and age, is widely existent. Practically every person has some pet belief or aversion, though few will honestly admit it. . . . The majority of people abide by their belief in these superstitions but when confronted with the accusation, they will deny their belief in superstitions, yet actually carry out the theory of superstitions.

He moves from there not to a dispelling of superstitions but to a positive trading on man's inclinations toward omens and signs.

In all the literature there is a striking absence of positive concern for ethics, a remarkable oversight in a nation where other religions have had to prove their worth by citing their moral contributions. Except for a few attacks on unscrupulous people in their own orbit, the morality of their audience is usually assumed by these writers; it is the quality of life which will be enhanced through occult practices. But there is never a hint of interest in the use these religious insights might have in the controversial realms of social justice. Like some forms of conservative orthodoxy, the occult establishment concentrates almost entirely on individual life and often on "other-worldly" concerns.

If there is one element in conventional religion which is often lacking here, it is the communal impulse. The advertisements offer opportunities to belong to metaphysical churches, to share worship with swamis, or to be part of cults or organizations like the Oahspe Circle (*Search,* March, 1970, pp. 49 ff.), but rarely are there injunctions to fellowship or community practice. In this sense, these mail-order- and magazine-based religious expressions are a modern phenomenon and may be a part of a wave of the future; their adherents no doubt seek one another out (seances are common experiences in community, for instance) but they also trade on nonreligious forms of interpersonality in a secular world.

If community is not central, symbols and sacramental objects are. *Zolar's Official Horoscope Magazine* (March, 1970, p. 33) offers a candle for lighting during prayer: "The most sincere way to achieve your desires is to ask the Supreme Being for guidance, you can call your prayers wishes if you want to but burn the seven knob candle regularly." Zolar seems to be one of the largest purveyors.

Proudly announcing that he is a member of the National Better Business Bureau, he "makes no claim to the supernatural or the authenticity of these items. They are offered for sale for what they may be worth to the purchaser." For sale? Mystic incense, commanding oil, fast luck powder, lucky planet incense, high conquering incense, astrological love secrets, directions for burning candles, Black Herman, etc., etc.

Since these primitive, Eastern, or eclectic entities are all reappearing on soil where Christianity has dominated, it is interesting to see the attitudes taken toward Christianity. These are sometimes negative, because Christians have opposed witches, astrology, sorcery, etc. On the other hand, there are few head-on confrontations, no doubt because selected Christian elements have been absorbed as well as for tactical reasons: Middle America has dual commitments, both to its historic but waning faiths and to these restored or novel offerings. Jesus is treated with special regard; Amherst Press sells L. Taylor Hansen's *He Walked the Americas,* a book tying Jesus into old Indian legends and claiming that he had been in the Western hemisphere. *Fate* (April, 1970, p. 30) advertises *Jesus Was a Beatnik,* recommended for all teachers, writers, scientists; and "for serious students of Zen, Vedanta, Sufism and mysticism . . . the most profound Philosophical views ever printed in English." Parts of the Bible are fused with Eastern books; Christians like Sherwood Eddy who write on occult themes ("You Will Survive after Death") are well treated. Innovators in the Christian tradition like Emanuel Swedenborg, of course, find their place in the new pantheon.

Sybil Leek is more critical of Christians than are most writers in the field. But there is not much positive interest in Christianity; the East holds more mystery, and Christian claims have become timeworn. At the same time, the astrology journals are pro-ecumenical, perhaps on the assumption that ecumenical Christianity will be more tolerant and more ready to blend and fuse with the occult. Law-and-order man Albert Fast (*Beyond,* March, 1970, p. 19) even worries about the travails of Pope Paul ("he will need to be exceptionally vigilant . . ."). Frank J. McCarthy, in "The Sizzling Seventies" in *Horoscope Guide* (March, 1970, pp. 106 ff.), discusses ecumenism: "There will have been Heavenly intervention in the affairs of Earth that will have made even the most extreme atheist take note. Religion will have unified to a great extent . . . in the face of a destructive secularism." David Techter (*Fate,* April, 1970, p. 124) reports with joy that his Unitarian Universalist church at Boston in its 1969 convention made room for the Spiritual Frontiers Fellowship and for the first time, before an overflow crowd, heard presentations of occult subject matter.

One thing the occult establishment shares with Christianity is a sense of being beleaguered and on the defensive. But in an era when many Christians write about the dwindling or even the collapse of their institutions and beliefs, the metaphysical-psychical-spiritual frontier regards the future optimistically; it is convinced it is winning. Douglas Hunt in *Prediction* (February, 1970, p. 37) speaks for all: "Be comforted. We are not a band of cranks but the van of a new army of light."

I have cited hardly more than a dozen magazines, all from the same season; dozens more repeat the motifs with monotonous predictability. They satisfy the religious needs of many thousands or millions—we cannot even begin to guess at the number—who have turned to their myriad advertisements, books, products, and claims, in an age often called secular and in a world surrounding them with conventional "high religions." They represent a stratum often overlooked by sensational discussions of the underground, and are securely and safely at home in middle America.

One of Marty's most valuable insights is that these different religious groups provide a refuge for people who have become disenchanted with secularized denominational religion. Ironically, he finds that many of these groups seem to embody the very same social and religious values that have been traditionally associated with established religion in the United States. To this extent it may well be that people who join such groups are not "dropping-out" from traditional religious values, but returning to them through a different set of religious institutions. The subsequent emergence of the "Jesus Freaks" and Key '73 support this interpretation. Most importantly these trends would seem to refute the notion of increasing secularization. Rather, the 1970s appear to be producing a religious revival, though surely a very different kind of revival than was experienced in the 1950s.

Name Index

Subject Index

PRINTED IN U.S.A.

ABOUT THE EDITOR

William M. Newman (M.A. Syracuse University; Ph.D. New School for Social Research) is associate professor of sociology at the University of Connecticut where he teaches courses on social theory, intergroup relations, and the sociology of religion. Professor Newman is the author of *American Pluralism* (1973) and a contributing editor to the *Review of Religious Research*. His essays have appeared in various journals including the *Journal for the Scientific Study of Religion, Sociological Analysis, Review of Religious Research,* and the *American Journal of Sociology*.